THE EQUINOX

No. V

THE great pressure on our space has made it necessary to hold over much promised matter. It is hoped to include in No. V:

VARIOUS OFFICIAL INSTRUCTION of the A∴ A∴

THE ELEMENTAL CALLS OR KEYS, WITH THE GREAT WATCH TOWERS OF THE UNIVERSE and their explanation. A complete treatise, fully illustrated, upon the Spirits of the Elements, their names and offices, with the method of calling them forth and controlling them. With an account of The Heptarchicall Mystery, The Thirty Aethyrs or Aires with " The Vision and the Voice," being the Cries of the Angels of the Aethyrs, a revelation of the highest truths pertaining to the grade of Magister Templi, and many other matters. Fully illustrated.

THE TEMPLE OF SOLOMON THE KING.

[Continuation.

This instalment, which deals with Frater P.'s communication from the A∴ A∴, is the most important of the Series. Fully Illustrated.

DIANA OF THE INLET. By KATHERINE S. PRITCHARD.

ACROSS THE GULF: An adept's memory of his incarnation in Egypt under the 26th dynasty; with an account of the Passing of the Equinox of Isis.

&c.   &c.   &c.

WILLIAM NORTHAM,

ROBEMAKER,

9, Henrietta Street, Southampton Street, Strand

TELEPHONE—5400 Central.

MR. NORTHAM begs to announce that he has been entrusted with the manufacture of all robes and other ceremonial apparel of members of the A∴ A∴ and its adepts and aspirants.

No. 0.	PROBATIONER'S ROBE			£5	0	0
1.	„ „ superior quality			7	0	0
2.	NEOPHYTE'S			6	0	0
3.	ZELATOR	Symbol added to No. 2		1	0	0
4.	PRACTICUS	„ „ 3		1	0	0
5.	PHILOSOPHUS	„ „ 4		1	0	0
6.	DOMINUS LIMINIS	„ „ 5		1	0	0
7.	ADEPTUS (without)	„ „ 0 or 1		3	0	0
8.	„ (within)			10	0	0
9.	ADEPTUS MAJOR			10	0	0
10.	ADEPTUS EXEMPTUS			10	0	0
11.	MAGISTER TEMPLI			50	0	0

The Probationer's robe is fitted for performance of all general invocations and especially for the I. of the H. G. A.; a white and gold nemmes may be worn. These robes may also be worn by Assistant Magi in all composite rituals of the White.

The Neophyte's robe is fitted for all elemental operations. A black and gold nemmes may be worn. Assistant Magi may wear these in all composite rituals of the Black.

The Zelator's robe is fitted for all rituals involving I O, and for the infernal rites of Luna. In the former case an Uraeus crown and purple nemmes, in the latter a silver nemmes should be worn.

The Practicus' robe is fitted for all rituals involving I I, and for the rites of Mercury. In the former case an Uraeus crown and green nemmes, in the latter a nemyss of shot silk, should be worn.

The Philosophus' robe is fitted for all rituals involving O O, and for the rites of Venus. In the former case an Uraeus crown and azure nemmes, in the latter a green nemmes, should be worn.

The Dominus Liminis' robe is fitted for the infernal rites of Sol, which must never be celebrated.

The Adeptus Minor's robe is fitted for the rituals of Sol. A golden nemmes may be worn.

The Adeptus' robe is fitted for the particular workings of the Adeptus, and for the Postulant at the First Gate of the City of the Pyramids.

The Adeptus Major's Robe is fitted for the Chief Magus in all Rituals and Evocations of the Inferiors, for the performance of the rites of Mars, and for the Postulant at the Second Gate of the City of the Pyramids.

The Adeptus Exemptus' robe is fitted for the Chief Magus in all Rituals and Invocations of the Superiors, for the performance of the rites of Jupiter, and for the Postulant at the Third Gate of the City of the Pyramids.

The Babe of the Abyss has no robe.

For the performance of the rites of Saturn, the Magician may wear a black robe, close-cut, with narrow sleeves, trimmed with white, and the Seal and Square of Saturn marked on breast and back. A conical black cap embroidered with the Sigils of Saturn should be worn.

The Magister Templi Robe is fitted for the great Meditations, for the supernal rites of Luna, and for those rites of Babylon and the Graal. But this robe should be worn by no man, because of that which is written: "Ecclesia abhorret a sanguine."

Any of these robes may be worn by a person of whatever grade on appropriate occasions.

To be obtained of

THE EQUINOX, 124, Victoria Street, S.W.

And through all Booksellers

Crown 8vo, Scarlet Buckram, pp. 64.

This Edition strictly limited to 500 copies

PRICE 10s.

A ∴ A ∴

PUBLICATION IN CLASS B.

BOOK

777

THIS book contains in concise tabulated form a comparative view of all the symbols of the great religions of the world; the perfect attributions of the Taro, so long kept secret by the Rosicrucians, are now for the first time published; also the complete secret magical correspondences of the G ∴ D ∴ and R. R. et A. C. It forms, in short, a complete magical and philosophical dictionary; a key to all religions and to all practical occult working.

For the first time Western and Qabalistic symbols have been harmonized with those of Hinduism, Buddhism, Mohammedanism, Taoism, etc. By a glance at the Tables, anybody conversant with any one system can understand perfectly all others.

The *Occult Review* says:

"Despite its cumbrous sub-title and high price per page, this work has only to come under the notice of the right people to be sure of a ready sale. In its author's words, it represents 'an attempt to systematise alike the data of mysticism and the results of comparative religion,' and so far as any book can succeed in such an attempt, this book does succeed; that is to say, it condenses in some sixty pages as much information as many an intelligent reader at the Museum has been able to collect in years. The book proper consists of a Table of 'Correspondences,' and is, in fact, an attempt to reduce to a common denominator the symbolism of as many religious and magical systems as the author is acquainted with. The denominator chosen is necessarily a large one, as the author's object is to reconcile systems which divide all things into 3, 7, 10, 12, as the case may be. Since our expression 'common denominator' is used in a figurative and not in a strictly mathematical sense, the task is less complex than appears at first sight, and the 32 Paths of the Sepher Yetzirah, or Book of Formation of the Qabalah, provide a convenient scale. These 32 Paths are attributed by the Qabalists to the 10 Sephiroth, or Emanations of Deity, and to the 22 letters of the Hebrew alphabet, which are again subdivided into 3 mother letters, 7 double letters, and 12 simple letters. On this basis, that of the Qabalistic 'Tree of Life,' as a certain arrangement of the Sephiroth and 22 remaining Paths connecting them is termed, the author has constructed no less than 183 tables.

"The Qabalistic information is very full, and there are tables of Egyptian and Hindu deities, as well as of colours, perfumes, plants, stones, and animals. The information concerning the tarot and geomancy exceeds that to be found in some treatises devoted exclusively to those subjects. The author appears to be acquainted with Chinese, Arabic, and other classic texts. Here your reviewer is unable to follow him, but his Hebrew does credit alike to him and to his printer. Among several hundred words, mostly proper names, we found and marked a few misprints, but subsequently discovered each one of them in a printed table of errata, which we had overlooked. When one remembers the misprints in 'Agrippa' and the fact that the ordinary Hebrew compositor and reader is no more fitted for this task than a boy cognisant of no more than the shapes of the Hebrew letters, one wonders how many proofs there were and what the printer's bill was. A knowledge of the Hebrew alphabet and of the Qabalistic Tree of Life is all that is needed to lay open to the reader the enormous mass of information contained in this book. The 'Alphabet of Mysticism,' as the author says—several alphabets we should prefer to say—is here. Much that has been jealously and foolishly kept secret in the past is here, but though our author has secured for his work the *imprimatur* of some body with the mysterious title of the A. ∴ A. ∴, and though he remains himself anonymous, he appears to be no mystery-monger. Obviously he is widely read, but he makes no pretence that he has secrets to reveal. On the contrary, he says, 'an indicible arcanum is an arcanum which *cannot* be revealed.' The writer of that sentence has learned at least one fact not to be learned from books.

"G. C. J."

The New Thought Library

Crown 8vo. Crimson cloth extra, gilt tops, 3s. 6d. net per volume.

The NEW THOUGHT LIBRARY has been designed to include only the best works in this class of literature. No volume will find a place in this series unless it has already an established position in the popular favour. The first eight volumes are now ready.

HAVE YOU A STRONG WILL? How to Develop and Strengthen Will Power, Memory, or any other Faculty, or Attribute of the Mind by the Easy Process of Self-Hypnotism. By CHARLES GODFREY LELAND. Third and enlarged edition, containing the Celebrated Correspondence between Kant and Hufeland, and an additional Chapter on Paracelsus and his Teaching.

CONTENTS.—Preface. Introduction. How to Awaken Attention and Create Interest as preparatory to Developing the Will. Faculties and Powers latent in man. Mesmerism, Hypnotism and Self-Hypnotism. Pomponatius, Gassner, and Paracelsus. Medical Cures and Benefits which may be realised by Auto-Hypnotism. Forethought and its Value. Corrupt and Pure Will. Instinct and Suggestion. The Process of Developing Memory. The *Artes Memorandi* of Old Time. The Action of Will and Hypnotism on the Constructive Faculties. Fascination. The Voice. Telepathy and the Subliminal Self. The Power of the Mind to Master Disordered Feelings as set forth by Kant. Paracelsus, his Teaching with regard to Self-Hypnotism. Last Words.

"Why can we not will ourselves to do our very best in all matters controllable by the individual will? Mr. Leland answers triumphantly that we can."—*The Literary World*.
"An earnestly written work entirely free from charlatanism."—*Birmingham Post*.

THE SCIENCE OF THE LARGER LIFE. A Selection from the Essays of URSULA N. GESTEFELD.

CONTENTS.—Preface. Part I. *How we Master our fate.*—The Inventor and the Invention The Ascension of Ideas. Living by Insight or by Outsight. Destiny and Fate. The Origin of Evil. What is within the "Heir"? Words as Storage Batteries. How to Care for the Body. The Way to Happiness. You Live in your Thought-World. The Language of Suggestion. Constructive Imagination. The Power of Impression. How to Remove Impressions. Your Individualism. Making Things go Right. Utilizing Energy. Master, or be Mastered. The Voice that is heard in Loneliness. The Ingrafted Word. The Law of Liberty. Part II. —*The Evolution of an Invalid;* The Invalid's Alter Ego. The Evolution of a Thief: The Honest Man. The Evolution of a Liar; The Truthful Man. The Evolution of a Miser; The Benefactor. The Evolution of an Egotist; The Self-Forgetful Man. The Evolution of a Drunkard; The Self-Possessed Man. The Evolution of a Libertine; The Strong Man. The Evolution of a Flirt; The Divine Womanly. Part III.—*Stilling the Tempest.* Live in the Eternal, not in Time. Affirmation of Being. Affirmation for the Morning. Affirmation for the Evening. Affirmation for Fear of Heredity. Affirmation for Fear of Death.

EVERY MAN A KING, or Might in Mind Mastery. By ORISON SWETT MARDEN.

This very popular American handbook on the subject of the practical conduct of life, is now offered to the British Public as a new volume of the "New Thought Library" at the popular price of 3s. 6d. net.

"Strong, wise, sound, pleasant, helpful, well-written—these are only a few of the complimentary adjectives which can honestly be applied to this book."—ALICE BROWN in *Ohio State Journal*.
"Admirable! It is a long time since we have read a book on the fascinating subject of mind's influence over matter, especially in the building of character, with as much pleasure as this has afforded. Characterized throughout by a cheery optimism, the perusal of it is as good as any tonic, and far better than most."—*Pall Mall Gazette*.

MENTAL MEDICINE: Some Practical Suggestions from a Spiritual Standpoint. By OLIVER HUCKEL, S.T.D. With an Introduction by LEWELLYS F. BARKER, M.D.

SUMMARY OF CONTENTS—The New Outlook for Health. The Unique Powers of Mind. The Spiritual Mastery of the Body. Faith as a Vital Force. The Healing Value of Prayer. Glimpses of the Sub-conscious Self. The Training of the Hidden Energies. The Casting Out of Fear. The Cause and Cure of the Worry Habit. The Gospel of Relaxation. Work as a Factor in Health. Inspiration of the Mental Outlook. Best Books for Further Reading.

"It is a cheerful, inspiring book, and should fulfil its object to give mental galvanic shocks to spiritual paralytics."—*Sunday Times*.
"A serious exposition of the way a spiritual guide may helpfully minister to the diseased."—*Bristol Times and Mirror*.

Write for full Catalogue to

WILLIAM RIDER AND SONS, Ltd., 164, Aldersgate Street, London, E.C.

The Star in the West

BY

CAPTAIN J. F. C. FULLER

FOURTH LARGE EDITION NOW IN PREPARATION

THROUGH THE EQUINOX AND ALL BOOKSELLERS

SIX SHILLINGS NET

A highly original study of morals and religion by a new writer, who is as entertaining as the average novelist is dull. Nowadays human thought has taken a brighter place in the creation: our emotions are weary of bad baronets and stolen wills; they are now only excited by spiritual crises, catastrophes of the reason, triumphs of the intelligence. In these fields Captain Fuller is a master dramatist.

A
GREEN GARLAND

By

V. B. NEUBURG

Green Paper Cover.   1s. 6d. net.

"As far as the verse is concerned there is in this volume something more than mere promise; the performance is at times remarkable; there is beauty not only of thought and invention—and the invention is of a positive kind— but also of expression and rhythm. There is a lilt in Mr. Neuburg's poems; he has the impulse to sing, and makes his readers feel that impulse."

The Morning Post, May 21, 1908.

"There is a certain given power in some of the imaginings concerning death, as 'The Dream' and 'The Recall,' and any reader with a liking for verse of an unconventional character will find several pieces after his taste."

The Daily Telegraph, May 29, 1908.

"Here is a poet of promise."—*The Daily Chronicle*, May 13, 1908.

"It is not often that energy and poetic feeling are united so happily as in this little book."—*The Morning Leader*, July 10, 1908.

"There is promise and some fine lines in these verses."

The Times, July 11, 1908.

Very few copies remain

London: PROBSTHAIN & CO.   And all Booksellers.

THE EQUINOX

THE EQUINOX

THE OFFICIAL ORGAN OF THE A∴A∴

THE REVIEW OF SCIENTIFIC ILLUMINISM

An VI   VOL. I. No. IV   ☉ in ♎

SEPTEMBER MCMX

O. S.

"THE METHOD OF SCIENCE—THE AIM OF RELIGION"

LONDON

PRINTED FOR ALEISTER CROWLEY AND PUBLISHED BY
HIM AT THE OFFICE OF THE EQUINOX
124 VICTORIA STREET, S.W.

The Equinox
The Review of Scientific Illuminism
Vol. I.   No. IV.

First published in London in 1910

An CXIV    ☉ in ♋

CONTENTS

SPECIAL SUPPLEMENT

ILLUSTRATIONS

Persons wishing for information, assistance, further interpretation, etc., are requested to communicate with

THE CHANCELLOR OF THE A∴ A∴

c/o THE EQUINOX,

124 Victoria Street,

S.W.

Telephone: 3210 VICTORIA,

or to call at that address by appointment. A representative will be there to meet them.

———

Probationers are reminded that the object of Probations and Ordeals is one: namely, to select Adepts. But the method appears twofold: (i) to fortify the fit; (ii) to eliminate the unfit.

———

The Chancellor of the A∴ A∴ views without satisfaction the practice of Probationers working together. A Probationer should work with his Neophyte, or alone. Breach of this rule may prove a bar to advancement.

EDITORIAL

WE shall be glad if all subscribers to, and readers of, THE EQUINOX will make themselves personally known to the staff at the offices at 124, Victoria Street.

Various meetings are held, lectures given, and experiments carried out, from time to time, which cannot be advertised effectively in a paper appearing at intervals of six months, and those wishing to attend must therefore be privately notified of the dates as they are fixed.

* * * * *

It should, moreover, be remembered, that although knowledge can be imparted through books, skill cannot be attained except by practice; and in most cases it is better that practice should be carried out under instruction.

* * * * *

Further, research work continually proceeds, and cannot be published, perhaps, for years, when it has been collated and criticised. To be *au courant* the seeker should be on the spot.

* * * * *

After the 21st of October 1910 the price of No. 1 of THE EQUINOX, of which only a few copies remain, will be increased to ten shillings.

THE EQUINOX

The subscription for 1911 will be raised from ten to twelve shillings.

*   *   *   *   *

A library for the use of subscribers is in progress of formation at 124, Victoria Street. The Editor will be glad to receive any books on mysticism, magic, Egyptology, philosophy, and similar subjects. Old books out of print are especially welcome.

*   *   *   *   *

Another feather in the cap of H. P. B. That incomparable dodderer, Franz Hartmann, has published a portrait of Cagliostro which she had given him. (She had it taken when she *was* Cagliostro, you understand.)

This sounds all very reasonable and likely; but the difficulty is that the portrait is not of Cagliostro at all, but of Stanislas Augustus, the last King of Poland.

So this is not a common simple miracle, you see; but a very wonderful miracle. However, I'm not going to be done; so I've bought a shilling photograph of Queen Victoria and intend to publish it next March as

ME When I Was CLEOPATRA.

*   *   *   *   *

As if this was not enough, we find The Annals of Psychical Research publishing in all good faith as a serious account "The Apparition of Mrs. Veal to Mrs. Bargrave," which was written by Daniel Defoe as a puff of some ass's Meditations on Death!

*   *   *   *   *

EDITORIAL

We do not blame the Editors of these papers for nodding; but we do think they owe us some poetry as good as Homer's or some erotic adventures to match Jove's.

*   *   *   *   *

I had almost forgotten dear old Mathers.

Yet it was only last December that a colleague of mine was told by some greasy old harridan, in her best nominal $7° = 4°$ voice (she has paid hundreds of pounds for that nominal $7° = 4°$, and never got initiated into any mysteries but those of Over-eating) that Imperrita (? Imperator) was coming over from Paris to *crush* Perdurabo; and Perdurabo has *fled* before his *face*.

Anyhow, I sneaked back from Algeria, trembling all over, and began to enjoy the comedy of a lawyer pretending that he could not serve a writ on a man with an address in the telephone directory, who was spending hundreds of pounds on letting the whole world know where to find him. It was perhaps unkind of me not to warn Mr. Cran that he was putting his foot in it.

But if I had said a word, the case would have been thrown up; and then where would our advertisement have been?

So, even now, I restrict my remarks; there may be some more fun coming.

*   *   *   *   *

But at least there's a prophet loose! Some anonymous person wrote

Cran, Cran, McGregor's man,
Served a writ, and away he ran

3

before a writ was served! Though he might have guessed that it would be. But he couldn't possibly have known that the action would be dropped, as it has been.

And Mathers has run away too—without paying our costs.

    *   *   *   *   *

A word as to the sanctity of obligations seems necessary here. Some of my brother Masons (for example) have heard imperfectly and judged hastily. But if we apply our tools to our morals with patience and skill, we shall cure any defects in the building. Let me explain the situation carefully and clearly.

(1) Mathers and Dr. Wynn Westcott were the apparent heads of the Order calling itself Rosicrucian.

(2) This Order seriously claimed direct descent, and transmitted Authority, from the original Fratres R.C.

(3) It was founded on secret documents in the custody of Dr. Wynn Westcott, on whose honour and integrity we relied.

(4) Mathers and Westcott claimed to be working under one or more secret chiefs of the grade of $8° = 3°$.

(5) It was then to those chiefs that I and other members of the Order were pledged.

(6) When the "rebellion" took place in 1900, I thought Mathers a wolf, and Westcott a sheep; but, recognizing Truth in the knowledge issued by the Order, maintained my allegiance to the Secret Chiefs $8° = 3°$.

(7) In 1904 I was ordered directly and definitely by a person who proved himself to be the messenger of a

Secret Chief $8° = 3°$ to publish the knowledge and rituals of the Order (*a*) in order to destroy the value of that knowledge, so that the new knowledge to be revealed by himself might have room to grow (*b*) in order to stop the frauds of Mathers, which were a disgrace to arcane science.

The secrecy of his rituals, and of the MSS. in the custody of Dr. Wynn Westcott, was essential to the carrying on of these frauds.

(8) I was unable to comply with these orders until I had found a person competent to edit the enormous mass of papers. I showed my hand to some extent, however, in various references to the Order in my books. And now the task is accomplished.

(9) My defence against the accusation of having revealed secrets entrusted to me is then threefold.

(*a*) Secrets cannot be revealed, or even communicated from one person to another.

(*b*) One is not bound by an oath taken to any person who is a swindler trading upon the sanctity of one's oath to carry on his frauds. Especially is this the case when the person responsible for administering the oath assures you that it is "in no way contrary to your civil, moral, and religious obligations."

(*c*) I was not, in any case, bound to Mathers, but to the Secret Chiefs, by whose direct orders I caused the rituals to be published.

I wish expressly to dissociate from my strictures on

Mathers Brother Wynn Westcott his colleague; for I have heard and believe nothing which would lead me to doubt his uprightness and integrity. But I warn him in public, as I have (vainly) warned him in private, that by retaining the cipher MSS. of the Order, and preserving silence on the subject, he makes himself an accomplice in, or at least an accessory to, the frauds of his colleague. And I ask him in public, as I have (vainly) asked him in private, to deposit the MSS. with the Trustees of the British Museum with an account of how they came into his possession; or if they are no longer in his possession, to state publicly how he first obtained them, and why, and to whom, he parted with them.

I ask him in the name of faith between man and man; in the name of those unfortunates, who, for no worse fault than their aspiration to the Hidden Wisdom, have been and still are being befooled and betrayed and robbed by his colleague under the ægis of the respectability of his own name; and in the Name of Him, who, planning the Universe, employed the Plumb-line, the Level, and the Square.

*   *   *   *   *

Sweets to the sweet—and here is a press cutting for a Press Cutting Agency.

On 22nd March I felt the ache for fame and telephoned to Messrs. Romeike and Curtice of Ludgate Circus. An obsequious person appeared, louted him low, and took my guinea for 125 cuttings. [I hear you ask, " How can they do it?"]

For a fortnight Messrs. Romeike and Curtice were the most diligent of created beings. I got cuttings from obscure papers in Yorkshire and Ireland and other places that one has

6

never heard of. But then it dropped off to zero. I had received about 30 cuttings altogether. Then other people began to send me cuttings in a friendly way, and Messrs. Romeike and Curtice maintained a silence and immobility which would have done credit to a first-rate Mahatma.

They missed, for example, little things like an editorial par. in " John Bull," a full page in " The Sketch," the " Daily News," a page and a quarter in " The Nation," half a column in the " Daily Mail." . . .

[I hear you ask, " How can they make such oversights? Perhaps the Post Office is to blame."]

Well, if the Post Office is to blame, I can't answer your other question, " How can they do it? " and if it is by " oversight " or " clerical error " or " absence of mind," I am in a similar position. And it is a curious coincidence that exactly the same thing happened to me 12 years ago.

LIBER III

VEL JVGORVM

A ∴ A ∴ Publication in Class D.
Imprimatur:
D.D.S. $7°=4°$ Praemonstrator
O.S.V. $6°=5°$ Imperator
N.S.F. $5°=6°$ Cancellarius

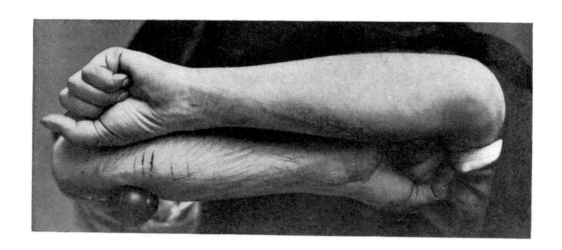

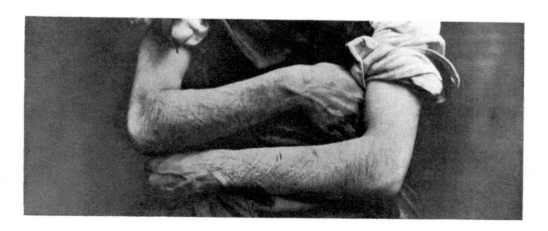

ARATRUM SECURUM

(Fra —— after one week avoiding the first person. His fidelity is good ; his vigilance bad.
Not nearly good enough to pass).

LIBER III

VEL JVGORVM

O

0. Behold the Yoke upon the neck of the Oxen! Is it not thereby that the Field shall be ploughed? The Yoke is heavy, but joineth together them that are separate—Glory to Nuit and to Hadit, and to Him that hath given us the Symbol of the Rosy Cross!

Glory unto the Lord of the Word Abrahadabra, and Glory unto Him that hath given us the Symbol of the Ankh, and of the Cross within the Circle!

1. Three are the Beasts wherewith thou must plough the Field; the Unicorn, the Horse, and the Ox. And these shalt thou yoke in a triple yoke that is governed by One Whip.

2. Now these Beasts run wildly upon the earth and are not easily obedient to the Man.

3. Nothing shall be said here of Cerberus, the great Beast of Hell that is every one of these and all of these, even as Athanasius hath foreshadowed. For this matter* is not of Tiphereth without, but Tiphereth within.

* (*I.e.* the matter of Cerberus).

11

I

o. The Unicorn is speech. Man, rule thy Speech! How else shalt thou master the Son, and answer the Magician at the Right Hand Gateway of the Crown?

1. Here are practices. Each may last for a week or more.

α. Avoid using some common word, such as " and " or " the " or " but "; use a paraphrase.

β. Avoid using some letter of the alphabet, such as " t " or " s " or " m "; use a paraphrase.

γ. Avoid using the pronouns and adjectives of the first person; use a paraphrase.

Of thine own ingenium devise others.

2. On each occasion that thou art betrayed into saying that thou art sworn to avoid, cut thyself sharply upon the wrist or forearm with a razor; even as thou shouldst beat a disobedient dog. Feareth not the Unicorn the claws and teeth of the Lion?

3. Thine arm then serveth thee both for a warning and for a record. Thou shalt write down thy daily progress in these practices, until thou art perfectly vigilant at all times over the the least word that slippeth from thy tongue.

Thus bind thyself, and thou shalt be for ever free.

LIBER III

II

0. The Horse is Action. Man, rule thou thine Action. How else shalt thou master the Father, and answer the Fool at the Left Hand Gateway of the Crown?

1. Here are practices. Each may last for a week or more.

α. Avoid lifting the left arm above the waist.

β. Avoid crossing the legs.

Of thine own ingenium devise others.

2. On each occasion that thou art betrayed into doing that thou art sworn to avoid, cut thyself sharply upon the wrist or forearm with a razor; even as thou shouldst beat a disobedient dog. Feareth not the Horse the teeth of the Camel?

3. Thine arm then serveth thee both for a warning and for a record. Thou shalt write down thy daily progress in these practices, until thou art perfectly vigilant at all times over the least action that slippeth from the least of thy fingers.

Thus bind thyself, and thou shalt be for ever free.

III

0. The Ox is Thought. Man, rule thou thy Thought! How else shalt thou master the Holy Spirit, and answer the High Priestess in the Middle Gateway of the Crown?

1. Here are practices. Each may last for a week or more.

α. Avoid thinking of a definite subject and all things connected with it, and let that subject be one which commonly occupies much of thy thought, being frequently stimulated by sense-perceptions or the conversation of others.

β. By some device, such as the changing of thy ring from one finger to another, create in thyself two personalities, the thoughts of one being within entirely different limits from that of the other, the common ground being the necessities of life.*

Of thine own ingenium devise others.

2. On each occasion that thou art betrayed into thinking that thou art sworn to avoid, cut thyself sharply upon the wrist or forearm with a razor; even as thou shouldst beat a disobedient dog. Feareth not the Ox the Goad of the Ploughman?

3. Thine arm then serveth thee both for a warning and for a record. Thou shalt write down thy daily progress in these practices, until thou art perfectly vigilant at all times over the least thought that ariseth in thy brain.

Thus bind thyself, and thou shalt be for ever free.

---

* For instance, let A be a man of strong passions, skilled in the Holy Qabalah, a vegetarian, and a keen "reactionary" politician; let B be a bloodless and ascetic thinker, occupied with business and family cares, an eater of meat, and a keen progressive politician. Let no thought proper to "A" arise when the ring is on the "B" finger; and *vice versa*.

LIBER A

VEL ARMORVM

SVB FIGVRÂ

CCCCXII

A ∴ A ∴ Publication in Class D.
Imprimatur:
D.D.S. 7°=4° Praemonstrator
O.S.V. 6°=5° Imperator
N.S.F. 5°=6° Cancellarius

LIBER A

VEL ARMORVM

SVB FIGVRÂ

CCCCXII

"The obeah and the wanga; the work of the wand and the work of the sword; these shall he learn and teach."—LIBER L. I. 37.

The Pentacle.

Take pure wax, or a plate of gold, silver-gilt or Electrum Magicum. The diameter shall be eight inches, and the thickness half an inch.

Let the Neophyte by his understanding and ingenium devise a symbol to represent the Universe.

Let his Zelator approve thereof.

Let the Neophyte engrave the same upon his plate, with his own hand and weapon.

Let it when finished be consecrated as he hath skill to perform, and kept wrapped in silk of emerald green.

The Dagger.

Let the Zelator take a piece of pure steel, and beat it, grind it, sharpen it, and polish it, according to the art of the swordsmith.

Let him further take a piece of oak wood, and carve a hilt. The length shall be eight inches.

IV   B   17

Let him by his understanding and ingenium devise a Word to represent the Universe.

Let his Practicus approve thereof.

Let the Zelator engrave the same upon his dagger with his own hand and instruments.

Let him further gild the wood of the hilt.

Let it when finished be consecrated as he hath skill to perform, and kept wrapped in silk of golden yellow.

The Cup.

Let the Practicus take a piece of Silver, and fashion therefrom a cup. The height shall be eight inches, and the diameter three inches.

Let him by his understanding and ingenium devise a Number to represent the Universe.

Let his Philosophus approve thereof.

Let the Practicus engrave the same upon his cup with his own hand and instrument.

Let it when finished be consecrated as he hath skill to perform, and kept wrapped in silk of azure blue.

The Baculum.

Let the Philosophus take a rod of copper, of length eight inches and diameter half an inch.

Let him fashion about the top a triple flame of gold.

Let him by his understanding and ingenium devise a Deed to represent the Universe.

Let his Dominus Liminis approve thereof.

Let the Philosophus perform the same in such a way that the Baculum may be partaker therein.

18

LIBER A

Let it when finished be consecrated as he hath skill to perform, and kept wrapped in silk of fiery scarlet.

The Lamp.

Let the Dominus Liminis take pure lead, tin, and quick-silver; with platinum, and, if need be, glass.

Let him by his understanding and ingenium devise a Magick Lamp that shall burn without wick or oil, being fed by the Aethyr.

This shall he accomplish secretly and apart, without asking the advice or approval of his Adeptus Minor.

Let the Dominus Liminis keep it when consecrated in the secret chamber of Art.

This then is that which is written: "Being furnished with complete armour, and armed, he is similar to the goddess."

And again " I am armed, I am armed."

I.NSIT N.ATURAE R.EGINA I.SIS

(*Obtained in invocation, June 9-10, 1910 O.S.*)

ALL the hot summer I lay in the darkness,
Calling on the winds to pass by me and slay me,
Slay me with light in the heat of the summer;
But the winds had no answer for one who was fallen
Asleep by the wayside, with no lyre to charm them,
No voice of the lyre, and no song to charm them.

Late as I lay there asleep by the wayside,
I heard a voice call to me, low in the silence,
There in the darkness the summer called to me:
"Thou who art hidden in the green silence,
Let a time of quietness come now upon thee.
Lay thine head on the earth and slumber on her bosom:
Time and the gods shall pass darkling before thee."
There in the silence I lay, and I heeded
The slow voice that called me, the grave hand that beckoned,
That beckoned me on through the hall of the silence.

There in the silence there was a green goddess,
Folden her wings, and her hands dumbly folden,
Lying in her lap, as though asleep in the darkness.

Then did I hail her: "O mother, my mother,
Syren of the silence, dumb voice of the darkness,

THE EQUINOX

How shall I have speech of Thee, who know not Thy speak-
  ing?
How shall I behold Thee, who art hidden in the darkness?
Lo! I bend mine eyes before Thee, and no sign dost Thou
  vouchsafe me;
I whisper love-words before Thee, and I know not if Thou
  hear me,
Thou who art the darling of the Night and of the Silence;
Yellow art Thou as the sunlight through the corn-fields,
Bright as the sun-dawn on the snow-clad mountains,
Slow as the voice of the great green gliding River.
Calmly in Thy silence am I come to rest me,
Now from the world the light hath slowly faded;
I have left the groves of Pan that I might gaze upon Thee,
Gaze upon the Virgin that before Time was begotten,
Mother of Chronos, and the old gods before him,
Child of the womb of the Silence, whose father
Is the unknown breath of the most secret Goddess,
Whose name whoso hath heard is smitten to madness.

" Now do I come before Thee in Thy temple,
With offerings from the oak-woods and the breath of the
  water
That girds the earth with a girdle of green starlight;
And all the austerity of the brooding summer,
And all the wonder of the starlit spaces
That stare down awesomely upon the lonely marshes,
And the bogs with sucking lips, and the pools that charm the
  wanderer
Till he forgets the world, and rushes to sleep upon them."
22

I . NSIT N . ATURAE R . EGINA I . SIS

And still there was silence, and the voice of the world swept
      by me,
Making in mine ears the noise of tumbling waters;
But two voices I heard, and they spake one to the other:
"Who stands with downcast eyes in the temple of our
      Lady?"
And the answer: "A wanderer from the world who hath sought
      the halls of silence;
Yet knoweth he not the Bride of the Darkness,
Her of the sable wings, and eyes of terrible blindness
That see through the worlds and find nothing and nothing,
Who would smite the worlds to peace, save that so she would
      perish,
And cannot, for that she is a goddess silent and immortal,
Utterly immortal in the gods' eternal darkness."

And the first voice cried: "Oh, that we might perish,
And become as pearls of blackness on the breast of the silence,
Lending the waste places of the world our darkness,
That the vision might burst in the brain of the seer,
And we be formed anew, and reborn in the light world."

But the other voice was silent, and the noise of waters
      swept me
Back into the world, and I lay asleep on a hill-side.
Bearing for evermore the heart of a goddess,
And the brain of a man, and the wings of the morning
Clipped by the shears of the silence; so must I wander lonely,
Nor know of the light till I enter into the darkness.

OMNIA VINCAM.

THE EQUINOX

How to Keep Fit. By C. T. Schofield, M.D. W. Rider and Sons. 1s. net.

There is a deal of sound sense in this little manual. The author castigates faddists, though to my mind not severely enough. However, I suppose that in this mealy-mouthed age the truth is not printable.

It is a little amusing, though, to see how he tries to make his commonsense fit into his Christianity.

It is the Puritan theory that theological sin, which means everything you like, is bad for you, that is responsible, according to statistics, for 79·403% of all the misery in England.

I suppose the bulk of the rest is due to having to review the outfall of the R.P.A.   A. C.

The Literary Guide. March-September, 1910.

We regret that the R.P.A. disliked our reviews of their sewerage. The said reviews were, however, written by one of the most prominent members of their own body. Rather like Epaminondas and the Cretans!

Anyhow, the "Guide" has wittily retorted on us that our reviews are "valueless." What a sparkler! What a crusher!   A. C.

Bhakti-Yoga. (Udvodhan Series.) By Swami Vivekânanda. 12 Gopal Chandra Neogi's Lane, Baghbazar, Calcutta. 8 annas.

If Swami Vivekânanda was not a great Yogi he was at least a very great expounder of Yoga doctrines. It is impossible here to convey to the reader a just estimate of the extreme value of this book. But we can say that this is the best work on the Bhakti-Yoga yet written. Union through devotion is Bhakti-Yoga, and union with Isvara or the Higher Self is the highest form this union can take—"man will be seen no more as man, but only as God; the animal will be seen no more as an animal, but as God; even the tiger will no more be seen a tiger, but as a manifestation of God" ... "love knows no bargaining ... love knows no reward ... love knows no fear ... love knows no rival ..." for "there are no men in this world but that One Man, and that is He, the Beloved."

In this excellent series can also be obtained Raja Yoga, one rupee; Karma Yoga, twelve annas; and Jnana Yoga, one rupee, which is worth knowing considering that the English edition of this last-mentioned work is priced at eleven shillings.   J. F. C. F.

[Yet we find Vivekânanda, at the end of his life, complaining, in a private letter to a friend, that his reputation for holiness prevented him from going "on the bust." Poor silly devil!—Ed.]

24

MY LADY OF THE BREECHES

A HISTORY—WITH A VENGEANCE

BY

GEORGE RAFFALOVICH

MY LADY OF THE BREECHES

O

THE FOOL

"Would you marry me, then?" the widow said.

"Yes, of course!" the man replied.

"You are a greater fool than I took you for."

"What do you mean?" he queried, vexed and puzzled. "Am I to take it that you had the intention—that you were prepared . . . ?"

"Go on."

"I don't know."

"I will be," she said, repressing a merry chuckle, "quite outspoken. I was prepared to . . . do nothing. Had you formulated some reasonable request . . . well, it might have ended otherwise. But marriage! Whom do you take me for?"

And the lady—she was dark-haired—whistled to her favourite monkey, a reddish animal, who bounded on her lap.

Lionel Tabard left them both, in their inspiring contrast; never unfrowning his well-shaped but delusive brow.

A few days later, he attempted to kiss the whimsical widow, who then horse-whipped him, meaning to teach him—not manners, but a-propos. Then she laughed. But he proved unintelligent, and never repeated his insult. Hence a nasty nickname from her lips.

THE EQUINOX

I

THE JUGGLER

" AND he well deserves it!"

"Oh! it must have been ripping. I do wish I had been there; . . . the horse-whip, and the monkey. He is such a silly fellow, poor ' cheval hongre!'"

"Ah, yes! the new nickname."

"Don't you think that it fits him?"

"Oh yes."

The silent man of the party moved uneasily in his arm-chair. He was slow of cogitation.

"Like the waistcoat of the late Nessus fitted Hercules, eh, what?" he suggested.

"A fool!"

"Hercules?"

"No, Lionel . . . and, er . . . yes, Hercules also. Tabard reminds me of that Bible chap."

"Potiphar's Joseph!" the silent man exclaimed triumphantly.

"Wrong again, Bernard. I meant Mary's Joseph."

The silent man threw his cigar over the fender.

II

LA PAPESSE

LIONEL TABARD had been horse-whipped by a woman; he had received—or taken—no compensation. This I attribute to his mother. One reads many tales, the paper thereof being

28

damnably wasted; in most of these, mothers are all author-made angels—sweet, loving, kind, forbearing, forgiving creatures, who feel the responsibility they undertook when they called upon a part of the spiritual world to come down among us. Of course, such mothers are the ideal mothers of a perfect human race, and the authors may consider themselves justified. Nevertheless, let us be true in this one history, and acknowledge the fact that some mothers are a thoroughly bad lot. They are mostly to be found among the well-to-do people, I suppose—and I do not wonder. When I see a mother smiling upon her grown-up son, I feel very sad. I remember my own parent . . .

There! I called this a history—with a vengeance. You have it. Now for a lesson in psychology.

Lionel's mother was queen and "regente" of bad parents. She was clever, but void of reasoning powers; inclined to religious mania, her immediate neighbourhood was crowded with foul larvæ. In a legal and womanly manner she had despatched her first husband to the night of a Sanatorium and thence to an early grave. She had suffered badly at the hands of her second. This we may take as being the coarsest form of that automatic justice, which is dealt only to the coarsest natures. It had not, however, extirpated an iota of her fund of self-esteem and lust for authority. To the latter, Lionel had often fallen a victim. He was born bright and happy; the Houses had done well by him. His mother gradually turned him into a self-concentrated, self-conscious, frightened and deceitful youth. She had mentally emasculated him; and, in his fits of understanding, he cursed her with no mean-spirited lips. He never forgave her the death of his father, her lying, under-handed ways, especially her brutality. His was a noble hatred, utter, blood-thirsty, virulent, eternal.

After years of melancholy and the physical consequences thereof, Lionel Tabard found himself free from his tyrannical parent. He soon forgot her, and, as the Divine Blinkings passed by, his recollection became less and less distinct. He only remembered two facts. She had once, during his sleep, broken a bone of his nose with a poker, because he snored; and, at another time, she had broken in two a valuable riding-crop on his shoulder.

Her death pleased him. But his constitution was much weakened by boyish exertions and the physical feeling of emptiness and marrowlessness, the consequences of his shyness and lack of sportsmanship.

The first use he had to make of his freedom and of his fortune was to book a cabin on the first liner bound for New Zealand, where he was led to expect a total recovery.

III

THE EMPRESS

LIONEL lived on a large estate, rode, hunted, played games, was made love to; discovered the joys of Nature, the pleasures kept in reserve for man by Isis, and the superiority of the numbers two and three over the unity. He found, to his surprise, that women could take interest in him. His shyness was apparent, but tempted them. In his eyes they met an eager hungry expression, a longing infinite for all things human, which tickled their desires. He seemed to be ever staring at an invisible goal. The goal was the Tree of the

30

full knowledge. Lionel felt within himself a tenacious longing, a perpetual desire. His lack of physical courage was counter-balanced by his intellectual daring; he meant to collar the Angel, and to re-enter the Paradise of that first victim of womanhood, Adam of the bent shoulders, Adam of the foolish resignation to the self-preserving decree of the frightened divinities.

His errors of tactics were caused by the fact that he hoped to test the apple without the help of Woman. Often enough, Lionel Tabard unwittingly repelled the advances of many a feminine would-be initiator.

VI*

THE LOVER

BUT he was not prompted by the wisdom of a Master; merely by cowardice and self-consciousness. He could not command love and desires; the angels of love and desires therefore digged a deep trap before his feet . . .

Tabard was sitting in the verandah. The men had gone to bed, the women also. He lighted his pipe, the use of which a life in the open air had permitted his lungs to tolerate. He was thinking, pondering, meditating upon the most important matter in life, the personal one. He looked at his hands, white, well shaped, well kept, but the left retaining a stiffer and curved appearance. Lionel felt ashamed of himself. He took his watch in his hand and looked at the time of night.

* For reasons which are obvious to anyone who has mixed the Gluten of the White Eagle with the Red Powder, or accomplished the Third Projection, the order of the Tarot trumps cannot any longer be preserved. Nor will their number here exceed seven.

THE EQUINOX

Twenty-one minutes past one o'clock—the day was marching towards its first duality. The door opened behind him, and the creaking wood caused him to jump up. The daughter of his host stood in her night-garments, a poem in pale green and white.

She said nothing; and he imitated the wisdom of her silence. His heart began a wild, unhealthy fandango; his temples ached; his legs shook under him. He felt himself paling; strange impulses prompted him to a return to ancestral savagery. Alas, he sadly lacked experience.

However, the woman had burned her vessels, and meant to help him.

"Lionel," she said, "I have come."

"I see," he managed to answer hoarsely, but the words in his throat seemed to feel like two huge hard lumps.

"Kiss me!"

Instinctively he stepped towards her and opened his arms. She fell heavily within their embrace. She hugged herself close against his breast and nestled on him, her eyes half-closed, her tongue and teeth searching blindly and savagely for his lips.

Contrary to his expectations, and more according to some of his past sensations and fears, Lionel Tabard felt more uneasiness than joy, more pain than pleasure. He congratulated himself upon the fact that the cool night had caused him to dress warmly, and that he had not trusted his body to the protection of the garment to which he owed his surname. As it was, the fierce Mænad was overcome by her passion ere she could have made him take a share in it.

Nevertheless, Woman often wins through sheer obstinacy,

and Lionel allowed himself to be conquered. Gradually, as the relations between them grew with the force of habit, his disgust increased, while his condescension plunged him deeper into the pit. He longed to tear himself away, and gradually discovered that she had become a necessity to him. He lost pleasure in himself and found none in her; finally he played an old trick and caused a telegram to be sent, calling him away. He swore to return speedily—which he didn't.

He sailed back to Europe, found himself in London, where his first experience caused him to waver between eagerness and self-consciousness. At that time, he met with the adventure which I related. A young widow horse-whipped him. Lionel was still very far from his salvation.

IX

THE HERMIT

He went to seek it in the wilderness. A cottage green as a lizard, surrounded by flowers and trees, well furnished, well kept by a couple of servants, male and female, such was the chosen retreat. It proved very comfortable—and lonely.

He pursued his education, often troubled by horrid visions, when he saw himself the centre of a stage where men and women crowded above, around, and beneath him. They reminded him of the terrible prediction of the French poet, who showed the two sexes dying away, irrevocably parted,

La femme ayant Gomorrhe et l'homme ayant Sodome.*

All the Messalines and Circes of an impure sex were

* Alfred de Vigny: "Colère de Samson."

balancing before him their tempting, repulsive, holy and foul, loose or firm, twin breasts. Himself, cloven-hoofed and curl-horned, had to flagellate his own flesh with iron chains, which failed to overcome the moral urtication, as had the repeated physical purgings of his early years. Narcissus, in a corner, pale and smiling, urged him to renewed efforts; Spirits, both incubi and succubae, thrusting themselves upon him, ate him away. . .

But all these dreams gradually faded out. Lionel had become a translucid set of bones, with two big eyes heavily crowned. The time of his knowledge had come.

XV

THE DEVIL

I TRUST I said nothing that could lead the reader into the belief that the cottage was a lonely spot. Men and women lived in its almost immediate neighbourhood. Among others, Sir Anthony Lawthon and his daughters. I propose that we concern ourselves solely with the eldest of these, Mary Lawthon.

I hardly know how to describe her. She was a woman of six and twenty, most easy to understand, very simple and very complex, simple in her complexity, complex in her simplicity. To men she seemed a man, strong, healthy, a rough-rider, a ski-runner, a champion in many sports, who smoked her pipe and emptied her glass passing well. To women she seemed a woman, whose hands were ever ready for a soft caress, whose lips were full and red, whose skin was velvet.

As a whole, she was very manly in her life, speech and

34

habit. She dressed often as a man; and, one day, riding by Lionel's cottage, she noticed the thin-armed youth whose eyes were big and haloed.

Their eyes met; she smiled, he trembled. Both were pleased. The next day rose and brought them again together. A formal introduction followed. Mary the male conquered Lionel the female. Thereafter, the "cheval hongre" lost his nick-name. Nor did he give any widow the chance of horse-whip-ping him again.

XVIII

THE MOON

THEY were very happy; he learnt the joy of health and the ineffable delectation of surrender; she the thrilling pain-pleasure of possession. Here, she, being the heroine of our tale, passes out of it.

They are very happy. Man and woman. The complete being. May their love last longer than the bee's!

GEORGE RAFFALOVICH.

THE EQUINOX

CAPTAIN MARGARET. By JOHN MASEFIELD. Thomas Nelson. 7d.

I bought this book thinking to find a jolly pirate yarn. Instead, in a style recalling now Bart Kennedy now Hall Caine, the meanderings and maunderings of a crew of ill-assorted sexual degenerates.

And I wasted sevenpence on this nauseous nastiness!

THE PORCH. Vol I, No. 1. THE OVERSOUL. By RALPH WALDO EMERSON. 21, Cecil Court, W.C. 3d.

"The Porch" promises to be a delightful addition to our periodical literature. Its first number gives in clear type on a nice page the magnificent essay which we all know so well, yet of which we never tire.

The one objection to Emerson is that he thinks all men know this Oversoul. They don't. It's a few holy illuminated men of God, and I hope that this includes John M. Watkins.   A. C.

Vol. I, No. 2. June. 1910. A TRUE CHRISTIAN. By JACOB BOEHME.

A most exquisite treatise on the life of the soul.

Boehme is a passive mystic, or quietist, of the very first water; he really perceives the underlying realities of Christianity, a religion which is so hidden by mounds of dirt and rubbish that it needs a very great mystic to get to the bottom of things without becoming defiled.

I hope Mr. Watkins is a true Christian.   V. B. N.

THE PORCH. Vol. I, No. 3. ON THE GOOD, OR THE ONE. By PLOTINUS.

We took up this book with avidity, thinking from the title that it was about Mr. Watkins. But no; at least not under that name.

Plotinus' method of mystic exercise is practically that of Liber XVI (A∴ A∴ publication in Class D), but it takes a deal of research to discover this in his dull pages. He drones on in such an exalted kind of way, don'tcherknow!

There is hardly a mystic living who wouldn't be a better man for reading Gal's Gossip now and then. I wish I had a copy here!

DORIS LESLIE ("BABY").

THINGS A FREEMASON SHOULD KNOW. By F. J. W. CROWE. G. Kenning and Son.

It is a pity that the title of this excellent manual should suggest the sexual sliminess of Sylvanus Stall, D.D., for it is a most admirable compilation, a capital handbook and *vade-mecum* which no Mason should be without. It is intensely interesting and beautifully illustrated with portraits of Masonic worthies past and present—there are no future celebrities; why the omission?—historic regalia and charitable institutions.   H. K. T.

AT BORDJ-AN-NUS

EL ARABI! El Arabi! Burn in thy brilliance, mine own!
O Beautiful! O Barbarous! Seductive as a serpent is
That poises head and hood, and makes his body tremble to
    the drone
Of tom-tom and of cymbal wooed by love's assassin sorceries!
    El Arabi! El Arabi!
The moon is down; we are alone;
May not our mouths meet, madden, mix, melt in the starlight
    of a kiss?
    El Arabi!

There by the palms, the desert's edge, I drew thee to my heart
    and held
Thy shy slim beauty for a splendid second; and fell moaning
    back,
Smitten by Love's forked flashing rod—as if the uprooted
    mandrake yelled!
As if I had seen God, and died! I thirst! I writhe upon the
    rack!
    El Arabi! El Arabi!
It is not love! I am compelled
By some fierce fate, a vulture poised, heaven's single ominous
    speck of black.
    El Arabi!

THE EQUINOX

There in the lonely bordj across the dreadful lines of sleeping
    men,
Swart sons of the Sahara, thou didst writhe slim, sinuous and
    swift,
Warning me with a viper's hiss—and was not death upon us
    then,
No bastard of thy maiden kiss? God's grace, the all-surpassing
    gift!
               El Arabi! El Arabi!
Yea, death is man's Elixir when
Life's pale wine foams and splashes over his imagination's
    rim!
               El Arabi!

El Arabi! El Arabi! witch-amber and obsidian
Thine eyes are, to ensorcell me, and leonine thy male caress.
Will not God grant us Paradise to end the music Earth
    began?
We play with loaded dice! He cannot choose but raise right
    hand to bless.
               El Arabi! El Arabi!
Great is the love of God and man
While I am trembling in thine arms, wild wanderer of the
    wilderness!
               El Arabi!

                          HILDA NORFOLK.

ΛΙΝΟΣ ΙΣΙΔΟΣ

Lo! I lament. Fallen is the sixfold Star:
Slain is Asar.
O twinned with me in the womb of Night!
O son of my bowels to the Lord of Light!
O man of mine that hast covered me
From the shame of my virginity!
Where art thou? Is it not Apep thy brother,
The snake in my womb that am thy mother,
That hath slain thee by violence girt with guile,
And scattered thy limbs on the Nile?

Lo! I lament. I have forged a whirling Star:
I seek Asar.
O Nepti, sister! Arise in the dusk
From thy chamber of mystery and musk!
Come with me, though weary the way,
To bring back his life to the rended clay!
See! are not these the hands that wove
Delight, and these the arms that strove
With me? And these the feet, the thighs
That were lovely in mine eyes?

Lo! I lament. I gather in my car
Thine head, Asar.

THE EQUINOX

And this—is this not the trunk he rended?
But—oh! oh! oh!—the task transcended,
Where is the holy idol that stood
For the god of thy queen's beatitude?
Here is the tent—but where is the pole?
Here is the body—but where is the soul?
Nepti, sister, the work is undone
For lack of the needed One!

Lo! I lament. There is no god so far
As mine Asar!
There is no hope, none, in the corpse, in the tomb.
But these—what are these that war in my womb?
There is vengeance and triumph at last of Maat
In Ra-Hoor-Khut and in Hoor-pa-Kraat!
Twins they shall rise; being twins they are one,
The Lord of the Sword and the Son of the Sun!
Silence, coeval colleague of Voice,
The plumes of Amoun—rejoice!

Lo! I rejoice. I heal the sanguine scar
Of slain Asar.
I was the Past, Nature the Mother.
He was the Present, Man my brother.
Look to the Future, the Child—oh paean
The Child that is crowned in the Lion-Aeon!
The sea-dawns surge and billow and break
Beneath the scourge of the Star and the Snake.
To my lord I have borne in my womb deep-vaulted
This babe for ever exalted!

ALEISTER CROWLEY.

THE TEMPLE OF SOLOMON
THE KING

IV

THE HERMIT

WITH the seventh stage in the Mystical Progress of Frater P. we arrive at a sudden and definite turning-point.

During the last two years he had grown strong in the Magic of the West. After having studied a host of mystical systems he had entered the Order of the Golden Dawn, and it had been a nursery to him. In it he had learnt to play with the elements and the elemental forces; but now having arrived at years of adolescence, he put away childish things, and stepped out into the world to teach himself what no school could teach him,—the Arcanum that pupil and master are one!

He had become a $6° = 5°$, and it now rested with him, and him alone, to climb yet another ridge of the Great Mountain and become a $7° = 4°$, an Exempt Adept in the Second Order, Master over the Ruach and King over the Seven Worlds.

By destroying those who had usurped control of the Order of the Golden Dawn, he not only broke a link with the darkening past, but forged so mighty an one with the gleaming future, that soon he was destined to weld it to the all encircling chain of the Great Brotherhood.

The Golden Dawn was now but a deserted derelict, mastless, rudderless, with a name of opprobrium painted across its battered stern. P. however did not abandon it to cast himself helpless into the boiling waters of discontent, but instead, he leapt on board that storm-devouring Argosy of Adepts which was destined to bear him far beyond the crimsoning rays of this dying dawn to the mystic land where stood the Great Tree upon the topmost branches of which hung the Golden Fleece.

Long was he destined to travel, past Lemnos and Samothrace, and through Colchis and the city of Æea. There, as a second Jason, in the Temple of Hecate, in the grove of Diana, under the cold rays of the Moon, was he to seal that fearful pact, that pledge of fidelity to Medea, Mistress of Enchantments. There was he to tame the two Bulls, whose feet were of brass, whose horns were as crescent moons in the night, and whose nostrils belched forth mingling columns of flame and of smoke. There was he to harness them to that plough which is made of one great adamantine stone; and with it was he determined to plough the two acres of ground which had never before been tilled by the hand of man, and sow the white dragons' teeth, and slay the armed multitude, that black army of unbalanced forces which obscures the light of the sun. And then, finally, was he destined to slay with the Sword of Flaming Light that ever watchful Serpent which writhes in silent Wisdom about the trunk of that Tree upon which the Christ hangs crucified.

All these great deeds did he do, as we shall see. He tamed the bulls with ease,—the White and the Black. He ploughed the double field,—the East and the West. He sowed the dragons' teeth,—the Armies of Doubt; and among them did he cast the stone of Zoroaster given to him by Medea, Queen of Enchantments, so that immediately they turned their weapons one against the other, and perished. And then lastly, on the mystic cup of Iacchus he lulled to sleep the Dragon of the illusions of life, and taking down the Golden Fleece accomplished the Great Work. Then once again did he set sail, and sped past Circe, through Scylla and Charybdis; beyond the singing sisters of Sicily, back to the fair plains of Thessaly and the wooded slopes of Olympus. And one day shall it come to pass that he will return to that far distant land where hung that Fleece of Gold, the Fleece he brought to the Children of Men so that they might weave from it a little garment of comfort; and there on that Self-same Tree shall he hang himself, and others shall crucify him; so that in that Winter which draweth nigh, he who is to come may find yet another garment to cover the hideous nakedness of man, the Robe that hath no Seam. And those who shall receive, though they cast lots for it, yet shall they not rend it, for it is woven from the top throughout.

For unto you is paradise opened, the tree of life is planted, the time to come is prepared, plenteousness is made ready, a city is builded, the rest is allowed, yea, perfect goodness and wisdom. The root of evil is sealed up from you, weakness and the moth is hid from you, and corruption is fled into hell to be forgotten: sorrows are passed, and in the end is shewed the treasure of immortality.*

Yea! the Treasure of Immortality. In his own words let us now describe this sudden change.

IN NOMINE DEI

אמן

Insit Naturae Regina Isis.

———

At the End of the Century:
At the End of the Year:
At the Hour of Midnight:
Did I complete and bring to perfection the Work of
L.I.L.†

---

* ii Esdras, viii, 52-54.

† Lamp of Invisible Light. L.I.L. The title of the first Æthyr derived from the initial letters of the Three Mighty Names of God. In all there are thirty of

THE EQUINOX

In Mexico: even as I did receive it from him who is reincarnated in me: and this work is to the best of my knowledge a synthesis of what the Gods have given unto me, as far as is possible without violating my obligations unto the Chiefs of the R. R. et A. C. Now did I deem it well that I should rest awhile before resuming my labours in the Great Work, seeing that he, who sleepeth never, shall fall by the wayside, and also remembering the twofold sign: the Power of Horus: and the Power of Hoor-pa-Kraat.*

Now, the year being yet young, One D. A. came unto me, and spake.

And he spake not any more (as had been his wont) in guise of a skeptic and indifferent man: but indeed with the very voice and power of a Great Guru, or of one definitely sent from such a Brother of the Great White Lodge.

Yea! though he spake unto me words all of disapproval, did I give thanks and grace to God that he had deemed my folly worthy to attract his wisdom.

And, after days, did my Guru not leave me in my state of humiliation, and, as I may say, despair: but spake words of comfort saying: " Is it not written that if thine Eye be single thy whole body shall be full of Light?" Adding: " In thee is no power of mental concentration and control of thought: and without this thou mayst achieve nothing."

Under his direction, therefore, I began to apply myself unto the practice of Raja-yoga, at the same time avoiding all, even the smallest, consideration of things occult, as also he bade me.

Thus, at the beginning, I did meditate twice daily, three meditations morning and evening, upon such simple objects as—a white triangle; a red cross; Isis; the simple Tatwas; a wand; and the like. I remained after some three weeks for $59\frac{1}{2}$ minutes at one time, wherein my thought wandered 25 times. Now I began also to consider more complex things: my little Rose Cross;† the

---

these Æthyrs, " whose dominion extendeth in ever widening circles without and beyond the Watch Towers of the Universe." In one sense rightly enough did P. bring to completion the work L.I.L. at the end of the year 1900; but, in another, it took him nine long years of toil before he perfected it, for it was not until the last days of the year 1909 that the work of the Thirty Æthyrs was indeed brought to an end. In 1900 verily was the work conceived, but not until the year 1909 was it brought forth a light unto the darkness, a little spark cast into the Well of Time. (P. merely means that at this time he established a secret Order of this name.)

* The Signs are of Projection and Withdrawal of Force; necessary complements.

† Lost under dramatic circumstances at Frater P. A.'s house in 1909.

complex Tatwas; the Golden Dawn Symbol, and so on. Also I began the exercise of the pendulum and other simple regular motions. Wherefore to-day of Venus, the 22nd of February 1901, I being in the City of Guadalajara, in the Hotel Cosmopolita, I do begin to set down all that I accomplish in this work:

And may the Peace of God, which passeth all understanding, keep my heart and mind through Christ Jesus our Lord.

> Let my mind be open unto
> the Higher:
> Let my heart be the Centre
> of Light:
> Let my body be the
> Temple
> of the
> ROSY CROSS.

> Ex Deo Nascimur
> In Jesu Morimur
> Per Spiritum Sanctum Reviviscimus.

We must now digress in order to give some account of the Eastern theories of the Universe and the mind. Their study will clarify our view of Frater P's progress.

The reader is advised to study Chapter VII of Captain J. F. C. Fuller's "Star in the West" in connection with this exposition.

THE AGNOSTIC POSITION

DIRECT experience is the key to Yoga; direct experience of that Soul (Âtman) or Essence (Purusha) which acting upon Energy (Prâna) and Substance (Âkâsa) differentiates a plant from a stone, an animal from a plant, a man from an animal, a man from a man, and man from God, yet which ultimately is the underlying Equilibrium of all things; for as the Bhaga-vad-Gîta says: " Equilibrium is called Yoga."

Chemically the various groups in the organic and inorganic worlds are similar in structure and composition. One piece of limestone is very much like another, and so also are the actual bodies of any two men, but not so their minds. There-fore, should we wish to discover and understand that Power which differentiates, and yet ultimately balances all appearances, which are derived by the apparently unconscious object and received by the apparently conscious subject, we must look for it in the workings of man's brain.*

---

* Verworn in his "General Physiology" says: "It was found that the sole reality that we are able to discover in the world is mind. The idea of the physical world is only a product of the mind. . . . But this idea is not the whole of mind, for we have many mental constituents, such as the simple sensations of pain and of pleasure, that are not ideas of bodies . . . every process of know-ledge, including scientific knowledge, is merely a psychical event. . . . This fact cannot be banished by the well-known method of the ostrich " (pp. 39, 40).

"The real mystery of mysteries is the mind of man. Why, with a pen or brush, one man sits down and makes a masterpiece, and yet another, with the self-same instruments and opportunities, turns out a daub or botch, is twenty

48

THE TEMPLE OF SOLOMON THE KING

This is but a theory, but a theory worth working upon until a better be derived from truer facts. Adopting it, the transfigured-realist gazes at it with wonder and then casts Theory overboard, and loads his ship with Law; postulates that every cause has its effect; and, when his ship begins to sink, refuses to jettison his wretched cargo, or even to man the pumps of Doubt, because the final result is declared by his philosophy to be unknowable.

If any one cause be unknowable, be it first or last, then all causes are unknowable. The will to create is denied, the will to annihilate is denied, and finally the will to act is denied. Propositions perhaps true to the Master, but certainly not so to the disciple. Because Titian was a great artist and Rodin is a great sculptor, that is no reason why we should abolish art schools and set an embargo on clay.

If the will to act is but a mirage of the mind, then equally so is the will to differentiate or select. If this be true, and the chain of Cause and Effect is eternal, how is it then that Cause A produces effect B, and Cause B effect C, and Cause A + B + C effect X. Where originates this power of production? It is said there is no change, the medium remaining alike throughout. But we say there is a change—a change of form,* and not only a change, but a distinct birth and a distinct death of form. What creates this form? Sense perception. What will destroy this form, and reveal to us that which lies behind it?

times more curious than all the musings of the mystics, works of the Rosicrucians, or the mechanical contrivances which seem to-day so fine, and which our children will disdain as clumsy " (R. B. Cunninghame Graham in his preface to " The Canon ").

    * Form here is synonymous with the Hindu Mâyâ; it is also the chief power of the Buddhist devil, Mara, and even of that mighty devil, Choronzon.

IV   D   49

Presumably cessation of sense perception. How can we prove our theory? By cutting away every perception, every thought-form as it is born, until nothing thinkable is left, not even the thought of the unknowable.

The man of science will often say "I do not know, I really do not know where these bricks came from, or how they were made, or who made them; but here they are; let us build a house and live in it." Now this indeed is a very sensible view to take, and the result is we have some very fine houses built by these excellent bricklayers; but strange to say, this is the fatalist's point of view, and a fatalistic science is indeed a cruel kind of oxymoron. As a matter of fact he is nothing of the kind; for, when he has exhausted his supply of bricks, he starts to look about for others, and when others cannot be found, he takes one of the old ones and picking it to pieces tries to discover of what it is made so that he may make more.

What is small-pox? Really, my friend, I do not know where it came from, or what it is, or how it originated; when a man catches it he either dies or recovers, please go away and don't ask me ridiculous questions! Now this indeed would not be considered a very sensible view to adopt. And why? Simply because small-pox no longer happens to be believed in as a malignant devil, but is, at least partially, known and understood. Similarly, when we have gained as much knowledge of the First Cause as we have of small-pox, we shall no longer *believe* in a Benevolent God or otherwise, but shall, at least partially, know and understand Him as He is or is-not. "I can't learn this!" is the groan of a schoolboy and not the exclamation of a sage. No doctor who is worth his salt will say: "I can't tackle this disease"; he says: "I *will* tackle this disease." So also with the Unknowable, God, *à priori*, First Cause, etc., etc., this metaphysical sickness can be cured. Not certainly in the same manner as small-pox can be; for physicians have a scientific language wherein to express their ideas and thoughts, whilst a mystic too often has not; but by a series of exercises, or a system of symbolic teaching, which will gradually lead the sufferer from the material to the spiritual, and not leave him gazing and wondering at it, as he would at a star in the night.

A fourth dimensional being, outside a few mathematical symbols, would be unable to explain to a third dimensional being a fourth dimensional world, simply because he would be addressing him in a fourth dimensional language. Likewise, in a less degree, would a doctor be unable to explain the theory of inoculation to a savage, but it is quite conceivable that he might be able to teach him how to vaccinate himself or another; which would be after all the chief point gained.

Similarly the Yogi says: I have arrived at a state of Superconsciousness (Samâdhi) and you, my friend, are not only blind, deaf and dumb, and a savage, but the son of a pig into the bargain. You are totally immersed in Darkness (Tamas); a child of ignorance (Avidyâ), and the offspring of illusion (Mâyâ); as mad, insane and idiotic as those unfortunates you lock up in your asylums to convince you, as one of you yourselves has very justly remarked, that you are not all raving mad. For you consider not only one thing, which you insult by calling God, but all things, to be real; and anything which has the slightest odour of reality about it you pronounce an illusion. But, as my brother the Magician has told you, " he

51

who denies anything asserts something," now let me disclose to you this "Something," so that you may find behind the pairs of opposites what this Something is in itself and not in its appearance.

It has been pointed out in a past chapter how that in the West symbol has been added to symbol, and how that in the East symbol has been subtracted from symbol. How in the West the Magician has said: "As all came from God so must all proceed to God," the motion being a forward one, an acceleration of the one already existing. Now let us analyze what is meant by the words of the Yogi when he says: "As all came from God so must all return to God," the motion being, as it will be at once seen, a backward one, a slowing down of the one which already exists, until finally is reached that goal from which we originally set out by a cessation of thinking, a weakening of the vibrations of illusion until they cease to exist in Equilibrium.*

* "The forces of the universe are only known to us, in reality, by disturbances of equilibrium. The state of equilibrium constitutes the limit beyond which we can no longer follow them" (Gustave le Bon, "The Evolution of Matter," p. 94).

THE VEDÂNTA

BEFORE we enter upon the theory and practice of Yoga, it is essential that the reader should possess some slight knowledge of the Vedânta philosophy; and though the following in no way pretends to be an exhaustive account of the same, yet it is hoped that it will prove a sufficient guide to lead the seeker from the Western realms of Magic and action to the Eastern lands of Yoga and renunciation.

To begin with, the root-thought of all philosophy and religion, both Eastern and Western, is that the universe is only an appearance and not a reality, or, as Deussen has it:

> The entire external universe, with its infinite ramifications in space and time, as also the involved and intricate sum of our inner perceptions, is all merely the form under which the essential reality presents itself to a consciousness such as ours, but is not the form in which it may subsist outside of our consciousness and independent of it; that, in other words, the sum total of external and internal experience always and only tells us how things are constituted for us, and for our intellectual capacities, not how they are in themselves and apart from intelligences such as ours.*

Here is the whole of the World's philosophy in a hundred words; the undying question which has perplexed the mind of man from the dim twilight of the Vedas to the sweltering noon-tide of present-day Scepticism, what is the " Ding an sich "; what is the αὐτὸ καθ' αὐτό; what is the Âtman?

That the thing which we perceive and experience is not

* Deussen, "The Philosophy of the Upanishads," p. 40. See also Berkeley's " Three Dialogues between Hylas and Philonous."

the "thing in itself" is very certain, for it is only what "WE see." Yet nevertheless we renounce this as being absurd, or not renouncing it, at least do not live up to our assertion; for, we name that which is a reality to a child, and a deceit or illusion to a man, an apparition or a shadow. Thus, little by little, we beget a new reality upon the old reality, a new falsehood upon the old falsehood, namely, that the thing we see is "an illusion" and is not "a reality," seldom considering that the true difference between the one and the other is but the difference of name. Then after a little do we begin to believe in "the illusion" as firmly and concretely as we once believed in "the reality," seldom considering that all belief is illusionary, and that knowledge is only true as long as it remains unknown.*

Now knowledge is identification, not with the inner or outer of a thing, but with that which cannot be explained by either, and which is the essence of the thing in itself,† and which the Upanishads name the Âtman. Identification with this Âtman (Emerson's "Oversoul") is therefore the end of Religion and Philosophy alike.

"Verily he who has seen, heard, comprehended and known the Âtman, by him is this entire universe known." ‡ Because there is but one Âtman and not many Âtmans.

---

* Once the Unknown becomes known it becomes untrue, it loses its Virginity, that mysterious power of attraction the Unknown always possesses; it no longer represents our ideal, though it may form an excellent foundation for the next ideal; and so on until Knowledge and Nescience are out-stepped. General and popular Knowledge is like a common prostitute, the toy of any man. To maintain this purity, this virginity, are the mysteries kept secret from the multitude.

† And yet again this is a sheer deceit, as every conceit must be.

‡ Brihadâranyaka Upanishad, 2. 4. 5b.

THE TEMPLE OF SOLOMON THE KING

The first veil against which we must warn the aspirant is the entanglement of language, of words and of names. The merest tyro will answer, "of course you need not explain to me that, if I call a thing 'A' or 'B,' it makes no difference to that thing in itself." And yet not only the tyro, but many of the astutest philosophers have fallen into this snare, and not only once but an hundred times; the reason being that they have not remained silent* about that which can only be "known" and not "believed in," and that which can never be named without begetting a duality (an untruth), and consequently a whole world of illusions. It is the crucifixion of every would-be Saviour, this teaching of a truth under the symbol of a lie, this would-be explanation to the multitude of the unexplainable, this passing off on the "canaille" the strumpet of language (the Consciously Known) in the place of the Virgin of the World (the Consciously Unknown). †

No philosophy has ever grasped this terrible limitation so firmly as the Vedânta. "All experimental knowledge, the four Vedas and the whole series of empirical science, as they are enumerated in Chândogya, 7. 1. 2-3, are 'nâma eva,' 'mere name.'" ‡ As the Rig Veda says, "They call him Indra, Mitra, Varuna, Agni, and he is heavenly nobly-winged Garutmân. To what is One, sages give many a title: they call it Agni, Yama, Mâtirisvan." §

* The highest men are calm, silent and unknown. They are the men who really know the power of thought; they are sure that, even if they go into a cave and close the door and simply think five true thoughts and then pass away, these five thoughts of theirs will live through eternity. (Vivekânanda, "Karma Yoga," Udbodhan edition, pp. 164, 165.)

† Or the Unconsciously Known.　　　　　　‡ Deussen, *ibid.*, p. 76.

§ "Rigveda" (Griffiths), i. 164. 46. "You may call the Creator of all things

THE EQUINOX

Thus we find that "duality" in the East is synonymous with "a mere matter of words,"* and further, that, when anything is (or can be) described by a word or a name, the knowledge concerning it is Avidyâ, "ignorance."

No sooner are the eyes of a man opened † than he sees "good and evil," and becomes a prey to the illusions he has set out to conquer. He gets something apart from himself, and whether it be Religion, Science, or Philosophy it matters not; for in the vacuum which he thereby creates, between him and it, burns the fever that he will never subdue until he has annihilated both.‡ God, Immortality, Freedom, are appearances and not realities, they are Mâyâ and not Âtman; Space, Time and Causality§ are appearances and not realities, they also are Mâyâ and not Âtman. All that is not Âtman is Mâyâ, and Mâyâ is ignorance, and ignorance is sin.

Now the philosophical fall of the Âtman produces the Macrocosm and the Microcosm, God and not-God—the Universe, or the power which asserts a separateness, an indi-

---

by different names: Liber, Hercules, Mercury, are but different names of the same divine being" (Seneca, iv, 7. 8).

   * "Chândogya Upanishad," 6. 1. 3. Also of "form."

   † That is to say, when he gains knowledge.

   ‡ This is the meaning of "Nequaquam Vacuum."

   § Modern Materialism receives many a rude blow at the hands of Gustave le Bon. This great Frenchman writes: "These fundamental dogmas, the bases of modern science, the researches detailed in this work tend to destroy. If the principle of the conservation of energy—which, by the by, is simply a bold generalization of experiments made in very simple cases—likewise succumbs to the blows which are already attacking it, the conclusion must be arrived at that nothing in the world is eternal." ("The Evolution of Matter," p. 18.) In other words, all is full of birth, growth, and decay, that is Mâyâ. Form to the Materialist, Name to the Idealist, and Nothing to him who has risen above both.

56

viduality, a self-consciousness—I am! This is explained in Brihadâranyaka, I. 4. I. as follows:

> "In the beginning the Âtman alone in the form of a man * was this universe. He gazed around; he saw nothing there but himself. Thereupon he cried out at the beginning: 'It is I.' Thence originated the name I. Therefore to-day, when anyone is summoned, he answers first 'It is I'; and then only he names the other name which he bears." †

This Consciousness of "I" is the second veil which man meets on his upward journey, and, unless he avoid it and escape from its hidden meshes, which are a thousandfold more dangerous than the entanglements of the veil of words, he will never arrive at that higher consciousness, that super-consciousness (Samâdhi), which will consume him back into the Âtman from which he came.

As the fall of the Âtman arises from the cry "It is I," so does the fall of the Self-consciousness of the universe-man arise through that Self-consciousness crying "I am it," thereby identifying the shadow with the substance; from this fall arises the first veil we had occasion to mention, the veil of duality, of words, of belief.

This duality we find even in the texts of the oldest Upanishads, such as in Brihadâranyaka, 3. 4. I. "It is thy soul,

---

* "There are two persons of the Deity, one in heaven, and one which descended upon earth in the form of man (*i.e.*, the Adam Qadmon), and the Holy One, praised be It! unites them (in the union of Samâdhi, that is, of *Sam* (Greek σὺν, *together with*), and *Adhi*, Hebrew *Adonai, the Lord*). There are three Lights in the Upper Holy Divine united in One, and this is the foundation of the doctrine of Every-Thing, this is the beginning of the Faith, and Every-Thing is concentrated therein" ("Zohar III," beginning of paragraph. *She'-meneeh*, fol. 36a.

† It is fully realized that outside the vastness of the symbol this "Fall of God" is as impertinent as it is unthinkable.

which is within all." And also again in the same Upanishad
(I. 4. 10.), "He who worships another divinity (than the
Âtman), and says 'it is one and I am another' is not wise,
but he is like a house-dog of the gods." And house-dogs shall
we remain so long as we cling to a belief in a knowing subject and a known object, or in the worship of anything, even
of the Âtman itself, as long as it remains apart from ourselves. Such a dilemma as this does not take long to induce
one of those periods of "spiritual dryness," one of those
"dark nights of the soul" so familiar to all mystics and even
to mere students of mysticism. And such a night seems to
have closed around Yâjñavalkhya when he exclaimed:

> After death there is no consciousness. For where there is as it were a duality,
> there one sees the other, smells, hears, addresses, comprehends, and knows the
> other; but when everything has become to him his own self, how should he
> smell, see, hear, address, understand, or know anyone at all? How should he
> know him, through whom he knows all this, how should he know the knower? *

Thus does the Supreme Âtman become unknowable, on
account of the individual Âtman † remaining unknown; and
further, will remain unknowable as long as consciousness of a
separate Supremacy exists in the heart of the individual.

Directly the seeker realizes this, a new reality is born, and
the clouds of night roll back and melt away before the light
of a breaking dawn, brilliant beyond all that have preceded it.
Destroy this consciousness, and the Unknowable may become
the Known, or at least the Unknown, in the sense of the undiscovered. Thus we find the old Vedantist presupposing an
Âtman and a σύμβολον of it, so that he might better transmute

* Brihadâranyaka Upanishad, 2. 4. 12.

† The illusion of thinking ourselves similar to the Unity and yet separated
from It.

the unknown individual soul into the known, and the unknowable Supreme Soul into the unknown, and then, from the knowable through the known to the knower, get back to the Âtman and Equilibrium—Zero.

All knowledge he asserts to be Mâyâ, and only by paradoxes is the Truth revealed.

> Only he who knows it not knows it,
> Who knows it, he knows it not;
> Unknown is it by the wise,
> But by the ignorant known.*

These dark nights of Scepticism descend upon all systems just as they descend upon all individuals, at no stated times, but as a reaction after much hard work; and usually they are forerunners of a new and higher realization of another unknown land to explore. Thus again and again do we find them rising and dissolving like some strange mist over the realms of the Vedânta. To disperse them we must consume them in that same fire which has consumed all we held dear; we must turn our engines of war about and destroy our sick and wounded, so that those who are strong and whole may press on the faster to victory.

As early as the days of the Rig Veda, before the beginning was, there was "neither not-being nor yet being." This thought again and again rumbles through the realms of philosophy, souring the milk of man's understanding with its bitter scepticism.

> Not-being was this in the beginning,
> From it being arose.
> Self-fashioned indeed out of itself . . .
> The being and the beyond

---

* Kena Upanishad, 11.

59

THE EQUINOX

Expressible and inexpressible,
Founded and foundationless,
Consciousness and unconsciousness,
Reality and unreality.*

All these are vain attempts to obscure the devotee's mind
into believing in that Origin he could in no way understand,
by piling up symbols of extravagant vastness. All, as with
the Qabalists, was based on Zero, all, save one thing, and this
one thing saved the mind of man from the fearful palsy of
doubt which had shaken to ruin his brave certainties, his
audacious hopes and his invincible resolutions. Man, slowly
through all his doubts, began to realize that if indeed all were
Mâyâ, a matter of words, he at least existed. " I am," he cried,
no longer, " I am it." †

And with the Îsâ Upanishad he whispered:

Into dense darkness he enters
Who has conceived becoming to be naught,
Into yet denser he
Who has conceived becoming to be aught.

Abandoning this limbo of Causality, just as the Buddhist
did at a later date, he tackled the practical problem "What am
I? To hell with God! "

The self is the basis for the validity of proof, and therefore is constituted
also before the validity of proof. And because it is thus formed it is impossible
to call it in question. For we may call a thing in question which comes up to us
from without, but not our own essential being. For if a man calls it in question
yet is it his own essential being.

An integral part is here revealed in each of us which is a
reality, perhaps the only reality it is given us to know, and

* Taittirîya Brâhmana, 2. 7.   † *I.e.,* " Existence is " אהיה אשר אהיה.

60

one we possess irrespective of our not being able to understand it. We have a soul, a veritable living Âtman, irrespective of all codes, sciences, theories, sects and laws. What then is this Âtman, and how can we understand it, that is to say, see it solely, or identify all with it?

The necessity of doing this is pointed out in Chândogya, 8. 1. 6.

> He who departs from this world without having known the soul or those true desires, his part in all worlds is a life of constraint; but he who departs from this world after having known the soul and those true desires, his part in all worlds is a life of freedom.

In the Brihadâranyaka,* king Janaka asks Yâjñavalkhya, "what serves man for light?" That sage answers:

> The sun serves him for light. When however the sun has set?—the moon. And when he also has set?—the fire. And when this also is extinguished?—the voice. And when this also is silenced? Then is he himself his own light.†

This passage occurs again and again in the same form, and in paraphrase, as we read through the Upanishads. In Kâthaka 5. 15 we find:

> There no sun shines, no moon, nor glimmering star,
> Nor yonder lightning, the fire of earth is quenched;

---

* Brihadâranyaka Upanishad, 4. 3-4.

† These refer to the mystic lights in man. Compare this with the Diagram 2 "The Paths and Grades" in "The Neophyte." After the Âtman in the aspirant has been awakened by the trumpet of Israfel (The Angel) he proceeds by the path of ש. The next path the Aspirant must travel is that of ר—the Sun; the next that of ק—the Moon; the next that of צ—the Star. This path brings him to the Fire of Netzach. When this fire is extinguished comes the Voice or Lightning, after which the Light which guides the aspirant is Himself, his Holy Guardian Angel, the Âtman—Adonai.

61

From him,* who alone shines, all else borrows its brightness,
The whole world bursts into splendour at his shining.

And again in Maitrâyana, 6. 24.

When the darkness is pierced through, then is reached that which is not affected by darkness; and he who has thus pierced through that which is so affected, he has beheld like a glittering circle of sparks Brahman bright as the sun, endowed with all might, beyond the reach of darkness, that shines in yonder sun as in the moon, the fire and the lightning.

Thus the Âtman little by little came to be known and no longer believed in; yet at first it appears that those who realized it kept their methods to themselves, and simply explained to their followers its greatness and splendour by parable and fable, such as we find in Brihadâranyaka, 2. 1. 19.

That is his real form, in which he is exalted above desire, and is free from evil and fear. For just as one who dallies with a beloved wife has no consciousness of outer or inner, so the spirit also dallying with the self, whose essence is knowledge, has no consciousness of inner or outer. That is his real form, wherein desire is quenched, and he is himself his own desire, separate from desire and from distress. Then the father is no longer father, the mother no longer mother, the worlds no longer worlds, the gods no longer gods, the Vedas no longer Vedas. . . . This is his supreme goal.

As theory alone cannot for ever satisfy man's mind in the solution of the life-riddle, so also when once the seeker has become the seer, when once actual living men have attained and become Adepts, their methods of attainment cannot for long remain entirely hidden.† And either from their teachings directly, or from those of their disciples, we find in India

* The Âtman.

† As the light of a lamp brought into a dark room is reflected by all surfaces around it, so is the illumination of the Adept reflected even by his unilluminated followers.

62

sprouting up from the roots of the older Upanishads two great systems of practical philosophy:

     1. The attainment by Sannyâsa.
     2. The attainment by Yoga.

The first seeks, by artificial means, to suppress desire. The second by scientific experiments to annihilate the consciousness of plurality.

In the natural course of events the Sannyâsa precedes the Yoga, for it consists in casting off from oneself home, possessions, family and all that engenders and stimulates desire; whilst the Yoga consists in withdrawing the organs of sense from the objects of sense, and by concentrating them on the Inner Self, Higher Self, Augoeides, Âtman, or Adonai, shake itself free from the illusions of Mâyâ—the world of plurality, and secure union with this Inner Self or Âtman.

ATTAINMENT BY YOGA.

ACCORDING to the Shiva Sanhita there are two doctrines found in the Vedas: the doctrines of "Karma Kânda" (sacrificial works, etc.) and of "Jnana Kânda" (science and knowledge). "Karma Kânda" is twofold—good and evil, and according to how we live "there are many enjoyments in heaven," and "in hell there are many sufferings." Having once realized the truth of "Karma Kânda" the Yogi renounces the works of virtue and vice, and engages in "Jnana Kânda"—knowledge.

In the Shiva Sanhita we read : *

In the proper season, various creatures are born to enjoy the consequences of their karma.† As through mistake mother-of-pearl is taken for silver, so through the error of one's own karma man mistakes Brahma for the universe.

Being too much and deeply engaged in the manifested world, the delusion arises about that which is manifested—the subject. There is no other cause (of this delusion). Verily, verily, I tell you the truth.

If the practiser of Yoga wishes to cross the ocean of the world, he should renounce all the fruits of his works, having performed all the duties of his âshrama.‡

"Jnana Kânda" is the application of science to "Karma Kânda," the works of good and evil, that is to say of Duality.

* Shiva Sanhita, ii. 43. 45. 51.

† Work and the effects of work. The so-called law of Cause and Effect in the moral and physical worlds.

‡ The four âshramas are (1) To live as a Brahmachârin—to spend a portion of one's life with a Brahman teacher. (2) To live as a Grihastha—to rear a family and carry out the obligatory sacrifices. (3) To live as a Vânaprastha—

64

Little by little it eats away the former, as a strong acid would eat away a piece of steel, and ultimately when the last atom has been destroyed it ceases to exist as a science, or as a method, and becomes the Aim, *i.e.*, Knowledge. This is most beautifully described in the above-mentioned work as follows:

34. That Intelligence which incites the functions into the paths of virtue and vice "am I." All this universe, moveable and immoveable, is from me; all things are seen through me; all are absorbed into me; * because there exists nothing but spirit, and "I am that spirit." There exists nothing else.

35. As in innumerable cups full of water, many reflections of the sun are seen, but the substance is the same; similarly individuals, like cups, are innumerable, but the vivifying spirit like the sun is one.

49. All this universe, moveable or immoveable, has come out of Intelligence. Renouncing everything else, take shelter of it.

50. As space pervades a jar both in and out, similarly within and beyond this ever-changing universe there exists one universal Spirit.

58. Since from knowledge of that Cause of the universe, ignorance is destroyed, therefore the Spirit is Knowledge; and this Knowledge is everlasting.

59. That Spirit from which this manifold universe existing in time takes its origin is one, and unthinkable.

62. Having renounced all false desires and chains, the Sannyâsi and Yogi see certainly in their own spirit the universal Spirit.

63. Having seen the Spirit that brings forth happiness in their own spirit, they forget this universe, and enjoy the ineffable bliss of Samâdhi.†

As in the West there are various systems of Magic, so in the East are there various systems of Yoga, each of which purports to lead the aspirant from the realm of Mâyâ to that of Truth in Samâdhi. The most important of these are:

1. Gnana Yoga.   Union by Knowledge.
2. Raja Yoga.   Union by Will.
3. Bhakta Yoga.   Union by Love.

to withdraw into solitude and meditate. (4) To live as a Sannyâsin—to await the spirit's release into the Supreme Spirit.

* At the time of the Pralaya.   † "Shiva Sanhita," chap. i.

4. Hatha Yoga.	Union by Courage.
5. Mantra Yoga.	Union through Speech.
6. Karma Yoga.	Union through Work.*

The two chief of these six methods according to the Bhagavad-Gîta are: Yoga by Sâñkhya (Raja Yoga), and Yoga by Action (Karma Yoga). But the difference between these two is to be found in their form rather than in their substance; for, as Krishna himself says:

Renunciation (Raja Yoga) and Yoga by action (Karma Yoga) both lead to the highest bliss; of the two, Yoga by action is verily better than renunciation by action . . . Children, not Sages, speak of the Sâñkhya and the Yoga as different; he who is duly established in one obtaineth the fruits of both. That place which is gained by the Sâñkhyas is reached by the Yogis also. He seeth, who seeth that the Sâñkhya and the Yoga are one.†

Or, in other words, he who understands the equilibrium of action and renunciation (of addition and subtraction) is as he who perceives that in truth the circle is the line, the end the beginning.

To show how extraordinarily closely allied are the methods of Yoga to those of Magic, we will quote the following three verses from the Bhagavad-Gîta, which, with advantage, the reader may compare with the citations already made from the works of Abramelin and Eliphas Levi.

When the mind, bewildered by the Scriptures (Shruti), shall stand immovable, fixed in contemplation (Samâdhi), then shalt thou attain to Yoga.‡

Whatsoever thou doest, whatsoever thou eatest, whatsoever thou offerest,

---

* Besides these, there are several lesser known Yogas, for the most part variant of the above such as: Ashtânga, Laya, and Târaka. See " Hatha-Yoga Pradipika," p. iii.

† The " Bhagavad-Gîta." Fifth Discourse, 2-5.

‡ *Ibid.* Second Discourse, 53.

whatsoever thou givest, whatsoever thou doest of austerity, O Kaunteya, do thou that as an offering unto Me.

On Me fix thy mind; be devoted to Me; sacrifice to Me; prostrate thyself before Me; harmonized thus in the SELF (Âtman), thou shalt come unto Me, having Me as thy supreme goal.*

These last two verses are taken from " The Yoga of the Kingly Science and the Kingly Secret"; and if put into slightly different language might easily be mistaken for a passage out of " The Book of the Sacred Magic."

Not so, however, the first, which is taken from " The Yoga by the Sâñkhya," and which is reminiscent of the Quietism of Molinos and Madam de Guyon rather than of the operations of a ceremonial magician. And it was just this Quietism that P. as yet had never fully experienced; and he, realizing this, it came about that when once the key of Yoga was proffered him, he preferred to open the door of Renunciation and close that of Action, and to abandon the Western methods by the means of which he had already advanced so far rather than to continue in them. This in itself was the first great Sacrifice which he made upon the path of Renunciation—to abandon all that he had as yet attained to, to cut himself off from the world, and like an Hermit in a desolate land seek salvation by himself, through himself and of Himself. Ultimately, as we shall see, he renounced even this disownment, for which he now sacrificed all, and, by an unification of both, welded the East to the West, the two halves of that perfect whole which had been lying apart since that night wherein the breath of God moved upon the face of the waters and the limbs of a living world struggled from out the Chaos of Ancient Night.

* *Ibid.* Ninth Discourse, 27, 34.

THE YOGAS

DIRECT experience is the end of Yoga. How can this direct experience be gained? And the answer is: by Concentration or Will. Swami Vivekânanda on this point writes:

> Those who really want to be Yogis must give up, once for all, this nibbling at things. Take up one idea. Make that one idea your life; dream of it; think of it; live on that idea. Let the brain, the body, muscles, nerves, every part of your body, be full of that idea, and just leave every other idea alone. This is the way to success, and this is the way great spiritual giants are produced. Others are mere talking machines. . . . To succeed, you must have tremendous perseverance, tremendous will. "I will drink the ocean," says the persevering soul. "At my will mountains will crumble up." Have that sort of energy, that sort of will, work hard, and you will reach the goal.*

"O Keshara," cries Arjuna, "enjoin in me this terrible action!" This will TO WILL.

To turn the mind inwards, as it were, and stop it wandering outwardly, and then to concentrate all its powers upon itself, are the methods adopted by the Yogi in opening the closed Eye which sleeps in the heart of every one of us, and to create this will TO WILL. By doing so he ultimately comes face to face with something which is indestructible, on account of it being uncreateable, and which knows no dissatisfaction.

* Vivekânanda, "Raja Yoga," Udbodhan edition, pp. 51, 52. "Every valley shall be filled, and every mountain and hill shall be brought low; and the crooked shall be made straight, and the rough ways shall be made smooth. . . . Prepare ye the way of Adonai."—Luke, iii, 5, 4.

THE TEMPLE OF SOLOMON THE KING

Every child is aware that the mind possesses a power known as the reflective faculty. We hear ourselves talk; and we stand apart and see ourselves work and think. We stand aside from ourselves and anxiously or fearlessly watch and criticize our lives. There are two persons in us,—the thinker (or the worker) and the seer. The unwinding of the hoodwink from the eyes of the seer, for in most men the seer is, like a mummy, wrapped in the countless rags of thought, is what Yoga purposes to do: in other words, to accomplish no less a task than the mastering of the forces of the Universe, the surrender of the gross vibrations of the external world to the finer vibrations of the internal, and then to become one with the subtle Vibrator—the Seer Himself.

We have mentioned the six chief systems of Yoga, and now before entering upon what for us at present must be the two most important of them,—namely, Hatha Yoga and Raja Yoga, we intend, as briefly as possible, to explain the remaining four, and also the necessary conditions under which all methods of Yoga should be practised.

GNANA YOGA.   Union through Knowledge.

Gnana Yoga is that Yoga which commences with a study of the impermanent wisdom of this world and ends with the knowledge of the permanent wisdom of the Âtman. Its first stage is Viveka, the discernment of the real from the unreal. Its second Vairâgya, indifference to the knowledge of the world, its sorrows and joys. Its third Mukti, release, and unity with the Âtman.

In the fourth discourse of the Bhagavad-Gîta we find Gnana Yoga praised as follows:

69

Better than the sacrifice of any objects is the sacrifice of wisdom, O Parantapa. All actions in their entirety, O Pârtha, culminate in wisdom.

As the burning fire reduces fuel to ashes, O Arjuna, so doth the fire of wisdom reduce all actions to ashes.

Verily there is nothing so pure in this world as wisdom; he that is perfected in Yoga finds it in the Âtman in due season.*

KARMA YOGA.   Union through Work.

Very closely allied to Gnana Yoga is Karma Yoga, Yoga through work, which may seem only a means towards the former.   But this is not so, for not only must the aspirant commune with the Âtman through the knowledge or wisdom he attains, but also through the work which aids him to attain it.

A good example of Karma Yoga is quoted from Chuang-Tzu by Flagg in his work on Yoga.   It is as follows:

Prince Hui's cook was cutting up a bullock. Every blow of his hand, every heave of his shoulders, every tread of his foot, every thrust of his knee, every *whshh* of rent flesh, every *chhk* of the chopper, was in perfect harmony,—rhythmical like the dance of the mulberry grove, simultaneous like the chords of Ching Shou." "Well done," cried the Prince; "yours is skill indeed." "Sire," replied the cook, "I have always devoted myself to *Tao* (which here means the same as Yoga). *It is better than skill.* When I first began to cut up bullocks I saw before me simply whole *bullocks*. After three years' practice I saw no more whole animals. And now I work with my mind and not with my eye. When my senses bid me stop, but my mind urges me on, I fall back upon eternal

* "The Bhagavad-Gîtâ," iv, 33, 37, 38. Compare with the above "The Wisdom of Solomon," *e.g.*: "For wisdom, which is the worker of all things, taught me: for in her is an understanding spirit, holy, one only, manifold, subtle, lively, clear, undefiled, plain, not subject to hurt, loving the thing that is good, quick, which cannot be letted, ready to do good. . . . for wisdom is more moving than any motion: she passeth and goeth through all things by reason of her pureness. For she is the breath of the power of God." (Chap. VII, 22, 24, 25.)

70

principles. I follow such openings or cavities as there may be, according to the natural constitution of the animal. A good cook changes his chopper once a year, because he cuts. An ordinary cook once a month—because he hacks. But I have had this chopper nineteen years, and although I have cut up many thousand bullocks, its edge is as if fresh from the whetstone.*

MANTRA YOGA. Union through Speech.

This type of Yoga consists in repeating a name or a sentence or verse over and over again until the speaker and the word spoken become one in a perfect concentration. Usually speaking it is used as an adjunct to some other practice, under one or more of the other Yoga methods. Thus the devotee to the God Shiva will repeat his name over and over again until at length the great God opens his Eye and the world is destroyed.

Some of the most famous mantras are:
"Aum mani padme Hum."
"Aum Shivaya Vashi."
"Aum Tat Sat Aum."
"Namo Shivaya namaha Aum."

The pranava AUM† plays an important part throughout the whole of Indian Yoga, and especially is it considered sacred by the Mantra-Yogi, who is continually using it. To pronounce it properly the "A" is from the throat, the "U" in the middle, and the "M" at the lips. This typifies the whole course of breath.

* "Yoga or Transformation," p. 196. Control, or Restraint, is the Key to Karma Yoga; weakness is its damnation. Of the Karma Yogi Vivekânanda writes: "He goes through the streets of a big city with all their traffic, and his mind is as calm as if he were in a cave, where not a sound could reach him; and he is intensely working all the time." "Karma Yoga," p. 17.

† See Vivekânanda's "Bhakti-Yoga," pp. 62-68.

It is the best support, the bow off which the soul as the arrow flies to Brahman, the arrow which is shot from the body as bow in order to pierce the darkness, the upper fuel with which the body as the lower fuel is kindled by the fire of the vision of God, the net with which the fish of Prâna is drawn out, and sacrificed in the fire of the Âtman, the ship on which a man voyages over the ether of the heart, the chariot which bears him to the world of Brahman.[*]

At the end of the " Shiva Sanhita " there are some twenty verses dealing with the Mantra. And as in so many other Hindu books, a considerable amount of mystery is woven around these sacred utterances. We read:

190. In the four-petalled Muladhara lotus is the seed of speech, brilliant as lightning.

191. In the heart is the seed of love, beautiful as the Bandhuk flower. In the space between the two eyebrows is the seed of Shakti, brilliant as tens of millions of moons. These three seeds should be kept secret.[†]

These three Mantras can only be learnt from a Guru, and are not given in the above book. By repeating them a various number of times certain results happen. Such as: after eighteen lacs, the body will rise from the ground and remain suspended in the air; after an hundred lacs, " the great yogi is absorbed in the Para-Brahman.[‡]

BHAKTA YOGA. Union by love.

In Bhakta Yoga the aspirant usually devotes himself to some special deity, every action of his life being done in honour and glory of this deity, and, as Vivekânanda tells us, " he has not to suppress any single one of his emotions, he only strives to intensify them and direct them to God." Thus, if he devoted himself to Shiva, he must reflect in his life to his utmost the life of Shiva; if to Shakti the life of Shakti, until the seer and the seen become one in the mystic union of attainment.

* Deussen. " The Upanishads," p. 390.
† " Shiva Sanhita," chap. v. The seed in each case is the Mantra.
‡ The Absolute.

THE TEMPLE OF SOLOMON THE KING

Of Bhakta Yoga the " Nârada Sûtra " says :

58. Love (Bhakti) is easier than other methods.
59. Being self-evident it does not depend on other truths.
60. And from being of the nature of peace and supreme bliss.*

This exquisite little Sûtra commences :

1. We will now explain Love.
2. Its nature is extreme devotion to some one.
3. Love is immortal.
4. Obtaining it man becomes perfect, becomes immortal, becomes satisfied.
5. And obtaining it he desires nothing, grieves not, hates not, does not delight, makes no effort.
6. Knowing it he becomes intoxicated, transfixed, and rejoices in the Self (Âtman).

This is further explained at the end of Swâtmârâm Swâmi's " Hatha-Yoga."

Bhakti really means the constant perception of the form of the Lord by the Antahkarana. There are nine kinds of Bhaktis enumerated. Hearing his histories and relating them, remembering him, worshipping his feet, offering flowers to him, bowing to him (in soul), behaving as his servant, becoming his companion and offering up one's Âtman to him. . . . Thus, Bhakti, in its most transcendental aspect, is included in Sampradnyâta Samâdhi.‡

---

* Nârada Sûtra. Translated by T. Sturdy. Also see the works of Bhagavan Ramanuja, Bhagavan Vyasa, Prahlada, and more particularly Vivekânanda's " Bhakti Yoga." Bhakta Yoga is divided into two main divisions. (1) The preparatory, known as "Gauni"; (2) The devotional, known as "Pará." Thus it very closely resembles, even in detail, the Operation of Abramelin, in which the aspirant, having thoroughly prepared himself, devotes himself to the invocation of his Holy Guardian Angel.

‡ In Bhakta Yoga the disciple usually devotes himself to his Guru, to whom he offers his devotion. The Guru being treated as the God himself with which the Chela wishes to unite. Eventually " He alone sees no distinctions! The mighty ocean of love has entered into him, and he sees not men, animals and plants or the sun, moon and the stars, but beholds his Beloved everywhere and in everything. Vivekânanda, "Bhakti Yoga," Udbodham edition, p. 111. The Sufis were Bhakti Yogis, so was Christ. Buddha was a Gnani Yogi.

The Gnana Yoga P., as the student, had already long practised in his study of the Holy Qabalah; so also had he Karma Yoga by his acts of service whilst a Neophyte in the Order of the Golden Dawn; but now at the suggestion of D. A. he betook himself to the practice of Hatha and Raja Yoga.

Hatha Yoga and Raja Yoga are so intimately connected, that instead of forming two separate methods, they rather form the first half and second half of one and the same.

Before discussing either the Hatha or Raja Yogas, it will be necessary to explain the conditions under which Yoga should be performed. These conditions being the conventional ones, each individual should by practice discover those more particularly suited to himself.

i. *The Guru.*

Before commencing any Yoga practice, according to every Hindu book upon this subject, it is first necessary to find a Guru,* or teacher, to whom the disciple (Chela) must entirely devote himself: as the " Shiva Sanhita " says:

11. Only the knowledge imparted by a Guru is powerful and useful; otherwise it becomes fruitless, weak and very painful.

12. He who attains knowledge by pleasing his Guru with every attention, readily obtains success therein.

13. There is not the least doubt that Guru is father, Guru is mother, and Guru is God even: and as such, he should be served by all, with their thought, word and deed.†

ii. Place. *Solitude and Silence.*

The place where Yoga is performed should be a beautiful and pleasant place, according to the Shiva Sanhita.‡ In the

* A Guru is as necessary in Yoga as a Music Master is in Music.
† " Shiva Sanhita," chap. iii.
‡ *Ibid.*, chap. v, 184, 185. The aspirant should firstly, join the assembly of

74

Kshurikâ Upanishad, 2. 21, it states that " a noiseless place " should be chosen; and in S'vetâs'vatara, 2. 10:

Let the place be pure, and free also from boulders and sand,
Free from fire, smoke, and pools of water,
Here where nothing distracts the mind or offends the eye,
In a hollow protected from the wind a man should compose himself.

The dwelling of a Yogi is described as follows:

The practiser of Hathayoga should live alone in a small Matha or monastery situated in a place free from rocks, water and fire; of the extent of a bow's length, and in a fertile country ruled over by a virtuous king, where he will not be disturbed.

The Matha should have a very small door, and should be without any windows; it should be level and without any holes; it should be neither too high nor too long. It should be very clean, being daily smeared over with cow-dung, and should be free from all insects. Outside it should be a small corridor with a raised seat and a well, and the whole should be surrounded by a wall. . . .*

iii. *Time.*

The hours in which Yoga should be performed vary with the instructions of the Guru, but usually they should be four times a day, at sunrise, mid-day, sunset and mid-night.

iv. *Food.*

According to the " Hatha-Yoga Pradipika ": " Moderate

good men but talk little; secondly, should eat little; thirdly, should renounce the company of men, the company of women, all company. He should practise in secrecy in a retired place. " For the sake of appearances he should remain in society, but should not have his heart in it. He should not renounce the duties of his profession, caste or rank, but let him perform these merely as an instrument without any thought of the event. By thus doing there is no sin." This is sound Rosicrucian doctrine, by the way.

* " Hatha-Yoga Pradipika," pp. 5, 6. Note the similarity of these conditions to those laid down in " The Book of the Sacred Magic." Also see " Gheranda Sanhita," p. 33.

diet is defined to mean taking pleasant and sweet food, leaving one fourth of the stomach free, and offering up the act to Shiva." *

Things that have been once cooked and have since grown cold should be avoided, also foods containing an excess of salt and sourness. Wheat, rice, barley, butter, sugar, honey and beans may be eaten, and pure water and milk drunk. The Yogi should partake of one meal a day, usually a little after noon. "Yoga should not be practised immediately after a meal, nor when one is very hungry; before beginning the practice, some milk and butter should be taken." †

v. *Physical considerations.*

The aspirant to Yoga should study his body as well as his mind, and should cultivate regular habits. He should strictly adhere to the rules of health and sanitation. He should rise an hour before sunrise, and bathe himself twice daily, in the morning and the evening, with cold water (if he can do so without harm to his health). His dress should be warm so that he is not distracted by the changes of weather.

vi. *Moral considerations.*

The Yogi should practise kindness to all creatures, he should abandon enmity towards any person, "pride, duplicity, and crookedness" . . . and the "companionship of women." ‡ Further, in Chapter 5 of the "Shiva Sanhita" the hindrances

---

* "Hatha-Yoga Pradipika," p. 22. On the question of food Vivekânanda in his "Bhakti Yoga," p. 90, says: "The cow does not eat meat, nor does the sheep. Are they great Yogins? . . . Any fool may abstain from eating meat; surely that alone gives him no more distinction than to herbivorous animals." Also see "Gheranda Sanhita," pp. 34-36.

† "Shiva Sanhita," iii, 37.   ‡ *Ibid.*, iii, 33.

of Enjoyment, Religion and Knowledge are expounded at some considerable length. Above all the Yogi "should work like a master and not like a slave." *

HATHA YOGA. Union by Courage.

It matters not what attainment the aspirant seeks to gain, or what goal he has in view, the one thing above all others which is necessary is a healthy body, and a body which is under control. It is hopeless to attempt to obtain stability of mind in one whose body is ever leaping from land to water like a frog; with such, any sudden influx of illumination may bring with it not enlightenment but mania; therefore it is that all the great masters have set the task of courage before that of endeavour.† He who *dares* to *will*, will *will* to know, and knowing will keep silence; ‡ for even to such as have entered the Supreme Order, there is no way found whereby they may break the stillness and communicate to those who have not ceased to hear.§ The guardian of the Temple is Adonai, he alone holds the key of the Portal, seek it of Him, for there is none other that can open for thee the door.

Now to dare much is to will a little, so it comes about that though Hatha Yoga is the physical Yoga which teaches the aspirant how to control his body, yet is it also Raja Yoga

* Vivekânanda, "Karma-Yoga," p. 62.

† As in the case of Jesus, the aspirant, for the joy that is set before him, must *dare* to endure the cross, despising the shame; if he would be "set down at the right hand of the throne of God." Hebrews, xii, 2.

‡ "If there be no interpreter, let him keep silence in the church; and let him speak to himself, and to God" (1 Corinthians, xiv, 28) has more than one meaning.

§ "And when he had opened the seventh seal, there was silence in heaven about the space of half an hour" (Rev. viii, 1).

which will teach him how to control his mind. Little by little, as the body comes under control, does the mind assert its sway over the body; and little by little, as the mind asserts its sway, does it come gradually, little by little under the rule of the Âtman, until ultimately the Âtman, Augoeides, Higher Self or Adonai fills the Space which was once occupied solely by the body and mind of the aspirant. Therefore through the death of the body as it were is the resurrection of the Higher Self accomplished, and the pinnacles of that Temple, whose foundations are laid deep in the black earth, are lost among the starry Palaces of God.

In the " Hatha-Yoga Pradipika " we read that " there can be no Raja Yoga without Hatha Yoga, and *vice versa*, that to those who wander in the darkness of the conflicting Sects unable to obtain Raja Yoga, the most merciful Swâtmârâma Yogi offers the light of Hathavidya." *

In the practice of this mystic union which is brought about by the Hatha Yoga and the Raja Yoga exercises the conditions necessary are:

1. *Yama*: Non-killing (Ahinsa); truthfulness (Satya); non-stealing (Asteya); continence (Brahmacharya); and non-receiving of any gift (Aparigraha).
2. *Niyama*: Cleanliness (S'ancha); contentment (Santosha); mortification (Tapasaya); study and self surrender (Swádhyáya); and the recognition of the Supreme (I's'wara pranidhâná).
3. *Â'sana*: Posture and the correct position of holding the body, and the performance of the Mudras.

* " Hatha-Yoga Pradipika," p. 2.

4. *Prânâyâma*: Control of the Prâna, and the vital forces of the body.

5. *Pratyâhâra*: Making the mind introspective, turning it back upon itself.

6. *Dhâranâ*: Concentration, or the *will* to hold the mind to certain points.

7. *Dhyâna*: Meditation, or the outpouring of the mind on the object held by the will.

8. *Samâdhi*: Ecstasy, or Superconsciousness.

As regards the first two of the above stages we need not deal with them at any length. Strictly speaking, they come under the headings of Karma and Gnana Yoga, and as it were form the Evangelicism of Yoga—the " Thou shalt " and " Thou shalt not." They vary according to definition and sect.* However, one point must be explained, and this is, that it must be remembered that most works on Yoga are written either by men like Patanjali, to whom continence, truthfulness, etc., are simple illusions of the mind; or by charlatans, who imagine that, by displaying to the reader a mass of middle-class "virtues," their works will be given so exalted a flavour that they themselves will pass as great ascetics who have out-soared the bestial passions of life, whilst in fact they are running harems in Boulogne or making indecent proposals to flower-girls in South Audley Street. These latter ones gener-ally trade under the exalted names of *The* Mahatmas; who,

* In all the Mysteries the partakers of them were always such as had not committed crimes. It will be remembered that Nero did not dare to present himself at the Eleusinia (Sueton. *vit. Nero*, e. 3A). And Porphyry informs us that "in the Mysteries honour to parents was enjoined, and not to injure animals" ("de Abstinentia," iv, 22).

79

coming straight from the Shâm Bazaar, retail their wretched *băk băk* to their sheep-headed followers as the eternal word of Brahman—"The shower from the Highest!" And, not infrequently, end in silent meditation within the illusive walls of Wormwood Scrubbs.

The East, like the West, has for long lain under the spell of that potent but Middle-class Magician—St. Shamefaced sex; and the whole of its literature swings between the two extremes of Paederasty and Brahmachârya. Even the great science of Yoga has not remained unpolluted by his breath, so that in many cases to avoid shipwreck upon Scylla the Yogi has lost his life in the eddying whirlpools of Charybdis.

The Yogis claim that the energies of the human body are stored up in the brain, and the highest of these energies they call "Ojas." They also claim that that part of the human energy which is expressed in sexual passion, when checked, easily becomes changed into Ojas; and so it is that they invariably insist in their disciples gathering up the sexual energy and converting it into Ojas. Thus we read:

It is only the chaste man and woman who can make the Ojas rise and become stored in the brain, and this is why chastity has always been considered the highest virtue. . . . That is why in all the religious orders in the world that have produced spiritual giants, you will always find this intense chastity insisted upon. . . .* If people practise Raja-Yoga and at the same time lead an impure life, how can they expect to become Yogis? †

---

* Certainly not in the case of the Mahometan Religion and its Sufi Adepts, who drank the vintage of Bacchus as well as the wine of Iacchus. The question of Chastity is again one of those which rest on temperament and not on dogma. It is curious that the astute Vivekânanda should have fallen into this man-trap.

† Swami Vivekânanda, "Raja Yoga," p. 45.

This argument would appear at first sight to be self-contradictory and therefore fallacious; for, if to obtain Ojas is so important, how then can it be right to destroy a healthy passion which is the chief means of supplying it with the renewed energy necessary to maintain it? The Yogi's answer is simple enough: Seeing that the extinction of the first would mean the ultimate death of the second the various Mudra exercises were introduced so that this healthy passion might not only be preserved, but cultivated in the most rapid manner possible, without loss of vitality resulting from the practices adopted. Equilibrium is above all things necessary, and even in these early stages, the mind of the aspirant should be entirely free from the obsession of either ungratified or over-gratified appetites. Neither Lust nor Chastity should solely occupy him; for as Krishna says:

Verily Yoga is not for him who eateth too much, nor who abstaineth to excess, nor who is too much addicted to sleep, nor even to wakefulness, O Arjuna.
Yoga killeth out all pain for him who is regulated in eating and amusement, regulated in performing actions, regulated in sleeping and waking.*

This balancing of what is vulgarly known as Virtue and Vice,† and which the Yogi Philosophy does not always appreciate, is illustrated still more forcibly in that illuminating work "Konx om Pax," in which Mr. Crowley writes:

As above so beneath! said Hermes the thrice greatest. The laws of the physical world are precisely paralleled by those of the moral and intellectual sphere. To the prostitute I prescribe a course of training by which she shall

---

* The Bhagavad-Gita, vi, 16, 17.
† Or more correctly as the Buddhist puts its—skilfulness and unskilfulness.

comprehend the holiness of sex. Chastity forms part of that training, and I should hope to see her one day a happy wife and mother. To the prude equally I prescribe a course of training by which she shall comprehend the holiness of sex. Unchastity forms part of that training, and I should hope to see her one day a happy wife and mother.

To the bigot I commend a course of Thomas Henry Huxley; to the infidel a practical study of ceremonial magic. Then, when the bigot has knowledge and the infidel faith, each may follow without prejudice his natural inclination; for he will no longer plunge into his former excesses.

So also she who was a prostitute from native passion may indulge with safety in the pleasure of love; and she who was by nature cold may enjoy a virginity in no wise marred by her disciplinary course of unchastity. But the one will understand and love the other.*

Once and for all do not forget that nothing in this world is permanently good or evil; and, so long as it appears to be so, then remember that the fault is the seer's and not in the thing seen, and that the seer is still in an unbalanced state. Never forget Blake's words:

"Those who restrain desire do so because theirs is weak enough to be restrained; and the restrainer or reason usurps its place and governs the unwilling." † Do not restrain your desires, but equilibrate them, for: "He who desires but acts not, breeds pestilence." ‡ Verily: "Arise, and drink your bliss, for everything that lives is holy." §

The six acts of purifying the body by Hatha-Yoga are Dhauti, Basti, Neti, Trataka, Nauli and Kapâlabhâti,‖ each of

---

* "Konx om Pax," by A. Crowley, pp. 62, 63.
† The Marriage of Heaven and Hell.   ‡ *Ibid.*
§ Visions of the Daughters of Albion.
‖ "Hatha Yoga Pradipika," p. 30. Dhauti is of four kinds: Antardhauti (internal washing); Dantdhauti (cleaning the teeth); Hriddhauti (cleaning the heart); Mulashodhana (cleaning the anus). Basti is of two kinds, Jala Basti (water Basti) and Sukshma Basti (dry Basti) and consists chiefly in dilating and contracting the sphincter muscle of the anus. Neti consists in inserting a thread

which is described at length by Swâtmârân Swami. But the two most important exercises which all must undergo, should success be desired, are those of Â'sana and Prânâyâma. The first consists of physical exercises which will gain for him who practises them control over the muscles of the body, and the second over the breath.

The Â'sanas, or Positions.

According to the " Pradipika " and the " Shiva Sanhita," there are 84 Â'sanas; but Goraksha says there are as many Â'sanas as there are varieties of beings, and that Shiva has counted eighty-four lacs of them.* The four most important are: Siddhâsana, Padmâsana, Ugrâsana and Svastikâsana, which are described in the Shiva Sanhita as follows:†

The *Siddhâsana*. By "pressing with care by the (left) heel the yoni,‡ the other heel the Yogi should place on the lingam; he should fix his gaze upwards on the space between the two eyebrows . . . and restrain his senses."

The *Padmâsana*. By crossing the legs "carefully place the feet on the opposite thighs (the left on the right thigh and *vicê versâ*), cross both hands and place them similarly on the thighs; fix the sight on the tip of the nose."

The *Ugrâsana*. "Stretch out both the legs and keep them apart; firmly take hold of the head by the hands, and place it on the knees."

The *Svastikâsana*. "Place the soles of the feet completely under the thighs, keep the body straight and at ease."

For the beginner that posture which continues for the

into the nostrils and pulling it out through the mouth, Trataka in steadying the eyes, Nauli in moving the intestines, and Kapâlabhâti, which is of three kinds, Vyût-krama, Vâma-krama, and Sit-krama, of drawing in wind or water through the nostrils and expelling it by the mouth, and *vice versâ*. Also see " Gheranda Sanhita," pp. 2-10. This little book should be read in conjunction with the " Hatha Yoga Pradipika."

* The " Gheranda Sanhita " gives thirty-two postures.
† The " Shiva Sanhita," pp. 25, 26.
‡ The imaginary " triangle of flesh " near the perinaeum.

greatest length of time comfortable is the correct one to adopt; but the head, neck and chest should always be held erect, the aspirant should in fact adopt what the drill-book calls "the first position of a soldier," and never allow the body in any way to collapse. The "Bhagavad-Gîta" upon this point says:

> In a pure place, established in a fixed seat of his own, neither very much raised nor very low . . . in a secret place by himself. . . . There . . . he should practise Yoga for the purification of the self. Holding the body, head and neck erect, immovably steady, looking fixedly at the point of the nose with un-wandering gaze.

When these postures have been in some way mastered, the aspirant must combine with them the exercises of Prânâyâma, which will by degrees purify the Nâdi or nerve-centres.

These Nâdis, which are usually set down as numbering 72,000,* ramify from the heart outwards in the pericardium; the three chief are the Ida, Pingala and Sushumnâ,† the last of which is called "the most highly beloved of the Yogis."

Besides practising Prânâyâma he should also perform one

* Besides the 72,000 nerves or veins there are often 101 others mentioned. These 101 chief veins each have 100 branch veins which again each have 72,000 tributary veins. The total ($101 + 101 \times 100 + 101 \times 100 \times 72,000$) equals 727,210,201. The 101st is the Sushumnâ. Yoga cuts through all these, except the 101st, stripping away all consciousness until the Yogi "is merged in the supreme, indescribable, ineffable Brahman." Also see "Gheranda Sanhita," p. 37. The Nâdis are known to be purified by the following signs: (1) A clear skin. (2) A beautiful voice. (3) A calm appearance of the face. (4) Bright eyes. (5) Hearing constantly the Nâda.

† The Sushumnâ may in more than one way be compared to Prometheus, or the hollow reed, who as the mediator between heaven and earth transmitted the mystic fire from the moon. Again the Mahalingam or ὁ φαλλός. For further see "The Canon," p. 119.

84

or more of the Mudras, as laid down in the "Hatha Yoga Pradipika" and the "Shiva Sanhita," so that he may arouse the sleeping Kundalini, the great goddess, as she is called, who sleeps coiled up at the mouth of the Sushumnâ. But before we deal with either of these exercises, it will be necessary to explain the Mystical Constitution of the human organism and the six Chakkras which constitute the six stages of the Hindu Tau of Life.

THE CONSTITUTION OF THE HUMAN ORGANISM

Firstly, we have the Âtman, the Self or Knower, whose being consists in a trinity in unity of, Sat, Absolute Existence; Chit, Wisdom; Ânanda, Bliss. Secondly, the Anthakârana or the internal instrument, which has five attributes according to the five elements, thus:

1. Spirit.
   - Spirit . Âtma.
   - Air . . Manas.* The mind or thought faculty.
   - Fire . . Buddhi. The discriminating faculty.
   - Water . Chittam.* The thought-stuff.
   - Earth . Ahankâra. Egoity.

2. Air. The five organs of knowledge. Gnanendriyam.
3. Fire. The five organs of Action. Karmendriyam.
4. Water. The five subtle airs or Prânas.
5. Earth. The five Tatwas.

The Âtma of Anthakârana has 5 sheaths, called Kos'as.†

* Manas and Chittam differ as the movement of the waters of a lake differ from the water itself.

† H. P. Blavatsky in "Instruction No. 1" issued to members of the first degree of her Eastern School of Theosophy (marked "Strictly Private and Confidential!") deals with those Kos'as on p. 16. But it is quite impossible here

1. Ânandamâyâkos'a, Body of Bliss, is innermost. It is still an illusion. Âtma, Buddhi and Manas at most participate.

2. Manomâyâkos'a. The illusionary thought-sheath including Manas, Buddhi, Chittam, and Ahankâra in union with one or more of the Gnanendriyams.

3. Viññanamâyâkos'a. The consciousness sheath, which consists of Anthakârana in union with an organ of action or of sense—Gnan- and Karm-endriyam.

4. Prânâmâyâkos'a. Consists of the five airs. Here we drop below Anthakârana.

5. Annamâyâkos'a. Body of Nourishment. The faculty which feeds on the five Tatwas.

Besides these there are three bodies or Shariras.

1. Karana Sharira. The Causal body, which almost equals the protoplast.

2. Sukshma Sharira. The Subtle body, which consists of the vital airs, etc.

3. Sthula Shirara. The Gross body.

THE CHAKKRAS

According to the Yoga,* there are two nerve-currents in

to attempt to extract from these instructions the little sense they may contain on account of the numerous Auric Eggs, Âkâsic envelopes, Karmic records, Dêvâchanic states, etc., etc. On p. 89 of " Instruction No. III " we are told that the Sushumnâ *is* the Brahmarandhra, and that there is " an enormous difference between Hatha and Raja Yoga." Plate III of Instructions No. II is quite Theosophical, and the third rule out of the Probationers' pledge, " I pledge myself never to listen, without protest, to any evil thing spoken falsely, or yet unproven, of a brother Theosophist, and to abstain from condemning others," seems to have been consistently acted upon ever since.

* Compare with the Kundalini the Serpent mentioned in paragraph 26 of

the spinal column called respectively Pingala and Ida, and between these is placed the Sushumnâ, an imaginary tube, at the lower extremity of which is situated the Kundalini (potential divine energy). Once the Kundalini is awakened it forces its way up the Sushumnâ,* and, as it does so, its progress is marked by wonderful visions and the acquisition of hitherto unknown powers.

The Sushumnâ is, as it were, the central pillar of the Tree of Life, and its six stages are known as the Six Chakkras.† To these six is added a seventh; but this one, the Sahasrâra, lies altogether outside the human organism.

These six Chakkras are:

1. *The Mûlâdhara-Chakkra.* This Chakkra is situated between the lingam and anus at the base of the Spinal Column. It is called the Adhar-Padma, or fundamental lotus, and it has four petals. "In the pericarp of the Adhar lotus there is the triangular beautiful yoni, hidden and kept secret in all the Tantras." In this yoni dwells the goddess Kundalini; she surrounds all the Nadis, and has three and a half coils. She catches her tail in her own mouth, and rests in the entrance of the Sushumnâ.‡

"The Book of Concealed Mystery." Note too the lotus-leaf that backs the throne of a God is also the hood of the Cobra. So too the Egyptian gods have the serpent upon the brow.

* Provided the other exits are duly stopped by Practice. The danger of Yoga is this, that one may awaken the Magic Power before all is balanced. A discharge takes place in some wrong direction and obsession results.

† The forcing of the Kundalini up the Sushumnâ and through the six Chakkras to the Sahasrâra, is very similar to Rising on the Planes through Malkuth Yesod, the Path of ס, Tiphereth, the Path of ט, and Daäth to Kether, by means of the Central Pillar of the Tree of Life.

‡ The following Mystical Physiology is but a symbolic method of expressing

58. It sleeps there like a serpent, and is luminous by its own light . . . it is the Goddess of speech, and is called the vija (seed).

59. Full of energy, and like burning gold, know this Kundalini to be the power (Shakti) of Vishnu; it is the mother of the three qualities—Satwa (good) Rajas (indifference), and Tamas (bad).

60. There, beautiful like the Bandhuk flower, is placed the seed of love; it is brilliant like burnished gold, and is described in Yoga as eternal.

61. The Sushumnâ also embraces it, and the beautiful seed is there; there it rests shining brilliantly like the autumnal moon, with the luminosity of millions of suns, and the coolness of millions of moons. O Goddess! These three (fire, sun and moon) taken together or collectively are called the vija. It is also called the great energy.*

In the Mûlâdhara lotus there also dwells a sun between the four petals, which continuously exudes a poison. This venom (the sun-fluid of mortality) goes to the right nostril, as the moon-fluid of immortality goes to the left, by means of the Pingala which rises from the left side of the Ajna lotus.†

The Mûlâdhara is also the seat of the Apâna.

2. *The Svadisthâna Chakkra.* This Chakkra is situated at the base of the sexual organ. It has six petals. The colour of this lotus is blood-red, its presiding adept is called Balakhya and its goddess, Rakini.‡

He who daily contemplates on this lotus becomes an object of love and adoration to all beautiful goddesses. He fearlessly recites the various Shas-

---

what is nigh inexpressible, and in phraseology is akin to Western Alchemy, the physiological terms taking the place of the chemical ones.

* " Shiva Sanhita," chap. v.

† *Ibid.*, chap. v, 107, 108, 109. This is probably wrong, as the sun is usually placed in the Manipûra Chakkra. In the body of a man the Pingala is the solar current, the Ida the lunar. In a woman these are reversed.

‡ *Ibid.*, chap. v, 75.

tras and sciences unknown to him before . . . and moves throughout the universe.*

This Chakkra is the seat of the Samâna, region about the navel and of the Apo Tatwa.

3. *The Manipûra Chakkra.* This Chakkra is situated near the navel, it is of a golden colour and has ten petals (sometimes twelve), its adept is Rudrakhya and its goddess Lakini. It is the " solar-plexus " or " city of gems," and is so called because it is very brilliant. This Chakkra is the seat of the Agni Tatwa. Also in the abdomen burns the " fire of digestion of food " situated in the middle of the sphere of the sun, having ten Kalas (petals). . . . †

He who enters this Chakkra

Can make gold, etc., see the adepts (clairvoyantly) discover medicines for diseases, and see hidden treasures.‡

4. *The Anahata Chakkra.* This Chakkra is situated in the heart, it is of a deep blood red colour, and has twelve petals. It is the seat of Prâna and is a very pleasant spot; its adept is Pinaki and its goddess is Kakini. This Chakkra is also the seat of the Vâyu Tatwa.

He who always contemplates on this lotus of the heart is eagerly desired by the daughters of gods . . . has clairaudience, clairvoyance, and can walk in the air. . . . He sees the adepts and the goddesses. . . . §

5. *The Vishuddha Chakkra.* This Chakkra is situated in the throat directly below the larynx, it is of a brilliant gold

* " Shiva Sanhita," chap. v, 76, 77. Compare this Chakkra to the lunar and sexual Yesod of the Qabalah; also note that the power here attained to is that of Skrying.

† *Ibid.*, chap. ii, 32. This Chakkra corresponds to Tiphareth.

‡ *Ibid.*, chap. v, 82.   § *Ibid.*, chap. v, 85, 86, 87.

colour and has sixteen petals. It is the seat of the Udana and the Âkâsa Tatwa; its presiding adept is Chhagalanda and its goddess Sakini.

6. *The Ajna Chakkra.* This Chakkra is situated between the two eyebrows, in the place of the pineal gland. It is the seat of the Mano Tatwa, and consists of two petals. Within this lotus are sometimes placed the three mystical principles of Vindu, Nadi and Shakti.* "Its presiding adept is called Sukla-Mahakala (the white great time; also Adhanari— 'Adonai') its presiding goddess is called Hakini." †

97. Within that petal, there is the eternal seed, brilliant as the autumnal moon. The wise anchorite by knowing this is never destroyed.

98. This is the great light held secret in all the Tantras; by contemplating on this, one obtains the greatest psychic powers, there is no doubt in it.

99. I am the giver of salvation, I am the third linga in the turya (the state of ecstasy, also the name of the thousand petalled lotus.‡ By contemplating on this the Yogi becomes certainly like me.§

The Sushumnâ following the spinal cord on reaching the Brahmarandhra (the hole of Brahman) the junction of the sutures of the skull, by a modification goes to the right side of the Ajna lotus, whence it proceeds to the left nostril, and is called the Varana, Ganges (northward flowing Ganges) or Ida. By a similar modification in the opposite direction the

* "Shiva Sanhita," chap. v, 110.   † *Ibid.*, chap. v, 49.

‡ Though all Hindu works proclaim that the Sahasrâra has but one thousand petals, its true number is one thousand and one as depicted in the diagram called the Yogi. $1001 = 91 \times 11$ (אדני $\times$ אמן); $91 =$ יהוה $+$ אדני $11 = $ ABRA-HADABRA $= 418 \ (38 \times 11) = $ Achad Osher, or one and ten, $=$ the Eleven Averse Sephiroth $=$ Adonai. Also $91 = 13 \times 7$ אחד $\times$ ARARITA, etc., etc. 11 is the Number of the Great Work, the Uniting of the Five and the Six, and $91 =$ mystic number $(1+2+3 \ldots +13)$ of $13 = $ Achad $= 1$.

§ *Ibid.*, chap. v, 50.

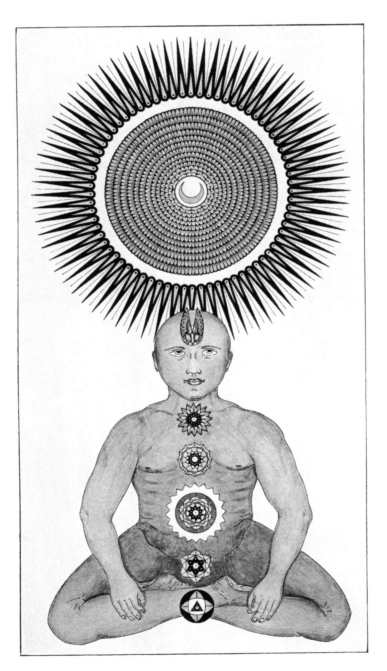

DIAGRAM 83.

The Yogi (showing the Cakkras).

Sushumnâ goes to the left side of the Ajna lotus and proceeding to the right nostril is called the Pingala, Jamuna or
Asi. The space between these two, the Ida and Pingala, is
called Varanasi (Benares), the holy city of Shiva.

111. He who secretly always contemplates on the Ajna lotus, at once
destroys all the Karma of his past life, without any opposition.

112. Remaining in the place, when the Yogi meditates deeply, idols appear
to him as mere things of imagination, *i.e.*, he perceives the absurdity of idolatry.*

The Sahasrâra, or thousand-and-one-petalled lotus of the
brain, is usually described as being situated above the head,
but sometimes in the opening of the Brahmarandhra, or at
the root of the palate. In its centre there is a Yoni which
has its face looking downwards. In the centre of this Yoni
is placed the mystical moon, which is continually exuding an
elixir or dew †—this moon fluid of immortality unceasingly
flows through the Ida.

In the untrained, and all such as are not Yogis, " Every
particle of this nectar (the Satravi) that flows from the Ambrosial
Moon is swallowed up by the Sun (in the Mûlâdhara Chakkra) ‡
and destroyed, this loss causes the body to become old. If
the aspirant can only prevent this flow of nectar by closing
the hole in the palate of his mouth (the Brahmarandra), he
will be able to utilize it to prevent the waste of his body. By

* " Shiva Sanhita," chap. v. It does not follow that missionaries are Yogis.

† Compare. " From the Skull of the Ancient Being wells forth Dew, and
this Dew will wake up the dead to a new life."—The Zohar, *Idra Rabba*.

" I will be as a dew unto Israel: he shall grow as the lily, and cast forth his
roots as Lebanon."—Hosea, xiv, 5.

‡ This is according to the " Shiva Sanhita." " The Hatha Yoga Pradipika "
places the Sun in the Svadisthâna Chakkra. The Manipûra Chakkra is however
probably the correct one.

drinking it he will fill his whole body with life, and "even though he is bitten by the serpent Takshaka, the poison does not spread throughout his body." *

Further the "Hatha Yoga Pradipika" informs us that: "When one has closed the hole at the root of the palate . . . his seminal fluid is not emitted even though he is embraced by a young and passionate woman."

Now this gives us the Key to the whole of this lunar symbolism, and we find that the Soma-juice of the Moon, dew, nectar, semen and vital force are but various names for one and the same substance, and that if the vindu can be retained in the body it may by certain practices, which we will now discuss, be utilized in not only strengthening but in prolonging this life to an indefinite period.† These practices are called the Mudras, they are to be found fully described in the Tantras, and are made use of as one of the methods of awakening the sleeping Kundalini.‡

There are many of these Mudras, the most important being the Yoni-Mudra, Maha Mudra, Maha Bandha, Maha Vedha, Khechari, Uddiyana, Mula and Salandhara Bandha, Viparitakarani, Vajroli and Shakti Chalana.

1. *The Yoni Mudra.*

With a strong inspiration fix the mind in the Adhar lotus;

* "Hatha Yoga Pradipika," p. 53.

† Fabulous ages are attributed to many of the Yogis. See Flagg's "Yoga," chap. xxviii; and "OM" by Sabhapaty Swami, p. vi.

‡ We believe this to be the exoteric explanation of this symbolism, the esoteric one being that Shiva represents the Solar or Spiritual Force, and Shakti the lunar or Bodily, the union of these two cancels out the pairs of opposites and produces Equilibrium.

then engage in contracting the yoni (the space between the lingam and anus). After which contemplate that the God of love resides in the Brahma-Yoni, and imagine that an union takes place between Shiva and Shakti.

A full account of how to practise this Mudra is given in the "Shiva Sanhita"; * but it is both complicated and difficult to carry out, and if attempted should most certainly be performed under the instruction of a Guru.

2. *Maha Mudra.*

Pressing the anus with the left heel and stretching out the right leg, take hold of the toes with your hand. Then practise the Jalandhara Bandha † and draw the breath through the Sushumnâ. Then the Kundalini becomes straight just as a coiled snake when struck. . . . Then the two other Nadis (the Ida and Pingala) become dead, because the breath goes out of them. Then he should breathe out very slowly and never quickly.‡

3. *Maha Bandha.*

Pressing the anus with the left ankle place the right foot upon the left thigh. Having drawn in the breath, place the chin firmly on the breast, contract the anus and fix the mind on the Sushumnâ Nadi. Having restrained the breath as long as possible, he should then breathe out slowly. He should practise first on the left side and then on the right.§

4. *Maha Vedha.*

As a beautiful and graceful woman is of no value without a husband, so Maha Mudra and Maha Bandha have no value without Maha Vedha.

The Yogi assuming the Maha Bandha posture, should draw in his breath

---

* "Shiva Sanhita," chap. iv, 1-11. Also see "Gheranda Sanhita," p. 23.

† The Jalandhara Banda is performed by contracting the throat and pressing the chin firmly against the breast.

‡ "Hatha Yoga Pradipika," pp. 45, 46. Also see "Shiva Sanhita," chap. iv, 11-20. The breath is always exhaled slowly so as not to expend the Prâna.

§ "Hatha Yoga Pradipika," p. 47; "Shiva Sanhita," chap. iv, 21, 22.

with a concentrated mind and stop the upward and downward course of the Prâna by Jalandhara Bandha. Resting his body upon his palms placed upon the ground, he should strike the ground softly with his posteriors. By this the Prâna, leaving Ida and Pingala, goes through the Sushumnâ. . . . The body assumes a death-like aspect. Then he should breathe out.*

5. *Khechari Mudra.*

The Yogi sitting in the Vajrâsana (Siddhâsana) posture, should firmly fix his gaze upon Ajna, and reversing the tongue backwards, fix it in the hollow under the epiglottis, placing it with great care on the mouth of the well of nectar.†

6. *Uddiyana Mudra.*

The drawing up of the intestines above and below the navel (so that they rest against the back of the body high up the thorax) is called Uddiyana Bandha, and is the lion that kills the elephant Death.‡

7. *Mula Mudra.*

Pressing the Yoni with the ankle, contract the anus and draw the Apâna upwards. This is Mula Bandha.§

8. *Jalandhara Mudra.*

Contract the throat and press the chin firmly against the breast (four inches from the heart). This is Jalandhara Bandha. . . . ‖

9. *Viparitakarani Mudra.*

This consists in making the Sun and Moon assume exactly reverse positions. The Sun which is below the navel and the Moon which is above the palate change places. This Mudra

* " Hatha-Yoga Pradipika," p. 48; " Shiva Sanhita," vol. iv, 23-30.
† " Shiva Sanhita," chap iv, 31. This is perhaps the most important of the Mudras. The " Hatha Yoga Pradipika " gives a long description of how the *fraenum linguae* is cut. See pp. 49-56.
‡ " Hatha Yoga Pradipika," p. 57; " Shiva Sanhita," chap. iv, 48-52.
§ " Hatha Yoga Pradipika," p. 58; " Shiva Sanhita," chap. iv, p. 41-44.
‖ " Hatha Yoga Pradipika," p. 60; " Shiva Sanhita," chap. iv, 38-40.

must be learnt from the Guru himself, and though, as we are
told in the "Pradipika," a theoretical study of crores of
Shastras cannot throw any light upon it, yet nevertheless in
the "Shiva Sanhita" the difficulty seems to be solved by
standing on one's head.*

10. *Shakti Chalana Mudra.*

Let the wise Yogi forcibly and firmly draw up the goddess Kundalini
sleeping in the Adhar lotus, by means of the Apana-Vâyu. This is Shakti-
Chalan Mudra. . . .†

The "Hatha Yoga Pradipika" is very obscure on this
Mudra, it says:

As one forces open a door with a key, so the Yogi should force open the
door of Moksha (Deliverance) by the Kundalini.

Between the Ganges and the Jamuna there sits the young widow inspiring
pity. He should despoil her forcibly, for it leads one to the supreme seat of
Vishnu.

You should awake the sleeping serpent (Kundalini) by taking hold of its
tail. . . .‡

As a special form of Kumbhaka is mentioned, most probably this Mudra is but one of the numerous Prânâyâma
practices, which we shall deal with shortly.

11. *The Vajroli-Mudra.*

In the "Shiva Sanhita"§ there is a long account of this
Mudra in which the God says: "It is the most secret of all

* "Hatha Yoga Pradipika," p. 62; "Shiva Sanhita," chap. iv, 45-47. Again
this is the union of Shiva and Shakti, and that of the solar and lunar Pingala
and Ida by means of the Sushumnâ—the path of the gods.

† "Shiva Sanhita," chap. iv, 76-81.

‡ "Hatha Yoga Pradipika," pp. 63, 69.

§ "Shiva Sanhita," chap. iv, 53-75.

the secrets that ever were or shall be; therefore let the prudent Yogi keep it with the greatest secrecy possible." It consists chiefly in uniting the linga and yoni, but in restraining the vindu.*

If by chance the Vindu begins to move let him stop it by practice of the Yoni Mudra. . . . After a while let him continue again . . . and by uttering the sound *hoom*, let him forcibly draw up through the contraction of the Apana Vâyu the germ cells. . . .

Know Vindu to be moon-like, and the germ cells the emblem of the sun; let the Yogi make their union in his own body with great care.†

I am the Vindu, Shakti is the germ fluid; when they both are combined, then the Yogi reaches the state of success, and his body becomes brilliant and divine.

Ejaculation of Vindu is death, preserving it within is life. . . . Verily, verily, men are born and die through Vindu. . . . The Vindu causes the pleasure and pain of all creatures living in this world, who are infatuated and subject to death and decay.‡

There are two modifications of the Vajroli Mudra; namely, Amarani and Sahajoni. The first teaches how, if at the time of union there takes place a union of the sun and moon, the lunar flux can be re-absorbed by the lingam. And the second how this union may be frustrated by the practice of Yoni Mudra.

These practices of Hatha Yoga if zealously maintained bring forth in the aspirant psychic powers known as the Siddhis,§ the most important of which are (1) Anima (the

* On the doctrines of this Mudra many popular American semi-occult works have been written, such as " Karezza," " Solar Biology," and " The Goal of Life."

† It is to be noted here that the union is again that of the mystical Shakti and Shiva, but now within the man. All this symbolism is akin to that made use of by the Sufis.

‡ " Shiva Sanhita," chap. iv, 56, 58, 59, 60, 61, 63.

§ " Any person if he actively practises Yoga becomes a Siddha; be he

power of assimilating oneself with an atom). (2) Mahima (the power of expanding oneself into space). (3) Laghima (the power of reducing gravitation). (4) Garima (the power of increasing gravitation). (5) Prapti (the power of instantaneous travelling). (6) Prakamya (the power of instantaneous realization). (7) Isatva (the power of creating). (8) Vasitva (the power of commanding and of being obeyed).*

The Prâna.

We now come to the next great series of exercises, namely those which control the Prâna (breath); and it is with these exercises that we arrive at that point where Hatha Yoga merges into Raja Yoga, and the complete control of the physical forces gives place to that of the mental ones.

Besides being able by the means of Prânâyâma to control the breath, the Yogi maintains that he can also control the Omnipresent Manifesting Power out of which all energies arise, whether appertaining to magnetism, electricity, gravitation, nerve currents or thought vibrations, in fact the total forces of the Universe physical and mental.

Prâna, under one of its many forms,† may be in either a static, dynamic, kinetic or potential state, but, notwithstanding the form it assumes, it remains Prâna, that is in common language the " will to work " within the Âkâsa, from which it evolves the Universe which appeals to our senses.

The control of this World Soul, this " will to work " is

young, old or even very old, sickly or weak. Siddhis are not obtained by wearing the dress of a Yogi, or by talking about them; untiring practice is the secret of success " (" Hatha Yoga Pradipika," p. 25).

* For further powers see Flagg's " Transformation or Yoga," pp. 169, 181.

† Such as: Apana, Samana, Udana, Vyana, Naga, Kurma, Vrikodara, Devadatta, Dhanajaya, etc., etc.

called Prânâyâma. And thus it is that we find the Yogi saying that he who can control the Prâna can control the Universe. To the perfect man there can be nothing in nature that is not under his control.

If he orders the gods to come, they will come at his bidding. . . . All the forces of nature will obey him as his slaves, and when the ignorant see these powers of the Yogi, they call them miracles.*

PRÂNÂYÂMA

The two nerve currents Pingala and Ida correspond to the sensory and motor nerves, one is afferent and the other efferent. The one carries the sensations to the brain, whilst the other carries them back from the brain to the tissues of the body. The Yogi well knows that this is the ordinary process of consciousness, and from it he argues that, if only he can succeed in making the two currents, which are moving in opposite directions, move in one and the same direction, by means of guiding them through the Sushumnâ, he will thus be able to attain a state of consciousness as different from the normal state as a fourth dimensional world would be from a third. Swami Vivekânanda explains this as follows:

Suppose this table moves, that the molecules which compose this table are moving in different directions; if they are all made to move in the same direction it will be electricity. Electric motion is when the molecules all move in the same direction. . . . When all the motions of the body have become perfectly rhythmical, the body has, as it were, become a gigantic battery of will. This tremendous will is exactly what the Yogi wants.†

And the conquest of the will is the beginning and end of Prânâyâma.

* Raja-Yoga, "Vivekânanda," p. 23. See Eliphas Levi's "The Dogma and Ritual of Magic," pp. 121, 158, 192, and Huxley's "Essay on Hume," p. 155.
† Raja-Yoga, "Vivekânanda," pp. 36, 37.

THE TEMPLE OF SOLOMON THE KING

Arjuna says: "For the mind is verily restless, O Krishna; it is impetuous, strong and difficult to bend, I deem it as hard to curb as the wind."

To which Krishna answers: "Without doubt, O mighty-armed, the mind is hard to curb and restless, but it may be curbed by constant practice and by indifference." *

The Kundalini whilst it is yet coiled up in the Mûlâdhara is said to be in the Mahâkâsa, or in three dimensional space; when it enters the Sushumnâ it enters the Chittâkâsa or mental Space, in which supersensuous objects are perceived. But, when perception has become objectless, and the soul shines by means of its own nature, it is said to have entered the Chidâkâsa or Knowledge space, and when the Kundalini enters this space it arrives at the end of its journey and passes into the last Chakkra the Sahasrâra. Vishnu is United to Devaki or Shiva to Shakti, and symbolically, as the divine union takes place, the powers of the Ojas rush forth and beget a Universe unimaginable by the normally minded man.†

---

* "Bhagavad-Gîtâ," vi, 34, 35.

† The whole of this ancient symbolism is indeed in its very simplicity of great beauty. The highest of physical emotions, namely, love between man and woman, is taken as its foundation. This love, if allowed its natural course, results in the creation of images of ourselves, our children, who are better equipped to fight their way than we on account of the experiences we have gained. But, if this love is turned into a supernatural channel, that is to say, if the joys and pleasures of this world are renounced for some higher ideal still, an ideal super-worldly, then will it become a divine emotion, a love which will awake the human soul and urge it on through all obstructions to its ultimate union with the Supreme Soul. To teach this celestial marriage to the children of earth even the greatest masters must make use of worldly symbols; thus it has come about that corruption has cankered the sublimest of truths, until man's eyes, no longer seeing the light, see but the flameless lantern, because of the filth that has been cast about it.

How to awake the Kundalini is therefore our next task.

We have seen how this can partially be done by the various Mudra exercises, but it will be remembered that the Shakti Chalana mentioned the practice of Kumbhaka or the retention of breath. Such an exercise therefore partially falls under the heading of Prânâyâma.

It is a well-known physiological fact that the respiratory system, more so than any other, controls the motions of the body. Without food or drink we can subsist many days, but stop a man's breathing but for a few minutes and life becomes extinct.* The air oxydises the blood, and it is the clean red blood which supports in health the tissues, nerves, and brain. When we are agitated our breath comes and goes in gasps, when we are at rest it becomes regular and rhythmical.

In the "Hatha Yoga Pradipika" we read:

He who suspends (restrains) the breath, restrains also the working of the mind. He who has controlled the mind, has also controlled the breath.

. . . .

If one is suspended, the other also is suspended. If one acts, the other also does the same. If they are not stopped, all the Indriyas (the senses) keep actively engaged in their respective work. If the mind and Prâna are stopped, the state of emancipation is attained.†

There are three kinds of Prânâyâma: Rechaka Prânâyâma (exhaling the breath), Puraka Prânâyâma (inhaling the breath) and Kumbhaka Prânâyâma (restraining the breath). The first kind consists in performing Rechaka first; the second in doing Puraka first; and the third in suddenly stopping the breath without Puraka and Rechaka.‡

* Malay pearl divers can remain from three to five minutes under water.
† "Hatha Yoga Pradipika," p. 79.
‡ Also see "The Yogasara-Sangraha," p. 54.

THE TEMPLE OF SOLOMON THE KING

Kumbhaka is also of two kinds—Sahita and Kevala. The Sahita is of two sorts, the first resembling the first kind of Prânâyâma, namely Rechaka Kumbhaka Puraka; the second resembling the second kind of Prânâyâma, namely Puraka Kumbhaka Rechaka. The Sahita should be practised till the Prâna enters the Sushumnâ, which is known by a peculiar sound * being produced in the Sushumnâ; after which the Kevala Kumbhaka should be practised. This Kumbhaka is described in the " Hatha-Yoga Pradipika " as follows:

When this Kumbhaka has been mastered without any Rechaka or Puraka, there is nothing unattainable by him in the three worlds. He can restrain his breath as long as he likes through this Kumbhaka.

He obtains the stage of Raja-Yoga. Through this Kumbhaka, the Kundalini is roused, and when it is so roused the Sushumnâ is free of all obstacles, and he has attained perfection in Hatha-Yoga.†

Of the many Prânâyâma exercises practised in the East the following are given for sake of example.

1. Draw in the breath for four seconds, hold it for sixteen, and then throw it out in eight. This makes one Prânâyâma.

At the same time think of the triangle (the Mûlâdhara Chakkra is symbolically represented as a triangle of fire) and concentrate the mind on that centre. At first practice this four times in the morning and four times in the evening, and as it becomes a pleasure to you to do so slowly increase the number.

2. Assume the Padmâsana posture; draw in the Prâna through the Ida (left nostril), retain it until the body begins to perspire and shake, and then exhale it through Pingala (right nostril) slowly and never fast.

* The Voice of the Nada.
† " Hatha Yoga Pradipika," p. 43.

101

THE EQUINOX

He should perform Kumbhakas four times a day—in the early morning, midday, evening, and midnight—till he increases the number to eighty.*

This will make 320 Kumbhakas a day. In the early stages the Prâna should be restrained for 12 matras (seconds) increasing as progress is made to 24 and to 36.

In the first stage, the body perspires; in the second, a tremor is felt throughout the body; and in the highest stage, the Prâna goes to the Brahmarandhra.†

This exercise may also be practised with an additional meditation on the Pranava OM.

3. Close with the thumb of your right hand the right ear, and with that of the left hand the left ear. Close with the two index fingers the two eyes, place the two middle fingers upon the two nostrils, and let the remaining fingers press upon the upper and the lower lips. Draw a deep breath, close both the nostrils at once, and swallow the breath. . . . Keep the breath inside as long as you conveniently can; then expire it slowly.‡

---

* " Hatha Yoga Pradipika," p. 28; the " Svetasvatara Upanishad;" and the " Shiva Sanhita," chap. iii, 25.

† " Hatha Yoga Pradipika," p. 28.

‡ " Shiva Sanhita," p. xlix. This in the " Hatha Yoga Pradipika," p. 91, is called the Shanmukhi Mudra. Enormous concentration is needed in all these Prânâyâma exercises, and, if the aspirant wishes to succeed, he must inflame himself with a will to carry them out to their utmost, just as in the Ceremonial Exercises of Abramelin he inflamed himself to attain to the Holy Vision through Prayer. The mere act of restraining the breath, breathing it in and out in a given time, so occupies the mind that it has "no time" to think of any external object. For this reason the periods of Kumbhaka should always be increased in length, so that, by making the exercise little by little more difficult, greater concentration may be gained.

Fra. P. writes: "If Kumbhaka be properly performed, the body and mind become suddenly 'frozen.' The will is for a moment free, and can hurl itself toward Adonai perhaps with success, before memory again draws back the attention to the second-hand of the watch."

102

THE TEMPLE OF SOLOMON THE KING

PRATYÂHÂRA

The next step in Raja Yoga is called Pratyâhâra, or the making of the mind introspective, by which the mind gains will to control the senses and to shut out all but the one object it is concentrating upon.

He who has succeeded in attaching or detaching his mind to or from the centres of will, has succeeded in Pratyâhâra, which means "gathering towards," checking the outgoing powers of the mind, freeing it from the thraldom of the senses. When we can do this we shall really possess a character; then alone we shall have made a long step towards freedom; before that we are mere machines.*

The absorption of the mind in the ever-enlightened Brahman by resolving all objects into Âtman, should be known as Pratyâhâra.†

The mind in ordinary men is entirely the slave of their senses. Should there be a noise, man hears it; should there be an odour, man smells it; a taste, man tastes it; by means of his eyes he sees what is passing on around him, whether he likes it or not; and by means of his skin he feels sensations pleasant or painful. But in none of these cases is he actually master over his senses. The man who is, is able to accommodate his senses to his mind. To him no longer are external things necessary, for he can stimulate mentally the sensation desired. He can hear beautiful sounds without listening to beautiful music, and see beautiful sights without gazing upon them; he in fact becomes the creator of what he wills, he can exalt his imagination to such a degree over his senses, that by a mere act of imagination he can make those senses instantaneously respond to his appeal, for he is lord over the senses,

---

* Raja Yoga, "Vivekânanda," p. 48. It will be noticed that Prânâyâma itself naturally merges into Pratyâhâra as concentration on the breath increases.

† "The Unity of Jîva and Brahman, Srimat Sânkarâchârya," paragraph 121.

and therefore over the Universe as *it appears*, though not as yet as *it is*.

The first lesson in Pratyâhâra is to sit still and let the mind run on, until it is realized what the mind is doing, when it will be understood how to control it. Then it will find that the thoughts which at first bubbled up, one over the other, become less and less numerous; but in their place will spring up the thoughts which are normally sub-conscious. As these arise the Will of the aspirant should strangle them; thus, if a picture is seen, the aspirant by means of his will should seize hold of it before it can escape him, endow it with an objectivity, after which he should destroy it, as if it were a living creature, and have done with it. After this mastership over the senses has been attained to, the next practice namely that of Dhârana must be begun.

DHÂRANÂ

Dhârana consists in concentrating the will on one definite object or point. Sometimes it is practised by concentrating on external objects such as a rose, cross, triangle, winged-globe, etc., sometimes on a deity, Shiva, Isis, Christ or Buddha; but usually in India by forcing the mind to feel certain parts of the body to the exclusion of others, such as a point in the centre of the heart, or a lotus of light in the brain.

"When the Chitta, or mind stuff, is confined and limited to a certain place, this is called Dhârana."

"The Steadiness of the mind arising from the recognition of Brahma, wherever it travels or goes, is the real and great Dhârana." *

* "Unity of Jîva and Brahman, Srimat Sânkarâchârya," paragraph 122.

The six Chakkras are points often used by the Yogi when in contemplation. Thus seated in the Padmâsana he will fix his attention in the Ajna lotus, and by contemplating upon this light the "Shiva Sanhita"* informs us "all sins (unbalanced forces) are destroyed, and even the most wicked (unbalanced) person obtains the highest end."

Those who would practise Dhârana successfully should live alone, and should take care to distract the mind as little as possible. They should not speak much or work much, and they should avoid all places, persons and food which repel them.† The first signs of success will be better health and temperament, and a clearer voice. Those who practise zealously will towards the final stages of Dhârana hear sounds as of the pealing of distant bells,‡ and will see specks of light floating before them which will grow larger and larger as the concentration proceeds. "Practice hard!" urges Swami Vivekânanda, "whether you live or die, it does not matter. You have to plunge in and work, without thinking of the result. If you are brave enough, in six months you will be a perfect Yogi."§

DHYÂNA.

After Dhârana we arrive at Dhyâna, or meditation upon the outpouring of the mind on the object held by the will.‖

---

* See Chapter V, 43-51.
† Compare the Abramelin instructions with these.   ‡ The Nada.
§ Compare Eliphas Levi, "Doctrine and Ritual of Magic," p. 195.
‖ Imagine the objective world to be represented by a sheet of paper covered with letters and the names of things, and our power of concentration to be a magnifying glass: that power is of no use, should we wish to burn that paper, until the rays of light are *focussed*. By moving the glass or paper with our hand

When once Dhâranâ or Concentration has progressed so far as to train the mind to remain fixed on one object then Dhyâna or meditation may be practised. And when this power of Dhyâna becomes so intensified as to be able to pass beyond the external perception and brood as it were upon the very centre or soul of the object held by the will, it becomes known as Samâdhi or Superconsciousness. The three last stages Dhâranâ, Dhyâna and Samâdhi, which are so intimately associated, are classed under the one name of Samyâma.*

Thus meditation should rise from the object to the object-less. Firstly the external cause of sensations should be perceived, then their internal motions, and lastly the reaction of the mind. By thus doing will the Yogi control the waves of the mind, and the waters of the great Ocean will cease to be disturbed by their rise and fall, and they will become still and full of rest, so that like a mirror will they reflect the unimaginable glory of the Âtman.

And I saw a new heaven and a new earth: for the first heaven and the first earth were passed away; and there was no more sea. And I John saw the Holy City, new Jerusalem, coming down from God out of heaven, prepared as a bride adorned for her husband.† And I heard a great voice out of heaven saying, Behold the tabernacle of God is with men, and he will dwell with them, and they shall be his people, and God himself shall be with them and be their God. And God shall wipe away all tears from their eyes; and there shall be no more death, neither sorrow, nor crying, neither shall there be any more pain: for the former things are passed away.‡

we obtain the right distance. In the above the Will takes the place of the hand.

* See also "The Yogasara-Sangraha," p. 74.

† It is to be noted that the symbolism made use of here is almost identical with that so often made use of in the Yoga Shastras and in the Vedanta. The union of Kundalini (Shakti) and Shiva.

‡ Revelation, xxi, 1-4.

THE TEMPLE OF SOLOMON THE KING

Compare this with the following:

That which is the night of all beings, for the disciplined man is the time of waking; when other beings are waking, then is it night for the Muni who seeth.

He attaineth Peace, into whom all desires flow as rivers flow into the ocean, which is filled with water but remaineth unmoved—not he who desireth desires.

He who, through the likeness of the Âtman, O Arjuna, seeth identity in everything, whether pleasant or painful, he is considered a perfect Yogi.*

Now that we have finished our long account of the Vedânta Philosophy and the theories of Yoga which directly evolved therefrom, we will leave theory alone and pass on to practical fact, and see how Frater P. turned the above knowledge to account, proving what at present he could only believe.

The following is a condensed table of such of his meditation practices as have been recorded between January and April 1901.

OBJECT MEDITATED UPON.	TIME.	REMARKS.
Winged-Globe.†	4 min.	The entire meditation was bad.
Tejas-Âkâsa.‡	3 „	There was no difficulty in getting the object clear; but the mind wandered.
Apas-Vâyu.§	? „	Result not very good.
Winged-Globe and Flaming Sword.‖	? „	Meditation on both of these was only fair.

---

* "The Bhagavad-Gîta," ii, 69, 70; vi, 32. Cf. "Konx om Pax," pp. 73-77.

† The ordinary Egyptian Winged-Globe is here meant, but as visualized by the mind's eye; the meditation then takes place on the image in the mind. So with the following practices.

‡ Tejas-Âkâsa is the Element of Fire. It is symbolized by a red triangle of fire with a black egg in the centre. See 777, col. LXXV, p .16. See Diagram 84.

§ Apas-Vâyu is the Element of Water and is symbolized by a black egg of Spirit in the Silver Crescent of Water. See 777, col. LXXV, p. 16. See Diagram 84.

‖ The Golden Dawn symbol of the Flaming Sword. See Diagram 12.

THE EQUINOX

OBJECT MEDITATED UPON.	TIME.	REMARKS.
Pendulum * (E).†	? ,,	Good as regards plane kept by the pendulum; but thoughts wandered.
Winged-Globe.	? ,,	The result was pretty good.
Tejas-Vâyu (E).	? ,,	Fair.
Ankh ‡ (a green).	? ,,	Not bad.
Pentagram (E).	? ,,	Rather good.
The L. I. L.§ (E).	? ,,	Burning till extinct. Rather good, but oil level descended very irregularly.‖
Cross.	? ,,	Result fair.
Cross.	10 m. 15 s.	Three breaks.
Isis ¶ (E).	18 m. 30 s.	Five breaks. A very difficult practice, as Isis behaved like a living object.**
Winged-Globe.	29 m.	Seven breaks. Result would have been much better but for an epicene eunuch with an alleged flute. My mind revolved various methods of killing it.
Tejas-Âkâsa.	18 ,,	Seven breaks.
R. R. et A. C.††	19 ,,	Seven breaks.
Pendulum.	? ,,	After 3 m. lost control and gave up.
Winged-Globe (E).‖	10 ,,	Ten breaks.‡‡

* By this is meant watching the swing of an imaginary pendulum. The difficulty is to keep it in one plane, as it tries to swing round; also to change its rate.

† In these records "M" means morning and "E" evening.

‡ The Egyptian Key of Life. See Diagram 61.

§ Lamp of the Invisible Light.

‖ In the mind.

¶ The visualized form of the goddess Isis.

** That is to say she kept on moving out of the line of mental sight.

†† See Diagram 80. A scarlet rose on a gold cross.

‡‡ At this point P. made the following resolve: "I resolve to increase my powers very greatly by the aid of the Most High, until I can meditate for twenty-four hours on one object."

108

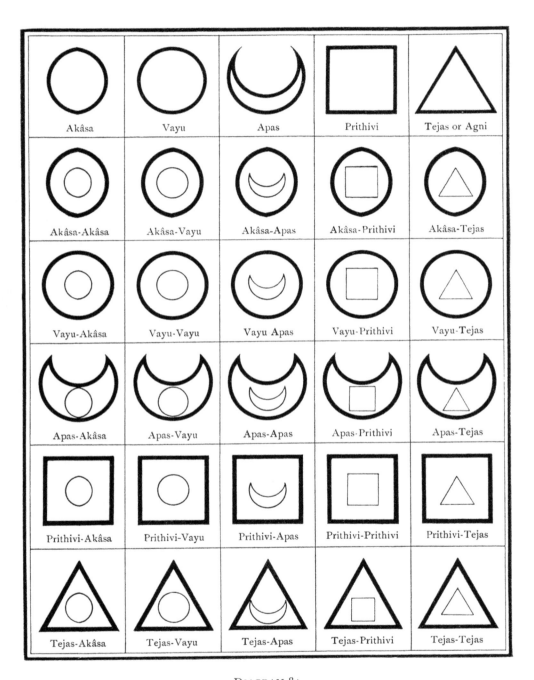

DIAGRAM 84.

The Five Tatwas, with their twenty-five sub-divisions.

OBJECT MEDITATED UPON.	TIME.	REMARKS.
Black egg and white ray between pillars * (E).	10 „	Five breaks.
Golden Dawn Symbol † (E).	? „	Very bad. Bad cold, dust, shaking, etc., prevented concentration.‡
Golden Dawn Symbol (E).	10 „	Four breaks.
R. R. et A. C.	23 „	Nine breaks.

Against this particular practice P. wrote: "I think breaks are longer in themselves than of old; for I find myself concentrating on them and forgetting the primary altogether. But I have no means of telling how long it is before the error is discovered."

Some very much more elaborate and difficult meditations were attempted by P. at this time; in nature they are very similar to many of St. Loyola's. We give the account in his own words:

I tried to imagine the sound of a waterfall. This was very difficult to get at; and it makes one's ears sing for a long time afterwards. If I really got it, it was however not strong enough to shut other physical sounds. I also tried to imagine the " puff-puff" of an engine. This resulted better than the last, but it caused the skin of my head to commence vibrating. I then tried to imagine the taste of chocolate; this proved extremely difficult; and after this the ticking of a watch. This proved easier, and the result was quite good; but there was a tendency to slow up with the right ear, which however was easy to test by approaching a watch against the ear."§

During this whole period of rough travel, work is fatiguing, difficult and uncertain. Regularity is impossible, as regards hours and even days, and the

---

* The Âkâsic egg of spirit set between the Pillars of Mercy and Severity with a ray of light descending upon it from Kether.

† The Golden Dawn Symbol here meditated upon consisted of a white triangle surmounted by a red cross. See Diagram 4.

‡ This meditation took place whilst P. was on a journey.

§ These meditations are called Objective Cognitions, by concentrating on certain nerve centres super-physical sensations are obtained.

mind, being so full of other things, seems to refuse to compose itself. Nearly always I was too tired to do two (let alone three) meditations; and the weariness of the morrow was another hostile factor. Let me hope that my return here (Mexico City) will work wonders.

Three days after this entry on a certain Wednesday evening we find a very extraordinary mental experiment recorded in P.'s diary.

D. A. made to P. the following suggestion for a meditation practice.

1. Imagine that I am standing before you in my climbing clothes.
2. When you have visualized the figure, forbid it to move its limbs, etc.
3. Then allow the figure to change, *as a whole*, its illumination, position and appearance.
4. Carefully observe and remember any phenomenon in connection therewith.

All this P. attempted with the following result:

The figure of D.A.: leaning on an ice-axe was clearly seen, but at first it was a shade difficult to fix.

The figure at once went 35° to my left, and stayed there; then I observed a a scarlet Tiphereth above the head and the blue path of ג (gimel) going upwards. Around the head was bluish light, and Tiphereth was surrounded by rays as of a sun. I then noticed that the figure had the power to reduplicate itself at various further distances; but the main figure was very steady.

Above and over the figure there towered a devil in the shape of some antediluvian beast. How long I mentally watched the figure I cannot say, but after a period it became obscure and difficult to see, and in order to prevent it vanishing it had to be willed to stay. After a further time the Plesiosaurus (?) above the figure became a vast shadowy form including the figure itself.

The experiment being at an end D.A. put the following question to P. "How do you judge of distance of secondary replicas of me?"

P. answered: "By size only."

D.A. comments on the above were as follows:

1. That the test partially failed.
2. That he expected his figure to move more often.*

---

* Normally in these experiments the figure does move more often.

3. The vast shadowy form was very satisfactory and promising.*

On the following day P. records first: Meditation upon Winged-Globe to compose himself. He then imagined D. A. sitting forward with his arms around his knees and his hands clasped. Around the figure was an aura of heaving surfaces, and then a focussing movement which brought the surfaces very close together. " The figure then started growing rapidly in all dimensions till it reached a vast form, and as it grew it left behind it tiny emaciated withered old men sitting in similar positions, but with changed features, so much so that I should think it were due to other reasons besides emacia-tion."

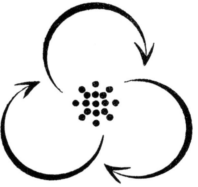

DIAGRAM 85.

Aura of Heaving Surfaces.

D. A. considered this medita-tion very satisfactory, but that nevertheless P. should attempt it again the next day.

This, however, was impossible; as on the next day, Friday, he was suffering severely from headache and neuralgia; so instead, in order to compose himself, he meditated upon a cross for an hour and a quarter.

The next living object meditation he attempted is described in the diary as follows:

To meditate upon the image of D. A. sitting with his hands on his knees like a God.† Spirals were seen moving up him to a great height, and then descending till they expanded to a great size. Besides this no other change took place.

D. A.'s comments on these remarkable experiments are as follows:

The hidden secret is that the change of size and distance is not in accord-ance with optical laws. No one has kept living objects " dead still."‡ One of two things may occur:

(a) The figure remains in one spot, but alters in size.

(b) The figure remains same apparent size, but alters in distance.

---

* Normally this is so. † In the position many of the Egyptian gods assume.

‡ Qy.: Is this from habit of expecting living things to move? I can, I think, succeed in keeping them still.—*Note by P.*

Further that the Yogi theories on this experiment were:

(1) That a living object is the reflection of the Actual, the living object being purely unreal.

(2) That from this type of meditation can be discovered the character of the person meditated upon.

e.g. Q. Is A. pious?

    A. If he grows large, yes he is very pious.

    Q. Is B. a villain?

    A. If he shrivels, he is a *small* villain, not a man to be afraid of.

Also of ordinary occult things—*e.g.* change of face, expressions, etc. There are also further theories regarding the disintegration of man. Theories concerning the danger of this process to the meditator and meditatee alike.*

The next practice was to meditate upon the image of D. A. standing.

The figure remained in the same place, but altered much like a form reflected in glasses of various curves. The general tendency was to increase slightly, but the most fixed idea was of a figure about 9 feet high but of normal breadth. Next, of normal height and of about double normal breadth.

D. A.'s comment on this meditation was that the result was not good.

This practice was attempted again on the following day: and resulted in many superposed images of various sizes and at various distances. One of the figures had moustaches like the horns of a buffalo. The expression of the figures became bold and fierce; especially at four feet distance, where there were two very real images, one small and one large respectively.

The comment of D. A. on this meditation was that it was most clear, and represented complete success.

On the fifteenth of April 1901 we find P. writing in his diary:

"I agree to project my astral to Soror F.† in Hong-Kong every Saturday evening at nine o'clock, which should reach her at 4.6 p.m. on Sunday by Hong-Kong time. She is to start at 10 a.m. Sunday by Hong-Kong time to reach me by 12.2 p.m. Saturday.

These spirit journeys were to commence on the 31st of

---

* This danger is also experienced by such as carry out Black Magical Operations. The Current of will often returns and injures the Magician who willed it.

† Soror F. the same as Soror S.S.D.F.

May; but this date seems to have been anticipated, for two days later we read the following:

10 p.m. Enclosing myself in an egg of white light I travelled to Hong-Kong. This city is white and on a rocky hill, the lower part is narrow and dirty. I found F. in a room of white and pale green. She was dressed in a white soft stuff with velvet lapels. We conversed awhile. I remember trying to lift a cloisonné vase from the shelf to a table, but cannot remember whether I accomplished the act or not. I said " Ave Soror" aloud (and I think audibly) and remained some time.*

This astral projection is an operation of Chokmah; for the Chiah must vivify the Nephesch shell. After returning P. records that on his journey back he saw " his Magical Mirror of the Universe very clearly in its colours."

Towards the end of April P. drew up for himself the following daily Task:

(1) To work through the first five of the seven mental operations.†
(2) The assumption of God forms.‡
(3) To meditate on simple symbols with the idea of discovering their meaning.
(4) Rising on planes.
(5) Astral Visions.§
(6) Adonai ha Aretz.‖

---

* This description of Hong-Kong is as correct as can be expected from so short a visit. The conversation was subsequently verified by letter, and also again when they met several years later.

† He resolved the ש of ש Operation into seven parts.

‡ The ש of ש Operation, see also the Magical Invocation of the Higher Genius: chapter "The Sorcerer." And Liber O iii THE EQUINOX, vol. i, No. 2.

§ See chapter, "The Seer," also Liber O v THE EQUINOX, vol. i, No. 2.

‖ The invocation of the Guardian Angel under the form of a talisman.

How to draw it.

Draw the name אדני as follows:

א = A winged crown radiating white brilliance.

ד = The head and neck of a beautiful woman with a stern and fixed expression, and hair long dark and waving. (Malkuth.)

נ = The arms and hands, which are bare and strong, stretched out to the

(7) Meditation practices on men and things.*
(8) Elemental evocations.†
(9) Meditation to vivify telesmata.‡
(10) Astral projections.§

PHYSICAL WORK.

(2) Careful drawings of the Gods in their colours.
(6) Figure of Adonai ha Aretz in colour. [See Illustration.]

---

right and left at right angles to the body, in the left hand a gold cup and in right ears of ripe corn. From her shoulders dark spreading wings.
ı = A deep yellow-green robe, upon the breast of which is a square gold lamen decorated with four scarlet Greek crosses. Round her waist is a broad gold belt upon which in scarlet letters is written the name אדני ה ארץ in the letters of the alphabet of Honorius. Her feet are flesh coloured, and she wears golden sandals. Her long yellow-green drapery is rayed with olive, and beneath her feet roll black clouds lit with lurid patches of colour.

How to perform it.

(1) Commence with lesser pentagram Banishing Ritual.
(2) Formulate rose-cross round room (First, top to bottom; second left to right; third the rose as a circle dextro-rotary).
(3) The LVX signs in 5°=6° towards the four cardinal points.
(4) Formulate before you in white flashing brilliance the eight letters thus:

(5) Attach yourself to your Kether and imagine you see a white light there.

אדנינהארץ

(6) Having thus formulated the letters, take a deep breath and pronounce the name slowly making the letters flash.
(7) Invoke the Telesmatic image. Let it fill the Universe.
(8) Then whilst once again vibrating the Name absorb it into yourself; and then will your aura radiate with whiteness.

You should obtain your Divine White Brilliance before formulating the Image. There are two methods, the involving and the expanding whorls respectively.

* Similar to the D. A. Meditation Practices.
† Similar to Fra. I. A.'s ritual of Jupiter.
‡ This is done by making the telesmata flash by meditation.
§ This is done by projecting a physical image of the self in front of one by meditation.

DIAGRAM 86.
The Flashing Figure of Adonai-ha-Aretz.

(8) Completion of Watch-towers and instruments.*

(9) The making of simple talismans.

During each day this programme of work was to be divided as follows:

(1) In the Morning the ש of ש Operation, and Assumption of a God-form.

(2) Before Tiffin. An Astral projection practice.

(3) After Tiffin. Rising on a plane, or Vision, or Adonai ha Aretz.

(4) In the Evening. A magical ceremony of same sort, or any of above except astral projection.†

On March the 3rd we find P. wandering among the fastnesses of the Nevado de Colima. Here he lived for a fortnight, returning to Mexico City on the 18th only to leave it again two days later on an expedition to the Nevado de Toluca. On the 16th of April he journeyed to Amecameca, from which place he visited Soror F, by projection, and thence up Popocatapetl, encamped on whose slopes he resolved the ש of ש into seven Mental Operations:

1. Ray of Divine White Brilliance descending upon the Âkâsic Egg set between the two pillars.

2. Aspire by the Serpent, and concentrate on Flashing Sword. Imagine the stroke of the Sword upon the Daäth junction (nape of neck).

3. Make the Egg grow gray, by a threefold spiral of light.

4. Make the Egg grow nearly white. (Repeat spiral formula.)

5. Repeat 2. Above head. Triangle of Fire (red).

6. Invoke Light. Withdraw. See Golden Dawn Symbol.

7. Let all things vanish in the Illimitable Light.

On the 22nd of April P., having bidden farewell to D. A., who had been to him both friend and master, left for San Francisco.

* The Elemental Tablets of Dr. Dee; see Diagrams in "The Vision and the Voice."

† Ideas for mental Concentration. Concentration on Scarlet Sphere in Tiphereth. Let it slowly rise into Daäth and darken, after which into Kether and be a white brilliance; thence fling it flashing, or bring it down and keep it in Tiphereth.

THE EQUINOX

At this city, on the first of May, he solemnly began anew the Operations of the Great Work, and bought a steel rod for a wand, and tools to work it. On the second he bought gold, silver, and a jewel wherewith to make a Crown; and on the third set sail for Japan.

During the voyage the following practices have been recorded:

May 4th. Prithivi-Apas.*   45 m.

   Also went on an Astral Journey to Japan. In which I found myself crossing great quantities of Coral-pearl entangled with seaweed and shells. After having journeyed for some time I came to a spot where I saw the form of a King standing above that of Venus who was surrounded by many mermaids; they all had the appearance of having just been frozen. Above the nymphs bowing towards them were many pale yellow angels chained together, and amongst them stood Archangels of a pale silver which flashed forth rays of gold. Above all was the Formless Light. The Archangels showed me curious types of horned beings riding along a circle in different directions.

5th. Concentration on Position 1.†		This resulted in many strange dreams.
6th. Concentration on Position 1.	32 m.	Ten breaks. Better towards the end; but best after tenth break. Concentration must have then lasted quite 6 or 7 minutes.
7th. Position 1.	15 m.	Three breaks, but end very doubtful having become very sleepy.
Position 1.	6 m.	Three breaks. I seemed to collapse suddenly.

   Went to Devachan ‡ on Astral Journey. I found myself sur-

---

* In all cases when the name alone is mentioned a meditation practice is understood. Prithivi-Apas corresponds to water of earth. It is symbolized by a silver crescent drawn within a yellow square. See Diagram 84.

† *I.e.*, Self in Âkâsa between pillars with white ray descending.

‡ Heaven.

116

rounded by a wonderful pearly lustre, and then among great trees between the branches of which bright birds were flying. After this I saw a captain on his ship and also a lover contemplating his bride. The real inhabitants of this land to which I went were as of flame, and the imaginary ones were depicted as we physical beings are. Then the images of my vision sped past me rapidly. I saw a mountaineer; my father preaching with me in his old home; my mother; his mother; a man doing Rajayoga on white god-form. At last a wave of pale light, or rather of a silky texture passed through and over me; then one of the strange inhabitants passed through me unconscious of me, and I returned.

Golden Dawn symbol. 14 m. Three breaks.

May 8th. Position I. 22 m. Seven breaks.

       Calvary Cross. 50 m. Did I go to sleep?

    11th. Designed Abrahadabra
          for a pantacle.*

    12th. I performed a Magic Ceremonial at night, followed by attempt at Astral Projection. I prefer the Esoteric Theosophist Society's sevenfold division for these practical purposes. I think Physical Astral Projection should be preceded by a (ceremonial) "loosening of the girders of the soul."† How to do it is the great problem. I am inclined to believe in drugs—if one only knew the right drug.

    13th. Drew a pantacle.

    16th. Painted wicked black-magic pantacle.

       Held a magical ceremony in the evening.

       Lesser banishing Ritual of Pentagram and Hexagram.

       Invocation of Thoth and the Elements by Keys 1-6 ‡ and G.·. D.·. Opening Rituals.

       Consecrated Lamen Crown and Abrahadabra Wand with great force.

    16th. Did the seven ☿ of ☿ Operations.

       Worked at a Z for 5=6 Ritual.§

    17th. Position I. 12 m. Not good.

       Evening Invocation of Mercury, Chokmah and Thoth.

    18th. Completed Z for 5=6 Ritual.

---

  * An Eleven pointed Star.

  † P. at various times used the "Invocation of the Bornless one" as given in "The Goetia"; also the Pentagram rituals in Liber O.

  ‡ The first six Angelic Keys of Dr. Dee.

  § The explanation of the 5°=6° Ritual. See Chapter "The Adept."

THE EQUINOX

May 19th.   1. Assumption of the god-form of Harpocrates: it lasted nine minutes: the result was good, for I got a distinct aura around me.

2. Physical Astral Projection. I formed a sphere which took a human shape but rather corpse-like. I then projected a gray * ray from the left side of my head; this was very tiring and there was no result physically.

3. Concentrated on imaginary self for ten minutes, and then projected self into it with fearful force. Chiah *nearly* passed.†

4. Red sphere *darkened* and glorified and returned to lighten Tiphereth. The result was good.

20th.   1. Tejas-Apas Meditation.

2. Meditation on living object with the usual two figure result.

3. Astral Vision.‡ I found myself in a boiling sea with geysers spouting around me. Suddenly monsters shaped like lions and bulls and dragons rose from the deep, and about them sped many fiery angels, and Titanic god-forms plunged and wheeled and rose amongst the waters. Above all was built a white temple of marble through which a rose-flame flickered. There stood Aphrodite with a torch in one hand and a cup in the other,§ and above her hovered Archangels. Then suddenly all was an immense void, and as I looked into it I beheld the dawn of creation. Gusts of liquid fire flamed and whirled through the darkness. Then nothing but the brilliance of fire and water. I was away fifteen minutes.

4. Seven minutes breathing exercise fifteen seconds each way. (Breathing in, withholding, and breathing out.)

5. White Lion on Gray.   5 m.   Result bad.

21st. Position 1.   45 m.   Fair.

Worked out a "double" formula for Physical Astral Projection. First project with Enterer sign; Simulacrum answers with Harpocrates sign.‖ Then as soon as Enterer sign weakens change consciousness as for Astral Visions. After which attack body from Simulacrum

---

* The colour of Chokmah.

† See Plate VI. "The Kabbalah Unveiled," S. L. Mathers.

‡ It is to be noted that this Vision is of a fiery nature, and that it was experienced shortly after meditating upon Tejas-Apas.

§ Very similar to the older form of "Temperance" in the Taro.

‖ See Liber O, THE EQUINOX, vol. i, No. 2; Plate, "Signs of the Grades," i; and vol. i, No. 1; Plates the "Silent Watcher" and "Blind Force."

118

with sign of Enterer to draw force. This cycle repeat until Simulacrum is at least capable of audible speech.

I tried this and started by invoking the forces of Chokmah and Thoth, but omitted stating purpose of Operation in so many words. Yet with three projections (each way) I obtained a shadowy grayness somewhat human in shape. But found difficulty where least expected —in transferring consciousness to Simulacrum.

May 22nd. God-form Thoth.   16 m.   Result fair.

Âkâsa-Âkâsa. During the meditation the following Vision was seen. All things around me were surrounded by silver flashes or streaks. But about the human corpse which I saw before me there were fewer, and they moved more slowly. Above me was a pyramid of flashing light, and around me purple hangings. Five silver candlesticks were brought in, and then I saw a throne with pentagram in white brilliance above it. There was a rose of five by five petals within; and above Qesheth the rainbow. Rising from the ground were formless demons—all faces! Even as X. A. R. P.* etc. are evil. Above were the Gods of E.H.N.B.; and above them svastika wheels whirling, and again above this the Light Ineffable.

24th. Green ankh.   7 m.   Poor.

Worked at $5° = 6°$ explanation.

Cross in brilliance.   10 m.   Medium result.

Thoth in front of me.   5 m.   Poor.

June 3rd. Astral Vision. Dressed in white and red Abramelin robes with crown, wand, ankh, and rose-cross, etc., etc., went on an Astral Journey to

---

* The four letters of the Air line in the "Little Tablet of Union" which unites the four great Watch Towers of the Elements (see Dr. Dee's system, also Golden Dawn MS. entitled "The Concourse of the Forces)." Thus the T of Nanta represents Earth of Earth —the Empress of Pantacles in the Taro, and that letter is used as an initial for names of angels drawn from the Earthy corner of the Earth tablet. For further see the EQUINOX, vol. i, No. 5.

DIAGRAM 87.
The Spirit Tablet.

Hong-Kong. I found Soror F. sitting or kneeling in a temple. On the Altar were elemental instruments also Symbol of Golden Dawn. She was waiting in awe, almost in fear. On my entering she saw me and started. Then I heard the words "carry it" or "wish to carry"; apparently with reference to idea of carrying away a physical token. The room was full of incense, which I took to materialize myself. At the time I was very tired and really not fit to travel.

June 15th. The Buddha appeared to me in the Northern Heaven and said: "Fear not for money.* Go and work, as thou hast intended." *I go.*

July 14th.	Triangle of Fire.	10 m.	Middling to bad.
	Winged-Globe.	6 m.	Not good.
	R.R. et A.C.	?	Fairly good.

[Somewhere on this journey (Yokohama to Hong-Kong) BECAME the GREAT PEACE.

15th.	R.R. et A.C.	16 m.	An improvement.
16th.	Svastika.	6 m.	Very poor.
	R.R. et A.C.	4 m.	Very bad.
	H.P.K.†	10 m.	Better.
	Pentagram.	16 m.	Not at all bad.
18th.	Calvary Cross.	15 m.	Bad, but I was very sleepy.
	H.P.K. on lotus.	16 m.	Ten breaks; very strictly counted.
	R.R. et A.C.	8 m.	One break. Got very sleepy; but this seems surprisingly good.
	Scarlet Sphere Operation (Tiphereth).	10 m.	Good. One or two breaks only.
	Buddha position.	5 m.	Hopeless; I was nearly asleep.
19th.	Winged-Globe.	9 m.	Five breaks.
	H.P.K. on Lotus.	9 m.	Five breaks. The God was not very clear.
	R.R. et A.C.	8 m.	Bad.
	Position 1.	13 m.	Middling.
	Thoth.	?	Hopelessly sleepy.

Attempted meditation on solar spectrum as a band. By working

---

* A draft had been sent only payable in Hong-Kong on personal application. He was consequently afraid lest by staying too long in Japan he should become "stranded."

† Harpocrates.

at each colour separately, or lighting each one by one, it is not bad; but taken altogether is no good.

July 20th.	Thoth.	10 m.	Rather poor.
	Cross.	15 m.	Not very good.
	Golden Dawn Symbol.	10 m.	Not good.

[My thought seems terribly wandering nowadays.]

	Isis.	19 m.	Not so bad.
	Winged-Globe.	12 m.	Bad, sleepy.
23rd.	Triangle of Fire with Cross in centre.	15 m.	Very wandering.
	Abrahadabra pantacle.	17 m.	Pretty good, though perhaps the whole was hardly ever absolutely clear.

25th. Tried Physical Astral Projection twice. In the first one the person employed to watch—my beloved Soror F.— saw physical arm *bent* whilst my own was straight.

26th. I did the H.P.K. ritual at night to enter into the silence. I think the result was rather good.

| 27th. | Nirvana.* | 38 m. | If I was not asleep, result pretty good. |
| | White circle. | 13 m. | Fair. |

[This day I got my first clear perception *in consciousness* † of the illusory nature of material objects.]

	H.P.K. on Lotus.	17 m.	Good, as I employed my identity to resolve problems.‡
	R.R. et A.C.	5 m.	Very bad.
28th.	Nirvana.	15 m.	
	Calvary Cross.	24 m.	Ten breaks. Never got settled till after 8 breaks.

29th. Rising on planes. Malkuth to Kether; this took **thirty-six minutes.** The result was not very good.

	Calvary Cross.	22 m.	Four breaks.
30th.	Buddha.	15 m.	
	Calvary Cross.	11 m.	Five breaks, but had headache.

---

* Meditation upon Nirvana.
† *I.e.*, no longer through reason or imagination.
‡ Harpocrates being the meditative God.

One hundred indrawn breaths in reclining position with belt on. 7 minutes 50 seconds. (4.7 secs. per breath.)

Ten indrawn breaths as slow as possible 7 m. 26 sec. (44.6 secs. per breath.)

July 31st. Went to sleep doing Buddha.

Buddha.	32 m.	It seemed much more.
Pendulum 1,000 single strokes.	23½ m.	The pendulum kept in its plane.* At end of 940 strokes pendulum wanted to swing right over several times.
Calvary Cross.		Too tired to settle at all.

August 1st. Position 1. — 10 m. — Not bad.

2nd. Buddha. — 8 m. — It seems very difficult nowadays to settle down.

Red Cross.	22 m.	Ten breaks.
Nirvana.†	13 m.	Not bad.

I tried to put (astrally) a fly on a man's nose. It seemed to disturb him much; but he did not try to brush it off.

Tried the same with Chinaman, great success.

Tried to make a Chinaman look round, instant success.

Tried the same with a European, but failed.

3rd. Tried in vain two "practical volitions" but was too unwell to do any work.

4th. Nirvana, Selfishness, Magical Power Hierophantship, etc. — 28 m.

After this meditation I arrived at the following decision: I must not cling to the Peace.‡ It certainly has become real to me, but if

---

* In this exercise the pendulum tends to swing out of plane. Here are Frater P.'s two methods of correcting it:

(a) Fix mind on the two points of a pendulum-swing and move pendulum sharply like chronograph hand, keeping them fixed and equal in size. Pendulum recovers its plane.

(b) Follow swing carefully throughout keeping size exact. This more legitimate but more difficult.

† Invoked angel of Nirvana as H.P.K. on lotus. Note P.'s complete ignorance of Buddhism, at this date.

‡ I.e., the Peace which had been enfolding him for so many days. See entry July 14th.

I make a God of it it will become but an illusion. I am ready to receive the Magical Power as I should not abuse it. I must needs accomplish the Finished Work.

Buddha.   33 m.   The best Meditation I have so far done. I regard this as a *real* meditation; for 13 minutes quite forgot time.

Rose on planes of כ׳נ׳ת׳ס׳י׳ת * from Malkuth to Kether.
August 5th. Meditated on Thoth concerning Frater I.A.
6th. Arrived at Colombo.

We now arrive at another turning-point in the progress of P. Up to the first of this year 1901 he had studied Western methods of Magic alone, from this date, at first under the tuition of D. A., and then solely under his own mastership, he had begun to study Raja Yoga, practising meditation and a few simple breathing exercises. Now he was going, if not entirely under a Guru, to work daily with one with whom he had, before his departure from England, carried out so many extraordinary magical operations. And this one was no other than Frater I. A.

On account of ill health Frater I. A. had journeyed to Ceylon to see if a warmer climate would not restore to him what a colder one had taken away; and now, that once again his old friend P. had joined him, these two determined to work out the Eastern systems under an Eastern sky and by Eastern methods alone.

On the 1st of August we find P. writing:

" I exist not: there is no God: no place: no time: wherefore I exactly particularize and specify these things." And

---

* כ=Kether   ג=Path of Gimel   ת=Tiphereth.
  ס=Path of Samech   י=Yesod   ת=Path of Tau.

five days later he began what he called "The Writings of Truth." Before we begin these, it will be necessary to enter upon the doctrines of Buddhism at some little length, for Frater I. A. was now at heart a follower of Gotama, being rather disgusted with his Tamil Guru; and under his guidance it was that P. grasped the fundamental importance of Concentration through meditation.

THE DOCTRINES OF BUDDHISM

Having sat for seven long years under the Bôdhi tree Gotama opened his eyes and perceiving the world of Samsâra* exclaimed: "Quod erat demonstrandum!" True, he had attained to the spotless eye of Truth and had become Buddha the Enlightened One; he had entered the Nothingness of Nibbâna,† and had become one with the Uncreated and the Indestructible. And now he stood once again on the shore line of existence and watched the waves of life roll landwards, curve, break and hiss up the beach only to surge back into the ocean from which they came. He did not deny the existence of the Divine, (how could he when he had become one with it?) but so filled was he with the light of Amitâbha,‡ that he fully saw that by Silence alone could the world be saved, and that by the denial of the Unknowable of the uninitiate, the Kether, the Âtman, the First Cause, the God of the unenlightened, could he ever hope to draw mankind to that great illimitable LVX, from which he had

---

* The world of unrest and transiency, of birth and death.

† The Great Attainment of Buddhism. Our terminology now degenerates into the disgusting vulgarity of the Pali dialect.

‡ The Mahâyâna Buddhists' Boundless Light. Compared with the canonical Nibbâna it bears a very similar relation to it as the Ain Soph Aur, the Illimitable Light, does to the Ain, the negatively Existent One. In the Brihadâranyka Upanishad 4. 4. 66. Brahman is termed "jyotishâm jyotis" which means "the light of lights"—a similar conception.

125

descended a God-illumined Adept. He fully realized that to admit into his argument the comment of God was to erase all hope of deliverance from the text, and therefore, though he had become The Buddha, nevertheless, in his selflessness he stooped down to the level of the lowest of mankind, and abandoning as dross the stupendous powers he had acquired, helped his fellows to realize the right path by the most universal of all symbols—the woe of the world, the sorrow of mankind.

Like the Vedântist, he saw that the crux of the whole trouble was Ignorance (Avijjâ). Dispel this ignorance, and illumination would take its place, that insight into the real nature of things, which, little by little, leads the Aspirant out of the world of birth and death, the world of Samsâra, into that inscrutable Nibbâna where things in themselves cease to exist and with them the thoughts which go to build them up. Ignorance is the greatest of all Fetters, and, "he who sins inadvertently," as Nâgasena said, "has the greater demerit."

Enquiring into the particular nature of Ignorance Buddha discovered that the Tree of Knowledge of Good and Evil had three main branches, namely: Lobha, Dosa and Moha; Craving, Passion and the Delusion of Self, and that these three forms of Ignorance alone could be conquered by right understanding the Three Great Signs or Characteristics of all Existence, namely: Change, Sorrow and Absence of an Ego— Anikka, Dukkha, and Anatta, which were attained by meditating on the inmost meaning of the Four Noble Truths:

"The Truth about Suffering; the Truth about the Cause of Suffering; the Truth about the Cessation of Suffering; and the Truth about the Path which leads to the Cessation of

126

Suffering." These consist of the above Three Characteristics with the addition of the Noble Eightfold Path, which contains as we shall presently see the whole of Canonical Buddhism.

Up to this point, save for the denial of the Ego, the whole of the above doctrine might have been extracted from almost any of the Upanishads. But there is a difference, and the difference is this. Though the Vedântist realized that Ignorance (Avidyâ) was the foundation of all Sorrow, and that all, possessing the essence of Change, was but illusion or Mâyâ, a matter of name and form; * Buddha now pointed out that the true path of deliverance was through the Reason (Ruach) and not through the senses (Nephesh), as many of the Upanishads would give one to believe. Further, this was the path that Gotama had trod, and therefore, naturally he besought others to tread it. The Vedântist attempted to attain unity with the Âtman (Kether) † by means of his Emotions (Nephesh) intermingled with his Reason (Ruach), but the Buddha by means of his Reason (Ruach) alone. Buddha attempted to cut off all joy from the world, substituting in its place an implacable rationalism, a stern and inflexible morality, little seeing that the sorrows of Earth which his system substituted in place of the joys of Heaven, though they might not ruffle his self-conquered self, must perturb the minds of his followers,

---

* We have seen how in the Chândogya Upanishad that all things, including even the four Vedas, are called "nâma eva"—mere name. Now in "The Questions of King Milinda" we find Nâgasena stating that all things but "name and form," the difference between which lies in that "Whatever is gross therein is form:'" whatever is subtle, mental, is "name." But that both are dependent on each other, and spring up, not separately, but together. "The Questions of King Milinda," ii. 2. 8.

† It must not be forgotten that in its ultimate interpretation the Âtman is the Ain, however we use this reading as seldom as possible, as it is so very vague.

and produce emotions of an almost equal intensity though perhaps of an opposite character to those of his opponents. Yet nevertheless, for a space, the unbending Rationalism of his System prevailed and crushed down the Emotions of his followers, those Emotions which had found so rich and fertile a soil in the decaying philosophy of the old Vedânta. The statement in the Dhammapada that: "All that we are is the result of what we have thought: it is founded on our thoughts, it is made up of our thoughts:" * is as equally true of the Vedânta as it is of Buddhism. But, in the former we get the great doctrine and practice of the Siddhis directly attributable to a mastering of the emotions and then to a use of the same, which is strictly forbidden to the Buddhist, but which eventually under the Mahâyâna Buddhism of China and Tibet forced itself once again into recognition, and which, even as early as the writing of "The Questions of King Milinda," unless the beautiful story of the courtesan Bindu-mati be a latter day interpolation, was highly thought of under the name of an "Act of Truth." Thus, though King Sivi gave his eyes to the man who begged them of him, he received others by an Act of Truth, by the gift of Siddhi, or Iddhi as the Buddhists call it. An Act, which is explained by the fair courtesan Bindumati as follows. When King Asoka asked her by what power she had caused the waters of the Ganges to flow backwards. She answered:

Whosoever, O King, gives me gold—be he a noble, or a brahman, or a tradesman, or a servant—I regard them all alike. When I see he is a noble I make no distinction in his favour. If I know him to be a slave I despise him

---

* Dhammapada, v. 1.

not. Free alike from fawning and from dislike do I do service to him who has bought me. This, your Majesty, is the basis of the Act of Truth by the force of which I turned the Ganges back.*

In other words, by ignoring all accidents, all matters of chance, and setting to work, without favour or prejudice, to accomplish the one object in view, and so finally "to interpret every phenomenon as a particular dealing of God with the soul." In truth this is an "Act of Truth," the Power begot by Concentration and nothing else.

We have seen at the commencement of this chapter how the Âtman (that Essence beyond Being and Not Being) allegorically fell by crying "It is I," and how the great Hypocrisy arose by supposing individual Âtmans for all beings, and things which had to incarnate again and again before finally they were swallowed up in the One Âtman of the Beginning. This Individualistic Conception Gotama banned, he would have none of it; a Soul, a Spirit, a separate entity was anathema to him; but in overthrowing the corrupt Vedânta of the latter-day pundits, like Luther, who many centuries later tore the tawdry vanities from off the back of prostitute Rome, approximating his reformed Church to the communistic brotherhood of Christ, Gotama, the Enlightened One, the Buddha, now similarly went back to Vedic times and to the wisdom of the old Rishis. But, fearing the evil associations clinging to a name, he, anathematizing the Âtman, in

* "The Questions of King Milinda," iv, 1, 48. See also the story of the Holy Quail in Rhys Davids' "Buddhist Birth Stories," p. 302. These Iddhis are also called Abhijnyâs. There are six of them: (1) clairvoyance; (2) clairaudience; (3) powers of transformation; (4) powers of remembering past lives; (5) powers of reading the thoughts of others; (6) the knowledge of comprehending the finality of the stream of life. See also "Konx om Pax," pp. 47, 48.

IV   I   129

its place wrote Nibbâna, which according to Nâgasena is cessation,* a passing away in which nothing remains, an end.† Soon however, under Mahâyâna-Buddhism, was the Âtman to be revived in all its old glory under the name of Amitâbha, or that Source of all Light, which so enlightens a man who is aspiring to the Bodhi that he becomes a Buddha. "Amitâbha," so Paul Carus informs us, "is the final norm of wisdom and of morality ‡ (*sic*), the standard of truth and of righteousness, the ultimate *raison d'être* of the Cosmic Order." This of course is "bosh." Amitâbha, as the Âtman, is "the light which shines there beyond the heaven behind all things, behind each in the highest worlds, the highest of all." §

Once logically having crushed out the idea of an individual soul, a personal God and then an impersonal God had to be set aside and with them the idea of a First Cause or Beginning; concerning which question Buddha refused to give an answer. For, he well saw, that the idea of a Supreme God was the greatest of the dog-faced demons that seduced man from the path. "There is no God, and I refuse to discuss what is not!" cries Buddha, "but there is Sorrow and I intend to destroy it." If I can only get people to start on the upward journey they will very soon cease to care if there is a God or if there is a No-God; but, if I give them the slightest cause to expect any reward outside cessation of Sorrow, it would set them all

* "The Questions of King Milinda," iii, 4, 6.   † *Ibid.*, iii, 5, 10.

‡ It is curious how, inversely according to the amount of morality preached is morality practised in America; in fact there are almost as many moral writers there as there are immoral readers. Paul Carus is as completely ignorant of Buddhism as he is about the art of nursing babies—he has written on both these subjects and many more, all flatulently.

§ Chândogya, 3, 13, 7.

cackling over the future like hens over a china egg, and soon they would be back at the old game of counting their chickens before they were hatched. He also must have seen, that if he postulated a God, or First Cause, every unfledged rationalist in Pâtaliputta would cry, "Oh, but what a God, what a wicked God yours must be to allow all this sorrow you talk of . . . now look at mine . . ." little seeing that sorrow was just the same with the idea of God as without it, and that all was indeed Moha or Mâyâ—both God and No-God, Sorrow and Joy.

But Buddha being a practical physician, though he knew sorrow to be but a form of thought, was most careful in keeping it as real a calamity as he could; for he well saw, that if he could only get people to concentrate upon Sorrow and its Causes, that the end could not be far off, of both Sorrow and Joy; but, if they began to speculate on its illusiveness, this happy deliverance would always remain distant. His business upon Earth was entirely a practical and exoteric one, in no way mystical; it was rational not emotional, catholic and not secret.

What then is the Cause of Sorrow? and the answer given by Gotama is: Karma or Action, which when once completed becomes latent and static, and according to how it was accomplished, when once again it becomes dynamic, is its resultant effect. Thus a good action produces a good reaction, and a bad one a bad one. This presupposes a code of morals, furnished by what?* We cannot call it Âtman, Conscience,

* Twenty-three centuries later Kant falling over this crux postulated his "twelve categories," or shall we say "emanations," and thereby started revolving once again the Sephirothic Wheel of Fortune.

or Soul; and a Selecting Power, which however is strenuously denied by the rigid law of Cause and Effect. However the mental eyes of the vast majority of his followers were not so clear as to pierce far into the darkness of metaphysical philosophy, and so it happened that, where the idealism of the Vedânta had failed the realism of Buddhism succeeded.*

This denial of a Universal Âtman, and a personal Âtman, soon brought the ethical and philosophical arguments of Gotama up against a brick wall (Kant's "à priori"). As we have seen he could not prop up a fictitious beginning by the supposition of the former, and he dared not use Nibbâna as such, though in truth the Beginning is just as incomprehensible with or without an Âtman. But, in spite of his having denied the latter, he had to account for Causality and the transmission of his Good and Evil (Karma) by some means or another. Now, according to Nâgasena, the Blessed One refused to answer any such questions as "Is the universe everlasting?" "Is it not everlasting?" "Has it an end?" "Has it not an end?" "Is it both ending and unending?" "Is it neither the one nor the other?" And further all such questions as "Are the soul and the body the same thing?" "Is the soul distinct from the body?" "Does a Tathâgata exist after death?" "Does he not exist after death?" "Does

---

* In spite of the fact that Buddhism urges that "the whole world is under the Law of Causation," it commands its followers to lead pure and noble lives, in place of dishonourable ones, in spite of their having no freedom of choice between good and evil. "Let us not lose ourselves in vain speculations of profitless subtleties," says the Dhammapada, "let us surrender self and all selfishness, and as all things are fixed by causation, let us practise good so that good may result from our actions." Just as if it could possibly be done if "*all things are fixed.*" The Buddhist, in theory having postulated that all fowls lay hardboiled eggs, adds, the ideal man is he who can only make omelettes.

132

he both exist and not exist after death?" "Does he neither exist nor not exist after death?" . . . Because "the Blessed Buddhas lift not up their voice without a reason and without an object." * But in spite of their being no *soul* "in the highest sense," † Gotama had to postulate some vehicle which would transmit the sorrow of one generation to another, of one instant of time to the next; and, not being able to use the familiar idea of Âtman, he instead made that of Karma do a double duty. "He does not die until that evil Karma is exhausted," says Nâgasena. ‡

Now this brings us to an extraordinary complex question, namely the *practical* difference between the Karma minus Âtman of the Buddhists and the Karma plus Âtman of the later Vedântists?

The Brahman's idea, at first, was of one complete whole, this, as the comment supplanted the text, got frayed into innumerable units or Âtmans, which, on account of Karma, were born again and again until Karma was used up and the individual Âtman went back to the universal Âtman. Buddha erasing the Âtman, though he refused to discuss the Beginning, postulates Nibbâna as the end, which fact conversely also postulates the Beginning as Nibbâna. Therefore we have all things originating from an x sign, Âtman, Nibbâna, God, Ain or First Cause, and eventually returning to this primordial Equilibrium. The difficulty which now remains is the bridging over of this divided middle. To Gotama there is no unit, and existence *per se* is Ignorance caused as it were by a bad dream in the head of the undefinable Nibbâna; which itself, however,

* "The Questions of King Milinda," iv, 2, 5.　　† *Ibid.,* iii, 5, 6.
‡ *Ibid.,* iii, 4, 4.

is non-existent. Each man is, as it were, a thought in an universal brain, each thought jarring against the next and prolonging the dream. As each individual thought dies it enters Nibbâna and ceases to be, and eventually when all thoughts die the dream passes and Nibbâna wakes.* This bad dream seems to be caused by a separateness of Subject and Object which means Sorrow; when sleep vanishes this separateness vanishes with it, things assume their correct proportion and may be equated to a state of bliss or Non-Sorrow.

Thus we find that Nirvana and Nibbâna are the same † in

* Compare "Mândûkya Upanishad," 1, 16.

> In the infinite illusion of the universe
> The soul sleeps; when it awakes
> Then there wakes in it the Eternal,
> Free from time and sleep and dreams.

† Most Buddhists will raise a terrific howl when they read this; but, in spite of their statement that the Hindu Nirvana, the absorption into Brahman, corresponds not with their Nibbâna, but with their fourth Arûpa-Vimokha, we nevertheless maintain, that in essence Nirvana and Nibbâna are the same, or in detail, if logic is necessary in so illogical an argument, it certainly sided rather with Nirvana than Nibbâna. Nibbâna is Final says the Buddhist, when once an individual enters it there is no getting out again, in fact a kind of Spiritual Bastille, for it is Niccain, changeless; but Brahman is certainly not this, for all things in the Universe originated from him. This is as it should be, though we see little difference between proceeding from to proceeding to, when it comes to a matter of First and Last Causes. The only reason why the Buddhist does not fall into the snare, is, not because he has explained away Brahman, but because he refuses to discuss him at all. Further the Buddhist argues that should the Hindu even attain by the exaltation of his selfhood to Arûpa Brahma-loka, though for a period incalculable he would endure there, yet in the end Karma would once again exert its sway over him, "and he would die as an Arûpabrahmaloka-Deva, his Sankhâras giving rise to a being according to the nature of his unexhausted Karma." In "Buddhism," vol. i, No. 2, p. 323, we read: "To put it another way; you say that the Universe came from Brahman, and that at one

fact as in etymology, and that absorption into either the one or the other may be considered as re-entering that Equilibrium from which we originated.

The first and the last words have been written on this final absorption by both the Vedântist and the Buddha alike.

There no sun shines, no moon, nor glimmering star, nor yonder lightning, the fire of earth is quenched; from him, who alone shines, all else borrows its brightness, the whole world bursts into splendour at his shining.*

And—

There exists, O Brothers, a Realm wherein is neither Earth nor Water

---

time naught save the Brahman was. Then 'In the beginning Desire arose in it, which was the primal germ of Mind.' Where did that desire come from, if the Brahman was the All, and the Unchangeable. . . . Again, if the Brahman was the All, and was perfect, then what was the object of this emanation of a Sorrow-filled Universe?" The Vedântist would naturally answer to this: "To put it in another way; you say that the Universe will go to Nibbâna, and that at one time naught save Nibbâna will be. Then in the end Desire dies in it, which was the primal germ of mind. Where will that desire go to, if Nibbâna will be the All, and the Unchangeable. . . . Again, if Nibbâna will be the All, and will be perfect, then what will be the object of this emanation of a Sorrow-filled Universe?" This is all the merest twaddle of a Hyde Park atheist or Christian Evidence preacher. Granted the Hindu Brahman is rationally ridiculous, yet nevertheless it is more rational to suppose a continuous chain of Sorrowful universes and states of oblivion than an unaccounted-for State of Sorrow and an unaccountable Finality. It is as rational or irrational to ask where "Brahman" came from, as it is to ask where "Karma" came from. Both are illusions, and as discussion of the same will only create a greater tangle than ever, let us cut the Gordian knot by leaving it alone, and set out to become Arahats, and enter the house which so mysteriously stands before us, and see what is really inside it, instead of mooning in the back garden and speculating about its contents, its furniture, the size of its rooms, and all the pretty ladies that scandal or rumour supposes that it shelters. To work! over the garden wall, and with Romeo cry:

Can I go forward when my heart is here?
Turn back, dull earth, and find thy centre out.

* Kâthaka Upanishad, 5, 15.

neither Flame nor Air; nor the vast Aether nor the Infinity of Thought, not Utter Void nor the co-existence of Cognition and Non-cognition is there:—not this World nor Another, neither Sun nor Moon. That, Brothers, I declare unto you as neither a Becoming nor yet a Passing-away:—not Life nor Death nor Birth; Unlocalised, Unchanging and Uncaused:—That is the end of Sorrow.*

Gotama therefore had to hedge. Unquestionably the Soul-idea must go, but in order to account for the Universal law of Causation Karma must remain, and further, surreptitiously perform all the old duties the individual Âtman had carried out. He had abandoned the animism of a low civilization, it is true, but he could not, for a want of the exemption from morality itself, abandon the fetish of a slightly higher civilization, namely ethics. He saw that though mankind was tired of being ruled by Spirits, they were only too eager to be ruled by Virtues, which gave those who maintained these fictitious qualifications a sure standpoint from which to rail at those who had not. Therefore he banned Reincarnation and Soul and substituted in their place Transmigration and Karma (Doing) the Sankhârâ or Tendencies that form the character (individuality!) of the individual.

Ânanda Metteya in "Buddhism"† explains transmigration in contradistinction to reincarnation as follows. Two men standing on the shore of a lake watch the waves rolling land-wards. To the one who is unversed in science it appears that the wave travelling towards him retains its identity and shape, it is to him a mass of water that moves over the surface impelled by the wind. The other, who has a scientifically trained mind, knows that at each point upon the surface of the lake the particles of water are only rising and then falling in

* The Book of Solemn Utterances.   † Vol. i, No. 2, p. 293.

their place, that each particle in turn is passing on its motion to its neighbours. To the first there is a translation of matter, to the second one of force. "The Vedântist has seen Substance, an enduring Principle, an Ens; the Buddhist only Qualities, themselves in all their elements ever changing, but the sum-total of their Doing passing steadily on, till the wave breaks upon Nibbâna's shore, and is no more a wave for ever."

We have not space to criticise this, all we will ask is—what is the difference between Force and Matter, and if the annihilation of the one does not carry with it the annihilation of the other irrespective of which is first—if either?

Ânanda Metteya carries his illustration further still.

John Smith, then, in a sense, is immortal; nay, every thought he thinks is deathless, and will persist, somewhere, in the depths of infinity. . . . But it is not this part of his energy that results in the formation of a new being when he dies. . . . We may then consider the moment of John Smith's death. . . . During his life he has not alone been setting in vibration the great ocean of the Æther, he has been affecting the structure of his own brain. So that at the moment of his death all his own life, and all his past lives are existing pictured in a definite and characteristic molecular structure, a tremendous complicated representation of all that we have meant by the term John Smith—the record of the thoughts and doings of unnumbered lives. Each cell of the millions of his brain may be likened to a charged leyden-jar, the nerve-paths radiating from it thrill betimes with its discharges, carrying its meaning through man's body, and, through the Æther, even to the infinitude of space. When it is functioning normally, its total discharge is prevented, so that never at any time can more than a fraction of its stored up energy be dissipated. . . . And then Death comes; and in the moment of its coming, all that locked up energy flames on the universe like a new-born star.*

Ânanda Metteya then in a lengthy and lucid explanation demonstrates how the light of a flame giving off the yellow light of sodium may be absorbed by a layer of sodium vapour,

* Buddhism, vol. i, No. 2, p. 299, abridged.

so the Karma, released from the body of the dead man, will circle round until it finds the body of a new-born child tuned or syntonized to its particular waves.

Now we are not concerned here with stray children who like the receivers of a wireless telegraph pick up either good or evil messages; but it is an interesting fact to learn that at least certain orthodox Buddhists attribute so complex and considerable a power to the brain, that by the fact of leaving one body that body perishes, and of entering another that body revives. Can it be that we have got back to our old friend the Prâna which in its individual form so closely resembles the individual Karma, and in its entirety the totality of Nibbâna? Let us turn to Brihadâranyaka Upanishad. There in 1, 6, 3. we find a mystical formula which reads *Amritam satyena channam*. This means "The immortal (Brahman) veiled by the (empirical) reality;" and immediately afterwards this is explained as follows: "The Prâna (*i.e.* the Âtman) to wit is the immortal, name and form are the reality; by these the Prâna is veiled." Once again we are back at our starting-point. To become one with the Prâna or Âtman is to enter Nibbâna, and as the means which lead to the former consisted of concentration exercises such as Prânâyâma, etc.; so now shall we find almost identical exercises used to hasten the Aspirant into Nibbâna.

Frater P. by now was well acquainted with the Yoga Philosophy, further he was beginning to feel that the crude Animism employed by many of its expounders scarcely tallied with his attainments. The nearer he approached the Âtman the less did it appear to him to resemble what he had been taught to expect. Indeed its translation into worldly comments was a matter of education, so it came about that he discovered that the Great Attainment *per se* was identical in all systems irrespective of the symbol man sought it under. Thus Yahweh as a clay phallus in a band-box was as much a reality to the Jews of Genesis as Brahman in Brahma-loka was to the Aryas of Vedic India; that the vision of Moses when he beheld God as a burning bush is similar to the vision of the fire-flashing Courser of the Chaldean Oracles; and that Nibbâna the Non-existent is little removed, if at all, from the Christian heaven with its harps, halos and hovering angels. And the reason is, that the man who does attain to any of these states, on his return to consciousness, at once attributes his attainment to his particular business partner—Christ, Buddha, Mrs. Besant, etc., etc., and attempts to rationalize about the suprarational, and describe what is beyond description in the language of his country.

P., under the gentle guidance of Ânanda Metteya, at first found the outward simplicity most refreshing; but soon he discovered that like all other religious systems Buddhism was entangled in a veritable network of words. Realizing this, he went a step further than Gotama, and said: " Why bother about Sorrow at all, or about Transmigration? for these are not 'wrong viewyness,' as Mr. Rhys Davids would so poetically put it, but matters of the Kindergarten and not of the Temple; matters for police regulation, and for underpaid curates to chatter about, and matters that have nothing to do with true progress." He then divided life into two compartments; into the first he threw science, learning, philosophy and all things built of words—the toys of life; and into the second The Invocations of Adonai—the work of attainment.

Then he took another step forward. " Do as thou wilt!" Not only is Animism absurd, but so also is Morality; not only is Reincarnation absurd, but so also is Transmigration; not only is the Ego absurd, but so also is the Non-Ego; not only is Karma absurd, but so also is Nibbâna. For, all things and no-things are absurd save " I," who am Soul and Body, Good and Evil, Sorrow and Joy, Change and Equilibrium; who in the temple of Adonai, am beyond all these, and by the fire side in my study—Mr. X, one with each and all.

Thus it came about that the study of Buddhism caused Frater P. to abandon the tinsel of the Vedânta as well as its own cherished baubles, and induced him, more than ever, to rely on Work and Work alone and not on philosophizing, moralizing and rationalizing. The more rational he became, the less he reasoned outwardly; and the more he became endowed with the Spirit of the Buddha in place of the vapourings of Buddhism, the more he saw that personal endeavour was the key; not the Scriptures, which at best could but indicate the way.

It (the Dharma) is to be attained to by the wise, each one for himself. Salvation rests on Work and not on Faith, not in reforming the so-called fallen, but in conquering oneself. " If one man conquer in battle a thousand times a thousand men: and another conquer but himself;—he is the greatest of conquerors."*

This is the whole of Buddhism, as it is of any and all systems of self-control.

* Dhammapada, v, 103.

THE TEMPLE OF SOLOMON THE KING

Strenuousness is the Immortal Path—sloth is the way of death. The Strenuous live always,—the slothful are already as the dead.*

Impermanent are the Tendencies—therefore do ye deliver yourselves by Strenuousness.

Frater P. now saw more clearly than ever that this last charge of the Buddha was the one supremely important thing that he ever said.

* Dhammapada, v, 21.

THE NOBLE EIGHTFOLD PATH

In place of producing a dissolution of the individual Âtman in the universal Âtman, the method of Buddha produced a submersion of Karma in the bournless ocean of Nibbâna.

In Chapter I of Book II of "The Questions of King Milinda" Nâgasena lays down that he who escapes rebirth does so through Wisdom (Paññâ) and Reasoning (Yonisomanasikâra) and by other "Good Qualities." The Reason grasps the object and Wisdom cuts it off, whilst the good qualities seem to be the united action of these two, thus we get Good Conduct (Sîlam), Faith (Saddhâ), Perseverance (Viriyam), Mindfulness (Sati) and Meditation (Samâdhi), all of which rather than being separate states are but qualities of the one state of Meditation at various stages in that state of Samâdhi which Nâgasena calls "the leader" . . . "All good qualities have meditation as their chief, then incline to it, lead up towards it, are as so many slopes up the side of the mountain of meditation."* Just as Yama, Niyama, Prânâyâma, Pratyâhâra, Dhâranâ and Dhyâna are of Samâdhi. Further Nâgasena says "Cultivate in yourselves O Bhikkhus, the habit of meditation. He who is established therein knows things as they really are."†

Under Faith, is classed Tranquillization (Sampasâdana) and

---

* "The Questions of King Milinda," ii, 1, 7, 9, 13.   † *Ibid.*, 13.

Aspiration (Sampakkhandana). Under Perseverance, the rendering of Support—tension (Paggaha). Under Mindfulness, Repetition (Apilâpana) and " keeping up " (Upaganhana). Under Good Conduct, the whole of the Royal Road from Aspirant to Arahat—The five Moral Powers (Indriyabalâin); The seven Conditions of Arahatship (Bogghangâ); The Path, readiness of memory, (Satipatthâna); The four kinds of Right Exertion (Sammappadhâna); The four Stages of Ecstasy (Ghâna); The eight forms of spiritual Emancipation (Vimokhâ); The four modes of Self-Concentration (Samâdhi);* The eight states of Intense contemplation (Samâpatti).

It would be waste of time to compare the above states with the states of the Hindu Yoga, or enumerate other similarities which exist by the score, but one point we must not overlook, and that is The Noble Eightfold Path, which contains the very essence of Gotama's teaching, as he said:

There is a Middle Path, O Monks, the Two Extremes avoiding, by the Tathâgata attained:—a Path which makes for Insight and gives Understanding, which leads to Peace of Mind, to the Higher Wisdom, to the Great Awakening, to Nibbâna! †

Let us now examine these eight truths.‡ The first is:

I. *Right Comprehension or Right Views.*

Right Comprehension is the first practical step in carrying

* It will be noticed that this is the third sense in which this hard-working word is employed.

† The Sutta of the Foundation of the Kingdom of Truth.

‡ [We respect the following noble attempt to rewrite Buddhism in the Universal Cipher, not unaware that the flatulent Buddhists of to-day will eructate their cacodylic protests. An orthodox Buddhist account is to be found in " The Sword of Song," by A. Crowley, article " Science and Buddhism."—ED.]

out the Four Noble Truths, that is in the understanding of the Three Characteristics—the three fundamental principles of Buddhism. Besides representing Malkuth, the Four Noble Truths (viewed in an elementary manner) represent the four lower Sephiroth—Malkuth, Yesod, Hod and Netzach, the state of Right Views carrying with its attainment a transcendency over all wrong views, that is to say all crude and unskilful views, all dogmas, assertions, all doubts, which are as unfertile as the elements are when uncombined, by applying to them what we have termed elsewhere the Pyrrhonic Serpent of Selection.

The attainment of Right Views is arrived at in three successive steps. (1) The Aspirant contemplates the ills of life; (2) he meditates upon them; (3) by strenuous will power he commences to strip the mind of the Cause of Sorrow, namely Change.

During this stage a series of humiliations must be undergone, and, not only must the Nephesch be conquered, but also the lower states of the Ruach, until the illumination of the Second Noble Truth of the Eightfold Path shatter the step of Right Views which the Aspirant is standing upon just as the fire of God consumed the Elemental Pyramid—the Tower of the Taro.

Having attained to mastery over Right Comprehension the aspirant begins to see things not as they are but in their right proportions. His views become balanced, he enters Tiphareth, the Solar Plexus, " He sees naked facts behind the garments of hypotheses in which men have clothed them, and by which they have become obscured; and he perceives that behind the changing and conflicting opinions of men there are permanent principles which constitute the eternal Reality in the Cosmic Order."*

In Tiphareth the aspirant attains to no less a state than that of conversation with his Holy Guardian Angel, his Jechidah, "The permanent principle behind the conflicting opinions." Once Right Comprehension has been attained to, he has discovered a Master who will never desert him until he become one with him.

II. *Right Resolutions or Right Aspirations.*

Having perceived the changing nature of all things, even of men's minds, and having acquired that glorified vision by which he can distinguish between the permanent and the impermanent, he aspires to the attainment of a perfect knowledge of that which is beyond change and sorrow, and resolves that he will, by strenuous effort,† reach to the peace beyond; to where his heart may find rest, his mind become steadfast, untroubled, and serene.‡

At this stage the Bodhi Satva of Work commences to revolve within the heart of the aspirant and to break up the harmony of the elements only to attune his aspirations for a time to a discord nobler than all harmony, and eventually to that Peace which passeth Understanding.

III. *Right Speech.*

Right Speech is a furthering of Right Aspirations. It consists of a discipline wherein a man not only converses with his Holy Guardian Angel, but outwardly and inwardly lives up to His holy conversation, turning his whole life into

---

* "The Noble Eightfold Path," by James Allen, in "Buddhism," vol. i, No. 2, p. 213. A most illuminating essay on this difficult subject.

† The same as the "inflamed by prayer" of Abramelin.

‡ *Ibid.*, p. 213.

one stupendous magical exercise to enter that Silence which is beyond all thought.

IV. *Right Acts or Right Conduct.*

Having become obedient to his Holy Guardian Angel (the aspirant's Spiritual Guru) or to the Universal Law as the Buddhist prefers to call it, man naturally enters the stage of Right Conduct, which brings with it supernormal or magical powers. Self is now put aside from action as well as from speech, and the striver only progresses by a stupendous courage and endurance. The canonical Buddhists however strenuously deny the value of these magical powers, Iddhis or Siddhis, and attribute the purification of the striver, the attainment of the state of " stainless deeds," to the great love wherein he must now enshrine all things. In detail the differences between Buddhism and the Yoga are verbal; in essence, man, at this stage, becomes the lover of the World, and love is the wand of the Magician, that wand which conquers and subdues, vivifies, fructifies and replenishes the worlds, and like the Caduceus of Hermes it is formed of two twining snakes.

V. *Right Livelihood.*

Up to this stage man has been but a disciple to his Holy Guardian Angel, but now he grows to be his equal, and in the flesh becomes a flame-shod Adept whose white feet are not soiled by the dust and mud of earth. He has gained perfect control over his body and his mind; and not only are his speech and actions right, but his very life is right, in fact his actions have become a Temple wherein he can at will
146

withdraw himself to pray. He has become a priest unto himself his own Guardian, he may administer to himself the holy sacrament of God in Truth and in Right, he has become Exempt from the shackles of Earth. He is the Supreme Man, one step more he enters the Sanctuary of God and becomes one with the Brotherhood of Light.

Up to this stage progress has meant Work, work terrible and Titanic, one great striving after union which roughly may be compared to the five methods of Yoga.

From this fifth stage work gives place to knowledge, Qabalistically the aspirant enters Daäth.

VI. *Right Effort.*

Man is now Master of Virtue and Vice and no longer their slave, servant, enemy or friend. The LVX has descended upon him, and just as the dew of the moon within the Sahasâra Chakkra falling upon the two-petalled Ajna-lotus causes the leaves to open out, so now does this celestial light lift him out and beyond the world, as wings lift a bird from the fields of earth, encompassing him, extending to his right hand and to his left like the wings of the Solar Globe which shut out from the ruby ball the twin serpents which twine beneath it.*

    ... Having purified himself, he understands the perfect life; being a doer of Holiness, he is a knower of Holiness; having practised Truth, he has become accomplished in the knowledge of Truth. He perceives the working of the inner Law of things, and is loving, wise, enlightened. And being loving, wise and

---

    * The two serpents and central rod of the Caduceus are in Yoga represented by the Ida, Pingala and Sushumnâ. The wings closed, to the Ajna-lotus; open and displaying the solar disk, to the Sahasâra Chakkra.

enlightened, he does everything with a wise purpose, in the full knowledge of what he is doing, and what he will accomplish. He wastes no drachm of energy, but does everything with calm directness of purpose, and with penetrating intelligence. This is the stage of Masterly Power in which effort is freed from strife and error, and perfect tranquillity of mind is maintained under all circumstances. He who has reached it, accomplishes everything upon which he sets his mind.*

VII. *Right Thought.*

So filled with Understanding is he now that he becomes, as it were, the actual mind of the Universe, nothing remains uncomprehended; he comes face to face with his goal, he sees HIMSELF as one who gazes into a mirror.

VIII. *Right Meditation, or the Right State of a Peaceful Mind.*

The glass vanishes and with it the reflection, the illusion of Mara or of Mâyâ. He is Reality! He is Truth! He is Âtman! He is God. Then Reality vanishes. Truth vanishes. Âtman vanishes. God vanishes. He himself vanishes. He is past; he is present; he is future. He is here, he is there. He is everything. He is nowhere. He is nothing. He is blessed, he has attained to the Great Deliverance. He IS; he IS NOT. He is one with Nibbâna.†

---

* *Ibid.*, p. 216.

† Another and perhaps a more comprehensive way of attributing the Noble Eightfold Path to the Tree of Life is as follows: The first and second steps—Right Comprehension and Right Resolution, may from their purging nature fitly be compared to Yama and Niyama and also to the Earthy and Lunar natures of Malkuth and Yesod. The third and fourth—Right Speech and Right Action, in their yearning and striving are by nature as unbalanced as Hod and Netzach which are represented by Fire and Water and by Mercury and Venus respectively. Then comes the fifth stage of poise—Right Livelihood; this is also a stage of exemption from worldly motion, and a stage which brings all

148

below it to a finality and which may be compared to Tiphereth in its Solar Aspect or to the Manipura Chakkra. The sixth and seventh stages—Right Effort and Right Thought, are stages of "definitely directed power" closely related to Geburah and Chesed—Mars and Jupiter. And then finally comes the eighth stage—Right Meditation, again a summary of the three stages below it, which may be compared as the Three Supernals or the Sahasâra Chakkra. [Compare with the essay " Science and Buddhism " in the " Sword of Song " by A. Crowley, and the writings of Ânanda Metteya. Here are then three men who have worked both severally and collectively, who yet apparently hold irreconcilable views as to what Buddhism is. What better proof is needed of the fact that all intellectual study ultimates in mental chaos?]

THE WRITINGS OF TRUTH *

The seeker after Wisdom, whose Bliss is non-existence, the Devotee of the Most Excellent Bhâvani,† the Wanderer in the Samsâra Câkkra, the Insect that crawls on Earth, on Seb beneath Nuit, the Purusha beyond Ishwara: He taketh up the Pen of the Ready Writer, to record those Mysterious Happenings which came unto Him in His search for Himself. And the beginning is of Spells, and of Conjurations and of Evocations of the Evil Ones: Things Unlawful to write of, dangerous even to think of; wherefore they are not here written. But he beginneth with his sojourning in the Isle of Lanka:‡ the time of his dwelling with Mâitrânanda Swâmi.§ Wherefore, O Bhâvani, bring Thou all unto the Proper End! To Thee be Glory—OM.

On the 6th of August P. landed in Colombo, and on the following day he went to see his old friend Frater I.A. who was now studying Buddhism with the view of becoming a Buddhist monk. On this very day he commenced, or rather continued his meditation practices; for we find him trying with Mâitrânanda the result of speech as a disturbing factor in Dhâr. (meditation). The experiment was as follows: P. sat and meditated for five minutes on a white Tau (T) during which Mâitrânanda spoke six times with the object of

---

* No rough working is given in this volume; it is only a compendium of Results.

† The goddess Isis, Deir, Kali, Sakti, etc, in her aspect as the patroness of Meditation. There are five principal meditations. Metta-Bhâvanâ, on love; Karunâ-Bhâvanâ, on pity; Mudita-Bhâvanâ, on joy; Asubha-Bhâvanâ, on impunity; and Upekshâ-Bhâvanâ, on serenity. But see 777, col. xxiii, p. 9.

‡ Old native name for Ceylon.

§ Frater I.A.'s Eastern name, afterwards changed to Ânanda Metteya.

seeing if it would interrupt P.'s meditation. The result on the first occasion was a bad break; second, two bad breaks; third to sixth, no breaks occurred. At the end of the experiment P. was able to repeat all Mâitrânanda had said except the last remark.*

August

9th. Practised Mental Muttering of the Mantra: "Namo Shivaya Namaha Aum." I found that with Rechaka the voice sounds as if from the Confines of the Universe: but with Puraka as if from the third eye. Whilst doing this in the Saivite Â'sana † I found the eyes, without conscious volition, are drawn up and behold the third eye. (Ajna Chakkra.)

10th. A day of revelation of Arcana. Ten minutes Â'sana and breathing exercise. Latter unexpectedly trying. Also practised Mental Muttering whilst in Â'sana. Repeating "Namo Shivaya Namaha Aum," which takes, roughly, 86 seconds for 50 repetitions, i.e. about 1,000 in half an hour. I practised this Mantra for thirty minutes: 10 minutes aloud; 10 minutes in silence; 10 minutes by hearing.‡

11th. Recited the Mantra for about 1½ hour while painting a talisman.

---

* Any who have undergone this test will readily understand how severe it is. The speaker says something with a view to break the meditation of the meditator. Meanwhile the meditator must so strengthen his will, that he *wills* to remain in his meditation uninterrupted; and yet in the end, though his mind has never wandered in contemplating the object meditated upon, he, nevertheless, has to repeat what the speaker said; which when the will is very strong may not even be heard as a sound, let alone as a coherent sentence. The will has to keep the thinking faculty of the meditator from interrupting the meditation; but meanwhile the thinking faculty without in any way breaking the meditation has to receive the message of the speaker and deliver it unimpaired to the meditator directly the meditation is at an end. This experiment, except that it is carried out by an act of will, differs very slightly, if at all, from those moments in which whilst absorbed in some work, we hear a clock strike, and only realize that the clock has struck a certain hour some considerable time after the event.

† The Thunderbolt: see Illustration in THE EQUINOX, vol. i, No. 1.

‡ *I.e.*, no longer uttering the Mantra, but listening to the Mystic Voice of the Universe saying it.

It was on this day I got a broken-bell-sound * in my head when not doing anything particular.

August

12th. Â'sana and Breathing 10 minutes. One fears to do Rechaka, so tremendous and terrible is the Voice of the Universe. But with Puraka is a still small Voice. Concerning which Mâitrânanda said to me: "Listen not to that Great and terrible Voice: but penetrate and hear the subtle soul thereof."

13th. Prânâyâma: Five cycles 5 minutes 15 seconds. Mantra (N.S.N.A.) † Half an hour. Ears begin to sing at about the twentieth minute. Towards the end I heard a soft sound as of a silver tube being struck very gently with a soft mallet.

These sounds are known as the Voice of the Nada, and are a sure sign that progress is being made. They, as already mentioned, are the mystical inner sounds which proceed from the Anahata Chakkra. According to the Hatha Yoga Pradipika these sounds proceed from the Sushumnâ. "They are in all of ten sorts; buzzing sound, sound of the lute, of bells, of waves, of thunder, of falling rain, etc."

Close the ears, the nose, the mouth and the eyes: then a clear sound is heard distinctly in the Sushumnâ (which has been purified by Prânâyâma).‡

The "Pradipika" further states that in all Yogi practices there are four stages. Arambha, Ghata, Parichaya and Nish-patti. In the first (Arambhâvasthâ) that is when the Anahata Chakkra is pierced by Prânâyâma various sweet tinkling sounds arise from the Âkâsa of the heart.

When the sound begins to be heard in the Shunya (Âkâsa), the Yogi possessed of a body resplendent and giving out sweet odour, is free from all diseases and his heart is filled (with Prâna).§

---

* These mystic sounds heard by the Yogi are supposed to proceed from the Anahata Chakkra.

† Short for Namo Shivaya Namaha Aum.

‡ "Hatha Yoga Pradipika," p. 91. The description here is of the Shanmukhi Mudra. § *Ibid.*, p. 92.

THE TEMPLE OF SOLOMON THE KING

In the second stage (Ghatâvasthâ) the Prâna becomes one with the Nada in the Vishuddhi Chakkra and make a sound like that of a kettledrum; this is a sign that Bramhânanda is about to follow. In the third stage (Parichayâvastha) a sound like a drum is heard in the Ajna Chakkra. Having overcome the blissful state arising from hearing the sounds the Yogi begins to experience a greater bliss from the increasing realization of the Âtman.

The Prâna, having forced the Rudra Granthi existing in the Ajna Chakkra goes to the seat of Ishwara. Then the fourth state (Nishpatti) sets in: wherein are heard the sounds of the flute and Vînâ (a stringed instrument).*

At this stage the Prâna goes to the Bramharandhra, and enters the Silence.

This is all most beautifully described in the various Shastras. In the Shiva Sanhita we read:

27. The first sound is like the hum of the honey-intoxicated bee, next that of a flute, then of a harp; after this, by the gradual practice of Yoga,† the destroyer of the darkness of the world, he hears the sounds of the ringing bells, then sounds like roars of thunder. When one fixes his full attention on this sound, being free from fear, he gets absorption, O My Beloved!

28. When the mind of the Yogi is exceedingly engaged in this sound, he forgets all external things, and is absorbed in this sound.‡

H. P. Blavatsky in " The Voice of the Silence " classifies these sounds under seven distinct heads.

The first is like the nightingale's sweet voice chanting a song of parting to its mate.

The second comes as the sound of a silver cymbal of the Dhyânis, awakening the twinkling stars.

---

* " Hatha Yoga Pradipika," p. 93.
† Chiefly by the Yoga of Nâda-Laya, a Dhyâna.
‡ " Shiva Sanhita," chap. v, p. 42.

The next is as the plaint melodious of the ocean-sprite imprisoned in its shell. And this is followed by the chant of vînâ.

The fifth like sound of bamboo-flute shrills in thine ear.

It changes next into a trumpet-blast.

The last vibrates like the dull rumbling of a thunder-cloud.

The seventh swallows all the other sounds. They die, and then are heard no more.*

The Hatha Yoga Pradipika is a great deal more exact in its description of these sounds than the famous Theosophist; concerning them Swâtmârâm Swâmi writes:

In the beginning, the sounds resemble those of the ocean, the clouds, the kettledrum, and Zarzara (a sort of drum cymbal); in the middle they resemble those arising from the Mardala, the conch, the bell and the horn.

In the end they resemble those of the tinkling bells, the flutes, the vînâ, and the bees. Thus are heard the various sounds from the middle of the body.

Even when the loud sounds of the clouds and the kettledrum are heard, he should try to fix his attention on the subtler sounds.

He may change his attention from the lull to the subtle sounds, but should never allow his attention to wander to other extraneous objects.

The mind fixes itself upon the Nâda to which it is first attracted until it becomes one with it.†

Many other passages occur in this little text book on Yoga dealing with these mystical sounds some of them of a combined beauty and wisdom which is hard to rival. Such as:

When the mind, divested of its flighty nature, is bound by the cords of the Nâda, it attains a state of extreme concentration and remains quiet as a bird that has lost its wings.

Nâda is like a snare for catching a deer, i.e., the mind. It, like a hunter, kills the deer.

The mind, having become unconscious, like a serpent, on hearing the musical sounds, does not run away.

---

* " The Voice of the Silence," pp. 24, 25.

† " Hatha Yoga Pradipika," iv, 96. For some of these sounds also see Brahmavidyâ, 13, Dhyânabindu, 18, and the Hamsa Upanishad, 4.

The fire, that burns a piece of wood, dies, as soon as the wood is burnt out. So the mind concentrated upon the Nâda gets absorbed with it.

When the Antahkarana, like a deer, is attracted by the sound of bells, etc., and remains immovable, a skilful archer can kill it.

Whatever is heard of the nature of sound is only Shakti.*

The conception of Âkâsa† (the generator of sound) exists, as long as the sound is heard. The Soundless is called Parabramha or Paramâtma.‡

August

14th. Bought a meditation-mat and also a bronze Buddha.

Nadi-Yama§ 10 minutes in the Saivite posture, in which my body-seat fits exactly into a square of about 18 inches forming the letter Aleph.

Mantra (N.S.N.A.). At the 28th minute got faint sounds like a musical box worked by a mallet on metal bars. As I stopped I heard a piano very distant. The intense attention requisite to try to catch the subtle sounds of the Universe when in Rechaka prevents Mantra, as my mental muttering is not yet absolutely automatic.

15th. By the five signs my Nadi are now purified.‖ But this appears to me as unlikely.

Eyes on tip of nose. 5 minutes. The nose grows very filmy and the rest of the field of vision loses its uprightness and is continually sliding into itself across itself. A most annoying phenomenon.

Nadi-Yama. 15 minutes. This becomes easier.

Mental Muttering of Aum Shivayavashi.

On the 17th August P. and Mâitrânanda left Colombo and journeyed to Kandy; Swami Mâitrânanda more particularly for his health; but P. so that he might escape the turmoil of a sea-port and to discover a suitable and secluded spot for a magical retirement, which he now had made up his mind to perform.

19th. Concentrated on point of base of brain. [To find this imagine cross-wires drawn between (a) ear to ear, as if a line had been stretched between

---

* Mental or bodily attributes. † See 777, col. lv, p. 17.

‡ "Hatha Yoga Pradipika," pp. 97-100. Also, Amritabindu Upanishad, 24.

§ Nadi-Yama or Control of the nerve-channels by regular breathing, without Khumbaka or holding the breath.

‖ He whose Nadi are pure has (1) a clear complexion; (2) a sweet voice; (3) a calm appearance; (4) bright eyes; (5) hearing constantly the Nada.

them, and from the centre of this line to the top of the skull. (*b*) from above the bridge of my nose horizontally backwards.]

The result was that I felt a throbbing in my head, principally at the spot concentrated on.

August

28th. I hereby formulate unto myself a Vow of Silence for a period of at least three days. My time to be occupied by Nadi-Yama and Â'sana, also by meditations of the Buddha and "Aum Mani Padme Hum." The vow to begin from Midnight. This vow I took ceremonially.

29th. 11.40-12.7 p.m. a.m.   Suddhi.*   Very painful and jerky, especially Rechaka. Â'sana much pain on moving.

7.40-7.55 a.m a.m.   Suddhi. Result was better, but goes off whilst meditating on "Aum Mani Padme Hum."

10.3-10.50 a.m a.m.   Began Mental Muttering of "Aum Mani Padme Hum" meditating upon Buddha. This developed into Pratyâhâric Dhâranâ; loss of Ego and a vision of mysterious power: loss of all objects mental and physical. I do not know how long this lasted I woke meditating Anahata.† The voice of Nada was like a far-off solemn song; it became "Aum" only, dropping "Mani Padme Hum," and then was more like thunder without harmonics.

Did Dhâranâ on Anahata.

11.45-12.15 a.m. p.m.   Suddhi. Â'sana very painful.

12.15-1.0 p.m. p.m.   Meditation on "Aum Mani Padme Hum," and sleep.

4.15-4.45 p.m. p.m.   Dhâranâ on Anahata with "Aum Mani Padme Hum." The latter sounds like the flight of a great bird in windy weather.

5.50-6.20 p.m. p.m.   Suddhi. When meditating on my bronze Buddha I obtained a great standing self-luminous but rayless Buddha.

30th. 12.12-12.42 a.m. am.   Suddhi.

I passed a bad night, and in the morning my will and control of thought seemed shortened.

8.45-9.15 a.m. a.m.   Suddhi.

Thoughts hopelessly wandering.

9.45-10.29 a.m. a.m.   Dhâranâ on Buddha with "Aum Mani Padme Hum." A much better meditation. I felt a spiral force whirring around

---

* The same as Nadi-Yama.

† Anahata Lotus, mystic ganglion in the heart. See diagram.

the top of my spine. This signifies an induction current of Prâna.

11.30-12.0 a.m. noon.	Suddhi.
6.15-6.45 p.m. p.m.	Suddhi.
9.34-10.4 p.m. p.m.	Suddhi.
12.30-1.0 a.m. a.m.	Suddhi.

August

31st. 6.10-6.40 a.m. a.m. Suddhi. "Sweet as a singing rain of silver dew" is the Voice of Nâda. Â'sana is evidently a question of training. At one point there were two or three distinct sharp throbs in the third eye. (Ajna.)

9.15-9.55 a.m. a.m. Dhâranâ on Ajna.* Tendency to become strained and rigid, with internal Kumbhaka, quite unconsciously. Exactly like a difficult stool, only the direction of force is upwards—very fatiguing.

10.24-10.28 a.m. a.m. Suddhi. Ida stopped up. Change of Nâda-note to a dull sound. Extreme excitement of Chitta, sleep impossible. Concentrating on Anahata gives sleepiness at once. I felt the pump action of the blood very plainly and also experienced Sukshma-Kumbhaka,† the subtle involuntary Kumbhaka.

6.10-6.40 a.m. p.m. Suddhi. One minute thirty-five seconds for a cycle. Repeated waking with nightmare. Test Kumbhaka, 45 and 55 seconds.

September

2nd. 12.5-12.35 p.m. p.m. Suddhi with Kumbhaka. Test Kumbhaka 85 seconds, 1 minute 25 seconds. Pain (or concentration of Prâna) in the back of head, level with eyes.

3rd. Sunset. Suddhi in the jungle. Concentration on Anahata, but did not go to sleep.

---

* Dhârâna on Ajna prevents sleep: ditto on Anahata causes it.

† In practising Prânâyâma, the breath may get convulsively withheld, all the muscles going suddenly rigid, without the will of the Yogi. This is called Sukshama-Kumbhaka, or Automatic holding in of the breath. This phenomenon marks a stage in attainment.

THE EQUINOX

Heard the following sounds:

(1) A noise as of blood filtering through.

(2) The tramp of armed men. This grew more distant on closing ears.

(3) The noise of a distant Siren. This grew stronger on closing ears.

(For a short time I distinctly saw the head of a nun in the centre of the Chakkra.)

September

5th. 12.15-12.52 p.m. p.m.   Fifty-two Suddhi-Kumbhakas or Prânâyâmas. 5. 10. 20 for 30 minutes. 10. 15. 30 for 6 minutes.

5.25-6.26 p.m. p.m.   Prânâyâma. 5. 10. 20 for 31 minutes without any breaks.

9.25-9.50 p.m. p.m.   Dhâranâ on the Shiva Pantacle given me by Mâitrânanda Swâmi, mentally muttering "Aum Shivaya Vashi." * Nothing particular occurred, though (were I not fixed in the knowledge of the vanity of physiological tests) I should judge my weight had diminished.† The Â'sana gave no pain till I moved. I had my eyes turned up to the third eye.

Vivekânanda says: "vibration of body" is the second stage of Prânâyâma. I get this, but put it down to weakness.

Dhâranâ on tip of nose for five minutes. Heard a voice saying: "And if you're passing, won't you?"

Concentration on any organ seems to make it very sensitive—a fleck of down lighting on my nose made me jump.

6th. 9.20-9.50 a.m. a.m.   Prânâyâma. Three cycles of 7 minutes (i.e. Twelve cycles of 5. 10. 20=one cycle of 7 minutes) with intervals of 3 minutes after each cycle.

6.10-6.40 p.m. p.m.   Prânâyâma. Two cycles of 5.10.20. The counting got mixed and things seem to tend to get buzzy and obscure. Found it difficult to follow clearly the second-hand of a watch. One cycle of 4 minutes of 10. 20. 30.

---

* A Mantra. Shi = Peace, Va = Power. It means "Thy peace by power increasing In me by power to peace."

† The four characteristic results of Prânâyâma are (1) perspiration; (2) rigidity; (3) jumping about like a frog; (4) levitation. P. never experienced this last result. But it is possible that, if there was an actual loss of weight, that this was at least a step towards it.

158

September

6th. 7.0 p.m.   Heard astral bell, not mine but Shri Mâitrânanda's.*

10.45-10.55 p.m. p.m.   Dhârana on tip of nose. I obtained a clear understanding of the unreality of that nose. This persists. An hour later whilst breathing on my arm as I was asleep, I said to myself: "What is this hot breath from?" I was forced to *think* before I could answer "my nose." Then I pinched myself and remembered at once; but again breathing the same thing happened again. Therefore the "Dhâranâtion" of my nose dividualizes Me and My Nose, affects my nose, disproves my nose, abolishes, annihilates and expunges my nose.

11.25-11.34 p.m. p.m.   Dhârana on end of Verendum.†

7th. 7.0-7.7 a.m. a.m.   Prânâyâma. 5. 10. 20.

7.15-7.37 a.m. a.m.   Prânâyâma. 5. 10. 20, and five minutes of 10. 20. 30. Tried external Kumbhaka with poorest of results.

8th. 11.0-11.5 a.m. a.m.   Dhârana on nose.

11.10-11.13 a.m. a.m.   Dhârana, covering face with a sheet of thick white paper. Very complex phenomena occur.

But this production of two noses seems to be the falling back of the eyes to parallel. Everything vanishes.

11.45-11.51 a.m. a.m.   Dhârana. Ditto. There are two noses all the time. The delusion is that you think your right eye is seeing your left nose!

6.10-6.50 p.m. p.m.   Prânâyâma 7 minutes 5. 10. 20; 6 minutes 10. 20. 30. Dhârana on nose 9 minutes 50 seconds. I actually lost the nose on one occasion, and could not think what I wished to find or where to find it; my mind having become a perfect blank. (Shri Mâitrânanda says this is very good, and means I approach "neighbourhood-concentration"). Six minutes more at 10. 20.30. Forty minutes in the Â'sana.

10.20-10.34 p.m. p.m.   Mentally muttering "Namo Shivaya Namaha Aum" I did Dhârana as before on my nose. I understand one Buddhist constipation now; for: I was (a) conscious of external things

---

* We do not know what this means, unless the note of Shri Mâitrânanda's bell was different from that of Frater P's.   † Wand.

seen behind, after my nose had vanished, *i.e.* altar, etc.; and (b) conscious that I was *not* conscious of these things. These two consciousnesses being simultaneous. This seems absurd and inexplicable, it is noted in Buddhist Psychology, *yet I know it.*

September

9th. 9.50-10.20 a.m. a.m. Prânâyâma. Ten minutes 5. 10. 20; 4 minutes 10. 25. 30; 6 minutes 10. 25. 30. Looking at the light at the top of my head. It was of a misty blue colour, its shape was that of an ordinary cone of flame, long and homogeneous. At intervals it dropped and opened out like a flower, its texture was that of fine hair. Mâitrânanda told me that this result was very good, and that these petals are of the Ajna Chakkra.*

2.10-2.42 p.m. p.m. Prânâyâma. Seven minutes. 5. 10. 20. Dhâranâ on nose thirteen minutes. During this Prânâyâma I heard the Astral Bell twice or thrice. Prânâyâma 8 minutes. 10. 20. 30.

Perspiration which has been almost suppressed of late has reappeared to excess.

6.12-6.38 p.m. p.m. Prânâyâma. Four minutes and 6 minutes 10. 29. 30.

Late Dhâranâ. Became quite unconscious. Recovered saying: "and not take the first step on Virtue's giddy road," with the idea that this had some reference to the instructions to begin Suddhi with Ida. Forgot that I had been doing Dhâranâ; but I felt quite pleased and a conviction that my thoughts had been very important.

10th. 7.12-7.34 a.m. a.m. Prânâyâma. Seven minutes 5. 10. 20; and 10 minutes 10. 20. 30. The last was very good and regular.

11.50-12.5 a.m. a.m. Prânâyâma. Fourteen minutes 5. 10. 20. Ida stopped up.

6.15-6.50 p.m. p.m. Dhâranâ on nose 22 minutes. Prânâyâma. 10. 20. 30.

9.15-9.34 p.m. p.m. Dhâranâ on nose. During this I heard a Siren-cooing Nâda; it sounded very audible and continuous; but loudest during Rechaka.

1.23 a.m. I awoke, lying on left side. This being unusual. . . . I did not know I had been asleep, and the time much surprised

---

* When Gods are near, or Kundalini arises thither, the petals bend down and out: thus is the Winged-Globe of Egypt formed. These petals are the same as the horns of Pan which open out as the God descends.

me. The one dominant thought in my brain was: "That is it," *i.e.*, Dhyâna. The characteristic perspiration which marks the first stage of success in Prânâyâma possesses the odour, taste, colour, and almost the consistency of semen.

September

11th. 6.25-6.45 a.m. a.m.   Prânâyâma. Fifteen minutes. 10. 20. 30. No perspiration.

10.30-10.45 a.m. a.m.   Prânâyâma. Twelve minutes: 10. 20. 30.

Prânâyâma. Eight minutes: 10. 20. 30.

6.0-6.30 p.m. p.m.   With great effort.

Cannot do Prânâyâma 30. 60. 15. more than once through, I tried twice.

Dhâranâ on nose ten minutes.

11.15 p.m.   Dhâranâ on nose.

12th. 7.35-7.55 a.m. a.m.   Prânâyâma. Six minutes 10. 20. 30.

Dhâranâ. Six minutes.

(P. was called away for a few days on business (or in disgust?) to Colombo.)

On the 20th of September P. returned from Colombo and then he made the following entry in his diary: "The Blessed Abhavânanda said: 'Thus have I heard. One day in Thy courts is better than a thousand'; let me recommence Prânâyâma." Thus he thought, and said. Further he said: "Let me abandon these follies of poesy and Vamacharya ("debauchery," *i.e.* normal life) and health and vain things and let me put in some work."

22nd.   Began Suddhi and "Namo Shivaya Namaha Aum."

10.15-11.15 a.m. am.   Â'sana. Prânâyâma. Nine minutes 10. 20. 30.

Dhâranâ on nose ten minutes.

5.55-6.25 p.m. p.m.   Prânâyâma. Four minutes: 10. 20. 30.

Prânâyâma. Ten minutes: 10. 20. 30.

Prânâyâma. One of 30. 15. 60. twice. Two such consecutively quite out of the question.

9.12-9.45 p.m. p.m.   Prânâyâma. Twelve minutes. 10. 20. 30.

Prânâyâma. Two consecutive cycles as above declared impossible!

23rd. 3.5-3.37 a.m. a.m.   Prânâyâma. Sixteen minutes. 10. 20. 30.

Dhâranâ on nose. Seven minutes.

5.20-5.50 p.m. p.m.   Dhâranâ on nose. Seventeen minutes.

Heard astral bell repeatedly, apparently from above my head, perhaps slightly to the left of median.

Two practices of Prânâyâma: 30. 15. 60.

Concentration on Ajna Chakkra. The effect was as of light gradually glimmering forth and becoming very bright.

September 24th.   Tried drinking through nose;* but could not accomplish it properly.

7.0-7.10 a.m. a.m.   Tried Dhârana on Nose as Ida was stopped up. Eyes watered, and the breathing was difficult, could not concentrate.

7.15-7.38 a.m. a.m.   Prânâyâma. Twenty-two minutes: 10. 20. 30. Could have gone on.

5.35-6.5 p.m. p.m.   Prânâyâma very difficult.

Dhârana on nose nine minutes. The nose is perhaps my least sensitive organ. Would I do better to try my tongue?

Dhârana, four minutes on tip of tongue. Burning feeling as usual. Can feel every tooth as if each had become a conscious being.

Prânâyâma. Broke down badly on second Rechaka of 30. 15. 60. I *will* do this, and often.

10.15-10.44 p.m. p.m.   Prânâyâma. Ten minutes 10. 20. 30.

Dhârana on nose seven minutes.

One Grand Prânâyâma. 30. 15. 60.

[N.B. For Prânâyâma be fresh, cool, not excited, not sleepy, not full of food, not ready to urinate or defaecate.]

25th. 6.0-6.42 a.m. a.m.   Prânâyâma. Twenty-six minutes: 10. 20. 30.

Dhârana on nose. Five minutes.

Dhârana on nose. Six minutes.

8.30-9.0 a.m. a.m.   Dhârana on nose. Twelve and a half minutes.

Grand Prânâyâma. 30. 15. 60. very difficult.

10.45-11.20 a.m. a.m.   Dhârana on nose. Thirty-four minutes. Stopped by an alarum going off—rather a shock—did not know where I was for a bit.

4.36-5.8 p.m. p.m.   Prânâyâma. Eight minutes: 10. 20. 30.

Prânâyâma. Eleven minutes: 10. 20. 30.

7.45-8.5 p.m. p.m.   Prânâyâma. Eleven minutes: 10. 20. 30.

Mental Muttering " Aum Shivayavashi."

8.40-9.23 p.m. p.m.   Thirty-seven minutes concentrated on Pentacle, right globe of ear throbs; left ear cold current; left hand tingles. I do

---

* A Hatha Yoga Practice. P.'s idea of the practice was to drink a pint right off! Hence disappointment.

get a sort of Sukshma-Kumbhaka which I cannot reproduce at will.

Rigidity of body and the fading of all vision are its stigmata. Curiously this happened on coming out of Mental Muttering back to audible, or rather at one loud slow Mantra, *i.e.* when no Kumbhaka was possible.

September 26th. 8.50-9.3 a.m. a.m.

Mental Muttering for ten minutes "Aum Shivayavashi." Results similar to last night's, somewhat more easily obtained.

5.25-5.57 p.m. p.m.

Mental Muttering of "Aum Shivayavashi." Result better than usual.

Prânâyâma. Seven minutes after 10 seconds of Kumbhaka. This seventh time I forgot all about everything and breathed out of both nostrils. Quite quietly—pure mental abstraction.

8.10-9.30 p.m. p.m.

Mental Muttering of "Aum Shivayavashi," for seventy-five minutes. Several times lost concentration or consciousness or something, *i.e.*, either vision or voice or both were interrupted.

(N.B. At one particular *rate* the third eye throbs violently in time with mantra.)

27th.

Constant dreams of Dhâr...

10.20-10.33 a.m. a.m.

Prânâyâma. Seven minutes 10. 20. 30. Twice forgot myself in Kumbhaka by exceeding the thirty seconds. I was trying to kill thoughts entering Ajna. On the first occasion I was still saying "Shiva" for this purpose; on the second I was meditating on Devi [a name of Bhâvani].

4.45-4.50 p.m. p.m.

One Grand Prânâyâma. 30. 15. 60.
New Prânâyâma of 25. 15. 50; twice.

5.12-5.40 p.m. p.m.

Prânâyâma. Seven minutes 10. 20. 30.
Mental Muttering. "Aum Shivayavashi" Fifteen minutes, at rate when Ajna throbs.

(N.B. Of late my many years' habit of sleeping only on the right side has vanished. I now sleep always on my left side.)

28th. 7 a.m.

Prânâyâma. 10. 20. 30.

4.35-5.16 p.m. p.m.

Prânâyâma. Four minutes: 10. 20. 30.
Mantra: "Aum Shivayavashi" Twenty minutes. I feel on the brink of something every time—Aid me, Lord Self!

His Holiness the Guru Swami says: "It is not well, O child, that thou contemplatest the external objects about thee. Let rather thy Chakkras be on-meditated. Aum!"

10.50 p.m.

Dhârnâ on Ajna eighteen minutes muttering "Aum Tat Sat Aum!"

September 29th. 12.0 m.n.	Dhâr`a`nâ on Ajna and "Aum Tat Sat Aum" thirty-one minutes. At one time Ajna seemed enormously, perhaps infinitely, elongated.
11.15-11.41 a.m. a.m.	Mantra "Aum Tat Sat Aum" with usual throbbing. Took 210 drops of Laudanum as an experiment under Mâitrânanda's guidance. (Absolutely no mental result, and hardly any physical result. I must be most resistant to this drug, which I had never previously taken).
30th.	Recovering from the Laudanum.
10.5 a.m.	Prânâyâma and Dhârânâ hopeless.*
October.	Another month of this great work commences, and though the toil has not been wasted the reward indeed seems still far off.

On the first of the month P. writes:—

"Blessed be thou, O Bhâvâni, O Isis my Sister, my Bride, my Mother! Blessed be Thou, O Shiva, O Amoun, Concealed of the Concealed. By Thy most secret and Holy Name of Apophis be Thou blessed, Lucifer, Star of the Dawn, Satan-Jeheshua, Light of the World! Blessed be Thou, Buddha, Osiris, by whatever Name I call Thee Thou art nameless to Eternity.

Blessed be Thou, O Day, that Thou hast risen in the Night of Time; First Dawn in the Chaos of poor P.'s poor mind! Accursed be Thou, Jehovah, Brahma, unto the Aeons of Aeons: thou who didst create Darkness and not Light! Mâra, vile Mask of Matter!

Arise, O Shiva, and destroy! That in destruction these at last be blest.

1st. 5.30 p.m.	Prânâyâma. Mantra seventeen minutes. Noise of glass being rubbed persistent.
9.30 p.m.	From now I decide to work more seriously, and follow out the following programme: Mantra "Aum Tat Sat Aum." Dhârânâ on Ajna Chakkra. Read Bhagavad-Gîta. Vegetarian diet.

---

* Probably at this time a period of "dryness" supervened.

164

Normal amount of sleep.
Speech only when necessary.
Prânâyâma.
A'sana with eyes turned up.

October	Walking as exercise.
2nd. 8.30 a.m.	Mantra " Aum Tat Sat Aum."
9.10-10.50 a.m. a.m.	A'sana with Mantra and eyes turned to Ajna Chakkra. Chittam distinctly slowing towards end.
10.50-12.5 a.m. p.m.	Continued lying down. [Did I sleep?]
12.35-1.45 p.m. p.m.	For a walk muttering Mantra.
2.20-2.45 p.m. p.m.	A'sana. Always forgetting to repeat the Mantra, Mâitra- nandra Swami says this is right. Ajna is now more steely in appearance and is open at a constant angle of about 30° to 40°.
3.10-3.45 p.m. p.m.	Prânâyâma. Thirty minutes 10. 20. 30.
4.10 p.m.	Resumed Â'sana. The "invading" thoughts are more and more fragmentary and ridiculous. I cannot mentally pro- nounce the Mantra with correctness, *e.g.*, " Op tap sapa " or " shastra " for " sat," etc. Now arose, with Music of the Vînâ the Golden Dawn.* At 5.15 I arose.
5.42 p.m.	Resumed my Â'sana and did three Prânâyâmas of 25. 15. 50. Also of 20. 10. 40.

Mâitrânanda Swami explained above as follows: Unto the sunset, moonrise, Agni;† then Vishvarupa Darshana,‡ and one's own Personal God;§ then Âtma-Darshana ‖ and Shiva-Darshana.¶

---

* The Golden Dawn, Dhyâna of the Sun.

† Or Rupa Visions. That is, visions of the three Lights of the Gunas. See "The Herb Dangerous." THE EQUINOX, vol. i, No. 2.

‡ The great Vision of Vishnu. See the Eleventh Discourse in the Bhagavad-Gîta. " Unnumbered arms, the sun and moon. Thine eyes. I see Thy face, as sacrificial fire blazing, its splendour burneth up the worlds." Verse 19.

§ Adonai. The Vision of the Holy Guardian Angel.

‖ Âtma-Darshana, the universal vision of Pan, or the vision of the Universal Peacock. It has many forms.

¶ Vision of Shiva, which destroys the Âtma-Darshana. The God Shiva opens his eye, and Equilibrium is re-established.

THE EQUINOX

October 3rd. 12.20. a.m.	Prânâyâma. Thirty-five minutes. 10. 20. 30. Â'sana terrible.
10-11.30 a.m. a.m.	Walk with Mantra.
11.30-12-41 a.m. a.m.	Â'sana. Always with Mantra and Ajna. Prânâyâma. Eighteen minutes. 10. 20. 30.
1.50-2.30 p.m. p.m.	Dhâranâ. Got very tired and lay down till 3.35 (not sleeping) then resumed Â'sana till 5.5 p.m. Now again at last the Golden Dawn. This, as my intuition had already taught me, had the effect of slowing the Dhyâna and also keeping me fixed therein. Yet, I fear, of partially destroying its perfection—He knows! Thus the disk came clear: but I began to be worried by body and clouded by doubt, and an effort to return only brought up a memory-picture.
	The flaming clouds are " thought "; the shadowy or hinted Form is Adonai!
5.35 p.m.	Three Prânâyâmas of 50. 25. 15.
5.40 p.m.	Prânâyâma. Twenty minutes 10. 20. 30.
9.30 p.m.	Holiday; which was fatal folly!

The full account of this wonderful realization of Dhyâna is set forth by P. in this note book entitled " The Writings of Truth," in which we find the following:

"After some eight hours' discipline by Prânâyâma arose 'The Golden Dawn.'

"While meditating, suddenly I became conscious of a shoreless space of darkness and a glow of crimson athwart it. Deepening and brightening, scarred by dull bars of slate-blue cloud arose the Dawn of Dawns. In splendour not of earth and its mean sun, blood-red, rayless, adamant, it rose, it rose! Carried out of myself, I asked not 'Who is the Witness?' absorbed utterly in contemplation of so stupendous and so marvellous a fact. For here was no doubt, no change, no wavering; infinitely more real than aught 'physical' is the Golden Dawn of this Eternal Sun! But ere the Orb of Glory rose clear of its banks of blackness —alas my soul!—that Light Ineffable was withdrawn beneath the falling veil of darkness, and in purples and greys glorious beyond imagining, sad beyond conceiving, faded the superb Herald of the Day. But mine eyes have seen it! And this, then, is Dhyâna! Walk with it, yet all but unremarked, came a melody as of the sweet-souled Vînâ.

.   .   .   .

Again, by the Grace Ineffable of Bhâvani to the meanest of Her devotees, arose the Splendour of the Inner Sun. As bidden by my Guru, I saluted the

166

THE TEMPLE OF SOLOMON THE KING

Dawn with Pranava. This, as I foresaw, retained the Dhyânic Consciousness. The Disk grew golden: rose clear of all its clouds, flinging great fleecy cumuli of rose and gold, fiery with light, into the aethyr of space. Hollow it seemed and rayless as the Sun in Sagittarius, yet incomparably brighter: but rising clear of cloud, it began to revolve, to coruscate, to throw off streamers of jetted fire! [This from a hill-top I beheld, dark as of a dying world. Covered with black decayed wet peaty wood, a few pines stood stricken, unutterably alone.*] But behind the glory of its coruscations seemed to shape, an idea less solid than a shadow! an Idea of some Human-seeming Form! Now grew doubt and thought in P.'s miserable mind; and the One Wave grew many waves and all was lost! Alas! Alas! for P.! And Glory Eternal unto Her, She the twin-Breasted that hath encroached even upon the other half of the Destroyer! "OM Namo Bhâvaniya OM."

Filled with the glory of the great light that had arisen in him, for many days P. communed in silence with the Vision that days upon days of labour had revealed to him, and then leaving his place of retirement near Kandy he journeyed to Anhuradhapura, and thence to many sacred shrines and temples throughout the island of Ceylon, gathering as he travelled spiritual knowledge, and learning the ancient customs of the people and the manner of their lives.

Towards the end of November his work in Ceylon being accomplished he arrived at Madura, and from there he journeyed to Calcutta. At this city he remained for about a month, during almost the whole of which time he suffered from sickness and fever. He however records one interesting incident, which took place during an early morning walk whilst he was in deep meditation:

" Whilst in this meditation, a kind of inverted Manichaeism seemed to develop and take possession of it, Nature appearing as a great evil and fatal force, unwittingly developing within

* This is a mere thought-form induced by misunderstanding the instruction of Mâitrânanda Swami as to observing the phenomenon.

itself a suicidal Will called Buddha or Christ:" This perhaps is most easily explained by imagining "Mâyâ" to be a circle of particles moving from right to left which after a time through its own intrinsic motion sets up within itself a counter motion, a kind of back-water current which moves in the opposite direction, from left to right, and little by little destroys the Mâyâ circle, marked "B"; and then becoming its Mâyâ, in its turn sets up a counter circle which in time will likewise be destroyed. The outer circle "B" is the world Mâyâ or the Samasâra Chakkra, the inner "A" the Bodhi Satva, the Buddha, the Christ.

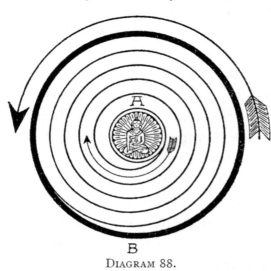

B

DIAGRAM 88.
The Bodhi Satva.

Thus is fulfilled again and again the great prophecy:

Whenever the dhamma decays, and a-dhamma prevails, then I manifest myself. For the protection of the good, for the destruction of the evil, for the firm establishment of the National Righteousness I am born again and again ! *

"It is a fallacy," wrote P., "that the Absolute must be the All-Good. There is *not* an Intelligence directing law; but only a line of least resistance along which all things move. Its own selfishness has not even the wit to prevent Buddha, and so its own selfishness proves its destruction.

"We cannot call Nature *evil*: Fatal is the exact word; for Necessity implies stupidity, and this stupidity is the chief attribute of Nature."

So P. argued, for the little Bodhi Satva had started whirl-

* *Cf.* Captain J. F. C. Fuller's "Star in the West," pp. 287, 288. " In his Essay 'Eleusis,' Crowley suggests that the world's history may roughly be divided into a continuous succession of periods, each embracing three distinct

ing within him, hungry and thirsty, slowly devouring its Mother Mâyâ.

On the 21st of January, 1902, P. left Calcutta for Burma, where for a short time he again joined Mâitrânanda. During the month of February he journeyed through the districts about Rangoon visiting many sacred cities and holy men, practising Dhâranâ on Maitri Bhâvana (Compassion) and taking his refuge in Triratna. (The triple jewel of Buddhism-Buddha, Dhamma and Sangha.) On the 14th of February he visited Lamma Sayadaw Kyoung and Bhikkhu Ânanda Metteyya, and on the 23rd shipped by S.S. Kapurthala from Rangoon to Calcutta, arriving there on the 26th.

For the first three months of 1902 no record was kept by P. of his meditations and mystical exercises, except one which is as curious as it is interesting, and which consists of a minutely detailed table showing the Classification of the Dreams he dreamt from the 8th of February to the 19th of March.

P., it may be mentioned, was much subjected to dreaming, but perhaps rarely were they so persistent and vivid as he now experienced. For he found that by trying to remember dreams he could remember more. Probably most men dream subconsciously; just as they breathe without knowing it unless the attention be directed to the act.

cycles—of Renaissance, Decadence, and Slime. In the first the Adepts rise as artists, philosophers, and men of science, who are sooner or later recognized as great men; in the second the adepts as adepts appear, but seem as fools and knaves; and in the third, that of Slime, vanish altogether, and are invisible. Then the chain starts again. Thus Crowley writes:

"'Decadence marks the period when the adepts, nearing their earthly perfection, become true adepts, not mere men of genius. They disappear, harvested by heaven: and perfect darkness (apparent death) ensues until the youthful forerunners of the next crop begin to shoot in the form of artists.'"

169

We append the following table. As it will be seen P. divides his dream-states into seven main divisions, each being again split up into further subdivisions to enable the various correspondences to be seen at a glance.

CLASSIFICATION OF DREAMS

A. *Depth of Impression.*

    1. Vivid. 2. Ordinary. 3. Slight. 4. Doubtful.

B. *Degree of Memory.*

    1. Detailed. 2. Outlined. 3. Partially outlined. 4. Central idea only. 5. Incident only. 6. Nothing save fact of dream.

C. *Cause.*

    1. Traceable to thoughts of previous day. 2. Traceable to local circumstances (*e.g.* Dream of river from rain falling on face). 3. Not so traceable.

D. *Character.*

    1. Surprising. 2. Ordinary.

E. *Character.*

    1. Rational. 2. Irrational.

F. *Character General.*

    1. Lascivious, (*a*) Finished, (*b*) Baffled. 2. Of travel. 3. Of literature. 4. Of art. 5. Of magic. 6. Of beauty. 7. Of religion. 8. Of social affairs. 9. Of disgust. 10. Of old friends (or foes). 11. Various. 12. Humorous. 13. Of very definite men not known to P. 14. Of combat. 15. Of money.

G. *Character Special.*

    1. Of losing a tooth. 2. Of beard being shaved off. 3. Of climbing a mountain. 4. Of being taken in adultery. 5. Of Poem or Magical book I have written (in dream). 6. Of being embarrassed. 7. Of flying, especially of escaping.

	A	B	C	D	E	F	G
February 8th	I	2	—	I	—	—	—
,, 9th	I	I	Probably 2	—	—	—	I
,, 12th	I	I	I	—	—	I (b)	—
,, 13th	I	I	I	I	—	6.12	—
,, 14th							
,, 15th	I	2	I	2	I	I	I
,, ,,	I	2	I	2	I	I	I
,, 16th	I	I	I	2	I	4.2.8	—
,, 17th	3	6	—	—	—	—	—
,, 18th	2	2	Probably I	2	I	II	—
,, 20th	I	?	?	I	?	?	—
,, 21st	4	—	—	—	—	—	—
,, 22nd	4	—	—	—	—	—	—
,, 23rd	I	I	2	I	2	I (a).2.10.9.11	—
,, 24th	I	4	I	2	—	I ?	—
,, 25th	2 (? I)	3	I	2	I	2	—
,, 28th	I	I	I	2	3	1.10.11	4 (?)
,, ,,	2	2	I	2	I	3.7	—
March 1st	3	6	—	—	—	—	—
,, 2nd	I	I	I (?)	2	I	8	6
,, ,,	I	I	I (?)	I	I	5	—
,, 3rd	2	I	I	2	I	2.8	—
,, 4th	I	4.5	I	I	—	8.10.13	—
,, 5th	(?) all						
,, ,,	2	2	I	2	I	2	—
,, 7th	I	I	1.2	2	2	I (b).2.9	6
,, 8th	I	6	—	—	—	—	—
,, 9th	I	I	I	I	I	I (b)2.5.8.10.13	4.6
,, 10th	I	I	3	2	I	8.10.13.14.15	—
,, 11th	I	I	I	I	2	3.5.7.12	5.7
,, ,,	I	I	I	I	2	I (b)	4
,, 12th	I	2	I	2	I	2	6
,, 13th	I	2	3	I	2	I (b)	—
,, 14th	4	—	—	—	—	—	—
,, 15th	I	I	3	2	I	1.2.8.10.13	—
,, ,,	I	I	2	2	2	2	—
,, 16th	I	2	I	I	2	3.10	—
,, 17th	2	2	3	2	I	7.8	—
,, 18th	I	5	I	I	I	5.6.11	—
,, 19th	2	5	—	—	I	II	—

On the 7th of March P. left Calcutta for Benares, arriving there on the following day, and lodging at the Hôtel de Paris he continued his concentration practices. In his diary on this date he writes: "The fear of the future seems practically destroyed, and during the last six months I have worked well. This removes all possible selfishness of incentive (after $4\frac{3}{4}$ years) Maitri-Bhâvana is left, and that alone. Aum!"

At Benares he visited the temples, and had a long conversation with Sri Swami Swayam Prakashânanda Maithila; and then after three days' sojourn there journeyed to Agra.

"I saw the Taj. A dream of beauty," he writes, "with appallingly evil things dwelling therein. I actually had to use H.P.K. formula! The building soon palls; the aura is apparent, and disgust succeeds. But the central hall is of strained aura, like a magic circle after the banishing."

At Agra P. met Astrologer and Geomancer Munshi Elihu Bux; who told him that by looking hard at a point on the wall constantly and without winking for many days he would be able to obtain an hypnotic power even to Deadly and Hostile Current of Will.

On the 16th P. left Agra and went to Delhi, and there on the 23rd he was joined by D. A., and these two with their companions on the following day journeyed to Rawal Pindi and from this city they set out together to travel for five months in the northern and little frequented districts of Baltistan, and to seek that great solemnity and solitude which is only to be found amongst the greatest mountains of earth.

With the Dhyâna Visions and Trance we arrive at another turning point in Frater P.'s magical ascent. For several years he had worked by the aid of Western methods, and with them he had laid a mighty and unshakable foundation upon which

172

he now had succeeded in building the great temple of Self-Control. Working upon Eastern lines he had laid stone upon stone, and yet when the work was completed, magnificent though it was, there was no God yet found to indwell it. It was indeed but an empty house.

Though we have now arrived at this turning point, it will be necessary before we review the contents of this chapter to narrate the events from the present date—March 1902, down to the 11th of August 1903; when, by the chance (destined) meeting with Ouarda the Seer, he was eventually enabled to set in motion the great power he had gained, and by wrestling with the deity, as Jacob wrestled with the Angel by the ford of Jabbok, see God face to face and LIVE.

For a space of nearly six months P. and D. A. journeyed amongst the vast mountains beyond Cashmir, and though during this period no record of his meditations has been preserved, time was not idled away and exercises in meditation of a more exalted kind, on the vastness of Nature and the ungraspable might of God, were his daily joy and consolation.

In September he returned to Srinnagar, and thence journeyed to Bombay where he remained for but a few days before his return journey to Europe.

Arriving in Egypt he remained in that ancient land for some three weeks, somehow feeling that it was here that he should find what he had so long now been seeking for in vain. But realizing the hopelessness of waiting in any definite country or city, without some clue to guide him to his goal, he left Egypt at the beginning of November and continued his journey back to England only to break it again at Paris.

In this city he remained until April the following year

173

(1903). In the month of January he met his old College friend H. L.

From the very first moment of this meeting H. L. showed considerable perturbation of mind, and on being asked by Frater P. what was exercising him, H. L. replied " Come and free Miss Q. from the wiles of Mrs. M. Being asked who Mrs. M. was, H. L. answered that she was a vampire and a sorceress who was modelling a sphinx with the intention of one day endowing it with life so that it might carry out her evil wishes; and that her victim was Miss Q. P. wishing to ease his friend's mind asked H. L. to take him to Miss Q.'s address at which Mrs. M. was then living. This H. L. did.

The following story is certainly one of the least remarkable of the many strange events which happened to Frater P. during his five months' residence in Paris, but we give it in place of others because it re-introduces several characters who have already figured in this history.

Miss Q. after an interview asked P. to tea to meet Mrs. M. After introductions she left the room to make tea—the White Magic and the Black were left face to face.

On the mantelpiece stood a bronze of the head of Balzac, and P., taking it down, seated himself in a chair by the fire and looked at it.

Presently a strange dreamy feeling seemed to come over him, and something velvet soft and soothing and withal lecherous moved across his hand. Suddenly looking up he saw that Mrs. M. had noiselessly quitted her seat and was bending over him; her hair was scattered in a mass of curls over her shoulders, and the tips of her fingers were touching the back of his hand.

No longer was she the middle aged woman, worn with strange lusts; but a young woman of bewitching beauty.

At once recognizing the power of her sorcery, and knowing that if he even so much as contemplated her Gorgon head all the power of his magic would be petrified, and that he would become but a puppet in her hands, but a toy to be played with and when broken cast aside, he quietly rose as if nothing unusual had occurred; and replacing the bust on the mantelpiece turned towards her and commenced with her a magical conversation; that is to say a conversation which outwardly had but the appearance of the politest small talk but which inwardly lacerated her evil heart, and burnt into her black bowels as if each word had been a drop of some corrosive acid.

She writhed back from him; and then again approached him even more beautiful than she had been before. She was battling for her life now, and no longer for the blood of another victim. If she lost, hell yawned before her, the hell that every once beautiful woman who is approaching middle age, sees before her the hell of lost beauty, of decrepitude, of wrinkles and fat. The odour of man seemed to fill her whole subtle form with a feline agility, with a beauty irresistible. One step nearer and then she sprang at Frater P. and with an obscene word sought to press her scarlet lips to his.

As she did so Frater P. caught her and holding her at arm's length smote the sorceress with her own current of evil, just as a would-be murderer is sometimes killed with the very weapon with which he has attacked his victim.

A blue-greenish light seemed to play round the head of the vampire, and then the flaxen hair turned the colour of muddy

175

snow, and the fair skin wrinkled, and those eyes, that had turned so many happy lives to stone, dulled, and became as pewter dappled with the dregs of wine. The girl of twenty had gone, before him stood a hag of sixty, bent, decrepit, debauched. With dribbling curses she hobbled from the room.

As Frater P. left the house, for some time he turned over in his mind these strange happenings, and was not long in coming to the opinion that Mrs. M. was not working alone, and that behind her probably were forces far greater than she. She was but the puppet of others, the slave that would catch the kids and the lambs that were to be served upon her master's table. Could P. prove this? could he discover who the masters were? The task was a difficult one; it either meant months of work, which P. could not afford to give, or the mere chance of a lucky stroke, which P. set aside as unworthy the attempt.

That evening whilst relating the story to his friend H. L. he asked him if he knew of any reliable clairvoyant. H. L. replied that he did, and that there was such a person at that very time in Paris known as The Sibyl, his own " belle amie." That night they called on her; and from her P. discovered, for he led her in the spirit, the following remarkable facts.

The vision at first was of little importance, then by degrees the seer was led to a house which P. at once recognised as that in which D.D.C.F. lived. He entered one of the rooms, which he also at once recognised but curious to say, instead of finding D.D.C.F. and V.N.R. there he found Theo and Mrs. Horos. Mr. Horos (M.S.R.) incarnated in the body of V.N.R. and Mrs. Horos (S.V.A.) in that of D.D.C.F. Their bodies were in prison; but their spirits were in the house of the fallen chief of the Golden Dawn.

At first Frater P. was seized with horror at the sight, he knew not whether to direct a hostile current of will against D.D.C.F. and V.N.R., supposing them to be guilty of cherishing within their bodies the spirits of two disincarnated vampires, or perhaps Abramelin demons under the assumed forms of S.V.A. and M.S.R., or to warn D.D.C.F.; supposing him to be innocent, as he perhaps was, of so black and evil an offence. But as he hesitated a voice entered the body of the Sibyl and bade him leave matters alone, which he did. Not yet was the cup full.

In April he journeyed to London, and the month of May 1903 once again found him amongst the fastnesses of the north in the house he had bought in which to carry out the Sacred Operation of Abramelin.

At this point of our history, in a prefatory note to one of Frater P.'s note-books, we find him recapitulating, in the following words, the events of the last four years:

In the year 1899 I came to C . . . House, and put everything in order with the object of carrying out the Operation of Abramelin the Mage.

I had studied Ceremonial Magic, and had obtained very remarkable success.

My Gods were those of Egypt, interpreted on lines closely akin to those of Greece.

In Philosophy I was a Realist of the Qabalistic School.

In 1900 I left England for Mexico, and later the Far East, Ceylon, India, Burma, Baltistan, Egypt and France. It is idle here to detail the corresponding progress of my thought; and passing through a stage of Hinduism, I had discarded all Deities as unimportant, and in Philosophy was an uncompromising Nominalist, arrived at what I may describe as an orthodox Buddhist; but however with the following reservations.

(1) I cannot deny that certain phenomena *do* accompany the use of certain rituals; I only deny the usefulness of such methods to the White Adept.

IV   M   177

(2) That I consider Hindu methods of meditation as possibly useful to the beginner, and should not therefore recommend them to be discarded at once.

With regard to my advancement, the redemption of the Cosmos, etc., etc., I leave for ever the " Blossom and Fruit " Theory and appear in the character of an Inquirer on strictly scientific lines.*

This is unhappily calculated to damp enthusiasm; but as I so carefully of old, for the magical path, excluded from my life all other interests, that life has now no particular meaning, and the Path of Research, on the only lines I can now approve of, remains the one Path possible for me to tread.

On the 11th of June P. records that he moved his bed into the temple that he had constructed at C . . . House, for convenience of more absolute retirement. In this temple he was afflicted by dreams and visions of the most appalling Abramelin devils, which had evidently clung to the spot ever since the operations of February 1900.

On the night of the 16th of June he began to practise Mahasatipatthana,† and found it easy to get into the way of it as a mantra which does not interfere much with sense-

---

* Till 1906. The theory of the Great White Brotherhood, as set forth in the story called " The Blossom and the Fruit," by Miss Mabel Collins.

† The practice of Mahasipatthana is explained by Mr. A. Crowley in his " Science and Buddhism " very fully. Briefly:

In this meditation the mind is not restrained to the contemplation of a single object, and there is no interference with the natural functions of the body. It is essentially an observation-practice, which later assumes an analytic aspect in regard to the question: " What is it that is really observed? "

The Ego-idea is excluded; all bodily motions are observed and recorded; for instance, one may sit down quietly and say: " There is a raising of the right foot." " There is an expiration," etc., etc., just as it happens. When once this habit of excluding the Ego becomes intuitive, the next step is to explain the above thus: " There is a sensation (Vedana) of a raising, etc." The next stage is that of perception (Sañña) " There is a perception of a (pleasant and unpleasant) sensation of a raising, etc." The two further stages Sankhara and Viññanam pursue the analysis to its ultimation. " There is a consciousness of a tendency

impressions, but remains as an undercurrent. After several days of this desultory Mahasatipatthana, he turned his mind once again to the Great Work and decided upon a fortnight's strict magical retirement. Though his retirement culminated in no definite state of illumination, it is most interesting from a scientific point of view, as it has been very carefully kept and the "breaks" that occurred in the meditations have been most minutely classified.

June
22nd. 10.20 p.m.   Mahasatipatthana for half an hour.
(1) Breathing gets deeper, rather sleepier. (I am tired.)
(2) Notable throbbing in Ajna and front of brain generally, especially with inspiring.
(3) Tendency to forget what I am doing. (I am tired.)
(4) Very bad concentration, but better than expected.

23rd. 10.11 a.m.   Walk with Mahasatipatthana. I obtained a very clear intuition that "I breathe" was a lie. With effort regained delusion.

11.30 a.m.   Entered Temple.
11.33 a.m.   Prânâyâma. 10. 20. 30. Resulting in a good deal of pain.
11.40 a.m.   Mahasatipatthana.
11.57 a.m.   Prânâyâma. 10. 20. 30. I do seem bad! My left nostril is not all it should be.
11.57 a.m.   Left Temple.
12.30 p.m.   Began Mahasatipatthana desultorily.
1.15 p.m.   In Mahasatipatthana. Doing it very badly. Seem sleepy.
1.35 p.m.   Went out for a walk feeling ill. Ill all the week.

28th.   During the night began again meditation upon Ajna, and "Mantra Aum Tat Sat Aum."

30th.   Decide to do tests on old principle to see how I really stand.

---

to perceive the (pleasant and unpleasant) sensation of a raising of the right foot" being the final form.

The Buddha himself said that if a man practises Mahasatipatthana honestly and intelligently a result is certain.

179

THE EQUINOX

BEGIN.	END.	OBJECT.	TIME.	NO. OF BREAKS.
10.21 a.m.	10.23 a.m.	Red Cross	2 m. 10 s.	Several breaks of the kind, "Oh, how well I'm doing it."

Seem quite to have forgotten what very long times I used to do.

		White tri-angle	10 m.	20 breaks.

[This about harmonic of good; 20 m. 10 breaks is a good performance.]

Apas-Âkâsa

[Very difficult: slightest noise is utterly disturbing.]

10.55 a.m.	11.1 a.m.	Red Cross	6 m.	7 breaks.

[But it is to be observed that a break may be of varying length. I doubt if this was as good as White Triangle *supra*.]

11.44 a.m.	11.56 a.m.	White tri-angle	12 m.	10 breaks.

[Above observation perhaps unimportant, as limit of variability is more or less constant (presumably) between 1901 and now.

It will be useless to attempt to devise any means of measuring the length of a break. The only possible suggestion is to count the links in thought back to the object. But I do not think it is worth the trouble.]

Note in White Triangle above:

I get considerably toward identification of self and object. This is probably a good result of my philosophy-work.

It will perhaps be more scientific if in these tests (and perhaps even in work) to stick to one or two objects and always go on to a special number of breaks—say 10. Then success will vary as time.*]

July 2nd.	3.14 p.m.	3.20 p.m.	White tri-angle	6 m. 30 s.	6 breaks. Disturbed by carpenter.
	10.40 p.m.	11.9 p.m.	White tri-angle	29 m.	23 breaks.

[A "break" shall be defined as: "a consciousness of the cessation of the object consciousness."

A simple outside thought arising shall not constitute a "break," since it may exist simultaneously with the object-consciousness.

---

* This, though a good system is a very difficult one to carry out.

It shall be meritorious to perform a rosary upon the Rudraksha-beads at least once (at one time) daily; for why? Because 108 is a convenient number of breaks, and the large number will aid determinations of rate progress.

If it be true, as I suppose, that fatigue to a great extent determines frequency, it will then be perhaps possible to *predict* a Geometrical Progression (or Mixed Progression.)]

	BEGIN.	END.	OBJECT.	TIME.	NO. OF BREAKS.
July 3rd.	10.58 a.m.	11.1 a.m.	White triangle	3 m.	5 breaks.

[I am in very bad state—nearly *all* breaks!—do a little Prânâyâma to steady me.]

	BEGIN.	END.	OBJECT.	TIME.	NO. OF BREAKS.
	11.10 a.m.	11.15½ a.m.	White triangle	5 m. 30 s.	4 breaks.

[Sneezed: totally forgot what I was doing. When I reflected, time as above.]

	BEGIN.	END.	OBJECT.	TIME.	NO. OF BREAKS.
4th.	9.45 a.m.	9.58½ a.m.	White triangle	13 m. 30 s.	20 breaks.
	10.25 a.m.	10.57½ a.m.	Ajna	32 m. 30 s.	20 breaks.

[With Mantra. Throbbing at once. "Invaders" nearly all irrational. Strong sub-current of swift thought noted. Quite the old times! Excellent: I require less food and less literary work. I wonder if it would be worth while to try irritation of skin over Ajna with tincture of Iodine.]

	BEGIN.	END.	OBJECT.	TIME.	NO. OF BREAKS.
5th.	11.30 a.m.	11.55 a.m.	Ajna	25 m.	20 breaks.
	9.36 p.m.	9.51½ p.m.	Ajna	15 m. 30 s.	20 breaks.
6th. 8th.	Ill.*				
9th.	10.57 a.m.	11.4 a.m.	Prânâyâma	7 m.	Nose not clear.
	11.16 a.m.	11.18 a.m.	Ajna	2 m.	6 breaks.

[Hyperaesthesia of sense. Various sounds disturbed me much.]

	BEGIN.	END.	OBJECT.	TIME.	NO. OF BREAKS.
10th.	Again ill.				
11th.	3.38 p.m.	3.46 p.m.	Prânâyâma	8 m.	Going easier.
	3.48 p.m.	3.51 p.m.	White triangle	3 m.	5 breaks.
	5.51 p.m.	6.10½ p.m.	Ajna	19 m. 30 s.	20 breaks.

---

* N.B. Frater P. did not practise when physically unfit.

	BEGIN.	END	OBJECT.	TIME.	NO. OF BREAKS.

July
11th. [Difficult to set the sound Hyperaesthesia. Began to forget Mantra.]*

| | 10.12½ p.m. | 10.19 p.m. | Prânâyâma | 6 m. 30 s. | Very hard. |

[The smallest quantity of food injures one's power immensely.]

| | 10.21 p.m. | 10.44 p.m. | Ajna | 23 m. | 20 breaks. |

[Used cotton wool in ears.]

Thoughts of Ajna go obliquely up (from opening of pharynx about) and direct horizontally forward. This gives an idea to *chase* consciousness, *i.e.*, find by the obvious series of experiments the spot in which the thoughts dwell. Probably however this moves about. If so, it is a clear piece of evidence for the idealistic position. If not, "thinking of it" equals "it thinking of itself," and its falsity will become rapidly evident.

July
12th.

| | 12.8 p.m. | 12.19 p.m. | Prânâyâma | 11 m. | |

[The best so far: the incense troubled me somewhat.]

| | 12.26 p.m. | 12.57 p.m. | | 31 m. | 30 breaks. |

[Mantra evolved into "tartsano."† I was not in good form and suspect many breaks of long duration.]

I keep Mantra going all day.

	4.58 p.m.	5.9 p.m.	Prânâyâma	11 m.	Perspiration.
	5.14 p.m.	5.25 p.m.	Prânâyâma	11 m.	Wound up with a Grand Prânâyâma.‡
	5.28 p.m.	6.6 p.m.		38 m.	30 breaks.

[Very tired towards end and difficult to get settled. To me it seems evident that the first ten breaks or so are rapid.]

| | 6.10 p.m. | 6.26 p.m. | Prânâyâma | 16 m. | |
| | 8.15 p.m. | 8.47 p.m. | Ajna with Mantra | 32 m. | 22 breaks. |

[Light coming a little, one very long break, and some sound.]

| | 10.5 p.m. | 10.17½ p.m. | Ajna | 12 m. 30 s. | 11 breaks. |

13th. Casual Mutterings of Mantra.

| | 10.44 a.m. | | Prânâyâma | | Quite hopeless. |
| | 10.48 a.m. | 11.20 a.m. | | 32 m. | 30 breaks. |

[Went to Edinburgh to meet H. L.]§

---

* Not understood.   † Om Tat Sat Aum.   ‡ 30.15.60.

§ This meeting with H. L., though of no importance in itself, led to one of the most important happenings in P.'s life; for it was through him that he again met Ouarda the seer, as we shall see at a later date.

THE TEMPLE OF SOLOMON THE KING

The following analysis of breaks which Frater P. deduced from his practices during this retirement is both of great interest and importance. It is the only analytical table of this character we know of, and must prove of very great use to investigator and aspirant alike.

THE CHARACTER OF BREAKS

1. Primary centres.
   The senses.

2. Secondary.
   These seem to assume a morbid activity as soon as the primaries are stilled. Their character is that of the shorter kind of memory. Events of the day, etc.

3. Tertiary.
   Partake of the character of "reverie." Very tempting and insidious.

4. Quaternary.
   Are closely connected with the control centre itself. Their nature is "How well I'm doing it," or "Wouldn't it be a good idea to . . .?" These are probably emanations from the control, not messages to it. We might call them: "Aberrations of control."

   Of a similar depth are the reflections which discover a break, but these are healthy warnings, and assist.

5. Quinary.
   Never rise into consciousness at all, being held down by the most perfect control. Hence the blank of thought, the forgetfulness of all things, including the object.

   Not partaking of any character at all, are the "meteor" thoughts which seem to be quite independent of anything the brain could think, or had ever thought. Probably this kind of thought is the root of irrational hallucinations, e.g., "And if you're passing, won't you?" *

---

* These interrupting voice suggestions have been named by P. Telephone-cross-voices on account of their close resemblance to disjointed conversations so often heard whilst using a telephone.

A similar phenomenon occurs in wireless telegraphy; chance currents make words, and are so read by the operator. They are called "atmospherics." I propose the retention of this useful word in place of the clumsy "Telephone-cross-voices."

6.

Perhaps as a result of the intense control, a nervous storm breaks. This we call Dhyâna. Its character is probably not determined by the antecedents in consciousness. Its essential characteristic being the unity of Subject and Object, a new world is revealed. Samâdhi is but an expansion of this, so far as I can see.

The slaying of any of these thoughts often leaves their echoes gradually dying away.

Now that we have come to the end of this long chapter, let us turn back on the upward slope and survey the road which winds beneath us, and lose not heart when but little of it can be seen, for the mountain's side is steep, and the distance from our last halting-place seems so short, not on account of our idleness, but because of the many twists and turnings that the road has taken since we left our last camp below, when the sun was rising and all was golden with the joy of great expectations. For, in truth, we have progressed many a weary league, and from this high spot are apt to misjudge our journey, and belittle our labours, as we gaze down the precipitous slope which sweeps away at our feet.

In the last two years and a half P. had journeyed far, further than he at this time was aware of; and yet the goal of his journey seemed still so distant that only with difficulty could he bring himself to believe that he had progressed at all. Indeed, it must have been discouraging to him to think that on the 6th of May 1901 he, in a meditation of thirty-two minutes had only experienced ten breaks, whilst during a meditation of similar length, on the 13th of July 1903, the number of breaks had been three times as many. But like most statistics, such a comparison is misleading: for the beginner, almost invariably, so clumsy is his will, catches quickly enough the gross breaks, but lets the minor ones dart away from his grasp, like the small fry which with ease swim in and out of the fisherman's net. Further, though in twelve meditations the number of breaks may be identical, yet the class of the breaks, much more so than the actual number, will tell the meditator, more certainly than anything else, whether he has progressed or has retrograded.

Thus at first, should the meditator practise with his eyes open, the number of breaks will in their swift succession form almost one unbroken interruption. Again, should the eyes be closed, then the ears detecting the slightest sound, the flow of the will will be broken, just as the faintest zephyr, on a still evening, will throw out of the perpendicular an ascending column of smoke. But presently, as the will gains power, the sense of hearing, little by little, as it comes under control, is held back from hearing the lesser sounds, then the greater, and at length all sounds. The vibrations of the will having re-pelled the sound vibrations of the air, and brought the sense of hearing into Equilibrium. Now the upward mounting fila-ment of smoke has become the ascending columns of a great volcano, there is a titanic blast behind it,—a will to ascend. And as the smoke and flame is belched forth, so terrific is its strength, that even a hurricane cannot shake it or drive it from its course.

As the five senses become subdued, fresh hosts of diffi-culties spring up irrationally from the brain itself. And, whichever way we turn, a mob of subconscious thoughts pull us this way and that, and our plight in this truculent multi-tude is a hundred times worse than when we commenced to wrestle with the five senses. Like wandering comets and

185

meteorites they seemingly come from nowhere, splash like falling stars through the firmament of our meditation, sparkle and are gone; but ever coming as a distraction to hamper and harass our onward march.

Once the mind has conquered these, a fresh difficulty arises, the danger of not being strong enough to overcome the occult powers which, though the reward of our toils, are liable, like the Queen in her bedchamber, to seduce the Conqueror in spite of his having conquered the King her husband, and secretly slay him as he sleeps in her arms. These are the powers known in the West as the Miraculous Powers, in the East as Siddhis.

The mind is now a blank, the senses have been subdued, the subconscious thoughts slain; it stretches before us like some unspotted canvas upon which we may write or paint whatever we will. We can produce entrancing sounds at will, beautiful sights at will, subtle tastes and delicious perfumes; and after a time actual forms, living creatures, men and women and elementals. We smite the rock, and the waters flow at our blow; we cry unto the heavens, and fire rushes down and consumes our sacrifice; we become Magicians, begetters of illusion, and then, if we allow ourselves to become obsessed by them, a time comes when these illusions will master us, when the children we have begotten will rise up and dethrone us, and we shall be drowned in the waters that now we can no longer control and be burnt up by the flames that mock obedience, and scorn our word.

Directly we perform a miracle we produce a change: a change is Mara the Devil, and not God the Changeless One. And though we may have scraped clean the palimpsest of our mind, our labours are in vain, if, when once it is stretched out spotless before us, we start scribbling over it our silly riddles, our little thoughts, our foolish "yeas" and "nays." The finger of God alone may write upon it, cleanly and beautifully, and the words that are written cannot be read by the eye or in the heart of man, for alone can they be understood by him who is worthy to understand them.

Now, though Frater P. had not as yet proved this, had not as yet accomplished the cleansing of the book of his mind, he had, however, built up on his own empirical observation so invulnerable a theory, that it now only remained for him to obtain that fine proportion, that perfect adjustment, that balancing of the Forces of the Will, which now lay before him like the chemicals in the crucible of a Chemist, before applying that certain heat which would dissolve all into one. He did not wish to rule by the sceptre he had won, but to transcend it; to rule the forces of this world, not by the authority that had been given him, but by his own essential greatness. And just as long before Mendeljeff had propounded the law of Periodicity, and by it had foreshadowed the existence of several undiscovered elements, so now did Frater P., by his law of the Correspondences of the Ruach, prove, not only historically, philosophically, theologically and mythologically the existence of the everywhere proclaimed Jechidah as being one, but in a lesser degree: that when an Egyptian thought of Ptah, a Greek of Iacchus, a Hindu of Parabrahman and a Christian of the Trinity as a Unity, they were not thinking of four Gods, but of one God, not of four conditions but of one condition, not of four results but of one result; and, that should they set out to attain unity with their ideal, the stages they would progress through would be in all cases essentially the same, the differences, if any, being due to the mental limitations of the experimenter, his education and prejudices, and not because the roads were dissimilar. Thus by this law could he with certainty predict that if a certain exercise were undertaken certain stages would be passed through, and what these stages meant relative to the final result, irrespective of the creed, caste, or sect of the practicer.

Further, he had proved beyond doubt or quibble, that the terrific strain caused by the Eastern breathing exercises was no whit greater or less than that resulting from The Acts of Worship in an operation of Ceremonial Magic, that Dhâranâ and the Mantra Yoga were in effect none other than a paraphrase of the Sacred Magic and the Acts of Invocation; and ultimately that the whole system of Eastern Yoga was but a synonym of Western Mysticism. Starting from the root, he had by now crept sufficiently far through the darkness of the black earth to predict a great tree above, and to prophecy concerning a Kingdom of Light and Loveliness; and, as a worm will detect its approach to the earth surface by the warmth of the mould, so did he detect by a sense, new and unknown to him, a world as different from the world he lived in as the world of awakenment differs from the world of dreams. Further, did he grow to understand, that, though as a sustenance to the tree itself one root might not be as important as another, yet that they all drew their strength from the self-same soil, and ultimately united in the one trunk above. Some were rotten with age, some dying, some again but feeders of useless shoots, but more sympathetically, more scientifically, they were all of one kind, the roots of one actual

188

living tree, dissimilar in shape but similar in substance, and all working for one definite end.

Thus did Frater P. by two years close and unabandoned experiment show, to his own satisfaction, that Yoga was but the Art of uniting the mind to a single idea; and that Gnana-Yoga, Raja-Yoga, Bhakta-Yoga and Hatha-Yoga * were but one class of methods leading to the same Result as attained to by The Holy Qabalah, The Sacred Magic, the Acts of Worship and The Ordeals of Western Ceremonial Magic; which again are but subsections of that One Art, the Art of uniting the mind to a Single Idea. And, that all these, The Union by Knowledge, The Union by Will, The Union by Love, The Union by Courage found their vanishing point in the Supreme Union through Silence; that Union in which understanding fails us, and beyond which we can no more progress than we can beyond the Equilibrium set forth as the Ultimate End by Gustave le Bon. There all knowledge ceases, and we like Bâhva, when he was questioned by Vâshkali, can only expound the nature of this Silence, as he expounded the nature of Brahman, by remaining silent, as the story relates:

And he said, "Teach me, most reverend Sir, the nature of Brahman." The other however remained silent. But when the question was put for a second or third time he answered, "I teach you indeed, but you do not understand; this Âtman is silent."

P. had not yet attained to this Silence; indeed it was the goal he had set out to accomplish, and though from the ridge

---

* To which may be added Mantra Yoga and Karma Yoga, which correspond with The Invocation and The Acts of Service and represent Union through Speech and Union through Work.

of the great mountain upon which he was standing the summit seemed but a furlong above him, it was in truth many a year's weary march away, and ridge upon ridge lay concealed, and each as it was gained presented an increasing difficulty.

This Silence or Equilibrium is described in the " Shiva Sanhita " * as Samâdhi:

" When the mind of the Yogi is absorbed in the Great God,† then the fulness of Samâdhi ‡ is attained, then the Yogi gets steadfastness.§

Though Frater P. had not attained to this Steadfastness, he had won a decisive victory over the lower states of Dhyanâ as far back as October 1901, which shows that though he was still distant he was by degrees nearing a state in which he would find no more Worlds to Conquer.

However, up to this point, there are several results to record, which are of extreme importance to the beginner, in so much that some of them are arrived at by methods diametrically opposed to those held by the dogmatic Yogins.

At the very commencement of his Yoga exercises Frater P. discovered, that in so lecherous a race as the Hindus it is absolutely necessary before a Chela can be accepted by a Guru to castrate him spiritually and mentally.‖ This being so, we

---

* " Shiva Sanhita," chap. v, 155.

† Âtman, Pan, Harpocrates, whose sign is silence, etc., etc. See 777.

‡ The Vision of the Holy Guardian Angel—Adonai.

§ Equilibrium, Silence, Supreme Attainment, Zero.

‖ As for women they are considered beyond the possibility of redemption, for in order of re-incarnation they are placed seven stages below a man, three below a camel, and one below a pig. Manu speaks of " the gliding of the soul through ten thousand millions of wombs." And if a man steal grain in the husk, he shall be born a rat; if honey, a great stinging gnat; if milk, a crow; if woven

therefore find almost every master of note, from Sankaracharya down to Agamya Paramahamsa, insisting on the maintenance to the letter of the rules of Yama and Niyama, that is absolute Chastity in body and mind amongst their pupils.*

Now P. proved that the strict letter of the law of Chastity had no more to do with the ultimate success of attainment than refusing to work on a Sabbath had to do with a free pass to the Celestial regions, unless every act of chastity was computed and performed in a magical manner, each act becoming as it were a link in one great chain, a formula in one great operation, an operation not leading to Chastity, the symbol, but beyond Chastity to the essence itself—namely the Âtman,—Adonai. Further he proved to his own satisfaction that, though absolute Chastity might mean salvation to one man, inducing in the lecherous a speedy concentration, it might be the greatest hindrance to another, who was by nature chaste.†

flax, a frog; if a cow, a lizard; if a horse, a tiger; if roots or fruit, an ape; if a woman, a bear. " Institutes of Manu," xii, 55-67.

* We find Christ insisting on this absolute chastity of body and mind, in a similar manner, and for similar reasons; for the Eastern Jew if he is not actually doing something dirty, is sure to be thinking about it.

† The reason for this is very simple. Take for example a glutton who lives for his palate and his stomach; he is always longing for tasty foods and spends his whole life seeking them. Let us now substitute the symbol of the Augoeides or Âtman for that of food and drink, let him every time he thinks of food and drink push the thought aside and in its place contemplate his Higher Self, and the result is a natural invocation of the Âtman, Augoeides, or Higher Self. If the aspirant be an artist let him do the same with his art; if a musician, with his music; if a poet, with his verses and rhymes. For the best foundation to build upon is always to be found upon that which a man *loves best*. It is no good asking a glutton who does not care a row of brass pins for music, to turn music into a magical formula, neither is it of the slightest use to impress upon a clean-minded individual the necessity of living a chaste life. It is like tapping Samson on the shoulder, just after he has carried the gates of Gaza on

He realized that there were in this world she-mules as well as she-asses, and that though the former would never foal in spite of all the stallions of Moultan, the latter seldom failed to do so after having been for a few minutes in the presence of a Margate jackass.

Discarding Chastity (Brahmachârya)—a good purgative for the prurient—he wrote in its place the word " Health." Do not worry about this code and that law, about the jibber of this crank or the jabber of that faddist. To hell with ethical pigs and prigs alike. *Do what you like*; but in the name of your own Higher Self wilfully *do no injury to your own body or mind* by over indulgence or under indulgence. Discover your normal appetite; satisfy it. Do not become a glutton, and do not become a nut-cracking skindlewig.

Soon after his arrival in Ceylon, and at the time that he was working with Frater I. A. the greatness of the Buddha, as we have already seen, attracted him, and he turned his attention to the dogmatic literature of Buddhism only to find that behind its unsworded Cromwellian colossus,* with all his rigid virtues, his stern reasoning, his uncharitableness, judicialism and impartiality, slunk a pack of pig-headed dolts, stubborn, asinine and mulish; slavish, menial and

to the top of the hill before Hebron, and saying: " My good boy, if you ever intend becoming strong, the first thing you must do is to buy a pair of my four pound dumb-bells and my sixpenny book on physical culture."

* The Buddha (it is true) did not encourage bloodshed, in spite of his having died from an overfeed of pork, but as Mr. A. Crowley has said, many of his present-day followers are quite capable of killing their own brothers for five rupees. The Western theory that Buddhists are lambs and models of virtue is due to the fact that certain Western vices are not so congenial to the Asiatic as they are to the European; and not because Buddhists are incapable of enjoying themselves.

gutless; puritanic, pharisaical and "suburban" as any seven-teenth century presbyter, as biliously narrow-minded as any of the present day Bethelites, Baptists, and Bible-beer brewers.*

The dogmatism of literal Buddhism appalled him. The Five Precepts, which are the Yama and Niyama of Buddhism, he at once saw, in spite of Nagasena and prig Milinda, must be broken by every Arahat each time he inhaled a breath of air. They were as absurd as they were valueless. But behind all this tantalizing *frou-frou*, this *lingerie de cocotte*, beautifully designed to cover the narded limbs of foolish virgins, sits the Buddha in silent meditation; so that P. soon discovered that by stripping his body of all these tawdry trappings, this feminine under-wear, and by utterly discarding the copy-book precepts of Baptistical Buddhists, the Four Noble Truths were none other than the complete Yoga, and that in The Three Characteristics † the summit of philosophy (The Ruach) had been reached.

The terrific strain of Âsana and Prânâyâma, the two chief exercises of Hathavidya, P., by months of trial proved to be

---

* Buddhism as a schism from the Brahminical religion may in many respects be compared with Lutheranism as a schism from the Catholic Church. Both Buddha and Luther set aside the authority of miracles, and appealed to the reason of the middle classes of their day. The Vedas were the outcome of aristocratic thought; and so in truth was the Christianity of Constantine and the Popes, that full-blooded Christianity which so soon swallowed the mystical Christ and the anaemic communism of the *canaille* which followed him. Conventional Buddhism is pre-eminently the "nice" religion of the bourgeoisie; it neither panders to the superstition of the masses nor palliates the gallantries of the aristocracy; it is essentially middle-class; and this no doubt is the chief reason why it has met with a kindly reception by this nation of shop-walkers.

† Anikka, Change; Dukka, Sorrow; Anatta, Absence of an Ego.

not only methods of great use as a sedative before commencing a Magical Operation, but methods of inordinate importance to such aspirants, who, having discarded the Shibboleths of sect, have adopted the fatuities of reason. For it is more difficult for one who has no natural magical aptitude, and one who perhaps has only just broken away from faith and corrupted ritual, to carry out an operation of Western Magic, than it is for him to sit down and perform a rational exercise, such as the Prânâyâma exercises of Yoga, which carry with them their own result, in spite of the mental attitude of the chela towards them, so long as the instructions of the Guru are properly carried out.*

As already pointed out, the mere fact of sitting for a time in a certain position, of inhaling, exhaling and of holding the breath, brings with it, even in the case of the most obdurate sceptic, a natural concentration, an inevitable Pratyâhâra, which develops in the aspirant the Siddhis, those seemingly miraculous powers which distinguish an Adeptus Major from an Adeptus Minor, and entitle the possessor to the rank of $6° = 5°$.

From this discovery † Frater P. made yet another, and this time one of still greater importance. And this was, that if the

---

* Prânâyâma acts on the mind just as Calomel acts on the bowels. It does not matter if a patient believes in Calomel or not. The physician administers it, and even if the patient be a most hostile Christian Scientist, the result is certain. Similarly with Prânâyâma, the Guru gives his chela a certain exercise, and as surely as the Calomel voided the noxious matter from the intestines of the sufferer, so will the Prânâyâma void the capricious thoughts from the mind of the disciple.

† By discovery here we mean individual experiment resulting in personal discovery; another person's discovery only begets illusion and comment. Individual discovery is the only true discovery worth consideration.

Adept, when once the Siddhis were attained, by a self-control (a still higher concentration) refused to expend these occult powers,* by degrees he accumulated within himself a terrific force; charged like a Leyden jar, instantaneously could he transmute this power into whatever he willed; but the act brought with it a recoil, and caused an exhaustion and a void which nullified the powers gained. Ultimately he proved that it was rather by the restraint of these occult (mental) powers than that of the bodily ones that Ojas is produced.†

By now he was beginning to learn that there was more than one way of opening the Lion's jaws; and that gentleness and humility would often succeed where brutality and much boasting were sure to fail. The higher he ascended into the realms of the Ruach the more he realized the irrational folly of performing wonders before a mob of gargoyle-headed apes, of pulling the strings of mystical marionettes and reducing himself to the level of an occult Punch and Judy showman. He had attained to powers that were beyond the normal, and now he carried them secretly like some precious blade of Damascus steel, hidden in a velvet sheath, concealed from view, but ever ready to hand. He did not display his weapon to the wanton, neither did he brandish it before the

* Nearly all the Masters have been cautious how they handled this power; generally refusing to expend it at the mere caprice of their followers or opponents. The Siddhis are like the Gold of the Alchemist. Once discovered it is kept secret, and the more secretly it is kept and the more it is hoarded the richer becomes the discoverer, and then one day will come wherein he will be able to pay his own ransom, and this is the only ransom that is acceptable unto God.

† Possibly the restraint of Brahmachârya produced the Siddhis, and that further restraint in its turn produced an accumulation of these occult powers, the benefit accruing from which is again placed to the credit of the bodily powers.

eyes of the gilded courtezan—Babylon, thou harlot of the Seven mansions of God's Glory! But he kept it free from rust, sharp and glittering bright, so that when the time came wherein he should be called upon to use it, it might leap forth from its sheath like a flash of lightning from betwixt the lips of God, and slay him who had ventured to cross his path, silently, without even so much as grating against his bones.

PAN TO ARTEMIS

UNCHARMABLE charmer
  Of Bacchus and Mars
In the sounding rebounding
  Abyss of the stars!
O virgin in armour,
  Thine arrows unsling
In the brilliant resilient
  First rays of the spring!

By the force of the fashion
  Of love, when I broke
Through the shroud, through the cloud,
  Through the storm, through the smoke,
To the mountain of passion
  Volcanic that woke—
By the rage of the mage
  I invoke, I invoke!

By the midnight of madness:—
  The lone-lying sea,
The swoon of the moon,
  Your swoon into me,
The sentinel sadness
  Of cliff-clinging pine,
That night of delight
  You were mine, you were mine!

THE EQUINOX

You were mine, O my saint,
 My maiden, my mate,
By the might of the right
 Of the night of our fate.
Though I fall, though I faint,
 Though I char, though I choke,
By the hour of our power
 I invoke, I invoke!

By the mystical union
 Of fairy and faun,
Unspoken, unbroken—
 The dusk to the dawn!—
A secret communion
 Unmeasured, unsung,
The listless, resistless,
 Tumultuous tongue!—

O virgin in armour,
 Thine arrows unsling,
In the brilliant resilient
 First rays of the spring!
No Godhead could charm her,
 But manhood awoke—
O fiery Valkyrie,
 I invoke, I invoke!

ALEISTER CROWLEY.

The Interpreter.

THE INTERPRETER

MOTHER of Light, and the Gods! Mother of Music, awake!
Silence and Speech are at odds; Heaven and Hell are at
    stake.
By the Rose and the Cross I conjure; I constrain by the
    Snake and the Sword;
I am he that is sworn to endure—Bring us the word of the
    Lord!

By the brood of the Bysses of Brightening, whose God was
    my sire;
By the Lord of the Flame and the Lightning, the King of
    the Spirits of Fire;
By the Lord of the Waves and the Waters, the King of the
    Hosts of the Sea,
The fairest of all of whose daughters was mother to me;

By the Lord of the Winds and the Breezes, the King of the
    Spirits of Air,
In whose bosom the infinite ease is that cradled me there;
By the Lord of the Fields and the Mountains, the King of
    the Spirits of Earth
That nurtured my life at his fountains from the hour of my
    birth;

THE EQUINOX

By the Wand and the Cup I conjure; by the Dagger and
   Disk I constrain;
I am he that is sworn to endure; make thy music again!
I am Lord of the Star and the Seal; I am Lord of the Snake
   and the Sword;
Reveal us the riddle, reveal! Bring us the word of the Lord!

As the flame of the sun, as the roar of the sea, as the storm
   of the air,
As the quake of the earth—let it soar for a boon, for a bane,
   for a snare,
For a lure, for a light, for a kiss, for a rod, for a scourge, for
   a sword—
Bring us thy burden of bliss—Bring us the word of the
   Lord!

Perdurabo.

THE DAUGHTER OF THE HORSELEECH

A FABLE

Tria sunt insaturabilia, et quartum, quod nunquam dicit : Sufficit.
Infernus, et os vulvae. . . . —Prov. xxx. 16.

THE Great White Spirit stretched Himself and yawned. He had done an honest six days' work if ever a man did ; yet in such physical training was He from His lengthy " cure " in that fashionable Spa Pralaya that he was not in the least fatigued. It was the Loi du Répos Hebdomadaire that had made Him throw down His tools.

" Anyway, the job's finished ! " He said, looking round Him complacently. Even His critical eye assured Him that it was very good.

And indeed it must be admitted that He had every right to crow. With no better basis than the Metaphysical Absolute of the Qabalists he had unthinkably but efficiently formulated Infinite Space, filled the said Space with Infinite Light, concentrated the Light into a Smooth-pointed Whitehead (not the torpedo) and emanated Himself as four hundred successive intelligences all the way from Risha Qadisha in Atziluth down to where intelligence ends, and England begins.

He took a final survey and again faintly murmured: "Very good! Beautifully arranged, too!" He added, "not a hole anywhere!"

It somewhat surprised Him, therefore, when a tiny, tiny silvery little laugh came bell-like in His ear. It was so tiny that he could hardly credit the audacity of the idea, but for all its music, the laugh certainly sounded as if some one were mocking Him.

He turned sharply round (and this was one of His own special attributes, as transcending the plane where activity and rotundity are incompatibles) but saw nothing; and putting His legs up, lighted His long pipe and settled down to a quiet perusal of a fascinating "cosmic romance" called Berashith by two pseudonymous authors, G. O. Varr and L. O. Heem— of ingenious fancy, exalted imaginative faculty, and a tendency, which would later be deemed undesirable, to slop over into the filthiest details whenever the love-interest became dominant. Oh, but it was a most enthralling narrative! Beginning with a comic account of the creation, possibly intended as a satire on our men of science or our men of religion—'twould serve equally well in either case—it went on to a thrilling hospital scene. The love-interest comes in chapter ii.; chapter iii. has an eviction scene, since when there have been no snakes in Ireland; chapter iv. gives us a first-rate murder, and from that moment the authors never look back.

But the Great White Spirit was destined to have his day of repose disturbed.

He had just got to the real masterpiece of literature "And Adam knew Hevah his woman," which contains all that ever has been said or ever can be said upon the sex-problem in its

202

THE DAUGHTER OF THE HORSELEECH

one simple, sane, clean truth, when glancing up, he saw that after all He had overlooked something. In the Infinite Universe which he had constructed there was a tiny crack.

A tiny, tiny crack.

Barely an inch of it.

Well, the matter was easily remedied. As it chanced, there was a dainty little Spirit (with gossamer wings like a web of steel, and scarlet tissue of silk for his robes) flitting about, brandishing his tiny sword and spear in a thoroughly warlike manner.

" Shun ! " said the Great White Spirit.

" By the right, dress !

" Sappers, one pace forward, march !

" Prepare to stop leak !

" Stop leak ! "

But the matter was not thus easily settled. After five hours' strenuous work, the little spirit was exhausted, and the hole apparently no nearer being filled than before.

He returned to the Great White Spirit.

" Beg pardon, sir ! " he said ; " but I can't fill that there 'ole nohow."

" No matter," answered the Great White Spirit, with a metaphysical double entendre. " You may go ! "

If anything, the crack was bigger than before, it seemed to Him. " This," He said, " is clearly the job for Bartzabel." And he despatched a " speed " message for that worthy spirit.

Bartzabel lost no time in answering the summons. Of flaming, radiant, far-darting gold was his crown ; flashing hither and thither more swiftly than the lightning were its rays. His head was like the Sun in its strength, even at high noon. His cloak was of pure amethyst, flowing behind him like a mighty river; his armour was of living gold, burnished with lightning even to the greaves and the armed feet of him; he radiated an intolerable splendour of gold and he bore the Sword and balance of Justice. Mighty and golden were his wide-flashing wings!

Terrible in his might, he bowed low before the Great White Spirit, and proceeded to carry out the order.

For five and twenty years he toiled at the so easy task; then, flinging down his weapons in a rage, he returned before the face of his Master and, trembling with passion, cast himself down in wrath and despair.

"Pah!" said the Great White Spirit with a smile; "I might have known better than to employ a low material creature like yourself. Send Graphiel to Me!"

The angry Bartzabel, foaming with horrid rage, went off, and Graphiel appeared.

All glorious was the moon-like crown of the great Intelligence Graphiel. His face was like the Sun as it appears beyond the veil of this earthly firmament. His warrior body was like a tower of steel, virginal strong.

Scarlet were his kingly robes, and his limbs were swathed in young leaves of lotus; for those limbs were stronger than any armour ever forged in heaven or hell. Winged was he with the wings of gold that are the Wind itself; his sword of green fire flamed in his right hand, and in his left he held the blue feather of Justice, unstirred by the wind of his flight, or the upheaval of the universe.

But after five and sixty centuries of toil, though illumined with intelligence almost divine, he had to confess himself defeated.

THE DAUGHTER OF THE HORSELEECH

"Sir," he cried strongly, "this is a task for Kamael the mighty and all his host of Seraphim!"

"I will employ them on it," said the Great White Spirit.

Then the skies flamed with wrath; for Kamael the mighty and his legions flew from the South, and saluted their Creator. Behold the mighty one, behold Kamael the strong! His crownless head was like a whirling wheel of amethyst, and all the forces of the earth and heaven revolved therein. His body was the mighty Sea itself, and it bore the scars of crucifixion that had made it two score times stronger than it was before. He too bore the wings and weapons of Space and of Justice; and in himself he was that great Amen that is the beginning and the end of all.

Behind him were the Seraphim, the fiery Serpents. On their heads the triple tongue of fire; their glory like unto the Sun, their scales like burning plates of steel; they danced like virgins before their lord, and upon the storm and roar of the sea did they ride in their glory.

"Sir," cried the Archangel, "sir," cried Kamael the mighty one, and his legions echoed the roar of his voice, "hast Thou called us forth to perform so trivial a task? Well, let it be so!"

"Your scorn," the Great White Spirit replied mildly, "is perhaps not altogether justified. Though the hole be indeed but a bare inch—yet Graphiel owns himself beaten."

"I never thought much of Graphiel!" sneered the archangel, and his serpents echoed him till the world was filled with mocking laughter.

But when he had left, he charged them straitly that the work must be regarded seriously. It would never do to fail!

205

So for æons three hundred and twenty and five did they labour with all their might.

But the crack was not diminished by an hair's breadth; nay, it seemed bigger than before—a very gape in the womb of the Universe.

Crestfallen, Kamael the mighty returned before the Great White Spirit, his serpents drooping behind him; and they grovelled before the throne of that All-powerful One.

He dismissed them with a short laugh, and a wave of His right hand. If He was disturbed, He was too proud to show it. "This," he said to himself, "is clearly a matter for Elohim Gibor."

Therefore He summoned that divine power before Him.

The crown of Elohim Gibor was Space itself; the two halves of his brain were the Yea and Nay of the Universe; his breath was the breath of very Life; his being was the Mahalingam of the First, beyond Life and Death the generator from Nothingness. His armour was the Primal Water of Chaos. The infinite moon-like curve of his body; the flashing swiftness of his Word, that was the Word that formulated that which was beyond Chaos and Cosmos; the might of him, greater than that of the Elephant and of the Lion and of the Tortoise and of the Bull fabled in Indian legend as the supports of the four letters of the Name; the glory of him, that was even as that of the Sun which is before all and beyond all Suns, of which the stars are little sparks struck off as he battled in the Infinite against the Infinite—all these points the Great White Spirit noted and appreciated. This is certainly the person, thought He, to do my business for me.

But alas! for five, and for twenty-five, and for sixty-five,

THE DAUGHTER OF THE HORSELEECH

and for three hundred and twenty-five myriads of myriads of myriads of kotis of crores of lakhs of asankhayas of maha-kalpas did he work with his divine power—and yet that little crack was in nowise filled, but rather widened!

The god returned. "O Great White Spirit!" he whispered —and the Universe shook with fear at the voice of him— "Thou, and Thou alone, art worthy to fill this little crack that Thou hast left."

Then the Great White Spirit arose and formulated Himself as the Pillar of Infinitude, even as the Mahalingam of Great Shiva the Destroyer, who openeth his eye, and All is Not. And behold! He was balanced in the crack, and the void was filled, and Nature was content. And Elohim Gibor, and Kamael the mighty and his Seraphim, and Graphiel, and Bartzabel, and all the inhabitants of Madim shouted for joy and gave glory and honour and praise to the Great White Spirit; and the sound of their rejoicing filled the Worlds.

Now for one thousand myriad eternities the Great White Spirit maintained Himself as the Pillar of Infinitude in the midst of the little crack that he had overlooked; and lo! He was very weary.

"I cannot stay like this for ever," He exclaimed; and returned into His human shape, and filled the bowl of His pipe, and lit it, and meditated. . . .

And I awoke, and behold it was a dream.

Then I too lit my pipe, and meditated.

"I cannot see," thought I, "that the situation will be in any way amended, even if we agree to give them votes."

ETHEL RAMSAY.

THE DREAMER

In the grey dim Dawn where the Souls Unborn
May look on the Things to Be ;
A tremulous Shade, a Thing Unmade,
Stood Lost by the silent Sea ;
And shuddering fought the o'erwhelming thought
Of Its own Identity.

Is the frenzied form that derides the storm
A ghost of the days to Be ?
And the restless wave but the troubled grave
Of Its own dread Imagery ?
Or merely a wraith cast up without faith
From the jaws of a Phantom Sea ?

To his Love Unborn in that grey dim Dawn
Did the Shade of the Dreamer flee ;
Nor marked he the Flood where the Vision had stood
Which mocks for Eternity.
For the Soul he would wed was the Hope that had fled
In the battle with Destiny.

Ethel Archer.

208

MR. TODD

A MORALITY

BY

THE AUTHOR OF "ROSA MUNDI"

In Memoriam
LILITH
Obiit Kal. Mai. 1906

MR. TODD

PERSONS OF THE PLAY

GRANDFATHER OSSORY (*eighty-one*)
ALFRED OSSORY (*fifty*), *his son, a shipowner*
EMILY OSSORY (*forty-five*), *his wife*
EUPHEMIA OSSORY (*eighteen*), *his daughter*
CHARLEY OSSORY (*ten*), *his son*
GEORGE DELHOMME (*twenty-four*), *of the Ministry of Foreign Affairs*
DIONYSUS CARR (*thirty-four*), *Professor of Experimental Eugenics in the
    University of Tübingen* ; and
MR. TODD

THOMAS, *a footman*
A HOSPITAL NURSE

SCENE : *The sitting-room in* OSSORY'S *house in Grosvenor Square.*

TIME : *Midday.*

The persons are in correct morning dress, except the invalid GRANDFATHER, *who is in a scarlet dressing-gown, with gold embroidery, and* CARR, *who affects a pseudo-Bohemian extravagance. He wears a low collar, a very big bow-tie of gorgeous colours, a pale yellow waistcoat, a rich violet lounge suit with braid, patent leather boots, pale blue socks. But the refinement and breeding of the man are never in question. His hair is reddish, curly, luxuriant. He is clean-shaved, and wears an eye-glass with a tortoiseshell rim.*

TODD *has a face of keen pallor; he is dressed in black, with a flowing black cape, black motor-cap. He gives the impression of great age combined with great activity.*

ACT I

GRANDFATHER *sunk in melancholy in his arm-chair;* MRS. OSSORY *red and weeping;* OSSORY (*a British heavy father*) *grief-stricken;* EUPHEMIA *sobbing at the table;* CARR *and* DELHOMME *cold and hot respectively in their expression of sympathy.* MR. TODD *is at the door, his cloak on, his hat in his hand.*

OSSORY. It is kind of you to have come so far to break the sad news, my dear sir. I hope that we shall see you again soon under—under—under happier circumstances.

[TODD *bows very low to the company as if deeply sympathising; but turning his face to the audience, smiles as if at some secret jest. The actor should study hard to make this smile significant of the whole character, as revealed in the complete play; for* TODD *does not develop through, but is explained by, the plot.* TODD *goes out;* OSSORY *follows, and returns in a minute. There is no sound in the room but that of* EUPHEMIA'S *sobs.*

OSSORY [*returning, throws himself into a chair near the door*]. Dear me! dear me! Poor, poor Henry!

DELHOMME. In the very flower of his life. . . .

CARR [*solemnly*]. Truly, my dear sir, in the midst of life we are in death.

213

THE EQUINOX

[EUPHEMIA *looks up and darts a furious glance at him; for she knows that he is mocking British solemnity and cant.*

DELHOMME. Crushed—crushed in a moment——

MRS. OSSORY [*very piously*]. Without a warning. Ah well, we must hope that—— [*Her voice becomes a mumble.*

DELHOMME. I will bid you good morning; I am sure you will not wish strangers to intrude upon your grief. If there is anything that I can do——

MR. OSSORY [*conventionally*]. Pray do not leave us yet, Monsieur Delhomme. Lunch is just ready.

DELHOMME. I really think that I should go.

[*He shakes hands.*

MRS. OSSORY. Good morning. We are so grateful for your sympathy and kindness. [*He turns to the old man.*] Grandfather is asleep.

[DELHOMME *shakes hands coldly with* CARR, *wondering why he does not offer to come with him. He goes to* EUPHEMIA.

EUPHEMIA. [*Jumps up and gives her hand, hiding her tear-stained face. She has a slight lisp.*] Good morning, monsieur. [*He bends over her hand and kisses it.*

DELHOMME. Always my sympathy and devotion, mademoiselle.

EUPHEMIA. Thank you—thank you.

[*Her real attitude to him is listlessness bordering on aversion, but constrained by politeness; he mistakes it for modesty striving with young love.*]

DELHOMME. Good morning, Mr. Ossory. Anything I can do, of course; anything I can do.

214

OSSORY. Thank you, my dear lad. Anything you can do, of course—I will let you know at once. By the way, you haven't asked her yet, I suppose?

DELHOMME. Not yet, sir. I am rather diffident: I do not care to precipitate affairs.

OSSORY. Well, I am really very anxious to see her future assured. And you know our proverb, "The early bird catches the worm." [*Points to him, and over his shoulder to her.*] There's our scientific friend, eh?

DELHOMME. Oh, I'm not afraid of him. A *farceur*, no more, though sometimes a pleasant one.

OSSORY. *Tu t'en f——, ça, mon vieux chameau? Quoi?*

DELHOMME [*very disgusted at* OSSORY'S *vulgarity, which mistakes* argot *for* chic]. Well, sir, as soon as I can find a favourable opportunity——

OSSORY. Grief is a good mood to catch them in, my boy. I know! I know! I've been a bit of a dog in my time.

[*Shakes hands as they go out.*

DELHOMME [*returning*]. One word in your ear, sir, if I may. It's purely instinctive—but—but—well, sir, I mistrust that man Todd!

OSSORY. Thanks: I believe you may be right.

DELHOMME. Good-bye, sir!

OSSORY. Good-bye.

MRS. OSSORY [*rising*]. Alfred, that man is a devil!

OSSORY. What, little Delhomme?

MRS. OSSORY. Of course not, Alfred. How can you be so silly? Todd!

OSSORY. Why, whatever do you mean?

MRS. OSSORY. I don't mean anything but what I say.

THE EQUINOX

He's a devil; I'm sure of it. I know it was his fault, some-how.

OSSORY. Nonsense, nonsense, my dear! He was not even in the car.

MRS. OSSORY. It was his car, Alfred.

OSSORY. You're a fool, Emily.

CARR. I think Mr. Ossory means that we could hardly hold him responsible if one of his steamers ran down a poor polar bear on a drifting iceberg.

MRS. OSSORY. I know I'm quite unreasonable; it's an instinct, an intuition. You know Saga of Bond Street said how psychic I was!

[*During the next few speeches* CARR *and* EUPHEMIA *correspond by signs and winks.*

GRANDFATHER. When I was in Australia forty-four years ago there was a very good fellow of the name of Brown in Ballarat. Brown of Buninyong we used to call him. I remember——

MRS. OSSORY [*bursting into tears*]. How can you, grandpa? Can't you realise that poor Henry is dead?

GRANDFATHER. Henry dead?

MRS. OSSORY. Didn't you hear? He was run over by Mr. Todd's motor-car this afternoon in Piccadilly.

GRANDFATHER. There, what did I tell you? I always disliked that man Todd from the first moment that I heard his name. Dear, dear! I always knew he would bring us trouble.

OSSORY. Well, this doesn't seem to have been his fault, as far as we can see at present. But I assure you that I share

216

your sentiments. I have heard very ill things said of him, I can tell you.

MRS. OSSORY. Who is he? Does any one know? A man of family, I hope. How dreadful for poor Henry if he had been run over by a plebeian!

OSSORY. Well, we hardly know—I wonder if his credit is good. [*His voice sinks to a whisper as the awful suspicion that he may be financially unsound strikes him.*]

CARR [*sharply, as if pained*]. Oh, oh! Don't suggest such a thing without the very best reason. It would be too terrible! [*This time* EUPHEMIA *laughs.*

OSSORY. My dear boy, I deliberately say it. I have the very best of reasons for supposing him to be very deeply dipped. Very deeply dipped.

CARR. [*Hides his head in his hands and groans, pretending to be overwhelmed by the tragedy. Looks up.*] Well, I was told the other day that he held a lot of land in London, and has more tenants than the Duke of Westminster!

OSSORY. Well, we'll hope it is true. But in these days one never knows. And he leaves a very unpleasant impression wherever he goes. If I were not an Englishman I should say that the feeling I had for him was not very far removed from actual fear!

CARR. Well said, sir. Hearts of oak in the City, eh?

[OSSORY *glares at him suspiciously.* EUPHEMIA *both enjoys the joke and is angry that her father is the butt of it.*

EUPHEMIA. Well, I'm not afraid of him—I think I rather like him. I'm sure he's a good man, when one knows him.

CARR. Oh, Todd's a good sort! I think I must be going, sir.

EUPHEMIA. I wish you would stay and help me with the letters, Mr. Carr. We shall have a great deal to do in the next day or two.

CARR. Well, if you really wish it, I will try and be of what service I can.

[CARR, *with his back to the audience, laughs with his hands, behind it.*

MRS. OSSORY. That is indeed kind of you, Professor!

[CARR'S *hand-laugh grows riotous.*

GRANDFATHER. Where is Nurse? I want my whisky and milk.

MRS. OSSORY. [*Rings.*] I shall go down to lunch, Alfred. Lunch when you like, please, everybody. I fear the house will be much upset for a day or two. You must go down to the mortuary at once. I am really too upset to do anything more.

CARR. [*Over* L. *To* EUPHEMIA.] She hasn't done much yet!

EUPHEMIA. What a brute you are!

MRS. OSSORY. And we can't possibly go to the dear Duchess on Friday!

CARR [*almost in tears*]. Forgive my seeming callousness! On my honour, I never thought of that. "Sunt lachrymæ rerum.'

[*A nurse and a footman appear. The latter wheels* GRAND-FATHER *out of the room, using the greatest care not to shake him.*

218

MR. TODD

GRANDFATHER. Oh, my sciatica! You careless scoundrel, you're shaking me to pieces! Emily, do get a gentler footman. Oh! Oh! Nobody cares for the poor old man. I am thrown on the dust-heap. Oh, Emily, may you suffer one day as I suffer! Oh! Oh! Oh!

[*The nurse comes forward and soothes him.*

NURSE. You must really be more careful of my patient, Thomas.

THOMAS. I humbly beg pardon, miss. I think the balls is gritty, miss. I'll ile 'em to-morrow.

GRANDFATHER. There, you see, Nurse is the only one that loves me. I should like to marry you, Nurse, eh? And cut 'em all out?

MRS. OSSORY. [*Glares at Nurse in silence, not trusting herself to speak to her.*] Now, grandpa, don't be silly! You know how we all love you! [*She goes to the chair and shakes it, unseen.*] Thomas, there you are again! How can you be so thoughtless?

GRANDFATHER. Oh! Oh! Oh!

[*They get him out of the room.*

MRS. OSSORY [*returning*]. Good-bye, Mr. Carr. It is so good of you to help.

CARR. Not at all, Mrs. Ossory, not at all. I am only too glad. You should try and get a nap after lunch.

MRS. OSSORY. I will—I really think I will.   [*Exit.*

CARR. [*Closes the door, turns to* EUPHEMIA, *executes a quiet hornpipe, goes to* EUPHEMIA, *holds out his arms.*] Sweetheart!

EUPHEMIA. How dare you! How can you! With poor Uncle Henry lying dead!

219

THE EQUINOX

CARR. Why have a long Latin name if you mean to play the English hypocrite? Who was poor Uncle Henry? Did you love poor Uncle Henry so dearly as all that? How old were you when your father quarrelled with poor Uncle Henry? About two and a half! The only thing you can know about poor Uncle Henry is that poor Uncle Henry once tickled your toes. [EUPHEMIA *gives a little scream of horror*.] Enough humbug about poor Uncle Henry! . . . Sweetheart!

EUPHEMIA. Mine own!

[*They embrace and kiss with great intensity.*

EUPHEMIA. Unhand me, villain! . . .

But one has to be decent about one's relations. Even the humbug of it is rather fun.

CARR. There speaks the daughter of Shakespeare's country. I am sure the Bacon imbroglio was a consummate practical joke on somebody's part. As I see the joke, I take no side in the controversy!

But we should look on the bright side of things!

[*Pompously.*]

Poor Uncle Henry, dead and turned to clay,
May feed the Beans that keep the Bile away.
Oh that whom all the world did once ignore
Should purge a peer or ease an emperor!

EUPHEMIA. But where is the bright side of our love?
CARR. Why, our love!
EUPHEMIA. Cannot you, cannot you understand?
CARR. Not unless you tell me!
EUPHEMIA. I can't tell you.

MR. TODD

CARR. —Anything I don't know.

EUPHEMIA. Oh, you laugh even at me!

CARR. Because I love you. So I laugh at humanity: if I took men seriously I should have to cut my throat.

EUPHEMIA. So you don't take me seriously either?

CARR. If I did, I should have to cut——

EUPHEMIA. What?

CARR. My lucky!

EUPHEMIA. What a dreadful expression! Where do you learn such things?

CARR. I notice you don't have to ask what it means.

EUPHEMIA. Stop teasing, darling!

CARR. I'm not teething! That's what I complain of; you always treat me as a baby!

EUPHEMIA. Come to his mummy, then!

CARR. You're not my mummy! That's what I complain of; you always treat me as a Cheops, ever since that night on the Great Pyramid!

EUPHEMIA. [*Hides her head in his bosom.*] Oh shame, shame!

CARR. Not a bit of it! Think of the infinite clearness of the night—

> "The magical green of the sunset,
> The magical blue of the Nile."

The rising of the great globed moon—the stars starting from their fastnesses like sentries on the alarm—the isolation of our stance upon the summit—the faery distance of Cairo and its spear-sharp minarets—and we—and we——

EUPHEMIA. Oh me! Oh me!

CARR. Shall I remind you——

THE EQUINOX

EUPHEMIA. Must *I* remind *you?*

CARR. No; my memory is excellent.

EUPHEMIA. Of what you swore?

CARR. I swore at the granite for not being moss.

EUPHEMIA. You swore to love me always.

CARR. The champagne at the Mena House is not champagne; it is—the cork of it is labelled " Good intentions."

EUPHEMIA. Then you didn't mean it?

CARR [*kissing her*]. Am I, or am I not—a plain question as between man and man—loving you now?

EUPHEMIA. Oh, I know! But I am so worried that everything most sure seems all shaken in the storm of it! I was glad—glad, glad!—when that Mr. Todd came in with his news, so that I could have a real good cry. [*Very close to him, in a tragic whisper.*] Something has happened—something is going to happen.

CARR. And something has not happened—I knew it was a long time since we missed a week. By the way, have you heard the terrible news about Queen Anne? Dead, poor soul! Never mind, silly, you told me most dramatically, and it shall be counted unto you for righteousness.

EUPHEMIA. I think you're the greatest brute in the world—and I love you.

CARR. How reciprocal of you!

EUPHEMIA. Sweet!

CARR. On my honour, I haven't a single chocolate on me. Have a cigar? [*Business with case.*

EUPHEMIA. Be serious! You must marry me at once.

CARR. Then how can I be serious? I understand from a gentleman named Shaw that marriage is only a joke—no,

222

not Shaw! Vaughan, or Gorell Barnes, or some name like that!

EUPHEMIA. But you will, won't you?

CARR. No, I won't, will I?

[*Sings.*] "I have a wife and bairnies three,
　　　　And I'm no sure how ye'd agree, lassie!"

EUPHEMIA. What?　　　　　　　　　[*She releases herself.*

CARR. Well, the wife's dead, as a matter of fact. Her name was Hope-of-ever-doing-something-in-the-Wide-Wide. But the bairns are alive: young Chemistry, already apt at repartee —I should say retort; little Biology, who's rather a worm between you and me and the gate-post; and poor puny, puling, sickly little Metaphysics, with only one tooth in his upper jaw!

Oh, don't cry! I love you as I always did and always shall. I'll see you through it somehow!

But don't talk foolishness about marriage! We are happy because when I come to see you I come to see you. If we were living together you would soon get to know me as the brute who grumbles at the cooking and wants to shut himself up and work—[*mimicking her voice*] "And I wouldn't mind so much if it were work, but all he does is to sit in a chair and smoke and stare at nothing and swear if any one comes in to ask him if my darling new old rose chiffon moiré Directoire corsets match my eau-de-Nil suede tussore appliqué garters." See?

EUPHEMIA. But—hush!

[*She flies away to the other end of the room. The door opens. Enter* THOMAS.

223

THE EQUINOX

THOMAS. Mr. Delomm would like to see you for a moment on urgent business.

[*The lovers exchange signals privately.*

EUPHEMIA. Show him up.

THOMAS. Yes, miss.   [THOMAS *goes out.*

CARR. I will go and get a snack. Trust me—love me——

EUPHEMIA. I will—I do.

[*They embrace.* CARR *goes to the door—turns.*

CARR. Love me—trust me.

[EUPHEMIA *flies to him, kisses him again, nods.*

EUPHEMIA. I will—I do—I love you—I trust you.

CARR. Sweetheart! [*They kiss, furtively, as if hearing footsteps.*] So long!

[*She retreats into the room, and blows him a kiss.*

CARR [*outside, loudly*]. Good morning, Miss Ossory!

EUPHEMIA [*sinking into a chair, faintly*]. Good-bye—no, no! Till—when?

[*She is almost crying, but sets her teeth and rises.*

THOMAS [*opening the door*]. Mr. Delomm.

[*Enter* DELHOMME.

DELHOMME. I am a thousand times sorry to intrude upon your grief, Miss Ossory, but——

EUPHEMIA. Uncle Henry was nothing to me.

DELHOMME. In any case, I should not have spoken to you, but my Embassy has suddenly called me. I am to go to Constantinople—I may be a month away—and—I want to see you first.

EUPHEMIA. Of course, to say good-bye. It is sweet of you to think of us, Monsieur Delhomme.

224

MR. TODD

DELHOMME. Of you—of thee.   How difficult is the English language to express subtle differences!

You must have seen, Miss Ossory——

EUPHEMIA [*dully*]. I have seen nothing.

DELHOMME. May I speak?

EUPHEMIA. What is this?   Oh!

DELHOMME. I need not tell you, I see.   My unspoken sympathy and devotion——

EUPHEMIA. Spare me, I pray you.

DELHOMME.   I must speak.   Mademoiselle, I am blessed in loving you.   I offer you the sympathy and devotion of a lifetime.

EUPHEMIA. I beg you to spare me.   It is impossible.

DELHOMME. It is the truth—it is necessary—I should kill myself if you refused.

EUPHEMIA. My father——

DELHOMME. Your respected father is my warmest advocate.

EUPHEMIA. You distress me, sir.   It is impossible.

DELHOMME. Ah, fairest of maidens, well I know your English coyness and modesty!   [*Taking her hand.*] Ah, give me this pure hand for good, for ever!   This hand which has been ever open to the misery of the poor, ever closed to box the enemies of your country!

EUPHEMIA. It is not mine!

DELHOMME.   I do not understand.   I am too worn a slave in the world's market for my fettered soul to grasp your innocence.   Ah! you are vowed to Our Lady, perhaps?   Yet, believe me——

EUPHEMIA. Oh, sir, you distress me—indeed you distress me!

THE EQUINOX

DELHOMME. I would not brush the bloom from off the lily—and yet——

EUPHEMIA. My God!—Monsieur Delhomme, I am going to shock you. Oh! Oh!

[*She buries her face in her hands. He starts back, surprised at the turn things are taking, and at the violence of her emotion and of its expression.*]

DELHOMME. What is it? Are you ill? Have I——

EUPHEMIA. [*Steady and straight before him.*] I am another man's—his—his mistress. There!

[*He reels, catches a chair and saves himself. Her breast heaves; swallowing a sob, she runs out of the room.*]

DELHOMME [*Utterly dazed*]. I—I—oh, my God! My father! My God! I thought her—oh, I dare not say it—I will not think it. [*On his knees, clutching at the chair.*] My God, what shall I do? She was my life, my hope, my flower, my star, my sun! What shall I do? Help me! help me! Who shall console me? [*He continues in silent prayer, sobbing*].

[*The door opens;* MR. TODD *steals into the room on tiptoe, bends over him and whispers in his ear. The expression of anguish fails from his face; a calm steals over him; he smiles in beatitude and his lips move in rapture. He rises, shakes* TODD *by the hand; they go out together.*]

[GRANDFATHER *wheeled into the room by* THOMAS, CHARLEY *walking by him. The servant leaves them.*]

GRANDFATHER. Bitter cold, Charley, for us old people!

Nothing right nowadays! Oh, my poor leg! Bitter, bitter cold! I mind me, more than sixty years ago now—oh dear! oh dear! run and tell Nurse I want my liniment! Oh dear! oh dear! what a wretched world. Sciatics—like rats gnawing, gnawing at you, Charley.

CHARLEY. You frighten me, grampa! Why doesn't Mr. Carr come and play with me?

GRANDFATHER. He has gone out with your mother. He'll come by-and-by, no doubt. Run and fetch Nurse, Charley! [CHARLEY *runs off.*

Oh dear! I wish I could find a good doctor. Nobody seems to do me any good. It's pain, pain all the time. Nurse! can't you tell me of a good doctor? For oh! for oh! [*he looks about him fearfully; his voice sinks to a thrilled whisper*] I am so afraid—afraid to die! Is there nobody——

[*Enter* TODD, *and stands by his chair, laying his hand on the old man's shoulder. He looks up.*

I wish you were a doctor, Mr. Todd. You have such a soothing touch. Perhaps you are a doctor? I can get nobody to do me any good.

[TODD *whispers in his ear. The old man brightens up at once.*

Why, yes! I should think that would relieve me at once. Very good! Very good!

[TODD *wheels him out of the room, the old man laughing and chuckling. Enter* OSSORY *and* EUPHEMIA, *talking.*

OSSORY. I want to say a word, girlie, about young Del-

227

homme. Er—well, we all grow older, you know—one day—er—ah! Nice young fellow, Delhomme!

EUPHEMIA. I refused him twenty minutes ago, father.

OSSORY. What? How the deuce did you know what I was going to say? Bless me, I believe there may be something in this psychic business after all!

EUPHEMIA. Yes, father, I feel I have strange powers!

OSSORY. But look here, girlie, why did you refuse him? *Reculer pour mieux sauter* is all very well, don't you know, but he gives twice who gives quickly.

EUPHEMIA. That's the point, father. If you accept a man the first time he asks you it's practically bigamy!

OSSORY. But—little girl, you ought to accept him at once. He will make you an excellent husband—I wish it. [*Pompously.*] It has ever been the desire of my heart to see my Phemie happily mated before I lay my old bones in the grave.

EUPHEMIA. But I don't love him. He's a quirk.

OSSORY. Tut! Nonsense! Appetite comes with eating.

EUPHEMIA. But I don't care for *hors d'œuvre*.

OSSORY. Euphemia, this is a very serious matter for your poor old father.

EUPHEMIA. What have you got to do with it? Really, father——

OSSORY. I have everything to do with it. The fact is, my child—here! I'll make a clean breast of it. I've been gambling, and things have gone wrong. Only temporarily, of course, you understand. Only temporarily. But—oh, if I had only kept out of Fidos!

EUPHEMIA. Is it a dog? [*Whistles.*] Here, Fido, Fido! Trust, doggie, trust!

OSSORY. That's it! they won't trust, those dogs! To put it short—[*a spasm of agony crosses his face*]—Good Lord alive, *I'm* short! If I can't find a couple of hundred thousand before the twelfth I'll be hammered.

EUPHEMIA. And so——?

OSSORY. Very decent young fellow, little Delhomme. I can borrow half a million from him if I want it; but I don't care to unless—unless things—unless you——

EUPHEMIA. I'm the goods, am I? You old bear!

OSSORY. I know, Phemie, I know. It's those damned bulls on Wall Street! How could I foresee——

EUPHEMIA. At least you might have foreseen that I was not a bale of cotton.

OSSORY. But I shall be hammered, my dear child. We shall all have to go to the workhouse!

EUPHEMIA. [*coldly*]. I thought mamma had three thousand a year of her own.

OSSORY. That's just what I say. The workhouse!

EUPHEMIA. My dear father, I really can't pity you. I think you're a fool, and you've insulted me. Good morning!

[*She goes out.*

OSSORY. Oh, the disgrace of it, the shame of it! She little knows—— How will the Receiver look at that Galapagos turtle deal? Receivers are damned fools. And juries are worse. Ah, Phemie, so little a sacrifice for the father who has given all for you—and she refuses! Cruel! Cruel! Which way can I turn? Is there nobody whose credit—— Let's think. Jenkins? No good. Maur? Too suspicious—a nasty, sly, sneaking fellow! Higginbotham, Ramspittle, Rosenbaum, Hoggenheimer, Flipp, Montgomery, MacAn—no, hang it!

229

no hope in a Mac—Schpliechenspitzel, Togahening, Adams, Blitzenstein, Cznechzaditzch—no use. I wonder where I caught that cold! Who the devil is there that I could ask?

[*Enter* THOMAS—OSSORY's *back toward door.*
THOMAS. Mr. Todd.   [*Enter* TODD—OSSORY *doesn't turn.*
OSSORY. I can't see him, Thomas. [*Turns.*] I beg your pardon, Mr. Todd. The fact is, I'm damnably worried over pay-day. I really don't know you well enough to ask you, perhaps, but the fact is, I've a good sound business proposition which I must put before some one, and I believe you're the very man to help me. Now——

[TODD *takes him by the shoulder and whispers in his ear.*

Why, really, that is good of you—damned good of you! Why, damme, sir! you're a public benefactor. Come, let us arrange the preliminaries——

[*They go out,* OSSORY *clinging tightly to* TODD's *arm.*
Enter MRS. OSSORY *and* CARR, *dressed for walking.*

MRS. OSSORY. She cut me! You saw it! She cut me absolutely dead!

CARR. Possibly she didn't see you.

[*As* MRS. OSSORY *is not looking, he employs a gesture which
lessens the likelihood of this, by calling attention to
her bulk.*

MRS. OSSORY. I know she saw me. My only Duchess!

CARR. There's better duchesses in Burke than ever came out of it, Mrs. Ossory. By the way, unless rumour lies, the jade! you can fly much higher than a paltry Duchess!

MRS. OSSORY. Why, why, what do you mean? Oh, dear Professor, how sweet of you! Or are you joking? Somehow

230

one never knows whether you are serious or not! But you wouldn't make fun of my embarrassments—Society is so serious, isn't it? But, oh do! do tell me what they say!

CARR. Well, Mrs. Ossory—you know our mysterious friend?

MRS. OSSORY. Mr. Todd?

CARR. Yes. Well, they say that—he is a King in his own country.

MRS. OSSORY. And I've always disliked and distrusted him so! But perhaps that was just the natural awe that I suppose one must always feel, even when one doesn't know, you know. I wonder, now, if we could get him to a little dinner. One could always pretend one didn't know who he was! Let me see, now! Caviar de sterlet royale——

CARR. Consommé royale, sole à la royale, timbale royale à l'empereur, bouchées à la reine, asperges à la royale, haunch of royal venison—can't insult him with mere baron of beef —pouding royale, glace à l'impératrice, canapé royale—you'll be able to *feed* him all right!

MRS. OSSORY. How clever you are, Professor! Thank you so much. Now who should we ask to meet him?

CARR. I rather expect you'll have to meet him *alone!*

MRS. OSSORY. *Tête-à-tête!* But would that be quite *proper,* Professor?

CARR. How very English!—all you English think that. But—royalty has its own etiquette.

[*Enter* CHARLEY.

Come along, Charley boy, and show me how the new engine works!

231

Never mind that old frump of a Duchess, Mrs. Ossory—perhaps Mr. Todd may call.   [*Goes out with* CHARLEY.

MRS. OSSORY. I do hope he meant it. But he's such a terrible man for pulling legs, as they call it.—I can't think where Euphemia picks up all her slang!—If that plain, quiet man should really be a crowned King! Oh! how I would frown at her! Ah! ah! Somebody coming.

        [*Enter* THOMAS.

THOMAS. Mr. Todd.   [*Enter* TODD.

MRS. OSSORY. Oh, my dear Mr. Todd, I am so glad to see you! I'm in such distress! You will help me, won't you?

    [TODD *bows, smiles, and whispers in her ear. She smiles all over.* TODD *offers his arm. She goes out on it, giggling and wriggling with pleasure. Enter* EUPHEMIA.

EUPHEMIA. I wonder where mother is! No, I don't want her. I'm too happy. How I love him! How proud I am—when another girl would be so shamed! I love him! I love him! Oh, what a world of ecstasy is this! To be his, and he mine! To be—oh! oh! I cannot bear the joy of it. I want to sit down and have a good cry. [*Sits, crying and laughing with the joy of it.*] Oh, loving Father of all, what a world Thou hast made! What a gift is life! How much it holds of love and laughter! Is there anything more, anything better? I cannot believe it. Is there anything, anybody that could make me happier?

THOMAS. Mr. Todd.   [*Enter* TODD.

EUPHEMIA. Good afternoon, Mr. Todd! So glad to see you! Why, how strange you look! What have you to say to me?   [TODD *whispers in her ear.*

EUPHEMIA. How splendid! You mean it? It is true? Better than all the rest! Come, come!

[*She throws her arm round his neck and runs laughing out of the room with him.*

[*Enter* CARR *and* CHARLEY, *a toy steam-engine puffing in front of them; they follow on hands and knees. The engine stops at the other end of the room.*

CHARLEY. Oh, my poor engine's stopped!

CARR. You must pour more spirit into it.

[CHARLEY *goes to the cupboard and gets it, busying himself until* CARR'S *exit.* CARR *sighs heavily, and sits down thoughtfully.*

Todd's been too frequently to this house. Well, Charley and I must get on as best we can. Life is a hard thing, my God!

" Meantime there is our life here. Well? "

It seems sometimes to me as if all the world's wisdom were summed up in that one Epicurus phrase. For if Todd has solved all their problems with a word, at least he supplies no hint of the answer to mine. For I—it seems I hardly know what question to ask!

Oh, Charley boy, the future is with you, and with your children—or, can humanity ever solve the great secret? Is progress a delusion? Are men mad? Is the great secret truly transcendental? We are like madmen, beating out our poor brains upon the walls of the Universe.

Is there no Power that might reveal itself?

[*Kneels.*] Who art Thou before whom all things are equal,

being as dust? Who givest his fame to the poet, his bankruptcy to the rich man? Who dost distinguish between the just and the unjust? Thou keeper of all secrets, of this great secret which I seek, and have nowise found! This secret for whose very shadowing-forth in parable I, who am young, strong, successful, beloved, most enviable of men, would throw it all away! Oh Thou who givest that which none other can give, who art Thou? How can I bargain with Thee? What shall I give that I may possess Thy secret? O question unavailing! For I know not yet Thy name! Who art Thou? Who art Thou?

THOMAS [*opening the door*]. Mr. Todd. [*Enter* TODD.

CARR [*rising*]. How are you? I'm afraid you find me distracted! Listen: all my life I have sought—nor counted the cost—for the secret of things. Science is baffled, for Knowledge hath no wings! Religion is baffled, for Faith hath no feet! Life itself—of what value is all this coil and tumult? Who shall give me the secret? What is the secret? [TODD *whispers in his ear.*

Why, thanks, thanks! What a fool I have been! I have always known who you were, of course, but how could I guess you had the key of things? Simple as A B C—or, rather, as A! And nothing to pay after all! "For of all Gods you only love not gifts." [*Ushers* TODD *to the door.*] I follow you.

[TODD *smiles kindly on him. They go out.*
[*The child turns; and, finding himself alone, begins to cry.*

CHARLIE. My nice man has gone away. Old Todd has taken him away. I think I hate that old Todd!

[*Enter* TODD.

MR. TODD

I hate you! I hate you! Where is my nice man?

[TODD *whispers in his ear.*

Oh, I see. It is when people get to be grown-ups that they don't like you any more. But I like you, Mr. Todd. Carry me pick-a-back!

[TODD *takes* CHARLIE *on his shoulder, and goes dancing from the room, the boy crowing with delight.*

CURTAIN.

THE GNOME

Lantern-light is over the fells
    When the sun has sunken low ;
Lantern-light and the moorland smells,
    The rain on the good brown soil.
Over the moorland we go, we go,
    Through the wet earth we toil. . . .

Sunken, sunken was the sun
    Ere ever the moon uprose,
And the tall dark trees cast shadows dun
    Over the lonely way ;
Over the moorland the long path goes
    We trod at the close of day.

We sped to reach the dark green hill,
    The Hill of the Bloody Bowl,
And the shadows were watching, watching us still
    As we crept in the shadowless path,
Over the moor to the Mother Troll
    With the heart that was pierced in wrath.

THE GNOME

Stumbling over the fallen leaves,
  Sliding over the dew,
Staring up at the barley sheaves
  That nod in the autumn wind,
We pushed and jostled the twilight thro',
  Shrilling to those behind.

And ere the night had grown to noon
  We were under the Bloody Bowl,
And then uprose a huge pale moon
  Behind the shivering trees ;
And so we found the Mother Troll
  Well-skilled in mysteries.

She heard our coming, and rose to the door,
  And we hurried eagerly through ;
We entered in with a breeze from the moor,
  And stood by the fading pyre.
The air was smoky, the flame was blue,
  And the face of the Troll like fire.

And so we gave her the heart of the slain,
  That was slain for a dead man's sake ;
She chuckled low at each blackened vein
  Gory and brown and torn ;
She wriggled her sides like a wounded snake
  As she squeezed the blood into a horn.

THE EQUINOX

Far into the fire she cast the blood,
    And the flames grew twisted and red;
Her breast heaved with her passion's flood
    As a hollow-eyed ghost arose
Like a cloud of stench from the rotting dead
    When a wind from a pest-house blows.

She clasped the ghost to her skinny dugs,—
    No other love might she know,—
The dead man squirmed at her panting hugs,
    But she had her passionate will,
And a sobbing breeze began to blow
    From the top of the lonely hill.

And then a dim grey streak of dawn
    Came, and the sad ghost fled,
With staring sockets and jaw-bone drawn,
    Back to the desolate place;
The morning breeze grew still and dead
    As it played around his face.

So we fled from the Mother Troll
    Under the dawning grey;
We left the Hill of the Bloody Bowl
    Ere ever the sun uprose,
But the dead man's heart till Judgment-day
    Shall there with the Troll repose.

VICTOR B. NEUBURG.

REVIEWS

DARE TO BE WISE. By JOHN MCTAGGART ELLIS MCTAGGART Doctor in
Letters Fellow and Lecturer of Trinity College in Cambridge, Fellow of
the British Academy. Watts and Co., 17 Johnson's Court, Fleet Street,
E.C. Price 3*d*.

Only the Price Threepence saved my reason.

"Dare to be Wise" is startling enough; but when one saw Who it was
that advised it . . .

"Our object," quoth he ("our" being the "Heretics"), "is to promote
discussion upon religion, philosophy, and art. . . ."

These desperate conspirators! What is the Parry-lytic Liar about to
allow such things in Trinity?

"In seeking truth of all sorts many virtues are needed." This daring
thinker!

"Happiness and misery have much to do with welfare." These burning
words may rekindle the fires of Smithfield.

"Here we find the need of courage. For, if we are to think on these
matters at all, we must accept the belief for which we have evidence, and we
must reject the belief for which we have no evidence. . . . And, sometimes,
this is not easy."

This unworthy right hand!

We should not think of calling this Martyr to His Convictions, this Revolutionary Thinker, an ass in a lion's skin. For asses can kick. Shall we say
a sheep in wolf's clothing? For the Heretics are too clearly Sheep—probably
descended from Mary's little lamb. If the Dean were to frown, they would
all take to their heels, and break the record for attending chapel.

In fact, this is what happened, when he did frown! Just like the
Rationalists themselves when they disowned and deserted Harry Boulter.

I am coming round to the belief that the best test of a religion is the
manhood of its adherents rather than its truth. Better believe a lie than act
like a coward!

And of all the pusillanimous puppies I have ever heard of, there are none
to beat the undergraduates who wagged their rudimentary tails round the
toothless old hound that yelped "Dare to be wise" on last 8th of December.

I hate Christianity as Socialists hate soap; but I would rather be saved

239

with Livingstone and Gordon, Havelock and Nicholson, than damned with Charles Watts and

> John McTaggart
> Ellis McTaggart
> Doctor in Letters
> Fellow and Lecturer
> Of Trinity College
> In Cambridge, and Fellow
> Of the Berritish
> Ac—ad—em—y.

I wonder, by the way, whether "letters" isn't a {misprint. If not, did he really qualify at the Sorbonne ?

ALEISTER CROWLEY.

THE ARCANE SCHOOLS. By JOHN YARKER. William Tait, 3 Wellington Park Avenue, Belfast. 12s. net.

The reader of this treatise is at first overwhelmed by the immensity of Brother Yarker's erudition. He seems to have examined and quoted every document that ever existed. It is true that he occasionally refers to people like Hargrave Jennings, A. E. Waite, and H. P. Blavatsky as if they were authorities ; but whoso fishes with a net of so wide a sweep as Brother Yarker's must expect to pull in some worthless fish. This accounts for Waite's contempt of him ; imagine Walford Bodie reviewing a medical book which referred to him as an authority on paralysis !

The size of the book, too, is calculated to effray : reading it has cost me many pounds in gondolas ! And it is the essential impossibility of all works of this kind that artistic treatment is not to be attained.

But Brother Yarker has nobly suppressed a Spencerian tendency to ramble ; he has written with insight, avoided pedantry, and made the dreary fields of archeology blossom with flowers of interest.

Accordingly, we must give him the highest praise, for he has made the best possible out of what was nearly the worst possible.

He has abundantly proved his main point, the true antiquity of some Masonic system. It is a parallel to Frazer's tracing of the history of the Slain God.

But why is there no life in any of our Slain God rituals ? It is for us to restore them by the Word and the Grip.

For us, who have the inner knowledge, inherited or won, it remains to restore the true rites of Attis, Adonis, Osiris, of Set, Serapis, Mithras, and Abel.

ALEISTER CROWLEY.

THE HERB DANGEROUS

PART IV

A FEW EXTRACTS FROM H. G. LUDLOW,

THE HASHEESH EATER

WHICH BEAR UPON THE PECULIAR CHARACTERISTICS OF THE DRUG'S ACTION

THE HASHEESH EATER

FOR a place, New York for instance, a stranger accounts, not by saying that any one of the many who testify to its existence copied from another, but by acknowledging " there is such a place." So do I account for the fact by saying " there is such a fact."

We try to imitate Eastern narrative, but in vain. Our minds can find no clew to its strange untrodden by-ways of speculation ; our highest soarings are still in an atmosphere which feels heavy with the reek and damp of ordinary life.

We fail to account for those storm-wrapped peaks of sublimity which hover over the path of Oriental story, or those beauties which, like rivers of Paradise, make music beside it.

We are all of us taught to say, " The children of the East live under a sunnier sky than their Western brethren : they are the *repositors* of centuries of tradition ; their semi-civilised imagination is unbound by the fetters of logic and the schools." But the Ionians once answered all these conditions, yet Homer sang no Eblis, no superhuman journey on the wings of genii through infinitudes of rosy ether. At one period of their history, France, Germany, and England abounded in all the characteristics of the untutored Old World mind, yet when did an echo of Oriental music ring from the lute of minstrel, *minnesinger,* or *trouvère* ? The difference can not be accounted for by climate, religion, or manners. It is not the supernatural in Arabian story which is inexplicable, but the peculiar phase of the supernatural both in beauty and terror.

I say inexplicable, because to me, in common with all around me, it bore this character for years. In later days, I believe, and now with all due modesty assert, I unlocked the secret, not by a hypothesis, not by processes of reasoning, but by journeying through those self-same fields of weird experience which are dinted by the sandals of the glorious old dreamers of the East. Standing on the same mounts of vision where they stood, listening to the same gurgling melody that broke from their enchanted fountains, yes, plunging into their rayless caverns of sorcery, and imprisoned with their genie in the unutterable silence of the fathomless sea, have I dearly bought the right to come to men with the chart of my wanderings in my hands, and unfold to them the foundations of the fabric of Oriental story.

The secret lies in the use of hasheesh. A very few words will suffice to tell what hasheesh is. In northern latitudes the hemp plant (*Cannabis sativa*) grows almost entirely to fibre, becoming, in virtue of this quality, the great resource for mats and cordage. Under a southern sun this same plant loses its fibrous texture, but secretes, in quantities equal to one-third of its bulk, an opaque and greenish resin. Between the northern and the southern hemp there is no difference, except the effect of diversity of climate upon the same vegetable essence ; yet naturalists, misled by the much greater extent of gummy secretion in the latter, have distinguished it from its brother of the colder soil by the name *Cannabis indica.* The

244

resin of the *Cannabis indica* is hasheesh. From time im-
memorial it has been known among all the nations of the East
as possessing powerful stimulant and narcotic properties ;
throughout Turkey, Persia, Nepaul, and India it is used at
this day among all classes of society as an habitual indulgence.
The forms in which it is employed are various. Sometimes
it appears in the state in which it exudes from the mature
stalk, as a crude resin ; sometimes it is manufactured into a
conserve with clarified butter, honey, and spices ; sometimes
a decoction is made of the flowering tops in water or arrack.
Under either of these forms the method of administration is by
swallowing. Again, the dried plant is smoked in pipes or
chewed, as tobacco among ourselves.

. . . a pill sufficient to balance the ten-grain weight of the
scales. This, upon the authority of Pereira and the Dispen-
satory, I swallowed without a tremor as to the danger of the
result.

Making all due allowance for the fact that I had not taken
my hasheesh bolus fasting, I ought to experience its effects
within the next four hours. That time elapsed without bring-
ing the shadow of a phenomenon. It was plain that my dose
had been insufficient.

For the sake of observing the most conservative prudence,
I suffered several days to go by without a repetition of the
experiment, and then, keeping the matter equally secret, I
administered to myself a pill of fifteen grains. This second
was equally ineffectual with the first.

Gradually, by five grains at a time, I increased the dose to
thirty grains, which I took one evening half an hour after
tea.

THE EQUINOX

I had now almost come to the conclusion that I was absolutely unsusceptible of the hasheesh influence. Without any expectation that this last experiment would be more successful than the former ones, and indeed with no realisation of the manner in which the drug affected those who did make the experiment successfully, I went to pass the evening at the house of an intimate friend. In music and conversation the time passed pleasantly. The clock struck ten, reminding me that three hours had elapsed since the dose was taken, and as yet not an unusual symptom had appeared. I was provoked to think that this trial was as fruitless as its predecessors.

Ha! what means this sudden thrill? A shock, as of some unimagined vital force, shoots without warning through my entire frame, leaping to my fingers' ends, piercing my brain, startling me till I almost spring from my chair.

I could not doubt it. I was in the power of the hasheesh influence. My first emotion was one of uncontrollable terror—a sense of getting something which I had not bargained for. That moment I would have given all I had or hoped to have to be as I was three hours before.

No pain anywhere—not a twinge in any fibre—yet a cloud of unutterable strangeness was settling upon me, and wrapping me impenetrably in from all that was natural or familiar.

As I heard once more the alien and unreal tones of my own voice, I became convinced that it was some one else who spoke, and in another world. I sat and listened ; still the voice kept speaking. Now for the first time I experienced that vast change which hasheesh makes in all measurements of time. The first word of the reply occupied a period suffi-

246

cient for the action of a drama ; the last left me in complete ignorance of any point far enough back in the past to date the commencement of the sentence. Its enunciation might have occupied years. I was not in the same life which had held me when I heard it begun.

And now, with time, space expanded also. At my friend's house one particular arm-chair was always reserved for me. I was sitting in it at a distance of hardly three feet from the centre table around which the members of the family were grouped. Rapidly that distance widened. The whole atmosphere seemed ductile, and spun endlessly out into great spaces surrounding me on every side. We were in a vast hall, of which my friends and I occupied opposite extremities. The ceiling and the walls ran upward with a gliding motion as if vivified by a sudden force of resistless growth.

Oh ! I could not bear it. I should soon be left alone in the midst of an infinity of space. And now more and more every moment increased the conviction that I was watched. I did not know then, as I learned afterward, that suspicion of all earthly things and persons was the characteristic of the hasheesh delirium.

In the midst of my complicated hallucination, I could perceive that I had a dual existence. One portion of me was whirled unresistingly along the track of this tremendous experience, the other sat looking down from a height upon its double, observing, reasoning, and serenely weighing all the phenomena. This calmer being suffered with the other by sympathy, but did not lose its self-possession.

The servant had not come.

THE EQUINOX

"Shall I call her again?" "Why, you have this moment called her." "Doctor," I replied solemnly, and in language that would have seemed bombastic enough to any one who did not realise what I felt, "I will not believe you are deceiving me, but to me it appears as if sufficient time has elapsed since then for all the Pyramids to have crumbled back to dust."

And now, in another life, I remembered that far back in the cycles I had looked at my watch to measure the time through which I passed. The impulse seized me to look again. The minute-hand stood half-way between fifteen and sixteen minutes past eleven. The watch must have stopped; I held it to my ear: no, it was still going. I had travelled through all that immeasurable chain of dreams in thirty seconds. "My God!" I cried, "I am in eternity." In the presence of that first sublime revelation of the soul's own time, and her capacity for an infinite life, I stood trembling with breathless awe. Till I die, that moment of unveiling will stand in clear relief from all the rest of my existence. I hold it still in unimpaired remembrance as one of the unutterable sanctities of my being. The years of all my earthly life to come can never be as long as those thirty seconds.

Before entering on the record of this new vision I will make a digression for the purpose of introducing two laws of the hasheesh operation, which, as explicatory, deserve a place here. First, after the completion of any one fantasia has arrived, there almost invariably succeeds a shifting of the action to some other stage entirely different in its surroundings. In this transition the general character of the emotion may remain unchanged. I may be happy in Paradise and happy at the sources of the Nile, but seldom, either in Paradise or on the Nile, twice in succession. I may writhe in Etna and burn unquenchably in Gehenna, but almost never, in the course of the same delirium, shall Etna or Gehenna witness my torture a second time.

Second, after the full storm of a vision of intense sublimity has blown past the hasheesh-eater, his next vision is generally of a quiet, relaxing, and recreating nature. He comes down from his clouds or up from his abyss into a middle ground of gentle shadows, where he may rest his eyes from the splendour of the seraphim or the flames of fiends. There is a wise philosophy in this arrangement, for otherwise the soul would soon burn out in the excess of its own oxygen. Many a time, it seems to me, has my own thus been saved from extinction.

When I woke it was morning—actually morning, and not a hasheesh hallucination. The first emotion that I felt upon opening my eyes was happiness to find things again wearing a natural air. Yes; although the last experience of which I had been conscious had seemed to satisfy every human want, physical or spiritual, I smiled on the four plain white walls of my bed-chamber, and hailed their familiar unostentatiousness with a pleasure which had no wish to transfer itself to arabesque or rainbows. It was like returning home from an eternity spent in loneliness among the palaces of strangers. Well may I say an eternity, for during the whole day I could not rid myself of the feeling that I was separated from the preceding one by an immeasurable lapse of time. In fact, I never got wholly rid of it.

I rose that I might test my reinstated powers, and see if the restoration was complete. Yes, I felt not one trace of bodily weariness nor mental depression. Every function had returned to its normal state, with the one exception mentioned; memory could not efface the traces of my having passed through a great mystery.

No. I never should take it again.

I did not know myself; I did not know hasheesh. There are temperaments, no doubt, upon which this drug produces, as a reactory result, physical and mental depression. With me this was never the case. Opium and liquors fix themselves as a habit by becoming necessary to supply that nervous waste which they in the first place occasioned. The lassitude which succeeds their exaltation demands a renewed indulgence, and accordingly every gratification of the appetite is parent to the next. But no such element entered into the causes which attached me to hasheesh. I speak confidently, yet without exaggeration, when I say that I have spent many an hour in torture such as was never known by Cranmer at the stake, or Gaudentio di Lucca in the Inquisition, yet out of the depths of such experience *I* have always come without a trace of its effect in diminished strength or buoyancy.

Had the first experiment been followed by depression, I had probably never repeated it. At any rate, unstrung muscles and an enervated mind could have been resisted much more effectually when they pleaded for renewed indulgence than the form which the fascination actually took. For days I was even unusually strong; all the forces of life were in a state of pleasurable activity, but the memory of the wondrous glories which I had beheld wooed me continually like an irresistible sorceress. I could not shut my eyes for midday musing without beholding in that world, half dark, half light, beneath the eyelids, a steady procession of delicious images which the severest will could not banish nor dim. Now through an immense and serene sky floated luxurious argosies of clouds continually changing form and tint through an infinite cycle of mutations.

Now, suddenly emerging from some deep embowerment of woods, I stood upon the banks of a broad river that curved far off into dreamy distance, and glided noiselessly past its jutting headlands, reflecting a light which was not of the sun nor of the moon, but midway between them, and here and there thrilling with subdued prismatic rays. Temples and gardens, fountains and vistas stretched continually through my waking or sleeping imagination, and mingled themselves with all I heard, or read, or saw. On the pages of Gibbon the palaces and lawns of Nicomedia were illustrated with a hasheesh tint and a hasheesh reality ; and journeying with old Dan Chaucer, I drank in a delicious landscape of revery along all the road to Canterbury. The music of my vision was still heard in echo; as the bells of Bow of old time called to Whittington, so did it call to me—"Turn again, turn again." And I turned.

It will be remembered that the hasheesh states of ecstasy always alternate with less intense conditions, in which the prevailing phenomena are those of mirth or tranquillity In accordance with this law, in the present instance, Dan, to whom I had told my former experience, was not surprised to hear me break forth at the final cadence of our song into a peal of unextinguishable laughter, **but** begged to know what was its cause, that he might laugh **too.** I could only cry out that my right leg was a tin case filled with stair-rods, and as I limped along, keeping that member perfectly rigid, both from fear of cracking the metal and the difficulty of bending it, I heard the rattle of the brazen contents shaken from side to side with feelings of the most supreme absurdity possible to the human soul. Presently the leg was restored to its former state, but in the interim its mate had grown to a size which would have made it a very respectable trotter for Brian Boru or one of the Titans. Elevated some few hundred feet into the firmament, I was compelled to hop upon my giant pedestal in a way very ungraceful in a world where two legs were the fashion, and eminently disagreeable to the slighted member, which sought in vain to reach the earth with struggles amusing from their very insignificance. This ludicrous affliction being gradually removed, I went on my way quietly until we again began to be surrounded by the houses of the town.

And now that unutterable thirst which characterises hasheesh came upon me. I could have lain me down and lapped dew from the grass. I must drink, wheresoever, howsoever. We soon reached home—soon, because it was not five squares off from where we sat down, yet ages, from the thirst which consumed me and the expansion of time in which I lived. I came into the house as one would approach a fountain in the desert, with a wild bound of exultation, and gazed with miserly eyes at the draught which my friend poured out for me until the glass was brimming. I clutched it—I put it to my lips. Ha! a surprise! It was not water, but the most delicious metheglin in which ever bard of the Cymri drank the health of Howell Dda. It danced and sparkled like some liquid metempsychosis of amber; it gleamed with the spiritual fire of a thousand chrysolites. To sight, to taste it was metheglin, such as never mantled in the cups of the Valhalla.

Hasheesh I called the " drug of travel," and I had only to direct my thoughts strongly toward a particular part of the world previously to swallowing my bolus to make my whole fantasia in the strongest possible degree topographical.

There are two facts which I have verified as universal by repeated experiment, which fall into their place here as aptly as they can in the course of my narrative. First: At two different times, when body and mind are apparently in precisely analogous states, when all circumstances, exterior and interior, do not differ tangibly in the smallest respect, the same dose of the same preparation of hasheesh will frequently produce diametrically opposite effects. Still further, I have taken at one time a pill of thirty grains, which hardly gave a perceptible phenomenon, and at another, when my dose had been but half that quantity, I have suffered the agonies of a martyr, or rejoiced in a perfect phrensy. So exceedingly variable are its results, that, long before I abandoned the indulgence, I took each successive bolus with the consciousness that I was daring an uncertainty as tremendous as the equipoise between hell and heaven. Yet the fascination employed Hope as its advocate, and won the suit. Secondly: If, during the ecstasy

of hasheesh delirum, another dose, however small—yes, though
it be no larger than half a pea—be employed to prolong the
condition, such agony will inevitably ensue as will make the
soul shudder at its own possibility of endurance without
annihilation. By repeated experiments, which now occupy
the most horrible place upon my catalogue of horrible remem-
brances, have I proved that, among all the variable phenomena
of hasheesh, this alone stands unvarying. The use of it
directly after any other stimulus will produce consequences as
appalling.

I extinguished my light. To say this may seem trivial,
but it is as important a matter as any which it is possible to
notice. The most direful suggestions of the bottomless pit
may flow in upon the hasheesh eater through the very medium
of darkness. The blowing out of a candle can set an un-
fathomed barathrum wide agape beneath the flower-wreathed
table of his feast, and convert his palace of sorcery into a
Golgotha. Light is a necessity to him, even when sleeping;
it must tinge his visions, or they assume a hue as sombre as
the banks of Styx.

It was an awaking, which, for torture, had no parallel in
all the stupendous domain of sleeping incubus. Beside my
bed in the centre of the room stood a bier, from whose
corners drooped the folds of a heavy pall; outstretched upon
it lay in state a most fearful corpse, whose livid face was
distorted with the pangs of assassination. The traces of a
great agony were frozen into fixedness in the tense position of
every muscle, and the nails of the dead man's fingers pierced

his palms with the desperate clinch of one who has yielded not without agonising resistance. Two tapers at his head, two at his feet, with their tall and unsnuffed wicks, made the ghastliness of the bier more luminously unearthly, and a smothered laugh of derision from some invisible watcher ever and anon mocked the corpse, as if triumphant demons were exulting over their prey. I pressed my hands upon my eye-balls till they ached, in intensity of desire to shut out the spectacle; I buried my head in the pillow, that I might not hear that awful laugh of diabolic sarcasm.

But—oh horror immeasurable! I behold the walls of the room slowly gliding together, the ceiling coming down, the floor ascending, as of old the lonely captive saw them, whose cell was doomed to be his coffin. Nearer and nearer am I borne toward the corpse. I shrunk back from the edge of the bed; I cowered in most abject fear. I tried to cry out, but speech was paralysed. The walls came closer and closer together. Presently my hand lay on the dead man's fore-head. I made my arm as straight and rigid as a bar of iron; but of what avail was human strength against the contraction of that cruel masonry? Slowly my elbow bent with the ponderous pressure; nearer grew the ceiling—I fell into the fearful embrace of death. I was pent, I was stifled in the breathless niche, which was all of space still left to me. The stony eyes stared up into my own, and again the maddening peal of fiendish laughter rang close beside my ear. Now I was touched on all sides by the walls of the terrible press; there came a heavy crush, and I felt all sense blotted out in darkness.

I awoke at last; the corpse was gone, but I had taken his

255

place upon the bier. In the same attitude which he had kept I lay motionless, conscious, although in darkness, that I wore upon my face the counterpart of his look of agony. The room had grown into a gigantic hall, whose roof was framed of iron arches ; the pavement, the walls, the cornice were all of iron. The spiritual essence of the metal seemed to be a combination of cruelty and despair. Its massive hardness spoke a language which it is impossible to embody in words, but any one who has watched the relentless sweep of some great engine crank, and realised its capacity for murder, will catch a glimpse, even in the memory, of the thrill which seemed to say, " This iron is a tearless fiend," of the unutterable meaning I saw in those colossal beams and buttresses. I suffered from the vision of that iron as from the presence of a giant assassin.

But my senses opened slowly to the perception of still worse presences. By my side there gradually emerged from the sulphurous twilight which bathed the room the most horrible form which the soul could look upon unshattered—a fiend also of iron, white-hot and dazzling with the glory of the nether penetralia. A face that was the ferreous incarnation of all imaginations of malice and irony looked on me with a glare withering from its intense heat, but still more from the un-conceived degree of inner wickedness which it symbolised. I realised whose laughter I had heard, and instantly I heard it again. Beside him another demon, his very twin, was rocking a tremendous cradle framed of bars of iron like all things else, and candescent with as fierce a heat as the fiend's.

And now, in a chant of the most terrific blasphemy which it is possible to imagine, or rather of blasphemy so fearful that no human thought has ever conceived of it, both the demons broke forth, until I grew intensely wicked merely by hearing it. I still remember the meaning of the song they sang, although there is no language yet coined which will convey it, and far be it from me even to suggest its nature, lest I should seem to perpetuate in any degree such profanity as beyond the abodes of the lost no lips are capable of uttering. Every note of the music itself accorded with the thought as symbol represents essence, and with its clangour mixed the maddening creak of the for ever oscillating cradle, until I felt driven into a ferocious despair. Suddenly the nearest fiend, snatching up a pitchfork (also of white-hot iron), thrust it into my writhing side, and hurled me shrieking into the fiery cradle. I sought in my torture to scale the bars; they slipped from my grasp and under my feet like the smoothest icicles. Through increasing grades of agony I lay unconsumed, tossing from side to side with the rocking of the dreadful engine, and still above me pealed the chant of blasphemy, and the eyes of demoniac sarcasm smiled at me in mockery of a mother's gaze upon her child.

"Let us sing him," said one of the fiends to the other, "the lullaby of Hell." The blasphemy now changed into an awful word-picturing of eternity, unveiling what it was, and dwelling with raptures of malice upon its infinitude, its sublimity of growing pain, and its privation of all fixed points which might mark it into divisions. By emblems common to all language rather than by any vocal words, did they sing this frightful apocalypse, yet the very emblems had a sound as distinct as tongue could give them. This was one, and the only one of their representatives that I can remember. Slowly they began, 'To-day is father of to-morrow, to-morrow hath a son that shall beget the day succeeding." With increasing rapidity they sang in this way, day by day, the genealogy of a thousand years, and I traced on the successive generations, without a break in one link, until the rush of their procession reached a rapidity so awful as fully to typify eternity itself; and still I fled on through that burning genesis of cycles. I feel that I do not convey my meaning, but may no one else ever understand it better.

Withered like a leaf in the breath of an oven, after millions of years I felt myself tossed upon the iron floor. The fiends had departed, the cradle was gone. I stood alone, staring into immense and empty spaces. Presently I found that I was in a colossal square, as of some European city, alone at the time of evening twilight, and surrounded by houses hundreds of stories high. I was bitterly athirst. I ran to the middle of the square, and reached it after an infinity of travel. There was a fountain carved in iron, every jet inimitably sculptured in mockery of water, yet dry as the ashes of a furnace. " I shall perish with thirst," I cried. " Yet one more trial. There must be people in all these immense houses. Doubtless they love the dying traveller, and will give him to drink. Good friends! water! water!" A horribly deafening din poured down on me from the four sides of the square. Every sash of all the hundred stories of every house in that colossal quadrangle flew up as by one spring. Awakened by my call, at every window stood a terrific maniac. Sublimely in the air above me, in front, beside me, on either hand, and behind my back, a wilderness of insane faces gnashed at me, glared, gibbered, howled, laughed horribly, hissed and cursed. At the unbearable sight

THE HASHEESH EATER

I myself became insane, and leaping up and down, mimicked them all, and drank their demented spirit.

Hasheesh is indeed an accursed drug, and the soul at last pays a most bitter price for all its ecstasies; moreover, the use of it is not the proper means of gaining any insight, yet who shall say that at that season of exaltation I did not know things as they are more truly than ever in the ordinary state? Let us not assert that the half-careless and uninterested way in which we generally look on nature is the normal mode of the soul's power of vision. There is a fathomless meaning, an intensity of delight in all our surroundings, which our eyes must be unsealed to see. In the jubilance of hasheesh, we have only arrived by an improper pathway at the secret of that infinity of beauty which shall be beheld in heaven and earth when the veil of the corporeal drops off, and we know as we are known. Then from the muddy waters of our life, defiled by the centuries of degeneracy through which they have flowed, we shall ascend to the old-time original fount, and grow rapturous with its apocalyptic draught.

I do not remember whether I have yet mentioned that in the hasheesh state an occasional awaking occurs, perhaps as often as twice in an hour (though I have no way of judging accurately, from the singular properties of the hasheesh time), when the mind returns for an exceedingly brief space to perfect consciousness, and views all objects in their familiar light.

Awaking on the morrow after a succession of vague and

259

delicious dreams, I had not yet returned to the perfectly natural state. I now began to experience a law of hasheesh which developed its effects more and more through all future months of its use. With the progress of the hasheesh life, the effect of every successive indulgence grows more per-during until the hitherto isolated experiences become tangent to each other ; then the links of the delirium intersect, and at last so blend that the chain has become a continuous band, now resting with joyous lightness as a chaplet, and now mightily pressing in upon the soul like the glowing hoop of iron which holds martyrs to the stake. The final months of this spell-bound existence, be it terminated by mental annihilation or by a return into the quiet and mingled facts of humanity, are passed in one unbroken yet chequered dream.

Moreover, through many ecstasies and many pains, I still supposed that I was only making experiments, and that, too, in the most wonderful field of mind which could be opened for investigation, and with an agent so deluding in its influence that the soul only became aware that the strength of a giant was needed to escape when its locks were shorn.

Upon William N—— hasheesh produced none of the effects characteristic of fantasia. There was no hallucination, no volitancy of unusual images before the eye when closed.

Circulation, however, grew to a surprising fulness and rapidity, accompanied by the same introversion of faculties and clear perception of all physical processes which startled me in my first experiment upon myself. There was stertorous breathing, dilatation of the pupil, and a drooping appearance of the eyelid, followed at last by a comatose state, lasting for hours, out of which it was almost impossible fully to arouse the energies. These symptoms, together with a peculiar rigidity of the muscular system, and inability to measure the precise compass and volume of the voice when speaking, brought the case nearer in resemblance to those recorded by Dr. O'Shaughnessy, of Calcutta, as occurring under his immediate inspection among the natives of India, than any I have ever witnessed.

At half-past seven in the evening, and consequently after supping instead of before, as I should have preferred, he took twenty-five grains of the drug. This may seem a large bolus to those who are aware that from fifteen grains I frequently got the strongest cannabine effect; but it must be kept in mind that, to secure the full phenomena, a much greater dose is necessary in the first experiment than ever after. Unlike all other stimuli with which I am acquainted, hasheesh, instead of requiring to be increased in quantity as existence in its use proceeds, demands rather a diminution, seeming to leave, at the return of the natural state (if I may express myself by rather a material analogy), an unconsumed capital of exaltation for the next indulgence to set up business upon.

For a while we walked silently. Presently I felt my companion shudder as he leaned upon my arm. "What is the matter, Bob?" I asked. "Oh! I am in unbearable horror," he replied. "If you can, save me!" "How do you suffer?" "This shower of soot which falls on me from heaven is dreadful!"

THE EQUINOX

I sought to turn the current of his thoughts into another channel, but he had arrived at that place in his experience where suggestion is powerless. His world of the Real could not be changed by any inflow from ours of the Shadowy. I reached the same place in after days, and it was then as impossible for any human being to alter the condition which enwrapped me as it would have been for a brother on earth to stretch out his hands and rescue a brother writhing in the pangs of immortality. There are men in Oriental countries who make it their business to attend hasheesh-eaters during the fantasia, and profess to be able to lead them constantly in pleasant paths of hallucination. If indeed they possess this power, the delirium which they control must be a far more ductile state than any I have witnessed occurring under the influence of hasheesh at its height. In the present instance I found all suggestion powerless. The inner actuality of the visions and the terror of external darkness both defeated me.

And now, in the midst of the darkness, there suddenly stood a wheel like that of a lottery, surrounded by one luminous spot, which illustrated all its movements. It began slowly to revolve; its rapidity grew frightful, and out of its opening flew symbols which indicated to him, in regular succession, every minutest act of his past life: from his first unfilial disobedience in childhood—the refusal upon a certain day, as far back as infancy, to go to school when it was enjoined upon him, to the latest deed of impropriety he had committed—all his existence fled before him like lightning in those burning emblems. Things utterly forgotten—things at the time of their first presence considered trivial acts—as small as the cutting of a willow wand, all fled by his sense in arrow-flight; yet he remembered them as real incidents, and recognised their order in his existence.

This phenomenon is one of the most striking exhibitions of the state in which the higher hasheesh exaltation really exists. It is a partial sundering, for the time, of those ties which unite soul and body. That spirit should ever lose the traces of a single impression is impossible.

In the morning he awoke at the usual time; but, his temperament being perhaps more sensitive than mine, the hasheesh delight, without its hallucination, continued for several days.

And now a new fact flashed before me. This agony was not new; I had felt it ages ago, in the same room, among the same people, and hearing the same conversation. To most men, such a sensation has happened at some time, but it is seldom more than vague and momentary. With me it was sufficiently definite and lasting to be examined and located as an actual memory. I saw it in an instant, preceded and followed by the successions of a distinctly recalled past life.

What is the philosophy of this fact? If we find no ground for believing that we have ever lived self-consciously in any other state, and cannot thus explain it, may not this be the solution of the enigma? At the moment of the soul's reception of a new impression, she first accepts it as a thing entirely of the sense; she tells us how large it is, and of what quality. To this definition of its boundaries and likeness succeeds, at times of high activity, an intuition of the fact that the sensation shall be perceived again in the future unveiling that is to throw open all the past. Prophetically she notes it down upon the indestructible leaves of her diary, assured that it is to come out in the future revelation. Yet we who, from the tendency of our thought, reject all claims to any knowledge of the future, can only acknowledge perceptions as of the present or the past, and accordingly refer the dual realisation to some period gone by. We perceive the correspondence of two sensations, but, by an instantaneous process, give the second one a wrong position in the succession of experiences. The soul is regarded as the historian when she is in reality the sibyl; but the misconception takes place in such a microscopic portion of time that detection is impossible. In the hasheesh expansion of seconds into minutes, or even according to a much mightier ratio, there is an opportunity thoroughly to scrutinise the hitherto evanescent phenomena, and the truth comes out. How many more such prophecies as these may have been rejected through the gross habit of the body we may never know until spirit vindicates her claim in a court where she must have audience.

In this world we are but half spirit; we are thus able to hold only the perceptions and emotions of half an orb. Once fully rounded into symmetry ourselves, we shall have strength to bear the pressure of influences from a whole sphere of truth and loveliness.

It is this present half-developed state of ours which makes the infinitude of the hasheesh awakening so unendurable, even when its sublimity is the sublimity of delight. We have no

264

longer anything to do with horizons, and the boundary which was at once our barrier and our fortress is removed, until we almost perish from the inflow of perceptions.

It would be no hard task to prove, to a strong probability, at least, that the initiation to the Pythagorean mysteries, and the progressive instruction that succeeded it, to a considerable extent consisted in the employment, judiciously, if we may use the word, of hasheesh, as giving a critical and analytic power to the mind, which enabled the neophyte to roll up the murk and mist from beclouded truths till they stood distinctly seen in the splendour of their own harmonious beauty as an intuition.

One thing related of Pythagoras and his friends has seemed very striking to me. There is a legend that, as he was passing over a river, its waters called up to him in the presence of his followers, " Hail ! Pythagoras."

Frequently, while in the power of the hasheesh delirium, have I heard inanimate things sonorous with such voices. On every side they have saluted me, from rocks, and trees, and waters, and sky, in my happiness filling me with intense exultation as I heard them welcoming their master ; in my agony heaping nameless curses on my head as I went away into an eternal exile from all sympathy. Of this tradition of Iamblichus I feel an appreciation which almost convinces me that the voice of the river was indeed heard, though only by the quickened mind of some hasheesh-glorified esoteric. Again, it may be that the doctrine of the metempsychosis was first communicated to Pythagoras by Theban priests ; but the astonishing illustration which hasheesh would contribute to

26

this tenet should not be overlooked in our attempt to assign its first suggestion and succeeding spread to their proper causes.

I looked, and lo! all the celestial hemisphere was one terrific brazen bell, which rocked upon some invisible adamantine pivot in the infinitudes above. When I came it was voiceless, but I soon knew how it was to sound. My feet were quickly chained fast to the top of heaven, and, swinging with my head downward, I became its tongue. Still more mightily swayed that frightful bell, and now, tremendously crashing, my head smote against its side. It was not the pain of the blow, though that was inconceivable, but the colossal roar that filled the universe, and rent my brain also, which blotted out in one instant all sense, thought, and being. In an instant I felt my life extinguished, but knew that it was by annihilation, not by death.

When I awoke out of the hasheesh state I was as overwhelmed to find myself still in existence as a dead man of the last century could be were he now suddenly restored to earth. For a while, even in perfect consciousness, I believed I was still dreaming, and to this day I have so little lost the memory of that one demoniac toll, that while writing these lines I have put my hand to my forehead, hearing and feeling something, through the mere imagination, which was an echo of the original pang. It is this persistency of impressions which explains the fact of the hasheesh state, after a certain time, growing more and more every day a thing of agony. It is not because the body becomes worn out by repeated nervous shocks; with some constitutions, indeed, this wearing may occur; it never did with me, as I have said, even to the extent of producing muscular weakness, yet the universal law of constantly accelerating diabolisation of visions held good as much in my case as in any others; but a thing of horror once experienced became a κτῆμα ἐς ἀεί, an inalienable dower of hell; it was certain to reproduce itself in some—to God be the thanks if not in all—future visions. I had seen, for instance, in one of my states of ecstasy, a luminous spot on the firmament, a prismatic parhelion. In the midst of my delight of gazing on it, it had transferred itself mysteriously to my own heart, and there became a circle of fire, which gradually ate its way until the whole writhing organ was in a torturous blaze. That spot, seen again in an after-vision, through the memory of its former pain instantly wrought out for me the same accursed result. The number of such remembered faggots of fuel for direful suggestion of course increased proportionally to the prolonging of the hasheesh life, until at length there was hardly a visible or tangible object, hardly a phrase which could be spoken, that had not some such infernal potency as connected with an earlier effect of suffering.

Slowly thus does midnight close over the hasheesh-eater's heaven. One by one, upon its pall thrice dyed in Acharon, do the baleful lustres appear, until he walks under a hemisphere flaming with demon lamps, and upon a ground paved with tiles of hell. Out of this awful domain there are but three ways. Thank God that over this alluring gateway is not written,

"Lasciate ogni speranza voi ch' entrate!"

The first of these exits is insanity, the second death, the third abandonment. The first is doubtless oftenest trodden,

267

yet it may be long ere it reaches the final escape in oblivion, and it is as frightful as the domain it leaves behind. The second but rarely opens to the wretch unless he prises it open with his knife ; ordinarily its hinges turn lingeringly. Towards the last let him struggle, though a nightmare torpor petrify his limbs—though on either side of the road be a phalanx of monstrous Afreets with drawn swords of flame— though demon cries peal before him, and unimaginable houris beckon him back—over thorns, through furnaces, but into —Life !

To the first restaurant at hand we hastened. Passing in, I called for that only material relief which I have ever found for these spiritual sufferings—something strongly acid. In the East the form in use is sherbet ; mine was very sour lemonade. A glass of it was made ready, and with a small glass tube I drew it up, not being able to bear the shock of a large swallow. Relief came but very slightly—very slowly. Before the first glass was exhausted I called most imperatively for another one to be prepared as quickly as possible, lest the flames should spread by waiting. In this way I kept a man busy with the composition of lemonade after lemonade, plunging my tube over the edge of the drained tumbler into the full one with a precipitate haste for which there were mortal reasons, until six had been consumed.

I returned to hasheesh, but only when I had become hopeless of carrying out my first intention—its utter and immediate abandonment. I now resolved to abandon it gradually—to retreat slowly from my enemy, until I had passed the borders of his enchanted ground, whereon he warred with me at vantage. Once over the boundaries, and the nightmare spell unloosed, I might run for my life, and hope to distance him in my own recovered territory.

This end I sought to accomplish by diminishing the doses of the drug. The highest I had ever reached was a drachm, and this was seldom necessary except in the most unimpressible states of the brain, since, according to the law of the hasheesh operation which I have stated to hold good in my experience, a much less bolus was ordinarily sufficient to produce full effect at this time than when I commenced the indulgence. I now reduced my daily ration to ten or fifteen grains.

The immediate result of even this modified resumption of the habit was a reinstatement into the glories of the former life. I came out of my clouds; the outer world was reinvested with some claim to interest, and the lethal torpor of my mind was replaced by an airy activity. I flattered myself that there was now some hope of escape by grades of renunciation, and felt assured, moreover, that since I now seldom experienced anything approaching hallucination, I might pass through this gradual course without suffering on the way.

As lemon-juice had been sometimes an effectual cure for the sufferings of excess, I now discovered that a use of tobacco, to an extent which at other times would be immoderate, was a preventive of the horrors of abandonment.

As, some distance back, I have referred to my own experience upon the subject, asserting my ability at times to *feel sights, see sounds*, &c., I will not attempt to illustrate the present discussion by a narrative of additional portions of my own case. It might be replied to me, " Ah! yes, all very likely; but probably you are an exception to the general rule;

nobody else might be affected so." This was said to me quite frequently when, early in the hasheesh life, I enthusiastically related the most singular phenomena of my fantasy.

But there is no such thing true of the hasheesh effects. Just as inevitably as two men taking the same direction, and equally favoured by Providence, will arrive at the same place, will two persons of similar temperament come to the same territory in hasheesh, see the same mysteries of their being, and get the same hitherto unconceived facts. It is this characteristic which, beyond all gainsaying, proves the definite existence of the most wondrous of the hasheesh disclosed states of mind. The realm of that stimulus is no vagary; it as much exists as England. We are never so absurd as to expect to see insane men by the dozen all holding to the same hallucination without having had any communication with each other.

As I said once previously, after my acquaintance with the realm of witchery had become, probably, about as universal as anybody's, when I chanced to be called to take care of some one making the experiment for the first time (and I always was called), by the faintest word, often by a mere look, I could tell exactly the place that my patient had reached, and treat him accordingly. Many a time, by some expression which other bystanders thought ineffably puerile, have I recognised the landmark of a field of wonders wherein I have travelled in perfect ravishment. I understood the symbolisation, which they did not.

Though as perfectly conscious as in his natural state, and capable of apprehending all outer realities without hallucination, he still perceived every word which was spoken to him in the form of some visible symbol which most exquisitely embodied it. For hours every sound had its colour and its form to him as truly as scenery could have them.

The fact, never witnessed by me before, of a mind in that state being able to give its phenomena to another and philosophise about them calmly, afforded me the means of a most clear investigation. I found that his case was exactly analogous to those of B. and myself; for, like us, he recognised in distinct inner types every possible sensation, our words making a visible emblematic procession before his eyes, and every perception of whatever sense becoming tangible to him as form and audible as music.

THE BUDDHIST

THERE never was a face as fair as yours,
    A heart as true, a love as pure and keen.
These things endure, if anything endures.
But, in this jungle, what high heaven immures
    Us in its silence, the supreme serene
Crowning the dagoba, what destined die
    Rings on the table, what resistless dart
Strikes me?   I love you ; can you satisfy
    The hunger of my heart ?

Nay ; not in love, or faith, or hope is hidden
    The drug that heals my life ; I know too well
How all things lawful, and all things forbidden
Alike disclose no pearl upon the midden,
    Offer no key to unlock the gate of Hell.
There is no escape from the eternal round,
    No hope in love, or victory, or art.
There is no plumb-line long enough to sound
    The abysses of my heart !

THE BUDDHIST

There no dawn breaks ; no sunlight penetrates
    Its blackness ; no moon shines, nor any star.
For its own horror of itself creates
Malignant fate from all benignant fates,
    Of its own spite drives its own angel afar.
Nay ; this is the great import of the curse
    That the whole world is sick, and not a part.
Conterminous with its own universe
    The horror of my heart !

ANANDA VIJJA.

THE AGNOSTIC

An Agnostic is one who thinks that he knows everything.

Victor B. Neuburg.

THE MANTRA-YOGI

I

How should I seek to make a song for thee
    When all my music is to moan thy name?
    That long sad monotone—the same—the same—
Matching the mute insatiable sea
That throbs with life's bewitching agony,
    Too long to measure and too fierce to tame!
    An hurtful joy, a fascinating shame
Is this great ache that grips the heart of me.

Even as a cancer, so this passion gnaws
Away my soul, and will not ease its jaws
    Till I am dead. Then let me die! Who knows
But that this corpse committed to the earth
May be the occasion of some happier birth?
    Spring's earliest snowdrop? Summer's latest rose?

II

Thou knowest what asp hath fixed its lethal tooth
    In the white breast that trembled like a flower
    At thy name whispered. Thou hast marked how hour
By hour its poison hath dissolved my youth,

275

THE EQUINOX

Half skilled to agonise, half skilled to soothe
   This passion ineluctable, this power
   Slave to its single end, to storm the tower
That holdeth thee, who art Authentic Truth.

O golden hawk! O lidless eye! Behold
How the grey creeps upon the shuddering gold!
   Still I will strive! That by the striving broken
I may exhaust this me! That thou mayst sweep
Swift on the dead from thine all-seeing steep—
   And the unutterable word be spoken.

ALEISTER CROWLEY.

THE VIOLINIST

THE room was cloudy with a poisonous incense: saffron, opoponax, galbanum, musk, and myrrh, the purity of the last ingredient a curse of blasphemy, the final sneer; as a degenerate might insult a Raphael by putting it in a room devoted to debauchery.

The girl was tall and finely built, huntress-lithe. Her dress, close-fitted, was of a gold-brown silk that matched, but could not rival, the coils that bound her brow—glittering and hissing like snakes.

Her face was Greek in delicacy; but what meant such a mouth in it? The mouth of a satyr or a devil. It was full and strong, curved twice, the edges upwards, an angry purple, the lips flat. Her smile was like the snarl of a wild beast.

She stood, violin in hand, before the wall. Against it was a large tablet of mosaic; many squares and many colours. On the squares were letters in an unknown tongue.

She began to play, her gray eyes fixed upon one square on whose centre stood this character, N. It was in black on white; and the four sides of the square were blue, yellow, red, and black.

She began to play. The air was low, sweet, soft, and slow. It seemed that she was listening, not to her own playing, but for some other sound. Her bow quickened; the air grew harsh and wild, irritated; quickened further to a rush like flames devouring a hayrick; softened again to a dirge.

Each time she changed the soul of the song it seemed as if she was exhausted: as if she was trying to sound a particular phrase, and always fell back baffled at the last moment.

Nor did any light infuse her eyes. There was intentness, there was weariness, there was patience, there was alertness. And the room was strangely silent, unsympathetic to her mood. She was the dimmest thing in that gray light. Still she strove. She grew more tense, her mouth tightened, an ugly compression. Her eyes flashed with—was it hate? The soul of the song was now all anguish, all pleading, all despair —ever reaching to some unattainable thing.

She choked, a spasmodic sob. She stopped playing; she bit her lips, and a drop of blood stood on them scarlet against their angry purple, like sunset and storm. She pressed them to the square, and a smear stained the white. She caught at her heart; for some strange pang tore it.

Up went her violin, and the bow crossed it. It might have been the swords of two skilled fencers, both blind with mortal hate. It might have been the bodies of two skilled lovers, blind with immortal love.

She tore life and death asunder on her strings. Up, up soared the phoenix of her song; step by step on music's golden scaling-ladder she stormed the citadel of her Desire. The blood flushed and swelled her face beneath its sweat. Her eyes were injected with blood.

The song rose, culminated—overleapt the barriers, achieved its phrase.

She stopped; but the music went on. A cloud gathered

278

upon the great square, menacing and hideous. There was a tearing shriek above the melody.

Before her, his hands upon her hips, stood a boy. Golden haired he was, and red were his young lips, and blue his eyes. But his body was ethereal like a film of dew upon a glass, or rust clinging to an airy garment; and all was stained hideously with black.

"My Remenu!" she said. "After so long!"

He whispered in her ear.

The light behind her flickered and went out.

The spirit laid her violin and bow upon the ground.

The music went on—a panting, hot melody like mad eagles in death struggle with mountain goats, like serpents caught in jungle fires, like scorpions tormented by Arab girls.

And in the dark she sobbed and screamed in unison. She had not expected this: she had dreamt of love more passionate, of lust more fierce-fantastic, than aught mortal.

And this?

This real loss of a real chastity? This degradation not of the body, but of the soul? This white-hot curling flame—ice cold about her heart? This jagged lightning that tore her? This tarantula of slime that crawled up her spine?

She felt the blood running from her breasts, and its foam at her mouth.

Then suddenly the lights flamed up, and she found herself standing—reeling—her head sagging on his arm.

Again he whispered in her ear.

In his left hand was a little ebony box, a dark paste was in it. He rubbed a little on her lips.

And yet a third time he whispered in her ear.

THE EQUINOX

With an angel's smile—save for its subtlety—he was gone into the tablet.

She turned, blew on the fire, that started up friendly, and threw herself in an armchair. Idly she strummed old-fashioned simple tunes.

The door opened.

A jolly lad came in and shook the snow from his furs.

"Been too bored, little girl?" he said cheerily, confident.

"No, dear!" she said. "I've been fiddling a bit."

"Give me a kiss, Lily!"

He bent down and put his lips to hers; then, as if struck by lightning, sprawled, a corpse.

She looked down lazily through half-shut eyes with that smile of hers that was a snarl.

Francis Bendick.

EHE!

A DROP FROM THE SPONGE OF KNOWLEDGE

Characters. SIMPLEX.
SIMPLICIOR.
SIMPLICISSIMUS.
THE MOB OF THE PHILISTINES.

SIMPLEX.
Behold, O men: a Tree deep-rooted—
A hundred branches from the mighty Trunk,
And on each branch a hundred leaves—
An Axe—a Child—a Hand—a Will!

THE MOB.
Down with the old tree!

SIMPLEX. [*Unperturbed.*]
And Oh, He, Ho, the Will so powerful!
(After one million years the tree fell)
See the result: Toys, TOys, TOYs, TOYS!

SIMPLICISSIMUS. [*Dogmatic.*]
The Spirit of Persistency unborn.

THE MOB.
Down with the Lords!

THE EQUINOX

SIMPLEX.

> Behold again: an empty well—
> A crystal pure—a dry sea—
> Birds—a dead bird, a live bird, a phœnix—
> A dying immortal harlot-goddess—
> A cage (alas! it broke open
> In the year of the sixteenth Funeral).

THE MOB.

> Down with the birds!

SIMPLICIOR.

> Yet, neither Bird could re-enter it!

THE MOB.

> Beer and Cup-ties!

SIMPLICISSIMUS. [*Pointedly.*]

> The Spirit of Persistency conceived!

THE MOB.

> Down with the Spirits!

SIMPLEX.

> Behold again, Impatients, and decide:
> Two centres I saw, that were but one—
> A thick set of hair upon a white skull—
> A Spider patient (with my qualities),
> Slowly webbing the slightly soiled cavities—
> A lute, a rapturing lute *aux sons clairs*,
> (But Oh, He, Ho, for three weary years
> The lute hath no song!)—

EHE!

THE MOB.
      Down with the foreign bands!

SIMPLEX. [*Pale, but firm.*]
                                    A rotten corpse,
      Coming to life again (for it cried)—
      A deep, deep hole—a beardy man—and
      Linking,

SIMPLICIOR. [*Radiant.*]
                  Clearly linking,

SIMPLEX.
                              the 6 (or 7—
      The Spider counting as the skull's paying guest)
      The Stream from Heaven unto Us poured—

THE MOB.
      Down with 'em!

SIMPLEX. [*Smiling.*]
      Proving our love's old age in a youth renewed!

SIMPLICISSIMUS. [*Exultant.*]
      The Spirit of Persistency growing!

THE MOB.
      Hooray!

                              GEORGE RAFFALOVICH.

HALF-HOURS WITH FAMOUS MAHATMAS. No. 1

YOGI MAHATMA SRI AGAMYA PARAMAHAMSA GURU SWAMIJI is a certain Punjabi lala, who, on account of his tremendous voice and ferocious temper, has well earned for himself the name of The Tiger Mahatma.

My first acquaintance with His Holiness was in November 1906, when he paid his second visit to England. I had seen his name in the daily press, but before calling upon him, I had read up what I could about him in his book: "Sri Brahma Dhara," in the preface of which he is praised as follows:

"He seeks to do good, he accepts money from no one, and lives a very simple, pure life . . . I . . . was much impressed by his great breadth of mind, his sweet charity, and his loving kindness for every living thing. . . . These teachings . . . breathe love and kindness, and dwell upon the joys of pure clean living."

Forewarned is to be forearmed, and I had read the same type of "puff" on many a patent pill box!

On entering 70, Margaret Street I was shown upstairs and ushered into the den of Tiger Sri Agamya. Besides himself, there were three people in the room, two men and a woman, and as I entered one of the men, an American, was saying:

"O Mahatma! I haven't the faith, I can't get it!"

To which His Holiness roared out:

"You sheep are!... I no want sheep!... tigers I make ... tigers tear up sheep, go away! . . . no good, get intellect . . . get English! . . . no more!!"

The three then departed, and I was left alone with the Blessed One. Neither of us spoke for about ten minutes, then at length, after a go or two at his snuff-box, he gave a loud grunt, to which I replied in a solemn voice:

"O Mahatma, what is Truth?"

"No Truth! All illusion," he answered, "I am the Master, you become my disciple; I show you all things; I lead you to the ultimate reality . . . the supreme stage of the Highest . . . the infinite Ultimatum . . . the unlimited omniscience of eternal Wisdom—All this I give you if you have faith in me."

As faith is exceedingly cheap in this country, I offered him unlimited oceans of it; and at this he seemed very pleased, and laughed:

"Ha! ha! You make good tiger cub . . . you tear sheep up . . . all is illusion!" Then after a pause: "De vouman," pointing to the door, "is no good!" And then, without further hesitation, he entered upon a veritable Don Juan description of his earthly adventures. This I thought strange of so sober-minded a saint, and so put to him several questions concerning the Vedanta philosophy, and its most noted exponents, to see what he really did know.

"Do you know Swami Vivekananda?" I asked.

"Ha," he replied, "he no good, he my disciple, I am the master!"

"And Swami Dayanand Sarasvati?" I continued. The same answer was vouched to me, although this latter teacher had died at the age of seventy, forty years ago. Thinking it about time to change the conversation, I said:

"O Thou Shower from the Highest! Tell thy grovelling disciple what then *is* a 'lie'?"

"Ha!" he replied, "it is illusion, this truth that has been diverged from its real point . . . an illusive spring in the primo-genial fermentation of 'fee-no-me-non,' in this typo-cosmy apparent to the senses which you call 'de Vurld'!!!"

With this, and promises of oceans of blissful reality from the highest eternality of ultimate ecstasy, he bade me sit in a chair and blow alternately through my nostrils; and, if I had faith, so he assured me, I should in six months' time arrive at the supreme stage of the Highest in the infinite Ultimatum, and should burst as a chance illusively fermented bubble in the purest atmosphere of the highest reality.

The next occasion on which I saw the Mahatma was at a business meeting of his disciples held at 60, South Audley Street. His Holiness called them tiger-cubs, nevertheless seldom have I seen such a pen full of sheep. A man from Ilfracombe proposed this, and a man from Liverpool seconded that; at last a London plumber arose, and with great solemnity declared: "Gintlemen, hi taik hit 'is 'oliness his really 'oly, hin fact gintlemen hi taik hit 'e his Gawd; . . . hand so hi proposes the very least we can do for 'im his to subscribe yearly towards 'im foive shillins!" (" 'ear, 'ear" from a comrade in the corner). However, the sheep wouldn't have it, and the

286

little man sat down to ruminate over lead piping, and solder at twopence a stick.

During the summer of '07 I had little time to waste at number 60, and had almost forgotten about the Mahatma, who, so I had been told, had left England for America, when I received a card announcing his return, and asking me to be present at a general meeting.

This I did, and as usual was more than bored. After business was over the Mahatma entered the room, all his sheep flocking round him to seek the turnips of his wisdom. On these occasions he would ask questions and select subjects upon which his disciples were supposed to write essays. One of these, I can still remember, was: "How to help the helpless hands"; another was: "What is dis-satisfaction, and what is true satisfaction?" And the answer was: "Love fixed on mortal things, without the knowledge of its source, increases vibration and creates dissatisfaction ('mortal things' is good!)."

In his book, "Sri Brahma Dhara," which contains some of the most astonishing balderdash ever put in print, may be found his philosophy. This is a stewed-up hash of Yoga, Vedanta, and outrageous verbosity. "Love," he writes, "is the force of the magician Maya, and is the cause of all disorder" (it seems to be so even in his exalted position). "This force of love—in the state of circumgyration in the extended world—is the cause of all mental movements towards the feeling of easiness or uneasiness: but the mind enjoys eternal beatitude with perfect calmness, when the force of love is concentrated over the unlimited extension of silence" ('silence' is really choice!).

THE EQUINOX

"Virtue," he defines as: "the bent of mind towards self-command" (and evidently practises it). His morals are good; but his scientific conceptions really "take the cake!" "There are three kinds of animate creations in the world," he writes: "They are the creations from (1) the womb; (2) Eggs; (3) Perspiration. . . ." Another gem: "how is it that some of the bodies are male and some are female?" Answer: "If the male seed preponderates, a male body is produced; and if female, a female. While, when both are equally proportioned, an eunuch is born" (!).

At one of his male meetings—there were also female ones; but mixed bathing in the ocean of infinite bliss was not allowed—he related to us his pet story, of how he had "flumoxed" the chief engineer and the captain of the liner which had brought him back from America.

He informed them that coal and steam were absurd; what you want, he said, is to have two large holes made in the sides of your ship, then the air will blow into them and turn the wheels, and make the ship go. When the captain pointed out to him, that if a storm were to arise the water might possibly flow into the ship and sink it, he roared out, "No! no! . . . get English! . . . get intellect! see! see! de vind vill fill de ship and blow it out of de vater and take it across over de vaves!" —Since this now becomes public property there probably will be a slump in turbines!

It was towards the close of last October, when I received from a friend of mine—also a so-called disciple—a letter in which he wrote: "There was a devil of a row at 60 last night. M: pressed me to come to his weekly entertainments; so I came. He urged me to speak; so I spoke. He then revealed his divine self in an exceptionally able manner; I refrained from revealing mine. His divine self reminded one rather of a 'Navvy's Saturday Night, by Battersea Burns.'" He further urged me to go and see the Mahatma himself on the following Sunday; and this I did.

I arrived at 60, South Audley Street at seven o'clock. There were already about twenty sheepish-looking tigers present, and when the Mahatma entered the room, I sat down next to him; for, knowing, in case a scrimmage should occur, that a Hindoo cannot stomach a blow in the spleen, I thought it wisest to be within striking distance of him.

The Mahatma opened the evening's discussion by saying: "Humph . . . I am Agnostic, you are believers. I say 'I don't know,' you contradict me." And during the next hour and a half more Bunkum was talked in that room than I should say in Exeter Hall during the whole course of the last century. At last it ended, and though I had made various attempts to draw His Holiness into argument, I had as yet failed to unveil his divinity. He now started dictating his precious philosophy, and in such execrable English, that it was quite impossible to follow him, and I once or twice asked him to repeat what he had said, and as I did so I noticed that several of the faithful shivered and turned pale. At length came the word "expectation" or "separation," and as I could not catch which, I exclaimed "what?"

"You pig-faced man!" shouted His Holiness, "you dirty fellow, you come here to take away my disciples . . . vat you vant vith this: vat! vat! vat! vat! . . . You do no exercise, else you understand vat I say, dirty man!" And then turning to his three head bell-wethers who were sitting at a separate table he sneered:

"X——" (my friend present at the previous revelation of his divinity) "send this pig-one . . . eh?"

"I don't know why . . ." I began.

"Grutch, butch!" he roared, "you speak to me, you cow-eater! . . . get intellect," he yelled, "get English," he bellowed, and up he sprang from the table.

As I did not wish to be murdered, for he had now become a dangerous maniac, I rose, keeping my eyes on him, and taking up my hat and stick, which I had purposely placed just behind me, I quietly passed round the large table at which his terror-stricken fold sat gaping, and moved towards the door.

The whole assembly seemed petrified with fear. At first the Blesséd One appeared not to realize what had happened, so taken aback was he by any one having the audacity to leave the room without his permission: then he recovered himself, and at the top of his tiger-roar poured out his curses in choicest Hindustani.

On reaching the door I opened it, and then facing him I exclaimed in a loud voice in his native tongue:

"*Chup raho! tum suar ke bachcha ho!*"

With gleaming eyes, and foaming lips, and arms flung wildly into the air,—there stood the Indian God, the 666th incarnation of Haram Zada, stung to the very marrow of his bones by this bitterest insult. Beside himself with fury he sprang up, murder written on every line of his face; tried to leap across the table—and fell in an epileptic fit. As he did so, I shut the door in his face.

Aum.

SAM HARDY.

290

THE THIEF-TAKER

Saïd Jellal ud din bin Messaoud
Trusted to Allah for his daily food;
And so with favour was the Saint anointed
That never yet had he been disappointed.

One day this pious person wished to shave
His head; a sly and sacrilegious knave
Passed; when the good man would resume his prayer,
Alas! his turban was no longer there.

In rushed Mohammed, Hassan, and Husein:
"See! there he goes, the bastard of a swine.
Hasten, and catch him!" But the good man went
With melancholy pace and sad intent

Unto the burying-ground without the wall;
And there he sat, stern and funereal,
Wrapped in deep thought from any outward sense,
A monument of earnest patience!

"Sire!" (a disciple dared at length to say)
"That wicked person took another way."
"Wide is the desert," said the saintly seer:
"But this is certain, that he must come here."

ALEISTER CROWLEY.

THE EQUINOX

SHELLEY. By FRANCIS THOMPSON. With an Introduction by the Rt. Hon. GEORGE WYNDHAM. Burns and Oates.

We would rather not refer to the Rt. Hon. George Wyndham in a paper of this character. Let us deal with Francis Thompson.

Had he no friend to burn this manuscript? To save him from blackening his own memory in this way? We were content to give him his appointed niche in the temple, that of a delicate, forceful spirit, if rarely capable of cosmic expansion. We did not look for eagle-flights; we thought of him as a wild goose sweeping from Tibet upon the poppy-fields of Yunnan. But the prose of a poet reveals the man in him, as his poetry reveals the god; and Francis Thompson the man is a pitiful thing enough. · It is the wounded earthworm cursing the harrow; the snipe blaspheming the lark. Shelley was a fine, pure, healthy man whose soul was habitually one with the Infinite Universe; Thompson was a wretch whose body was poisoned by drugs, whose mind by superstition. Francis Thompson was so much in love with his miserable self that he could not bear the thought of its extinction; Shelley was glad to die if thereby one rose could bloom the redder.

This essay is disgusting; we were all trying to forget Francis Thompson, to remember his songs; and here we have his putrid corpse indecently disinterred and thrust under our noses.

The worst of it all is the very perfection of the wrappings. What a poet Thompson might have been if he had never heard of Christ or opium; if he had revelled in Venice with its courtesans of ruddy hair, swan gracefulness, and tiger soul! Instead, he sold matches in the streets of London; from which abyss a church meant warmth, light, incense, music, and a pageant of hope.

To-day, as in the days of Nero, Christianity is no more than the slum-born shriek of the degenerate and undersized starvelings that inhabit the Inferno of Industrialism.

So also Thompson, impotent from abuse of opium, reviles Shelley and Byron for virility. "O che sciagura essere senza cogl "——

Dirt, dogma, drugs! What wonder and what hope lies in the soul of man if from such ingredients can be distilled such wine as "The dream tryst?" Requiescat in pace. Let the flowers grow on Thompson's grave; let none exhume the body!

A. QUILLER, JR.

THE EYES OF ST. LJUBOV:

DE LA RATIBOISIÈRE'S ACCOUNT OF THE TYPHLOSOPHISTS OF SOUTH RUSSIA

BY

J. F. C. FULLER AND GEORGE RAFFALOVICH

THE EYES OF ST. LJUBOV

I

"TELL it us! O tell us it!"

Elphénor Pistouillat de la Ratiboisière, the Master Magician, hearkened unto his disciples, who sat cross-legged around his incense-bowl. His lips parted in that unapeable grin of his, and he stopped his nostrils awhile with his two forefingers. Then he blew on the charcoal and began.

"Yes, I will tell it to you, intellectual infants, I will. Listen. Two hundred and one years ago—when I was thin and thirty—I chanced upon a couple, living in South Russia. Boy and girl they were still; but, as it were, they unwittingly founded a strange sect of self-mutilated followers, and, being the only man alive who witnessed the beginnings thereof, I will undertake to keep you interested for more than sixteen minutes with their history."

The room was now darkened, and three large globes of crystal, set under the rays of a lamp, stood alone, attracting the eyes. The first globe was limpid and colourless, the second was of the palest amethyst, the third of a rich yellow. Worlds were revolving within. Then Elphénor broke the silence again.

"She was a little girl and he was a little boy . . ."

"She looked like a penny toy," murmured the Neptunian of the party.

None of the others smiled, for the Ancient was already beginning:

"Per illud nomen per quod Solomo constringebat dae-mones, et conclusit . . ."

He stopped short, however, seeing that the irrelevant interruption had found no echo; and he went on with his narrative, moving his arms to the rhythm of his voice, and with his fingers kneading unseen shapes in the air.

II

"The boy comes in later. I want you to realize how beautiful was the little girl. Like a thick thread of scarlet were her lips, comely was her countenance, most pleasing to the sight was her earthly body, a temptation to the Angels her soul. Her eyes expressed the Infinite Sweetness, the Love Merciful; the Pure Innocence of the Eternal Equi-balanced. They were like crystalline drops of dew falling on a perfect rock of Carrara marble; eyes that looked upon you and created you holy; eyes clearer than the clearest rivulet, more beautiful than the most royal amethyst; eyes that illuminated the darkest corner of Hell; eyes that set the fashion to the stars of the Celestial Vault of Heaven; eyes that were but the imperfect mirror of the soul behind. Such was the ten-years-old Ljubov of the goodly countenance.

When, later on, the usual legend grew around her, it was said that wolves had once entered the village, in the midst of

296

winter, starved to madness, and had begun eating two cows in their shed, when little Ljubov chanced upon them and was discovered half an hour later, surrounded by two hundred of these wolves, which were pushing and kicking one another to lick her hands.

On another occasion, extraordinary miracle, one glance from her eyes had stopped the tongue of a drunken pope who was swearing at a peasant in the foulest of language.

She was, of course, a favourite with all in the village: the simpler and nearer Nature their souls, the more they gave the child her proper place. But it must not be inferred that little Ljubov was either worshipped or freed from such menial works as children of her age are called upon to perform. Nor did her playmates realize her superiority. The alleged miracles and the reported cases of healing were heard of some ten years after her death, when eye-witnesses had all departed from this world. Yet, of course, they were possible, quite possible, quite.

III

" ALL of you, suckling babes, have read the Russian tale of the Man who bought souls—or heard of it. Men of a similar turn of mind exist in Russia, and I want you to concentrate your mind upon such a man, albeit his bargains cost him even less, and were of a more physical reality.

From town to village he went, in search of treasures in the shape of eyes. The tools of his trade were a few walnut shells, enamelled within, and a certain magical liquid preparation, which he used to preserve the qualities, freshness and beauty of his acquisitions.

IV   X

THE EQUINOX

On the second day after his arrival in the village where Ljubov lived, he noticed the child and her marvellous beauty. For hours, having retired to the house belonging to a rich lady whose guest he was, he drivelled, with before him the enrapturing vision of Ljubov's priceless jewels. He proceeded carefully; made friends with all the children; and, the seventh day having come, he met her outside the village, by chance—so she thought—and made her a present of a few trifling ornaments. Then he placed over his own eyes two empty shells of walnut, and pretended to play some childish game of hide-and-seek.

After a few minutes, it was her turn to don the blinding apparel. But they were different from his, the empty shells he fixed under her eyebrows!

Ljubov felt no pain, rather an exquisite sensation of physical *bien-être*, of wondrous languor. Ay, but a few minutes later, the sun and moon and stars had lost their beauty for her. There were two large cavities under her eyelids. The force within the nutshells had drawn the eyes out of them.

The Man ran away, carrying a treasured little box, and no more was ever heard of him in those parts.

IV

" What boots it to tell of the long, awful days of darkness through which poor little Ljubov lived before she grew accustomed to her blindness? I am not a medical philosopher; I like home and comfort far too much. If I journey, I must needs travel in state, and my staff includes both a medical

298

man and a philosopher. Therefore, what need is there for me to think, to fathom the depths of childish or human sorrow, to send my brains into a tiring process of elucidation? far more pleasant it is to remain a contemplative individual. Therefore, O Mexican Gaucho, pass me thy pellote pouch and let me take a helping of the leaves and root of thy wonderful mescal plant. And without thought and without fatigue, I can then *SEE*.

Where was I, my little brethren, fathers of larvæ, sons of the she-goat? Ah, I know. Well, poor little Ljubov was saved by her magnificent soul from despairing thoughts. She lived, very miserable at first, more resigned later on.

And there was a boy, too. He was the blind-born son of an ex-soldier, and because of his father's queer and unsocial manner, few people in the village would condescend to take interest in him. But he was no mean child, nevertheless, and his heart was big.

Ljubov had denied herself the pitiful satisfaction of explaining her accident. No one ever heard from her lips the tale of her lost eyes. And, as the months passed by, all remembrance of her, as she had been, died away. Men, women and children passed her by, and took no notice of her. Her parents were kind, but over-worked. Only Piotr, the blind-born child, realized Ljubov's beauty. For if he had no eyes to see with, his other perceptions were sharpened for that very reason. He could not very well understand at first how, and why, it had come to pass that he, alone in the world— for he was but an ignorant peasant child—had not received the use of the five operations of the Lord. But the village deacon, who had been in trouble for some cause or another, and was almost a genius in disgrace—"*terribly clever*" the old men said—once told the little Piotr what it was to be blind. Fortunately for the child's mental equilibrium, he also spoke of the compensation.

"What they mean, boy, when they call you blind, is that you cannot see," he said; "that is, your eyes have been given unto you by the devil, and not by God. Your father must have been rather a bad fellow, you know. When you hear the women singing at the dance, it is that God has given you your ears; if you didn't enjoy the sounds it would mean that the devil has given you your ears, as the Book says, which God wrote in Russian for our people: "*They have ears and they hear not.*" However, you hear well, and smell well, and your two other senses are all right. What you miss, it's the colour of things. I cannot explain it to you, and it would do you no good if I did. Your compensation is that you do not see that which is ugly, ugly like old Ivan Semenovich, and also that you hear and feel and smell with more accuracy than we do. Of course, it is nice to see as well, and I will pray Christ for you, especially if you can give me a few coppers with which to buy tapers. You must have plenty of them; people seem to give you very freely."

Thus the tiresome brute, who had but a few chances of getting drunk in the place.

Happily, Piotr and little Ljubov taught one another a simpler and more natural theory. She was now twelve, and the boy fourteen years old. And I chanced to be staying in the neighbourhood. I met them, as hand in hand they cautiously crossed a lane, close to the spot where I was meditating. The girl I had seen before the accident, and only

300

by her golden voice did I recognize her. I listened to their childish talk, and joined in it, and heard it all from her lips. Then, a few days later, something happened. A lady entered.

There Elphénor became silent, for the door was violently shaken from the outside.

"Come in," he said.

The door was pushed open, then shut again, but no one had entered. The disciples exchanged a glance of amusement; one of them said:

"Has a lady entered?"

They were all made merry by that exhibition of Neptunian spirit of apropos. But Elphénor Pistouillat, like the French Southerner he was, missed the courteous element in life, and began to curse the twelve young men. He was a bad-tempered man, and a very theatrical one.

He rose and walked to him who had caused them all to laugh.

"I know you, sir," Elphénor said, purple in the face, "I know you, unwholesome monkey. Your father was a dealer in pork sausages and cooked ham, a trader in swine. Nothing better could be expected from you than your pig-like groans."

His blood was boiling already, and these few words he uttered were but a preliminary letting out of steam. He walked in the dark to a large cupboard at the far end of his room and took from a shelf twelve little wax figures which he stood on a small table. Rapidly he mumbled an invocation, an incantation, and a deprecation. Then he walked to the fireplace, took the red-hot poker which he kept ever ready for the purpose of lighting his charcoal, and returned with it to the table.

THE EQUINOX

The twelve disciples felt that something was going to happen, but knew not what. An awful feeling overcame their will; they dared not move. Then, suddenly, the twelve of them jumped up and fell on the floor, curling themselves, howling with intense pain and agony, all in a sweat, their bodies aching with all the torments of Fire. They could hear the old man, by his table, cursing them and hitting the wax figures with the hot poker, haphazard, careless of the spot where he struck; but he struck them all equally. The contortions of the men on the yellow painted floor were terrible. He took no heed of them, and went on, cursing them each by name and each time hitting one figure, corresponding to the name he was cursing.

Finally, the red-hot iron had turned black again; and Elphénor's arm was becoming tired. He gathered all the wax figures and went and threw them all into a large pail of water, pushing them down again and again as they came to the surface.

His victims were gradually coming back to their senses. Once more he gathered their waxen images and replaced them on the shelf. Then he turned to his disciples and shouted:

"Sit down, ye workers of Iniquity. Did you feel the draught—or not? Do not interrupt me again. And if anyone knocks again at the door, clear ye out of my visual path."

They were all trembling with excitement and a mixed feeling of anger and desire for a power equal to his. Elphénor blew on the charcoal and incense, turned out the lamp over the three crystal globes, so that they were now almost in utter darkness, and took up the thread of his narrative.

"The Lady who now comes before the footlights fell short

302

of being a great hysterical Countess Tarnowska; she had many lovers who went mad over her body, and whom she *could* drive to drink—or to murder, but she had not done so; she had only driven some of them to suicide, and some even to the loss of their self-respect. The Man who stole Eyes was one of these.

Without going into their respective or joint history let it be simply recorded that the proud collector of ocular jewels made present to the Lady of a pair of magnificent ear-rings— which were none other than the eyes of little Ljubov set in gold. When the Lady came to stay at the country house on the outskirts of the village, she wore her jewels. The simple peasants fell to gossip. The eyes they took for two weird precious stones resembling lapis lazuli. One of them spoke of his meeting with the Lady before poor blind little Piotr, who listened intently.

I will now, my friends, give you—nay, lend you—a piece of information of the utmost importance. It's a fine bit of psychology, too. *A man is not a wee bit interesting when he speaks of others, but let the beggar ride his own horse, expound his own experiences, and* (you can bet your shirt upon it) *he will be worth listening to.*

Thus the peasant-who-had-met-the-lady. He was usually very dull. But the poor fellow had not had any interesting experience in his life, until he met Her. She was walking in the garden, cutting flowers for the table, and, seeing a moujick digging the soil, summoned him.

"When thou hast done digging this hole, cut me some flowers," she said.

And he fell to work with all his might, his body seeming

303

young and beautiful in the precision of its mechanical actions. She let her eye fall upon him and wondered. . . . Presently he had done digging and set to cut her some flowers, looking at her all the while, already feeling strange and new sensations, sweating in an uncontrolled Sukshma-Pranayama.

Alack-a-day, fellows! That was a fine lady for a poor ignorant moujick to behold. She stood, to the end of his days, for a divine apparition. Had he known of OUR LADY HECATE, (blessed be he who murmurs her name with awe! may she gleefully look upon us!) he would have considered his vision to be a visit of the great Goddess (her name be rapidly uttered in the Vault of our beloved Brethren the Ka D Sh Knights of $\triangledown$ P.A. . . P.P. $\triangledown$).

To cut our tale short, for the time is approaching for our libations, the peasant heard the voice of the Lady. She thanked him, him, a poor peasant, her slave, and left him to his work. Her image, however, remained clear before his eyes and he did not fail in his description of her.

Well, little Piotr heard it all. As there was but one woman in the whole world whom he loved, the description of another woman did not in the least attract his attention. Only when mention was made of her magnificent jewels did his ears stand up.

"What are ear-rings?" he asked of Ljubov, when he felt her tiny hand in his, a little later.

"They are beautiful things, Piotr," she answered. "They are beautiful to the eye."

"Hah!" he sighed—for that was the one thing he could not well realize.

"They are stones with fire or water in them."

304

"What, do they burn? do they feel cool to the hand?"

"Only to the eye, dear. *I* remember. One sets them in gold and wears them hanging from the ear, or round one's neck."

"Would you like to *feel* some, Ljubov?"

"Oh yes! . . . But, it's no use, dear, I couldn't *see* them."

"Perhaps you would like just to pass your fingers over them, and try to imagine what they . . . er . . . look like?"

"I think I would. Then I could explain better to you what I mean."

Piotr sighed again and soon left her. In the evening he wandered around the house where the Lady was staying. She was walking in the garden and he listened to her voice while she sang softly to herself. Presently she sat down.

Piotr was well used to directing his steps without the use of eyes, and he managed to creep behind her. A fixed idea had taken possession of his childish brain. He would take the jewels everyone thought so beautiful, and take them to Ljubov.

Suddenly, he sprang forward and his hands searched in the darkness for the ears. A tiny little sound, made by the Lady, as she turned round, helped him to find the place. His fingers closed on each side over the ears and he pulled out with a violent movement. The Lady fell unconscious without having uttered a sound, so acute and sudden had been the pain.

Piotr went away slowly, his hands grasping two ear-rings with a little piece of human flesh attached to them.

THE EQUINOX

V

He sought Ljubov. She, who was like a shoot out of the stem of Jesse, who did not judge after the sight of her eyes, who could stretch out her hand on the den of the basilisk and play on the hole of the asp, without ever coming to grief, fell a-trembling with an unconscious knowledge of that which was going to happen. It dawned upon her that she had come to a point where the road was to become broad under her feet and of an easier walk than the dark path upon which she had of late journeyed. I was hiding behind a tree when Piotr approached her, and so I witnessed their meeting.

He, also, was quaking with excitement. Brandishing his two hands, somewhat red with the blood of his victim, he spoke pantingly.

"Ljubov, my little sister," he said, "I have two fine jewels for thee. Feel them."

But as she put her hand forward he withdrew his; and, instinctively, rubbed the two ear-rings with a corner of his blouse. The particles of flesh fell down during the process.

Then he took a step nearer to her and seized her shoulder, endeavouring to place one pendant where he knew it ought to be worn. But his hand trembled much; neither was her own body steady. They both laboured under great nervous excitement."

"I could not," Elphénor went on, "tell you how the thing happened, unless I used my imagination—and the whole pack of you are unworthy of that exertion—nor will I take the trouble to search the bottom drawers of my reason for any explanation of what I take to be a very scarce phenomenon."
306

THE EYES OF ST. LJUBOV

Briefly—for the time is approaching which we must better utilize—Piotr's hand shook so that he missed touching the lobe of little Ljubov's ear. The jewel he held up to her face touched, instead, one of the empty orbits of his little friend.

Our villain, the Man who bought and stole Eyes, must have done his job very properly indeed, for Ljubov, who, in a vain attempt to see that which was shewn her, had opened wide the dark cavities under her eyebrows. Well, I suppose the eye touched a still sensitive nerve. No sooner had it done so than she uttered an exclamation.

"I see! Piotr, I SEE! I SEE!"

And helping herself now, she rapidly unset the eyes from their golden crown and thrust them where they ought to have been all that time. Miracle of Miracles! She saw as you and I do. She saw poor little Piotr who stood before her, almost out of his mind, sharing her excitement.

She took his hand, drew him to her and kissed his forehead. Then she wept for a long time. Finally, she sat down by him and told him of her new sensations.

VI

But they were unsatisfactory. The sky she saw was, in spite of the Stars, inferior to the beauty she had endowed it with. The sweet face of her little friend even was less sweet to behold than it had been to her childish fancy. And, gently, with an extraordinary delicacy, she spoke of her disappointment.

"Oh! it was more beautiful as we thought it, Piotroushka!" she exclaimed.

And, acting upon an impulse, she dropped her eyes in her hand and threw them behind her without a sigh.

I picked them up, my friends, while the two children stood, their arms linked together, a sad but resigned expression gradually coming over their faces.

Ay, I picked them up, but I won't shew them to you, unworthy foxes.

And now, Lights please . . . let us take to the ritual. Brother H., fill the Holy Cups . . . Holy be the Lamps of Joy! Holy be the Lamps of Sorrow! Let us enter the Ark of Increased Knowledge!"

VII

A little later one of the Disciples inquired of the Master:

"You spoke of a strange sect of self-mutilated followers, O Master, what of them?"

"What of them?" Elphénor repeated. "Well, they were those who listened to Ljubov, and took her word for it—that one sees a better world if one has no human eyes. They put it into practice and their ranks were soon filled. They blinded themselves; they blinded their children almost in their cradles. Oh yes, there were soon hundreds of them who worshipped the Lord our God in that manner; and Ljubov and Piotr were their ministers. Is that all you want to know?

"Master, what of the Lady?"

"The Lady? Faugh! She went away; the Spirits of the Earth prevented her from lodging a complaint; she hid her

308

wounded ears under a thick ornament of pearls and gold. It was not bad with her! Besides, what is she to you, anyhow, billy-goat?

"And now, all of ye, clear out, and walk ye all to your rooms with the mantra."

FINIS

MIDSUMMER EVE

Faint shadows cross the shifting spears of light,
Pale gold and amethyst, or warmly white,
Till velvet shod, unseen, the wizard hours
Hold thus their elfin court amid the flowers,
That wake to wingèd music of the night.
And silken sighs scarce stir the amorous bowers
Where 'passioned sleep his poppy garland showers,
In dreams which mock the hastening moments' flight.

Up soars the moon, and higher still and higher
The dancers leap to catch some fairy fire
To steal and 'prison in the glow-worm's tail,
For pixie torches should the starlight fail;
Reflecting gems which deck the elfin choir,
Melting like snowflakes at the daybreak pale.

Ethel Archer.

THE POETICAL MEMORY

AN ESSAY

I AM one of those silly people (there are a lot of them—quite enough to make it pay) who are so irritated at the arrival of a bill that I nearly always throw it on the fire. For all that, I had been humbly proud of my memory, and it was an awful shock to me one morning when I received this bill,

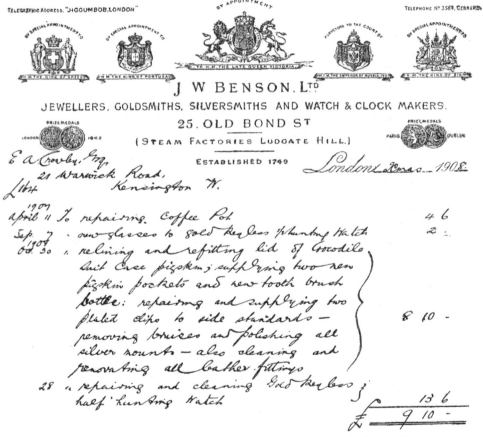

for I had a very clear impression in my mind that the contract was for £5.

Indeed, I wrote and said so.

But alas! my poor memory was most certainly at fault. Messrs. Bensons replied:

Sir

In reply to your letter respecting your account we beg to enclose statement herewith, from which you will see that the £5 you handed to our Assistant was in payment of your old account, the various items of which ranged from October 1906 to September 1907, and statements of which had been rendered to you each quarter. This payment of £5/1/- left a balance of 6/6, and with the 13/6 charged for repairing the old Watch and £8/10/- for repairing Chit Case, the total of your account to date is £9.10/-. With regard to the item of £8/10/- we cannot understand how you come to be under the impression that it should only be £5, as we are certain our Assistant did not quote this latter price for doing up the Chit Case.

Trusting that this explanation will make the matter quite clear to you,

We beg to remain, Sir,

Yours obediently,

J. W. Benson Ltd.

per G.B.

E. A. Crowley, Esq.,
21 Warwick Road,
Kensington. W.

312

THE POETICAL MEMORY

This explanation *did* make the matter quite clear to me; for I had all the time in my possession—not thrown in the fire after all!—their original account.

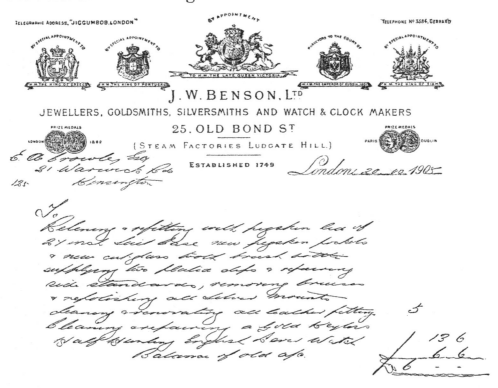

ALEISTER CROWLEY.

ADELA

♃ ☌ P ☽
VENEZIA, *May 19th*, 1910.

JUPITER'S foursquare blaze of gold and blue
Rides on the moon, a lilac conch of pearl,
As if the dread god, charioted anew
Came conquering, his amazing disk awhirl
To war down all the stars. I see him through
The hair of this mine own Italian girl,
Adela
That bends her face on mine in the gondola!

There is scarce a breath of wind on the lagoon.
Life is absorbed in its beatitude,
A meditative mage beneath the moon.
Ah! should we come, a delicate interlude,
To Campo Santo that, this night of June,
Heals for awhile the immitigable feud?
Adela!
Your breath ruffles my soul in the gondola!

ADELA

Through maze on maze of silent waterways,
Guarded by lightless sentinel palaces,
We glide; the soft plash of the oar, that sways
Our life, like love does, laps—no softer seas
Swoon in the bosom of Pacific bays!
We are in tune with the infinite ecstasies,
Adela!
Sway with me, sway with me in the gondola!

They hold us in, these tangled sepulchres
That guard such ghostly life. They tower above
Our passage like the cliffs of death. There stirs
No angel from the pinnacles thereof.
All broods, all breeds. But immanent as Hers
That reigns is this most silent crown of love,
Adela
That broods on me, and is I, in the gondola.

They twist, they twine, these white and black canals,
Now stark with lamplight, now a reach of Styx.
Even as our love—raging wild animals
Suddenly hoisted on the crucifix
To radiate seraphic coronals,
Flowers, flowers—O let our light and darkness mix,
Adela,
Goddess and beast with me in the gondola!

Come! though your hair be a cascade of fire,
Your lips twin snakes, your tongue the lightning flash,
Your teeth God's grip on life, your face His lyre,

THE EQUINOX

Your eyes His stars—come, let our Venus lash
Our bodies with the whips of Her desire.
Your bed's the world, your body the world-ash,
Adela!
Shall I give the word to the man of the gondola?

ALEISTER CROWLEY.

THE THREE WORMS

In the great vault is a coffin. In the coffin is the corpse of a very beautiful woman. The vault is deep under the ground and very still. Above its bricks is a layer of earth, and if any sound at all percolates into this chamber of death, it is only the delicate tremor and rustle of things growing, of the grass seed pushing its tiny way through the mould, to break at the last into its narrow slip of bright green flame. This, and the weak whisper of trailing rose-roots in whose brown and ugly stems glow such a tender sap and noiseless fervour of exquisite perfume. At intervals, maybe, this dark blue silence is wounded by strange creakings and indescribable tremors : noises that are really the wastings and settlings of decaying bone and flesh, just as if Death were feasting his lips at last with murderous kisses on the flesh of his latest mistress in the secret peace of his terrible bridal chamber. All around the vault are hung great blue-black carpets of shadow, and the floor is damp, and wriggling with the spawn of low life.

Let us look into the coffin of the beautiful dead woman, look into it as we would have strangers look into our own with the child eyes of fancy and imagination, rather than with the cold and scaly eyes of knowledge.

Only to vulgar and brutish eyes is there any horror, for

the sweet process of life is at work in every cell and particle of the dead. Truly, there is no such thing as death. Lips grown tired of speech, and outhonied of the honey of all kisses fade and whisper away into something else. The crude utterances of human language fail them, and they win instead the subtle perfumed conversation of flowers and vegetation. Thus their dust comes to lie about a rose-root, and with the lovely chemistry of earth they tremble back to the surface once more as crinkled and crimson perfume, or a frail flutter of yellow longing. Like flags, like tender waving pennons or messengers of hope and greeting from those beleaguered ones dissolving in the fastnesses of earth.

Every rose, every lily is a message from our dead: a sigh or a smile: something simple like the daisy from a simple heart, something of weird and oppressive beauty from some poet's brain, like the passion flower or the fuchsia.

In the coffin of the beautiful dead woman, there are three worms, sweet, clean, wavy, little maggots that will one day carry all the charm and delight of the dead back into the world again, will quicken and nourish seeds and roots, so that in the pink glamour of an April almond tree, the glory of the dead woman's hair shall be returned again.

One of these creatures is poised over her mouth, which again, to vulgar and unseeing eyes, looks ugly, though it is really more beautiful now than ever it was, for it is quick with frail seeds of countless existences, and is become a very factory and warehouse of Life Itself.

Another worm is coming out of the dead right eye of the woman, coined, as it were, like a little pink amethyst from the stuff of her brain. And yet another peers from the mysterious citadel of her heart, which like a faded and extinguished censer, rusts in the decadence of its scented memories.

The three worms dispose themselves and begin to talk.

The little worm which is issuing from her mouth begins:

"I am her mouth, her beautiful mouth, that sweet frail chalice where her soul delighted to dissolve itself and to lie. That mouth of hers, so nervous, so intimately sensible, that it is pleasant to think of it as the fragile rim of the holy and wonderful amphora of her strange exultant being.

"I am—since I was fed on them—all that litany of kisses which passion flung like a storm of wet rose-leaves on to her mouth—am, am I not?—all those dreams and pale blue shimmering fantasies that love drew like mists out of the hearts of all her lovers to expire in the stained fervour of an instant's rapture.

"I am—forgive it to me!—all the lies which floated from her lips as sweetly as caresses, all those lies which fled like arrows barbed with gall into the ravished brains of her adorers. One I sent to America, and another to pick out the green glint of Death's eye in the lustre of a glass of poison. I tore husband from wife with my wingèd scented words, redolent of the very nudity and flesh of love, yellow, crocus-tinted, opalescent, murderously sweet.

"I pricked the souls of little children with the crystal toys of speech that fell from the melting coral of my curvèd lips.

"I was East and West, and North and South, and sun and moon, and shuddering flight of stars to more than one, and it seems to me, as one of her heirs and sons, that she was not a good woman.

319

THE EQUINOX

" I fear she was bad, for from me were twisted such devious messages, such various, unalike reports, that yes and no became counters of speech almost indistinguishable to my thinking. Once, I remember, there trickled from me a vagrant little flow of words, so bitter and so inviting, so poisonous and yet so intoxicating, that the soul for whom they were meant held up the silver goblets of hearing for its own destruction with trembling, greedy hands, covetous and anxious, hungry and afraid. Her voice that purled and rippled and sang through me—ah! it was like a kiss caged in her throat, and to hear it made a man a father in longing. There are voices like that, and when men hear them, they live a lifetime in an instant, mate, rear children, are widowed, or have their eyes closed for them for the last time by these women whose souls they thus secretly and inviolately espouse."

After a little silence the worm which issued from her eyes then spoke:

" I am her eyes, and she was bad, bad as her mouth says. Some of that mouth's warm tribute came indeed to me, and I was shut from seeing with the close lips of men beating time to the superb madness of their love music with rhythmic kisses. And I saw—O what I saw!—mountains that bowed to her, and stringed necklaces of stars that flashed in ecstasy on Eternity's bosom from the very sight of her. Seas over which she passed on a sensuous errand as live and tremulous as the heave of their own great hearts—heaves that are the world's sighs for the little brood that teases it, and festers the green and waving glory of its skin and hair.

320

THE THREE WORMS

"Much have I looked upon—I, the now crawling, damp and sightless evidence of her sight.

"I am her eyes.

"Empires shone in me: suns set, moons arose, and were drowned like lovely naiads in the waters of the sky. I knew wild flowers so beautiful, that one dared not touch them lest their beauty start to mere ugly life.

"I am that quiver of fragile and delicious expectation that shone in the virgin eyes of her when . . . O happy hour!

"I am that greediness, that terrible woman's greediness, fierce as drought, relentless as Death, which devours its own portion in the feast of life.

"And I too, like her mouth, witness to it that she was evil. The senses are the person in so much as they are the sweet janitors to all that come and go. Through our five portals life only flows, and the flavour of its tides is with us always. I sit in judgment on myself—I where the world could gather itself in one, little, humble, focus-point of curiosity and peep into the garden of her soul—I—where seas could be held calm and captive in a little pool of blue—I—who could consume mountains in a flash, and devour the dawn, I who could bid the moon trail her white limbs for my pleasure through the windy bagnios of the sky.

"I sit in judgment and condemn, for often I was a sword when Truth was a·little child, and the breasts of my beauty I gave to Worthlessness in the stinking lupanars of Treachery and Deceit.

"Brothers, like the afterlight of day, I the light of her life consort with the shadows of evening, and I say it softly, gently, even as Spring's flying feet touch with unaccustomed primroses the wood, I say it—She was bad."

Then the third worm, which came from the woman's heart, turned to the other two, and said:

"I am her heart . . . her beautiful, beautiful heart.

"What do you know of the deeds of the Queen who were never in her council chamber?

"When you were bold, I was perhaps afraid, and when you exulted, there was I know not what trouble of sadness throbbing within me. All that you were I sustained: all your pleasure stirred through me, and you but harvested that which I sowed.

"When you were all aflame, it was I who lit you, and you could not even be sad without me.

"Not less tender than the inviting curl—like a curled and fluffy feather of coral—with which you who were her lips made welcome to some man, was the slow hypnotic wave of my thurible with whose essence I drenched ever cell of her body. I say that she was good, for she was human and she loved, oh! so sweetly, so delicately, so tenderly.

"What you did, you, her lips, her eyes and her other senses, was but to make vain effigies of our interior delight, to shatter in the broken shards of translation the mysterious silent beauty of the vase itself.

"I, the woman's heart of her, was like to a cave were thousands of voices of unborn children cried softly in the dark, where one felt their outstretching hands in pale and piteous appeal, as one may hear the early lilies break through the encompassing earth. In me were the seed of kisses that could only burst to flower in a hundred years to come.

322

THE THREE WORMS

"I am her heart, her ordinary, commonplace woman's heart. Commonplace! Ah! nothing is so mysterious as the commonplace, for it is only Subtlety sleeping and holding its hands a little while. A country clod is more interesting than the most awake and magnetic of geniuses, even as the veiled and cloistered odours of Spring with which one knows the earth is tingling in Winter are more delirious and exciting than the naked bosoms of May.

"Will you believe me, that, by I know not what exquisite contradiction, the sweetest kiss was ever a pang to her, and yielding was only less terrible than denial?

"On my small insistent beat have lain heads that were heavy with great dreams: men of action and men of fancy who loved her and were loved, it may be, a little of her too. I have been the couch of treaties and the pillow of financial strifes, and on me much uncoined gold has slept through dreamless transparent nights.

"Once a poet received her favours, and his head, bowed and weighted with its spongy amorphous magic, rested on me like a honeycomb, all giddy and vibrant with perfume and emotion.

"And once an old mother's head, gray and weary with its long rolling down the years, found on me the unexpected peace and happiness of the old. For the old are so lonely, and no one is their friend. . . . So, my brothers, I give you the key of all her secrets except that secret which she shares with Time and herself.

"I can make all plain except my own mystery, which is the tragedy of everyone, worm, or man, or God.

"Blaspheme no more in such childish, imitative fashion!

323

You are nearer the world than I, and its weak vanity has stained you. The eye looks at the world, and the world looks at the eye, and though each learns from the other, it is not often an even bargain and exchange. . . ."

Then, as the heart-worm ceased to speak, the other two, the eye-worm and the mouth-worm, drew closer to where during all his talking they had been magnetically moved. And all those years which they had passed unconsciously as the lips or the eyes of a woman became suddenly revealed, most vividly different to them.

They could not speak, the two detractors, for they had learnt the wisdom and merit of sin. They knew that good and evil are the same thing, that in a world of illusion he who has the most illusions is the richest man, that to be wise unto ignorance is the fairest counsel, that they knew nothing and yet all, that . . .

And the heart-worm, whose judgment and reasonings had been so readily accepted by the others, grew in his turn a sceptic, since faith cannot live without doubt, and truth is only co-existent with untruth, as day with night, as life with death, as, O beloved! my heart with thine, as vain and coloured chatterings like this with noble and inviolate silence.

EDWARD STORER.

THE FELON FLOWER

As the sighing of souls that are waiting the close of the light,
As the passionate kissings of Love in the Forest of Night,
  As the swish of the wavelets that beat on a cavernless shore,
  Or the cry of the sea-mew that echoes a moment or more,
So the voice of thy spirit soft-calling my soul in its flight.

As the breath of the wind that is borne from the island of Love,
As the swift-moving cloudlets that sail in the heaven above,
  As the warmth of the sunlight that breaks on the shimmer-
      ing sea,
  And the sweetness that lurks in the sting of the honey-
      fed bee,
So the joy of thy kiss, the dread offspring of serpent and dove.

As the trail of the fiery lightnings which gleam in the dark,
As the light from the measureless Bow of the sevenfold Arc,
  As the fires which glance o'er the face of the treacherous
      deep,
  When none but the furies may rest, and the nereids weep,—
So thy meteor eyes, brightest sirens alluring Love's barque.

When hid in the wonderful maze of thy whispering hair,
Alone with the shadows and thee, and away from the glare

THE EQUINOX

Of the burning and pitiless day, and the pitiless light,—
Thee only beside me, above me the mystical night,
No dream so created in darkness was ever more fair.

For then was thy touch as the light of a life-giving fire,
Which kindles, and scorches, and burns, with unsated desire,
Thy breath the warm essence of myrtle, the fragrance of pine,
The languorous smoke of a temple obscene yet divine,
Which gladdens the soul of a god in his passionate ire.

So silent those nights, I could fancy the uttermost deep
Engulfed us for ever,—for ever in silence to keep
The tale of our wooing: till sweetly the murderous hours
Had lulled us to rest; and the magical poison of flowers
Had stolen our brains, and our eyelids were heavy with sleep.

Ah love! They are banished, yet not so the strength of the
spell
Which holds both our beings in bondage, a bondage so fell
That even the angels above cannot alter its power;
It lives in the memory yet of one passionate hour,
When from the dark bosom of Hell sprang a fair felon flower.

ETHEL ARCHER.

326

THE BIG STICK

COUNTERPARTS. Vol. XVI of THE BROTHERHOOD OF THE NEW LIFE. An
Epitome of the Work and Teaching of Thomas Lake Harris. By
RESPIRO. 2s. 6d. net. A New Edition. C. W. Pearce and Co., 139, West
Regent Street, Glasgow.

If we are in any way to shadow forth the Ineffable, it must be by a degradation. Every symbol is a blasphemy against the Truth that it indicates. A
painter to remind us of the sunlight has no better material than dull ochre.

So we need not be surprised if the Unity of Subject and Object in Consciousness which is Samadhi, the uniting of the Bride and the Lamb which is
Heaven, the uniting of the Magus and the God which is Evocation, the uniting
of the Man and his Holy Guardian Angel which is the seal upon the work of
the Adeptus Minor, is symbolized by the geometrical unity of the circle and
the square, the arithmetical unity of the 5 and the 6, and (for more universality
of comprehension) the uniting of the Lingam and the Yoni, the Cross and the
Rose. For as in earth-life the sexual ecstasy is the loss of self in the Beloved,
the creation of a third consciousness transcending its parents, which is again
reflected into matter as a child; so, immeasurably higher, upon the Plane of
Spirit, Subject and Object join to disappear, leaving a transcendent unity. This
third is ecstasy and death; as below, so above.

It is then with no uncleanness of mind that all races of men have adored an
ithyphallic god; to those who can never lift their eyes above the basest plane
the sacrament seems filth.

Much, if not all, of the attacks upon Thomas Lake Harris and his worthy
successor "Respiro" is due to this persistent misconception by prurient and
degraded minds.

When a sculptor sees a block of marble he thinks "How beautiful a statue is
hidden in this! I have only to knock off the chips, and it will appear!"

This being achieved, the builder comes along, and says: "I will burn this,
and get lime for my mortar." There are more builders than sculptors in
England.

THE EQUINOX

This is the Magic Mirror of the Soul; if you see God in everything, it is because you are God and have made the universe in your image; if you see Sex in everything, and think of Sex as something unclean, it is because you are a sexual maniac.

True, it is, of course, that the soul must not unite herself to every symbol, but only to the God which every symbol veils.

And Lake Harris is perfectly clear on the point. The " counterpart " is often impersonated, with the deadliest results. But if the Aspirant be wise and favoured, he will reject all but the true.

And I really fail to see much difference between this doctrine and our own of attaining the Knowledge and Conversation of the Holy Guardian Angel, or the Hindu doctrine of becoming one with God. We may easily agree that Lake Harris made the error of thinking men pure-minded, and so used language which the gross might misinterpret; but sincere study of this book will make the truth apparent to all decent men. ALEISTER CROWLEY.

[We print this review without committing ourselves to any opinion as to how these doctrines may be interpreted in practice by the avowed followers of Harris.—ED.]

" No. 19." By EDGAR JEPSON. Mills and Boon, Ltd.

Arthur Machen wrote fine stories, " The Great God Pan," " The White People, etc.

Edgar Jepson would have done better to cook them alone; it was a mistake to add the dash of Algernon Blackwood. A. C.

RAINBOWS AND WITCHES. By WILL H. OGILVIE. 4th edition. 1s. Elkin Mathews.

A great deal of Mr. Ogilvie's verse rings true, an honest sensitive Scots heart in this brave world of ours. If he rarely—perhaps never—touches the summit of Parnassus, at least he is always on the ridge. A. C.

AN INTRODUCTION TO THE KABALAH. By W. WYNN WESTCOTT. John M. Watkins.

It is difficult to find words in which to praise this little book. It is most essential for the beginner. Lucid and illuminating, it is also illuminated. In particular, we are most pleased to find the correlation of the Qabalah with the philosophical doctrines of other religions; a task attempted by ourselves in

328

THE BIG STICK

"Berashith" and "777," perhaps not so successfully from the point of view of the beginner.

There is of course much beyond this elementary study, and the neophyte will find nothing in the book which he does not know; but the book is addressed to those who know nothing. It will supply them with a fine basis for Qabalistic research. ALEISTER CROWLEY.

THE PRIESTESS OF ISIS. By EDOUARD SCHURÉ. Translated by F. ROTH-WELL, B.A. W. Rider and Son. 3s. 6d. net.

Books I and II.

I have been trying to read this book for a week, but the rapidly recurring necessity to appear on the stage of "Pan, a comedy," in the name-part, has interfered, and I have not yet finished it. But it speaks well for the book that I have not been too bored by it.

I like both Hedonia and Alcyone, for I know them; but Memnones seems to lack cleanliness of line, and one understands Ombricius so little that one loses interest in his fortunes.

Books III and IV.

Book III did rather cheer me. But of course one knew all along that the Eruption was to be the God from the Machine. A great pity; why not another city and a less hackneyed catastrophe? But it's as well done as possible within these limits. The translation might have been better done in one or two places—Bother! here's Hedonia coming for lunch. What a wormy worm Ombricius was! D. CARR.

PETER THE CRUEL. By EDWARD STORER. John Lane.

This admirable story of a little-known monarch dresses once more the Middle Ages in robes of scarlet, winged and shot with a delicate impressionism. Mr. Storer wields a pen like the rod of Moses; he has struck the water of Romance from the Rock of History; such scenes have rarely been so vividly described since de Sade and Sacher-Masoch passed on to the Great Reward. CALIGULA II.

MORAG THE SEAL. By J. W. BRODIE-INNES. Rebman. 6s.

One must wish that Mr. Brodie-Innes' English were equal to his imagination. Again and again a lack of perfect control over his medium spoils one of the finest stories ever thought. All the glamour of the Highlands is here; all love, all magic—which is love—and Mr. Brodie-Innes' refinement avoids the crude detective solution of the mystery.

And that mystery is enticing and enthralling; Morag is delicious as dream or death, enticing, elusive, exquisite. One of the subtlest and truest women in literature.

Not many men have imagination so delicate and—dictame!—but Mr. Brodie-Innes writes "with authority, and not as the scribes." Why he allows Mathers to go about saying that he is a Jesuit and a poisoner will be revealed at the Last Day. Perhaps, like us, he can't catch him. Or perhaps it is that he is contented to be a great novelist—as he is, bar the weakness of his English and an occasional touch of Early Victorian prunes-and-prismism. He has every other qualification. God bless him!

BOLESKINE.

IN THE NAME OF THE MESSIAH. By E. A. GORDON. KEISERSHA. Tokyo. N.D. N.P.

The only way to read this book is to run at it, shouting a slogan, and to stick a skean dhuibh in it somewhere and read the sentence it hits. Thus, perhaps, with perseverance and a lot of luck, one may find a coherent paragraph in the porridge of disconnected drivel, defaced with italics and capitals and inverted commas like a schoolgirl's letter.

And this is the coherent paragraph.

"There are 3 apocryphal descriptions of the man Christ Jesus. . . . All *agree* in describing Him as 'strikingly tall,' '6 ft. high,' and with curled or wavy locks.

"This, to my mind, establishes the Identity of the Daibutsu with the curl-covered head and colossal stature."

This, to my mind, establishes the Identity of Mrs. Gordon with Mr. J. M. Robertson.

A. C.

OLD AS THE WORLD. By J. W. BRODIE-INNES. 6s. Rebman.

A rattling good novel, with hundreds of incidents on every page, a hero and heroine who seldom talk in anything meaner than capitals, and a happy ending:

"Wherever you are, there is my kingdom," he murmured, as he folded his beloved close against his heart.

Mr. Brodie-Innes belongs to what one may call the Exoteric Occult School

THE BIG STICK

of novelists; one feels throughout that his occultism is the result of study and not of experience. That is why I say exoteric.

Although the style of the book is comparatively undistinguished, and sometimes lapses into actual slovenliness, Mr. Brodie-Innes frequently attains beauty, and beauty of a positive and original kind. Some of his sea-pictures are quite fine. But the magic of style that renders Arthur Machen so marvellous is lacking. "Old as the World" is always interesting; it is never enthralling.

"Old as the World" is much better than "Morag the Seal," and there is a marked improvement in the style.

V. B. N.

BLACK MAGIC. BY MARJORIE BOWEN. Alston Rivers. 6s.

Marjorie Bowen knows nothing of the real magic, but she has learnt the tales spread by fools about sorcerers, and fostered by them as the best possible concealments of their truth.

Of these ingredients she has brewed a magnificent hell-broth. No chapter lacks its jewelled incident, and the web that she has woven of men's passions is a flame-red tapestry stained with dark patches of murder and charred here and there with fire of hell.

Marjorie Bowen has immense skill; has she genius? How can a stranger say? So many nowadays are forced by sheer starvation into writing books that will sell—and when they have taken the devil's money, find that it is in no figure that he has their souls in pawn.

I am told that it is the ambition of W. S. Maugham to write a great play.

A. C.

THE EDUCATION OF UNCLE PAUL. BY ALGERNON BLACKWOOD. Macmillan and Co. 6s.

I read this book on the Express Train from Eastbourne to London (change at Polegate, Lewes, Hayward's Heath, Three Bridges, Red Hill, and East Croydon—they ought to stop to set down passengers at Earlswood), and though it's a beautiful story, and I like Nixie, I must confess to being rather bored. Rather with a capital R and a sforzando *er*. I wanted George Macdonald's "Lilith," and Arthur Machen's "Hill of Dreams"—they have blood in them. And I was not in my library, but in a stuffy, dog-returneth-to-his-vomit-scented microbe-catcher labelled 1st Compo. Then, too, Algernon Blackwood began to remind me of Maeterlinck. There was too much bluebirdiness, and it gave me the blue devils. And then, again, though I've never read J. M. Barrie, I felt sure that he must be responsible for some of the oysters in the stew. And where was Sidney Blow?

Yes: it's a silly book; a book elaborately and deliberately silly; even laboriously silly with that silliness which cometh not forth but by prayer and fasting. . . .

And as I continued to read, it grew monotonously silly. Paul "slipped into the Crack" in several different ways, but there wasn't much difference in the result. I began to wonder if Mr. Blackwood has been drinking from the wisdom-fount of Ecclesiastes and Don Juan!

And oh dear! the conversations. Children don't talk bad metaphysics, nor do repatriated lumbermen. But Mr. Blackwood must dree his weird, I suppose.

And then, on a sudden, the monotony breaks up into a mixture of " La Morte Amoureuse," "Thomas Lake Harris," "The Yoke" (Mr. Hubert Wales' master-piece), and "The Autobiography of a Flea told in a Hop, Skip, and a Jump."

But I prefer Mr. Verbouc to Uncle Paul, and Bella to Nixie. From the point of view of pure literature, of course.

The book then slobbers off into Gentle-Darwin-meek-and-mild Theosophy.

Victoria at last, thank God! I think I'll slip into the Crack, myself!

ALEISTER CROWLEY.

THE LITERARY GUIDE. Messrs. Watts and Co. 2d. The Journeyings of Joseph.

Joseph has gone a-wandering; and, as he cannot even on the billowy waves keep his mouth shut, we are treated in the above official organ to an account of his itinerary as if he were the real original Vasco de Gama.

He reminds us rather of the Shoreditch lady who went for her first country walk, as an old song tells us:

" I've been roaming, I've been roaming
Where the meadow dew is sweet;
And I'm coming, and I'm coming
With its pearls upon my feet."

For, if he brings back with him "cockle shells from distant lands" like a certain Roman Caesar, akin to the information which now gushes from his lips, his pearls will indeed be from the land of Gophir, and must I am afraid be trampled by us with other flash fudge. Parisian ware back into the gutter whence they came, the gutter of phylogenic-ontogeny.

There was no other Joseph or Josephina aboard, no "helpmeet" worthy of Him, all Potiphar's wives—by the way, a Second Joseph would have been rather a tall order for either Mrs. Potiphar or Ernst Haeckel—so the Great and Only

THE BIG STICK

One was intensely bored as he had to restrict himself to his own society. And the more he restricted himself the more bored he became, and the more bored he became the more boorish did he grow, and the ruder did he become to his fellow passengers, who evidently had not sufficient "rationalism" to believe that Erasmus Darwin was born in 1788, or that the water upon which they floated was composed of HO_2. He wondered, "If it were they who were fools, or I myself,"—we, being mystics, don't; we know! Their conversation was "trivial chatter," so evidently it had nothing to do with ontogenic-phylogeny. The chaplain was "insufferable" twice over, and so were his prayers.

"The heavy mask of revelry was still on the faces of the men whom curiosity drew to the open rail: men in gay pyjamas and flaunting shirts, men with ends of cigarettes in their lax mouths, men whose language, up to a few hours before, had been too archaic for the dictionary. With open mouths they jostled each other to get a good view of the plunge of the white sewn outline of a man."

Now, Joseph, draw it mild; don't put the sugar in your tea with a trowel! we have seen many burials at sea, more than we should care to count, but we have never seen the corpse surrounded by "fag-ends" and a gay pyjamaed mob. Perhaps one of the passengers was on his way to the bath-room, in a Swan and Edgar "sleeping suit," when you went to have your own little peep—or have you borrowed a leaf from your former Jesuit brothers and write all this for the greater glory of God RPA?

We are travellers as well as mystics, we have been a score of journeys as long as yours and longer, right round the world twice—think of that, Jo! and all the cockle shells you could have collected! We know that the conversation "on board" is trivial, "very naughty," as a little Cape Dutch girl once said to us, "but rather nice," and that the ozone of the air and the brine of the waves make the ladies most charming on the boat deck. We are mystics and are never bored; we are mystics and are just as happy on board a Castle liner as behind Fleet Street in Johnson's Court. If we back a winner we ask our friends to come and have a "night out" with us; and if the wrong colours go by, well, we don't pawn our breeches to buy a revolver. If it were possible for boredom to descend upon us we should not say "sucks" to it, like Philpotts, but should retire into Dhyana or Samâdhi. You would call this "Self-induced-hypophylo-morphodemoniacal-auto-suggestion." Well, well, never mind! we will pass the words, we don't care a "tinker's curse" about them; it is the message we look for and not the special patents act under which the wire which conveyed it to us is registered. And if I say "hocuspocus" and down come a good dinner and a pretty girl, eat the one and don't be rude to the other—or she will run away, Joseph, she really will: and please, Josy, don't turn to me and say: You "insufferable" fool, you are not Romano's; what business have you to produce

THE EQUINOX

a " Pêche Melba "? You are not a " trivial " Mrs. Warren; what do you mean by " plumping down " before me this " little bit of fluff "?

Now don't be too bored or too serious, Joseph, be a good fellow even towards those who are unlike you, for a good heart is worth a dozen good heads and heaven only knows how many bad ones. Eat your " scoff " and enjoy it; give the girl a kiss—even if among the boats; and shake hands with the Chaplain—after all he probably agreed with you over the Boulter Case. Here surely is a link between you! Drop the " insufferable " and the " Christmas-card-curate " description of him, use your tea-spoon like an ordinary decent Christian and don't empty the sugar basin, shake hands with him, my boy, shake hands with him, and try and be a real good fellow, Joseph, a real good fellow, as well as an indifferent evolutionist!

A. QUILLER.

WITH THE ADEPTS. By FRANZ HARTMANN. William Rider and Son.

If you have never been to " The Shakespeare " or " The Elephant and Castle " please go; for, for the same price that you would pay for this book you will be able to obtain at either a good seat. Go there when they are playing " The Sorrows of Satan," and you will have no need to be " With the Adepts " of Franz Hartmann. Besides, if you are not amused by the play the back of the programme will surely never fail you. There you will learn the proximity of the nearest " Rag Shop " where old bones, scrap iron, india rubber and waste paper may be sold; and should you, like us, be so unfortunate as to possess a copy of this story, may with a little persuasion induce the ragman to relieve you of it. Besides, it will also tell you where you can obtain " Sausage and mash " for two pence—and who would not prefer so occult a dish to a " bun-worry " with Sisters Helen and Leila?

From page one to one hundred and eighty this is all warranted pure, like the white and pink sugar mice on a Christmas tree—quite wholesome for little children.

Not only can you meet the Adepts but the Adepts' " lady friends "; you might be in Bloomsbury, but no such luck. Polite conversation takes place upon " advanced occultism," which strongly reminds us of the pink and paunchy puddings of Cadogan Court. The lady adepts are bashful and shy, but always very proper. The Monastery might be in Lower Tooting. The hero asks silly questions so as to give the Adept the requisite opportunities of making sillier answers. " I was rather reluctant to leave the presence of the ladies . . . the ladies permitted me to retire." Outside bottles full of this sort of occult Potassium Bromide, this novelette is eminently suited as a moral sedative for young girls when they reach sixteen or thereabouts and are beginning to wonder how they got into this funny world.

334

THE BIG STICK

THE DEVIL: "Let us giggle."

THEODORUS: "Hush, you have committed a horrible black magical act, you have slept with" . . .

LEILA [*a creamy girl*]: "Good heavens, Sir, I faint; call a policeman."

THEODORUS: "Become acquainted with the Queen of the nymphs." . . .

SISTER HELEN [*nursing expert*]: "A douche, smelling salts, eau de Cologne, quinine . . .!"

THEODORUS: "From the abode of . . . Brotherhood you are expelled [*sobs*], to the British Museum you must go [*snuffles*], and read [*pause*] 'The Secret Symbols of the Rosicrucians'!"

THE DEVIL: "Tut, tut. . . . Dear Sisters, the train has stopped, we are at Streatham Hill—let us get out."   ALICIA DE GRUYS.

ON THE LOOSE. By GEORGE RAFFALOVICH. Publishing Office of THE
    EQUINOX, 124 Victoria Street, S.W.   1s. net.

The author of the Man-Cover is well-known to the readers of THE EQUINOX. His charm lays principally in the independence of his thought, the delicacy of his touch, in his spirit of pure joy, in his most holy childishness. He shows certainly a great lack of literary experience, an accumulation of various contradictory feelings which seem to fight one another for the conquest of his spirit. The scientific training of our order will give him that Mastery over self which alone can bring forth the full blossom of his rich imagination. There is every reason for us to expect much of Mr. Raffalovich. Is he not a Gemini man, with Jupiter and Saturn culminating? Somewhat Neronian, probably, as will be seen in his work.

We recommend especially the reading of the two sketches entitled "Demeter" and "A Spring Meeting," and we look forward to any future work of the author. There is more in his work than is met at first glance. Let him forget that he writes for English readers and subscribers to libraries!

                                           GEORGE RAFFALOVICH.

HISTORY OF CHEMISTRY. By SIR EDWARD THORPE. Watts and Co. Vol. ii.
    As excellent as vol. i. What is Sir Edward doing amongst this brainy
goody lot? H_2S.

HISTORY OF OLD TESTAMENT CRITICISM. By ARCHIBALD DUFF, D.D.
    Watts and Co. 1s. net.

An interesting little volume, as complete as can be expected for 146 pages. Duff, D.D., does not understand the Qabalah. We can assure him it is not a "fancied philosophy wherein everything was in reality brand new," as Zunz

335

THE EQUINOX

says. He does not understand it, but he is not alone in this. Few understand the Qabalah; and therefore few talk sense about the Pentateuch. We recommend Duff, D.D., to study " A Note on Genesis " in vol. i, No. 2, THE EQUINOX, after which if he still considers it " fancied " we shall be ready to discuss it with him.

B. RASHITH.

THE SACRED SPORTS OF SIVA. Printed at the Hindu Mission Press. Annas 8.

The editor in his preface does not see the objection to Gods and especially to Siva holding sports, neither do we. But you must play square, even if you are a God; it is not cricket to slay the whole of the opposing eleven each time you are bowled. But perhaps Siva had a reputation to keep up; we'll ask Kali.

VISHNU.

RITUAL, FAITH, AND MORALS. By F. H. PERRYCOSTE. Watts and Co.

If you should be so depraved as to desire to become a rationalistic author, you must buy a pair of scissors, some stickphast, and a parcel of odd vols. at Hodgson's, containing: Buckle, Draper, Gibbon, Lecky, an old dictionary or two of quotations and some of the Christian Fathers. The process then is easy; it consists in cutting these to pieces and in sticking them together in all possible combinations, and publishing each combination under a different name.

For fifteen years Mr. Perrycoste has been snipping hard, and the above work consists only of Chapters III and IV of one volume of a series of volumes. We are charitable enough to hope that Mr. Perrycoste may be spared to produce the rest, so long as we are spared reviewing them.   ELIAS ASHMOLE.

THE ANCIENT CONSTITUTIONAL CHARGES OF THE GUILD FREE MASONS. By JOHN YARKER. William Tait, 2s. 6d. net.

This is a most learned work; the author holds Solomon only knows how many exalted degrees; but besides the title-page there is much of interest to Masons in this little volume. Some of the ancient charges are quite amusing.

" That no Fellow go into town in the night time without a Fellow to bear witness that he hath been in honest company " seems, however, a bit rough on the girls.

F.

PAGANISM AND CHRISTIANITY. By J. A. FARRAR. Watts and Co. 6d.

A good book which makes us wish we had been born before Christ.

A. Q.

THE WHITE SLAVE TRAFFIC. Published at the Offices of M. A. P. 6d.

At one time I was acquainted with many of our London demi-mondaines, and many a charming girl and good-hearted woman had I the pleasure of meeting—and clean-minded withal. To say that all end in the Lock or the river is to say that you know nothing about the subject; for many marry, as Mayhew points out; in fact, Mayhew, in his classic " London Labour and the London Poor " is the only author I know—always excepting Charles Drysdale—who in any way saw the modern London hetaira as she really is. Drysdale in his courageous work, " The Elements of Social Science," also points out that the life of the ordinary prostitute is a very much healthier one than that of the average factory girl. The authoress of this work seems to understand this in a way, for in spite of " the awful degradation " which she harps upon, she contradicts herself by writing: " I may here remark that the girls I come in contact with, if they marry happily, make excellent wives " (p. 66).

The cure for the present degradation associated with prostitution is a common-sense one—one of not supposing that we are good and others are bad, of carting away our own manure before writing to the sanitary inspector about other people's dung, and to cease hatching mysteries between the sheets of our family four-poster.

If unions were sanctioned outside the marriage bond, even if such unions were only of an ephemeral nature, there would be no necessity to procure young girls, for natural love-making would take the place of state-fostered abduction. The root of the evil lies neither in the inherent lust of man after woman, which is natural, or of woman after gold, which shows her business-like capabilities; but in the unhealthy point of view adopted by the general public. There is nothing more disgusting in the act of generation, or even in the pleasures associated with it, than there is in alimentation, with its particular enjoyments. Dessert is quite a superfluous course after a good meal, and yet it is not considered degrading to eat it; and so, as it is not considered a crime to eat for the pleasure of eating, neither should it publicly (privately of course it is not) be considered a crime if unions take place without offspring resulting. This double-faced attitude must have the bottom knocked out of it as well as the front; it must utterly perish. From the natural, that is, the common-sense point of view, there are no such things as moral or immoral unions, for all nature demands is healthy parents and healthy children, healthy pleasures and healthy pains. The Church, the Chapel, and the Registry Office must go; for, so long as they remain, prostitution will spell degradation, and marriage falsehood and hypocrisy. Chaos will not result when Virtue weds with Vice, for what is possible to the savage is possible for us, and the children will be looked after better than ever. Once teach our children the nobility of love, and the pimp, the pander, and the puir-minded presbyter will simply be starved out. Continue to foster the present unhealthy aspect with its " unfortunate," its " fallen," its " awful," its " degradation " and its " doom," and, in spite of a million Vigilance Society men on every railway platform in the Kingdom, the White Slave Traffic will continue to flourish the more it is persecuted, and become more criminal and degrading than ever.

Money is not the basis of this so-called evil, as suggested, and public indignation will not work a cure any more than public indignation against the Metropolitan Water Board will stop people drinking water. We must cease globe-polishing virtue and sand-papering vice. Away with our moral Monkey Brand and our ethical Sapolio, and back to a little genuine common-sense elbow-grease.

When a girl ceases sowing her " wild oats " and can enter any phase of life without being spat upon and " chucked out," degradation will cease. And when such women as are *born* prostitutes are utilized by the State for the benefit of men who are not monogamists by nature, procuring will vanish. But, if these women be so used, it behoves the nation to care for these talented girls, just as she cares, or should care, for her soldiers; and when the time was expired, she should pension them off, and award them a long service and good-conduct medal should they deserve it.

This is a clean-minded book so far as it goes. We have no humbugging Horton, D.D., swooning at the thought of lace, frills, and a pretty ankle. But the remedies suggested are worse than the disease. Exalt the courtesan to her proper place, bracket her name with sweetheart, wife and mother, names which are rightly dear to us, and you will find a tender heart beneath the scarlet dress, and a charming lovable woman in spite of public opprobrium. Neglect this, and all other propositions of reform spell—Muck! A. QUILLER.

I like the legislation proposed by the blackguards of " vigilance "; who, never having met a gentleman, think that everybody is an avaricious scoundrel —though sometimes in another line of business. And this attack by M.A.P. on its trade rivals in the filth-purveying business (for all journalism is filth—must we exclude this White Slave "copy" from the indictment and class it as literature?) is only what is to be expected.

Anyhow, even our Government is hardly likely to pass the suggested Act, which thoughtfully provides that you may be arrested without a warrant for offering your umbrella in a shower to a strange lady, and makes it felony to raise your hat in the street.

I once had the pleasure of meeting Mr. Coote, well-groomed in ultra-respectable broadcloth, and flaunting Three Virtues in his button-hole. I looked for some others in his heart, but drew blank. If he had any others, too, I suppose he would have worn the appropriate ribbons.

The truth about Coote-Comstock crapulence is this. Manx Cats subscribe to the Society for the Suppression of Persian Cats. These funds go to support a lot of holy souteneurs in idleness—and they find it pays to foam at the mouth from time to time against the other souteneurs who live on poor prostitutes instead of wealthy virgins.

I should like, too, to ask Mr. Coote a rather curious question.

We were talking about paternity. His then secretary, Mr. Hewston, had given me to understand that the Vigilance Society made a practice of paying (on behalf of and at the expense of the fathers) allowances to the mothers of illegitimate children, of caring for the mothers, helping them to get work, and eventually marrying them to honest fellows of their own class.

This seemed too sensible to be true. Mr. Hewston's honest heart had led him to misunderstand.

Mr. Coote indignantly corrected this view of the Society's work. They never did that sort of thing, he said, *except in a few very special cases.*

Now I want to know about these very special cases. Are they by any chance those in which the fathers are reputable and pious persons, highly esteemed for their Evangelicalism and philanthropy? . . .

There have been some ill-disposed persons who were not ashamed to assert that some of the methods of Vigilance Societies reminded them of blackmail.

Is there another side to the medal?   A. QUILLER, JR.

THE CANON. An Exposition of the Pagan Mysteries perpetuated in the Cabala as the rule of all the arts. Elkin Mathews.

This is a very extraordinary book, and it should be a fair "eye-opener" to such as consider the Qabalah a fanciful concatenation of numbers, words, and names. Also it may come as rather a rude shock to some of our "fancied" knowalls, our "cocksureites," who are under the delusion that knowledge was born with their grandmothers, and has now reached perfection in themselves, for it proves conclusively enough by actual measurements of existing monuments and records that the ancients, hundreds of years ago, were perfectly well acquainted with what we are pleased in our swollenheadiness to call "the discoveries of modern science."

Every ancient temple was built on a definite symbolic design and was not a haphazard erection of brick and mortar dependent on £ s. d. On the contrary, it closely followed the measurements of the body of Christ or of a Man which it was supposed to represent.

The three great canonical numbers are 2,368 (IESOUS CHRISTOS), 1,480 (CHRISTOS) and 888 (IESOUS), Numerous other numbers also occur but most hinge on these three. Here is an example. 888, 1,480 and 2,368 are to each other in the ratio of 3, 5 and 8. 358 is numerically equal to Messiah, and and $358\frac{1}{2} \times 6 = 2,151$ which is again a symbol of the Hebrew Messiah. Alpha and Omega=2,152; and a hexagon described round a circle having a circumference of 2,151 has a perimeter of 2,368. 2,151 also is the sum of 1,480 (Christos) and 671 (Thora the Bride). A vesica 358 broad is 620 long, and 620 is the value of Kether, etc., etc. (see p. 124).

This book is a veritable model of industry and research, but in spite of an excellent index, an index in the ordinary sense is almost out of place in a work of so complicated a character as this; what is really needed is a table of the numerical correspondences, similar in type to those we have already published in our *777*. Then at a glance the student can see the various numerical values and what they refer to.   J. F. C. F.

KANT'S ETHICS AND SCHOPENHAUER'S CRITICISM. By M. KELLY. Swan Sonnenschein and Co., 2s. 6d.

Last year we had the pleasure of reviewing Major Kelly's " Kant's Philosophy as Rectified by Schopenhauer," and we hope that if in the future further volumes are to appear, and if they are as interesting as the present one, we may " continue the motion."

Kant's categories are in type similar to the Sephiroth of the Qabalah emanations from an unknown " x " sign or God, and whether this sign is called " à priori," " autonomy " or " categorical affirmative " matters no whit. Kant's ethics are futile, and to an intellect like Schopenhauer's absolutely childish. Kant never could understand " morality " because he never transcended the reason, practically, or even theoretically. If there is a moral law in the Formative World it is probably the line of least resistance. But the proof of the pudding is in the eating, and fixed laws of heteronomy and of autonomy are absurd, and if Kant had once transcended the Reason he would have had direct experience of this fact. On p. 126 Schopenhauer sets him right as follows:

"The essence of the world is will. . . . The only way of salvation is by negation of the will, or by self-denial and renunciation. . . ."

And again:

". . . life is the attainment of self-consciousness, in order that the will may acquire a right knowledge of its own nature. . . ." (p. 157).

"Evil and pleasure are but different manifestations of the one will to live " (p. 177).

"The tormentor and the tormented are one." . . . " Therefore what is good for one person may be just the opposite for another . . . all suffering is nothing but unfulfilled or crossed willing " (pp. 178-182).

"When a man has so far got rid of this veil that it no longer causes an egoistical distinction between his own person and that of another, he will recognize his innermost and true self in all beings, regard their endless suffering

THE BIG STICK

as his own, and so appropriate to himself the pain of the whole world " (p. 184).

Here the "true-self" is the Higher Self, Atman or Augoeides, unity with which is what we have called the Great Work of the A∴ A∴

When a soldier turns philosopher we always expect good work, and Major Kelly has not failed us; and to all such as would understand Kant as well as Schopenhauer's great work, "The World as Will and Idea"—of which an excellent English translation is published by Messrs. Paul, Trench, Trübner, we heartily recommend this masterful little volume. **F.**

THE SIGNS AND SYMBOLS OF PRIMORDIAL MAN. BY ALBERT CHURCHWARD. Swan Sonnenschein. 25s. net.

The first thing one has to do is to compose oneself in a comfortable position, for this book is large and weighs I don't know how many pounds; the next to remember that the author has an axe to grind, or at least has constituted himself leading counsel for his client Egypt, and in a learned and most convincing argument not only proves the undoubted antiquity of his client's claim, but that it was from Egypt, or rather Central Africa, that the human race originated, and that it is to Egyptian symbolism, and more particularly to the Ritual of the Dead, that we must go if we would rightly understand the temples, rites, ceremonies, and customs of mankind past and present. From Egypt they came and to Egypt must we go.

The book is in every sense a great book, and, by the way, it forms an excellent seventh volume to Gerald Massey's monumental work. Brother Wynne Westcott is very rightly condemned as displaying a peculiarly acute ignorance of both Freemasonry and Egyptology, and further on so is that chattering journalist, Mr. Andrew Lang—the Paul Carus of the British Isles.

Dr. Churchward is a Freemason of a very high degree, but yet not high enough to understand that secrets that need safeguarding are no secrets at all. " L. H." for left hand is excusable because it saves printers' ink; but "these need no explanation to R.A.M.'s" etc., etc., is ridiculous because R.A.M.'s need not be told about it, and if you are not going to divulge this frightful secret about a " Tau " why bother to say so? Remember that "an indicible arcanum is an arcanum which *cannot* be revealed," even by a R.A.M.! The Hebrew throughout is very faulty; either Dr. Churchward knows none, or else the proofs have been sadly neglected. But now let us turn to the subject over which he must have spent years of labour.

Man he traces back to the Pygmies of Central Africa, these or beings very like them hundreds of thousands of years ago emigrated all over the world— they were Paleolithic man, and whether these ape-like little beings had a Mythos or not would appear to be doubtful, but the next great exodus, that of Neolithic man, carried with it the Stellar Mythos,—that of the Seven Stars and the Pole Star, and the varied quarters to which these primitive men travelled is carefully indicated on the map at the end of the book. Though it may seem strange that they crossed vast oceans, it must be borne in mind that the configurations of the globe have changed since those remote periods; besides, primitive man did get about the world in a most extraordinary way, as such islands as Madagascar and Easter Island prove. The inhabitants of the former are Polynesian and not African, of the later, seemingly Melanesian, judging by their skulls, and the Solomon Islands, the nearest Melanesian islands to Easter Island, are thousands of miles away. Ducie Island, the nearest island to Easter Island, is many hundred miles away, and the coast of South America is no less than 2,300 miles distant. And yet in this tiny island we find proofs of very high civilization, and it is curious that Dr. Churchward has not mentioned the numerous hieroglyphics found there concerning which a very full account is given in the Smithsonian Reports of 1889. After these came another exodus, carrying with it the Lunar and Solar Mythos, and Horus became under varying names the supreme world-god, and his four sons, or emanations, the four quarters.

It is impossible here to enter into the numerous entrancing speculations that Dr. Churchward draws, or to give any adequate idea of the vast number of proofs that he marshals to convince us—they are quite bewildering. In fact, they completely reverse our conception of polytheism; for it is we who are the idolators, and not our ancestors; it is we who sacrifice to many gods, and not those little Bushmen who felt and saw and lived with the One Great Spirit. Let us therefore mention that the chief points, a few out of a score, that have struck us are—The Custom of the Mark Sacred Stone; the universality of Horus worship; the startling identity of hieroglyphics, all over the world, with the Egyptian; and the symbolism of the Great Pyramid, and its use as a Temple of Initiation.

A few others, however, do not understand. On p. 80 Dr. Churchward traces the "Bull Roarer" back to Egypt. But we can find no proofs of these ever having been used there. In Australia, as he states, they were used, and so also in New Zealand and New Guinea and over most of Europe; in Sussex, country boys to this day use them as toys. Again, the Egyptian throwing-stick (p. 67) is not a boomerang at all; it was made of thick rounded wood and will not return when thrown. It is as perfectly distinct from the Australian weapon as the Australian is from the throwing-clubs of Fiji. The double triangle symbol (?) is so common in the Pacific Islands that it is to be found on nearly every club and utensil; in some cases it represents figures of men with bent knees and arms akimbo. There are many combinations of it. In small details the author fails,

THE BIG STICK

he is so keen to find proof of Egyptian antiquity in everything. On p. 228 he quotes as an example of original sign-language that he "watched with interest our bluejackets leaning over the side of a man-of-war talking to one another" by means of their hands and fingers. Of course what they are really doing is semaphore signalling without flags after the official signalling with flags has ceased.

In spite of these small over-eagernesses, this book is a revolutionary volume, a work that should stimulate argument and comment; and we hope that it will induce others to collect and discover the secrets of the past before they are devoured by our Minotaurean Civilization. It is a melancholy fact that though amongst the rudest of rude savages secrets have been kept and great systems maintained for hundreds of thousands of years, the "clever" children of the present with all their arts and crafts are only destroyers of the past. We defame antiquity, annihilate those who still venerate it—mentally we destroy their minds with a corrupt and idolatrous Christianity, a veritable haggis of guts and blood, and their bodies with gunpowder and loathsome diseases. In a few years all will have gone; but (say you?) all will be saved, stored in our libraries and museums. But, we answer, even these in a few centuries will be dust and ashes; the very paper of this book which we are reviewing, beautiful though it be, will, like a girl's beauty, vanish before forty years are past. Our inventions are our curse, they are our destruction. What was coagulated in the minds of barbarians for thousands and tens of thousands of years we shall have destroyed utterly, utterly, in as many days and nights. Civilization has driven her plough over Stellar and Solar mythology, wantonly, and at haphazard, and in their place she has cultivated the Unknowable and Andrew Lang!

If the Utilitarian progress in the next few years as he has in the last, soon we shall have some socialistic fellah depriving the world of its last great monuments, and building labourers' cottages out of the stones and bricks of the Pyramids, because they are so very much more useful. "Solve" is the cry to-day; the Sabbatic finger of the Goat points upwards, yet on the clouds of darkness does it scrawl a sigil of light. A new God stirs in the Womb of its Mother; we can see his form, dim and red, in the cavern of Time. Dare we pronounce his name? Yea! It is Horus, Horus the Child, reborn Amsu the Good Shepherd, who will lead us out of the sheepish stupidity of to-day. How many understand this mystery? Perhaps none save those who have seen and subscribed to the Law of Thelema.   J. F. C. F.

THE LOST VALLEY. By ALGERNON BLACKWOOD. Nash. 6s.

It is the penalty of factitious success that the need of fuel increases like the dose of a drug-fiend. Instead of clothing his wit with silk from the loom of life

343

and embroidering it with gold thread drawn from the observation of things around him, the slave of popularity wears it threadbare. Morphia won't replace bread after the first month or so!

Now we see Mr. Blackwood and Nemesis. He gets a reputation by marketing his tiny scrap of knowledge of the Inner World; the public cries out for more, and the poor wage-slave, bankrupt in invention, does his best to fake—and fails.

It is the male equivalent of the harlot who has drifted from Piccadilly to Waterloo Bridge Road.

So here we see him, the shy smile changed to the open coarse appeal, the tawdry apparatus of his craft seen for what it is—rabbit-skin ermine!—and himself unmistakably the fifth-rate writer, like Baudelaire's "Old Mountebank"—surely no more pitiful—tumbling for no kindlier laugh than that of contempt. (And he might have been so fine!)

This is why success must in the nature of things spoil everybody. Make a hit with one arrow; you must never dare to do more than change the colour of the feathers—till your quiver is empty.

And how empty is Mr. Blackwood's! When it comes to a father hating his twin sons because (why?) he wanted one son very badly, going mad, and after his death turning the two into one in spite of a clergyman's reading aloud of Job——

Well, hang it, Mr. Blackwood, the woman has the best of it yet. It is a very foolish girl who cannot hold her own for ten years. But you who have been writing hardly half the time are only fit for the Literary Lock Hospital.

JONATHAN HUTCHINSON, Natu Minimus.

AMBERGRIS. A Selection of Poems by ALEISTER CROWLEY. Elkin Mathews. 3s. 6d. Printed by Strangeways and Sons, Great Tower Street, Cambridge Circus, W.C.

We don't like books of selections, and you can't make a nightingale out of a crow by picking out the least jarring notes.

The book is nicely bound and printed—as if that were any excuse! Mr. Crowley, however, must have been surprised to receive a bill of over Six Pounds for "author's corrections," as the book was printed from his volume of Collected Works, and the alterations made by him were well within the dozen!

[Yes; he was surprised; it was his first—and last—experience of these strange ways.—ED.]

If poets are ever going to make themselves heard, they must find some means of breaking down the tradition that they are the easy dupes of every —— [Satis.—ED.]

344

THE BIG STICK

Just as a dishonest commercial traveller will sometimes get a job by accepting a low salary, and look for profit to falsifying the accounts of "expenses," so —— [Here; this will never do.—Ed.]

We have had fine weather recently in Mesopotamia—— [I dare say; but I'm getting suspicious; stop right here.—Ed.] All right; don't be huffy; good-bye!   S. HOLMES.

SECRET REMEDIES. British Medical Association, 429, Strand, W.C. 1s.

Every person who has the welfare of the people at heart should buy this book for free distribution among the poor.

The major portion of the Press (which lives corruptly on the advertisements of the scoundrels exposed in this book, knaves who sell ginger at the price of gold) has done its best to boycott the book.

The public—the helpless, ignorant section of it—spends nigh $2\frac{1}{2}$ millions sterling every year on these quack nostrums.

We must safeguard them. We must register all "patent" remedies, insist on the ingredients and their cost being printed clearly on each box, and appoint a committee with funds at its disposal from the Treasury to recompense adequately and generously anyone who really should discover a cure for human affliction.

The Chancellor of the Exchequer need not worry about his third of a million yearly from the stamp duty. No country ever yet lost money by driving out its bloodsuckers, and saving its citizens from the penalties of ignorance.
                                                                A. C.

THE MAGNETIC MIRROR. By DR. CAROLUS REX. 1s.

This little work is very skilfully written; it is intended to induce members of the higher grades of the Universal Order of B∴ F∴ to pay "Dr." "Carolus" "Rex" sums of from Two to Twenty Guineas for "Magic Mirrors," which we hope are worth as many pence.   PROFESSOR JACOBUS IMPERATOR.

GLAZIERS' HOUSES:

OR,

THE SHAVING OF SHAGPAT

I will write him a very taunting letter.—*As You Like It.*

In these latter days, when (too often) a newspaper proprietor is like a Buddhist monk, afraid to scratch his head lest he should incommode his vermin, it is indeed a joy for a young and nameless author to be presented with a long sword by a cordial editor, with the injunction: "There, my lad, sweep away, never mind what you hit—I'll stand the racket."

Whoosh! off we go. One, two, three—crash! What's that? "Aere perennius"? Or a perennial ass?

Let us see—a very curious problem.

A problem not to be solved by mere surface scraping. Well then?

A thankless and invidious task it may seem to pierce deeper than the "wolf in Dr. Jaeger's clothing" of our wittiest woman and most alluring *morphinomane.* That task is ours. For last night in the visions of mine head upon my bed I beheld, strangely interwoven with this striking picture, the scene between Little Red Riding Hood and her sick grandmother—how perverted! For in my dream it seemed that the old lady had devoured the wolf and that the scourge of the

346

GLAZIERS' HOUSES

Tories was but a bed-ridden and toothless hag, mumbling the senile curses and jests which she could no longer articulate.

True it is that the Word of Shaw is quick and powerful, sharper than a two-edged sword. Yet the habit of sword-swallowing is probably fatal to the suicidal intentions of a Brutus, and it has certainly grown on him until he can no longer slay either himself or another.

A dweller in the glass houses of Fad, he has thrown stones at the fishy god. A Society Shimei, he has spat against the wind, and his beard is befouled.

True, every thought of Shaw is a great thought; and so equable and far-seeing is the artist, that its contradictory appears with it. His births are all Siamese twins; his god is Janus; his sign is Gemini . . . but his end is (I fear) not to rise above the equilibrium of contraries by a praeter-Hegelian dialectic, but to sink wearily between his two stools, a lamentable loon. . . . This Nulli Secundus, inflated with fermenting Grape-Nuts!

For in all that mass of analysis lucid and terrible I cannot recall a single line of beauty, rarely a note of ecstasy; with one exception (John Tanner), hardly a hero. Even he not a little absurd.

He has seen through the shams of romance, and marriage, and free love, and literary pose, and medical Ju-Ju, and religious rant, and political twaddle, and Socialist Buncombe and—every phase of falsehood. . . . But he has hardly grasped that each such falsehood is but a shadow of some sun of truth. He does not perceive the ineffable glory of the Universe in its whole and in each part. He has smitten at the shadow of a shadow: it falls—the world is filth. Let him rather new-edge his sword for a deeper analysis, and cut away the veil from the face of our Mother. 'Sdeath, man, is there nothing we may love?

He is wrong, anyway, to gibe at Scripture. For, like Balaam, I came to curse, and appear to be blessing him! (with scarce a monitory word). And, like Balaam, too, I have been reviewed by G. K. Chesterton.

To pass from this painful subject. . . .

Let me rouse myself to a really resolute effort to denounce Shaw as a niddering. Aha! I have it. The man is a journalist after all. We have to thank him for semi-educating a few of our noodles, for applying the caustic of Ibsen (right) and Wagner (wrong—the book's drivel) to that most indolent of ulcers, the British Public, but for nothing more. His own work, bar "Man and Overman" (why the hybrid Super-man?), is a glib sham. If it proves anything, it proves nothing.

But are we to writhe in the ecstasies of Pyrrhonism? For this prophet claims to be Zoroaster.

Can we be sure even of that? He has educated the British goat to caper to his discordant Pan-pipe, so that without the nuisance of crucifixion he may scourge the money-changers from the temple.

Yet is this true cynicism? Doth he delight, the surly Diogenes, in his solitary gambols—that insult both Lydia and Lalage? Or is he doing it to tempt them—to coquette with them? Is he a man deadly serious in positive constructive aim, yet so sensitive to ridicule that he will always seek to turn it off as a jest—and so a stultifier of himself? A Christ crucified, not upon Calvary, but upon Venusberg, and so no redeemer?

If so, *ave atque vale*, George Bernard Shaw, for a redeemer from the Overmen we want, and we will have; another we will not have. Rather than your mock-crucified castrato-devilry, Barabbas!

But if it be your serious livelong purpose to slay all ideas by ridicule. . . . Then we must claim you as an adept, one fit for the scourge and the buffets, for the gibes and the slaver of the lick-spittle English, whose only notion of a jest is a smutty story.

There is room for another hand at my bench.

See! If thou be indeed Achilles, why should we be in doubt? The gilded arms of Pandarus—the speech of Thersites. Sir, these things trouble us!

Thou seest it! If thou art journalist, the very journalists may rise from their slime, bubbling with foul breath, and suck thee down to their mother ooze unspeakable; but if not, then I too (no journalist, God knows!) must praise thee.

Thee—not thy work. For the manner thereof is wholly abominable. What have all we done, that for Pegasus we have this spavined and hamstrung Rosinante, for Bucephalus this hydrocephalic hydropath?

Even as god Gilbert begat the devil-brood musical comedy, so hast thou begotten the tedious stage-sermons to which our priest-loving, sin-conscious slaves now flock. Refinement of cruelty! Thou hast replaced the Trappist cell by the Court Theatre!

For this, I, who prefer the study to the theatre, forgive thee; for I love not the badger-reek of Suburbia and Bohemia in my nostrils. But for this also I praise thee, that lion-like thou turnest at last upon the jackal-crowd at thy heels. That ungainly dragon, the Chesterbelloc, hast thou ridden against,

349

good St. George Bernard Shaw! With a spear thou hast pierced its side, and there floweth forth beer and water.

Turn also, gramercy, upon the others, even unto the lowest. As Ibsen hawked at carrion birds with a Wild Duck, so do thou create some harpy to torment them. Who is this that followeth thee? Behold this mumbler born to butcher the English language, and educated to hack it with a saw! This stuttering babbler, this Harpocrates by the compulsion of a Sloane Square Mammurra! Who is this hanger-on to the bedraggled petticoats of thy lousy Thalia—this beardless, witless filcher of thy fallen crab-apples? This housemaid of the Court Theatre, the Gittite slut whose bleary eyes weep sexless crocodile tears over the crassness of the daughters of the Philistines?

Arise, and speak to this palsied megalomaniac, this frowsy Moll Flanders of a degenerated Chelsea, this down-at-heel *flâneur* on the outer boulevards of a prostituted literature, this little mongrel dog that fawneth upon the ill-cut trousers of thee, O St. Pancras Pulchinello—this little red-coated person that doth mouth and dance upon the kakophonous barrel-organ of New Thought fakirs and Modernity mountebanks.

Speak to this parasite—itself unspeakably verminous—of the long-haired brigade, who has "got on" for that it had neither sufficient talent to excite envy, nor manhood enough to excite apprehension, but wit well to comprehend the sycophancy of the self-styled court and the tittle-tattle of the servants' hall.

It is an Editor—dear Lord my God! it is an Editor; but he who employs it has an equally indefeasible title to employ the pronoun "We."

GLAZIERS' HOUSES

It hath never had aught to say; but, then, how affectedly it hath said it! . . .

Will not the late *New Quarterly* take note of this?

O these barbers, with their prattle, and their false expedients—and scarce even a safety razor among them!

For let each one who worships George Bernard Shaw, while ignorant of that magnificent foundation of literature and philosophy—the Cubical Stone of the Wise, on which a greater than Auguste Rodin hath erected the indomitable figure of Le Penseur—take these remarks individually to himself, and—oh! Thinker, think again. Let not posterity consider of this statue that its summit is no Overman, but a gibbering ape! Not filth, not sorrow, not laughter of the mocker is this universe; but laughter of a young god, a holy and beautiful god, a god of love and light.

And thou, since thou hast the ear of the British ass at thy lips, sing to it those starry songs. It can but bray. . . .

But why, as hitherto, shouldst thou bray also? Or if bray thou must, let us have the virile and portentous bray of the Ass of Apuleius, not (as hitherto) the plaintive bray of the proverbial ass who hesitated so long between the two thistles that he starved to death. I warn thee, ass! We who are gods have laughed with thee these many years; beware lest in the end we laugh at thee with the laughter of a mandrake torn up, whereat thou shouldst fall dead.

A. QUILLER, JR.

351

IN THE TEMPLE

The subtle-souled dim radiant queen
  Burns like a bale-fire through the mist;
The slender earth is bright and green,
  Emerald, gray and amethyst;
  The wavering breeze has slowly kissed
The way between
  Her zone and wrist.

Pale guardian of the altar-flame,
  Syren of old, perfidious song,
A murmuring runnel lately came
  In streaming hate of mortal wrong.
  Wait, for, my goddess, not for long
The snake is tame. . . .
  See! He is strong!

The wide-set temple-pillars gleam,
  As marble white, and tall as pines;
The doorway to immortal dream
  Lies through the temple's purple shrines.
  Behold, pure queen, the magic signs.
Let words out-stream
  As mingled wines! . . .

VICTOR B. NEUBURG.

THE HIGH HISTORY OF GOOD SIR PALAMEDES THE SARACEN KNIGHT AND OF HIS FOLLOWING OF THE QUESTING BEAST BY ALEISTER CROWLEY RIGHTLY SET FORTH IN RIME

TO ALLAN BENNETT

" Bhikkhu Ananda Metteyya "

my good knight comrade in the Quest, I dedicate this
imperfect account of it, in some small recognition of
his suggestion of its form.

MANDALAY, *November* 1905

ARGUMENT

i. Sir Palamede, the Saracen knight, riding on the shore of Syria, findeth his father's corpse, around which an albatross circleth.   He approveth the vengeance of his peers.

ii. On the shore of Arabia he findeth his mother in the embrace of a loathly negro beneath blue pavilions.   Her he slayeth, and burneth all that encampment.

iii. Sir Palamede is besieged in his castle by Severn mouth, and his wife and son are slain.

iv. Hearing that his fall is to be but the prelude to an attack on Camelot, he maketh a desperate night sortie, and will traverse the wilds of Wales.

v. At the end of his resources among the Welsh mountains, he is compelled to put to death his only remaining child.   By this sacrifice he saves the world of chivalry.

vi. He having become an holy hermit, a certain dwarf, splendidly clothed, cometh to Arthur's court, bearing tidings of a Questing Beast.   The knights fail to lift him, this being the test of worthiness.

vii. Lancelot findeth him upon Scawfell, clothed in his white beard.   He returneth, and, touching the dwarf but with his finger, hurleth him to the heaven.

viii. Sir Palamede, riding forth on the quest, seeth a Druid worship the sun upon Stonehenge.   He rideth eastward, and findeth the sun setting in the west.   Furious he taketh a Viking ship, and by sword and whip fareth seaward.

ix. Coming to India, he learneth that It glittereth.   Vainly fighting the waves, the leaves, and the snows, he is swept in the Himalayas as by an avalanche into a valley where dwell certain ascetics, who pelt him with their eyeballs.

x. Seeking It as Majesty, he chaseth an elephant in the Indian jungle.   The elephant escapeth ; but he, led to Trichinopoli by an Indian lad, seeth an elephant forced to dance ungainly before the Mahalingam.

xi. A Scythian sage declareth that It transcendeth Reason.   Therefore Sir Palamede unreasonably decapitateth him.

xii. An ancient hag prateth of It as Evangelical.   Her he heweth in pieces.

THE HIGH HISTORY OF GOOD

xiii. At Naples he thinketh of the Beast as author of Evil, because Free of Will. The Beast, starting up, is slain by him with a poisoned arrow ; but at the moment of Its death It is reborn from the knight's own belly.

xiv. At Rome he meeteth a red robber in a Hat, who speaketh nobly of It as of a king-dove-lamb. He chaseth and slayeth it ; it proves but a child's toy.

xv. In a Tuscan grove he findeth, from the antics of a Satyr, that the Gods still dwell with men. Mistaking orgasm for ecstasy, he is found ridiculous.

xvi. Baiting for It with gilded corn in a moonlit vale of Spain, he findeth the bait stolen by vermin.

xvii. In Crete a metaphysician weaveth a labyrinth. Sir Palamede compelleth him to pursue the quarry in this same fashion. Running like hippogriffs, they plunge over the precipice ; and the hermit, dead, appears but a mangy ass. Sir Palamede, sore wounded, is borne by fishers to an hut.

xviii. Sir Palamede noteth the swiftness of the Beast. He therefore climbeth many mountains of the Alps. Yet can he not catch It ; It outrunneth him easily, and at last, stumbling, he falleth.

xix. Among the dunes of Brittany he findeth a witch dancing and conjuring, until she disappeareth in a blaze of light. He then learneth music, from a vile girl, until he is as skilful as Orpheus. In Paris he playeth in a public place. The people, at first throwing him coins, soon desert him to follow a foolish Egyptian wizard. No Beast cometh to his call.

xx. He argueth out that there can be but one Beast. Following single tracks, he at length findeth the quarry, but on pursuit It eludeth him by multiplying itself. This on the wide plains of France.

xxi. He gathereth an army sufficient to chase the whole herd. In England's midst they rush upon them ; but the herd join together, leading on the knights, who at length rush together into a *mêlée*, wherein all but Sir Palamede are slain, while the Beast, as ever, standeth aloof, laughing.

xxii. He argueth Its existence from design of the Cosmos, noting that Its tracks form a geometrical figure. But seeth that this depends upon his sense of geometry ; and is therefore no proof. Meditating upon this likeness to himself—Its subjectivity, in short —he seeth It in the Blue Lake. Thither plunging, all is shattered.

xxiii. Seeking It in shrines he findeth but a money-box ; while they that helped him (as they said) in his search, but robbed him.

xxiv. Arguing Its obscurity, he seeketh It within the bowels of Etna, cutting off all avenues of sense. His own thoughts pursue him into madness.

SIR PALAMEDES, THE SARACEN KNIGHT

xxv. Upon the Pacific Ocean, he, thinking that It is not-Self, throweth himself into the sea. But the Beast setteth him ashore.

xxvi. Rowed by Kanakas to Japan, he praiseth the stability of Fuji-Yama. But, an earthquake arising, the pilgrims are swallowed up.

xxvii. Upon the Yang-tze-kiang he contemplateth immortal change. Yet, perceiving that the changes themselves constitute stability, he is again baulked, and biddeth his men bear him to Egypt.

xxviii. In an Egyptian temple he hath performed the Bloody Sacrifice, and cursed Osiris. Himself suffering that curse, he is still far from the Attainment.

xxix. In the land of Egypt he performeth many miracles. But from the statue of Memnon issueth the questing, and he is recalled from that illusion.

xxx. Upon the plains of Chaldea he descendeth into the bowels of the earth, where he beholdeth the Visible Image of the Soul of Nature for the Beast. Yet Earth belcheth him forth.

xxxi. In a slum city he converseth with a Rationalist. Learning nothing, nor even hearing the Beast, he goeth forth to cleanse himself.

xxxii. Seeking to imitate the Beast, he goeth on all-fours, questing horribly. The townsmen cage him for a lunatic. Nor can he imitate the elusiveness of the Beast. Yet at one note of that questing the prison is shattered, and Sir Palamede rusheth forth free.

xxxiii. Sir Palamede hath gone to the shores of the Middle Sea to restore his health. There he practiseth devotion to the Beast, and becometh maudlin and sentimental. His knaves mocking him, he beateth one sore; from whose belly issueth the questing.

xxxiv. Being retired into an hermitage in Fenland, he traverseth space upon the back of an eagle. He knoweth all things—save only It. And incontinent beseecheth the eagle to set him down again.

xxxv. He lectureth upon metaphysics—for he is now totally insane—to many learned monks of Cantabrig. They applaud him and detain him, though he hath heard the questing and would away. But so feeble is he that he fleeth by night.

xxxvi. It hath often happened to Sir Palamede that he is haunted by a shadow, the which he may not recognise. But at last, in a sunlit wood, this is discovered to be a certain hunchback, who doubteth whether there be at all any Beast or any quest, or if the whole life of Sir Palamede be not a vain illusion. Him, without seeking to conquer with words, he slayeth incontinent.

xxxvii. In a cave by the sea, feeding on limpets and roots, Sir Palamede abideth, sick unto death. Himseemeth the Beast questeth within his own bowels: he is the

SIR PALAMEDES, THE SARACEN KNIGHT

Beast. Standing up, that he may enjoy the reward, he findeth another answer to the riddle. Yet abideth in the quest.

xxxviii. Sir Palamede is confronted by a stranger knight, whose arms are his own, as also his features. This knight mocketh Sir Palamede for an impudent pretender, and impersonator of the chosen knight. Sir Palamede in all humility alloweth that there is no proof possible, and offereth ordeal of battle, in which the stranger is slain. Sir Palamede heweth him into the smallest dust without pity.

xxxix. In a green valley he obtaineth the vision of Pan. Thereby he regaineth all that he had expended of strength and youth; is gladdened thereat, for he now devoteth again his life to the quest; yet more utterly cast down than ever, for that this supreme vision is not the Beast.

xl. Upon the loftiest summit of a great mountain he perceiveth Naught. Even this is, however, not the Beast.

xli. Returning to Camelot to announce his failure, he maketh entrance into the King's hall, whence he started out upon the quest. The Beast cometh nestling to him. All the knights attain the quest. The voice of Christ is heard: "Well done." He sayeth that each failure is a step in the Path. The poet prayeth success therein for himself and his readers.

THE HIGH HISTORY
OF GOOD

SIR PALAMEDES

THE SARACEN KNIGHT; AND OF HIS FOLLOWING
OF

THE QUESTING BEAST

A

I

Sir Palamede the Saracen
  Rode by the marge of many a sea:
He had slain a thousand evil men
  And set a thousand ladies free.

Armed to the teeth, the glittering knight
  Galloped along the sounding shore,
His silver arms one lake of light,
  Their clash one symphony of war.

How still the blue enamoured sea
  Lay in the blaze of Syria's noon!
The eternal roll eternally
  Beat out its monotonic tune.

Sir Palamede the Saracen
  A dreadful vision here espied,
A sight abhorred of gods and men,
  Between the limits of the tide.

The dead man's tongue was torn away;
  The dead man's throat was slit across;
There flapped upon the putrid prey
  A carrion, screaming albatross.

THE HIGH HISTORY OF GOOD

So halted he his horse, and bent
  To catch remembrance from the eyes
That stared to God, whose ardour sent
  His radiance from the ruthless skies.

Then like a statue still he sate;
  Nor quivered nerve, nor muscle stirred;
While round them flapped insatiate
  The fell, abominable bird.

But coldest horror drave the light
  From knightly eyes.   How pale thy bloom,
Thy blood, O brow whereon the night
  Sits like a serpent on a tomb!

For Palamede those eyes beheld
  The iron image of his own;
On those dead brows a fate he spelled
  To strike a Gorgon into stone.

He knew his father.   Still he sate,
  Nor quivered nerve, nor muscle stirred;
While round them flapped insatiate
  The fell, abominable bird.

The knight approves the justice done,
  And pays with that his rowels' debt;
While yet the forehead of the son
  Stands beaded with an icy sweat.

SIR PALAMEDES, THE SARACEN KNIGHT

God's angel, standing sinister,
  Unfurls this scroll—a sable stain :
" Who wins the spur shall ply the spur
  Upon his proper heart and brain."

He gave the sign of malison
  On traitor knights and perjured men ;
And ever by the sea rode on
  Sir Palamede the Saracen.

II

BEHOLD! Arabia's burning shore
  Rings to the hoofs of many a steed.
Lord of a legion rides to war
  The indomitable Palamede.

The Paynim fly; his troops delight
  In murder of many a myriad men,
Following exultant into fight
  Sir Palamede the Saracen.

Now when a year and day are done
  Sir Palamedes is aware
Of blue pavilions in the sun,
  And bannerets fluttering in the air.

Forward he spurs; his armour gleams;
  Then on his haunches rears the steed;
Above the lordly silk there streams
  The pennon of Sir Palamede!

Aflame, a bridegroom to his spouse,
  He rides to meet with galliard grace
Some scion of his holy house,
  Or germane to his royal race.

SIR PALAMEDES, THE SARACEN KNIGHT

But oh! the eyes of shame! Beneath
   The tall pavilion's sapphire shade
There sport a band with wand and wreath,
   Languorous boy and laughing maid.

And in the centre is a sight
   Of hateful love and shameless shame:
A recreant Abyssinian knight
   Sports grossly with a wanton dame.

How black and swinish is the knave!
   His hellish grunt, his bestial grin;
Her trilling laugh, her gesture suave,
   The cool sweat swimming on her skin!

She looks and laughs upon the knight,
   Then turns to buss the blubber mouth,
Draining the dregs of that black blight
   Of wine to ease their double drouth!

God! what a glance! Sir Palamede
   Is stricken by the sword of fate:
His mother it is in very deed
   That gleeful goes the goatish gait.

His mother it his, that pure and pale
   Cried in the pangs that gave him birth;
The holy image he would veil
   From aught the tiniest taint of earth.

SIR PALAMEDES, THE SARACEN KNIGHT

She knows him, and black fears bedim
　　Those eyes ; she offers to his gaze
The blue-veined breasts that suckled him
　　In childhood's sweet and solemn days.

Weeping she bares the holy womb !
　　Shrieks out the mother's last appeal :
And reads irrevocable doom
　　In those dread eyes of ice and steel.

He winds his horn : his warriors pour
　　In thousands on the fenceless foe ;
The sunset stains their hideous war
　　With crimson bars of after-glow.

He winds his horn : the night-stars leap
　　To light ; upspring the sisters seven ;
While answering flames illume the deep,
　　The blue pavilions blaze to heaven.

Silent and stern the northward way
　　They ride ; alone before his men
Staggers through black to rose and grey
　　Sir Palamede the Saracen.

III

THERE is a rock by Severn mouth
  Whereon a mighty castle stands,
Fronting the blue impassive South
  And looking over lordly lands.

Oh ! high above the envious sea
  This fortress dominates the tides ;
There, ill at heart, the chivalry
  Of strong Sir Palamede abides.

Now comes irruption from the folk
  That live by murder : day by day
The good knight strikes his deadly stroke ;
  The vultures claw the attended prey.

But day by day the heathen hordes
  Gather from dreadful lands afar,
A myriad myriad bows and swords,
  As clouds that blot the morning star.

Soon by an arrow from the sea
  The Lady of Palamede is slain ;
His son, in sally fighting free,
  Is struck through burgonet and brain.

THE HIGH HISTORY OF GOOD

But day by day the foes increase,
  Though day by day their thousands fall:
Laughs the unshaken fortalice;
  The good knights laugh no more at all.

Grimmer than heathen hordes can scowl,
  The spectre hunger rages there;
He passes like a midnight owl,
  Hooting his heraldry, despair.

The knights and squires of Palamede
  Stalk pale and lean through court and hall;
Though sharp and swift the archers speed
  Their yardlong arrows from the wall.

Their numbers thin; their strength decays;
  Their fate is written plain to read.
These are the dread deciduous days
  Of iron-souled Sir Palamede.

He hears the horrid laugh that rings
  From camp to camp at night; he hears
The cruel mouths of murderous kings
  Laugh out one menace that he fears.

No sooner shall the heroes die
  Than, ere their flesh begin to rot,
The heathen turns his raving eye
  To Caerlon and Camelot.

SIR PALAMEDES, THE SARACEN KNIGHT

King Arthur in ignoble sloth
   Is sunk, and dalliance with his dame,
Forgetful of his knightly oath,
   And careless of his kingly name.

Befooled and cuckolded, the king
   Is yet the king, the king most high ;
And on his life the hinges swing
   That close the door of chivalry.

'Sblood ! shall it sink, and rise no more,
   That blaze of Time, when men were men ?
That is thy question, warrior
   Sir Palamede the Saracen !

IV

Now, with two score of men in life
  And one fair babe, Sir Palamede
Resolves one last heroic strife,
  Attempts forlorn a desperate deed.

At dead of night, a moonless night,
  A night of winter storm, they sail
In dancing dragons to the fight
  With man and sea, with ghoul and gale.

Whom God shall spare, ride, ride! (so springs
  The iron order).   Let him fly
On honour's steed with honour's wings
  To warn the king, lest honour die!

Then to the fury of the blast
  Their fury adds a dreadful sting :
The fatal die is surely cast.
  To save the king—to save the king!

Hail! horror of the midnight surge!
  The storms of death, the lashing gust,
The doubtful gleam of swords that urge
  Hot laughter with high-leaping lust!

SIR PALAMEDES, THE SARACEN KNIGHT

Though one by one the heroes fall,
  Their desperate way they slowly win,
And knightly cry and comrade-call
  Rise high above the savage din.

Now, now they land, a dwindling crew;
  Now, now fresh armies hem them round.
They cleave their blood-bought avenue,
  And cluster on the upper ground.

Ah! but dawn's dreadful front uprears!
  The tall towers blaze, to illume the fight;
While many a myriad heathen spears
  March northward at the earliest light.

Falls thy last comrade at thy feet,
  O lordly-souled Sir Palamede?
Tearing the savage from his seat,
  He leaps upon a coal-black steed.

He gallops raging through the press:
  The affrighted heathen fear his eye.
There madness gleams, there masterless
  The whirling sword shrieks shrill and high.

They shrink, he gallops. Closely clings
  The child slung at his waist; and he
Heeds nought, but gallops wide, and sings
  Wild war-songs, chants of gramarye!

SIR PALAMEDES, THE SARACEN KNIGHT

Sir Palamede the Saracen
   Rides like a centaur mad with war;
He sabres many a million men,
   And tramples many a million more!

Before him lies the untravelled land
   Where never a human soul is known,
A desert by a wizard banned,
   A soulless wilderness of stone.

Nor grass, nor corn, delight the vales;
   Nor beast, nor bird, span space.   Immense,
Black rain, grey mist, white wrath of gales,
   Fill the dread armoury of sense.

Nor shines the sun; nor moon, nor star
   Their subtle light at all display;
Nor day, nor night, dispute the scaur:
   All's one intolerable grey.

Black llyns, grey rocks, white hills of snow!
   No flower, no colour: life is not.
This is no way for men to go
   From Severn-mouth to Camelot.

Despair, the world upon his speed,
   Drive (like a lion from his den
Whom hunger hunts) the man at need,
   Sir Palamede the Saracen.

V

Sir Palamede the Saracen
  Hath cast his sword and arms aside.
To save the world of goodly men,
  He sets his teeth to ride—to ride!

Three days : the black horse drops and dies.
  The trappings furnish them a fire,
The beast a meal.   With dreadful eyes
  Stare into death the child, the sire.

Six days : the gaunt and gallant knight
  Sees hateful visions in the day.
Where are the antient speed and might
  Were wont to animate that clay?

Nine days ; they stumble on ; no more
  His strength avails to bear the child.
Still hangs the mist, and still before
  Yawns the immeasurable wild.

Twelve days : the end.   Afar he spies
  The mountains stooping to the plain ;
A little splash of sunlight lies
  Beyond the everlasting rain.

15

THE HIGH HISTORY OF GOOD

His strength is done ; he cannot stir.
  The child complains—how feebly now !
His eyes are blank ; he looks at her ;
  The cold sweat gathers on his brow.

To save the world—three days away !
  His life in knighthood's life is furled,
And knighthood's life in his—to-day !—
  His darling staked against the world !

Will he die there, his task undone ?
  Or dare he live, at such a cost ?
He cries against the impassive sun :
  The world is dim, is all but lost.

Then, with the bitterness of death
  Cutting his soul, his fingers clench
The piteous passage of her breath.
  The dews of horror rise and drench

Sir Palamede the Saracen.
  Then, rising from the hideous meal,
He plunges to the land of men
  With nerves renewed and limbs of steel.

Who is the naked man that rides
  Yon tameless stallion on the plain,
His face like Hell's ? What fury guides
  The maniac beast without a rein ?

SIR PALAMEDES, THE SARACEN KNIGHT

Who is the naked man that spurs
   A charger into Camelot,
His face like Christ's ?   What glory stirs
   The air around him, do ye wot ?

Sir Arthur arms him, makes array
   Of seven times ten thousand men,
And bids them follow and obey
   Sir Palamede the Saracen.

VI

Sir Palamede the Saracen
   The earth from murder hath released,
Is hidden from the eyes of men.

Sir Arthur sits again at feast.
   The holy order burns with zeal :
Its fame revives from west to east.

Now, following Fortune's whirling wheel,
   There comes a dwarf to Arthur's hall,
All cased in damascenèd steel.

A sceptre and a golden ball
   He bears, and on his head a crown ;
But on his shoulders drapes a pall

Of velvet flowing sably down
   Above his vest of cramoisie.
Now doth the king of high renown

Demand him of his dignity.
   Whereat the dwarf begins to tell
A quest of loftiest chivalry.

SIR PALAMEDES, THE SARACEN KNIGHT

Quod he : " By Goddes holy spell,
   So high a venture was not known,
Nor so divine a miracle.

A certain beast there runs alone,
   That ever in his belly sounds
A hugeous cry, a monster moan,

As if a thirty couple hounds
   Quested within him. Now God saith
(I swear it by His holy wounds

And by His lamentable death,
   And by His holy Mother's face !)
That he shall know the Beauteous Breath

And taste the Goodly Gift of Grace
   Who shall achieve this marvel quest."
Then Arthur sterte up from his place,

And sterte up boldly all the rest,
   And sware to seek this goodly thing.
But now the dwarf doth beat his breast,

And speak on this wise to the king,
   That he should worthy knight be found
Who with his hands the dwarf should bring

By might one span from off the ground.
   Whereat they jeer, the dwarf so small,
The knights so strong : the walls resound

With laughter rattling round the hall.
  But Arthur first essays the deed,
And may not budge the dwarf at all.

Then Lancelot sware by Goddes reed,
  And pulled so strong his muscle burst,
His nose and mouth brake out a-bleed ;

Nor moved he thus the dwarf. From first
  To last the envious knights essayed,
And all their malice had the worst,

Till strong Sir Bors his prowess played—
  And all his might availèd nought.
Now once Sir Bors had been betrayed

To Paynim ; him in traitrise caught,
  They bound to four strong stallion steers,
To tear asunder, as they thought,

The paladin of Arthur's peers.
  But he, a-bending, breaks the spine
Of three, and on the fourth he rears

His bulk, and rides away. Divine
  The wonder when the giant fails
To stir the fatuous dwarf, malign

Who smiles ! But Bors on Arthur rails
  That never a knight is worth but one.
" By Goddes death " (quod he), " what ails

SIR PALAMEDES, THE SARACEN KNIGHT

Us marsh-lights to forget the sun?
　There is one man of mortal men
Worthy to win this benison,

Sir Palamede the Saracen."
　Then went the applauding murmur round:
Sir Lancelot girt him there and then

To ride to that enchanted ground
　Where amid timeless snows the den
Of Palamedes might be found.

VII

BEHOLD Sir Lancelot of the Lake
   Breasting the stony screes : behold
How breath must fail and muscle ache

Before he reach the icy fold
   That Palamede the Saracen
Within its hermitage may hold.

At last he cometh to a den
   Perched high upon the savage scaur,
Remote from every haunt of men,

From every haunt of life afar.
   There doth he find Sir Palamede
Sitting as steadfast as a star.

Scarcely he knew the knight indeed,
   For he was compassed in a beard
White as the streams of snow that feed

The lake of Gods and men revered
   That sitteth upon Caucasus.
So muttered he a darkling weird,

SIR PALAMEDES, THE SARACEN KNIGHT

And smote his bosom murderous.
  His nails like eagles' claws were grown ;
His eyes were wild and dull ; but thus

Sir Lancelot spake : "Thy deeds atone
  By knightly devoir !"   He returned
That "While the land was overgrown

With giant, fiend, and ogre burned
  My sword ; but now the Paynim bars
Are broke, and men to virtue turned :

Therefore I sit upon the scars
  Amid my beard, even as the sun
Sits in the company of the stars ! "

Then Lancelot bade this deed be done,
  The achievement of the Questing Beast.
Which when he spoke that holy one

Rose up, and gat him to the east
  With Lancelot ; when as they drew
Unto the palace and the feast

He put his littlest finger to
  The dwarf, who rose to upper air,
Piercing the far eternal blue

Beyond the reach of song or prayer.
  Then did Sir Palamede amend
His nakedness, his horrent hair,

SIR PALAMEDES, THE SARACEN KNIGHT

His nails, and made his penance end,
   Clothing himself in steel and gold,
Arming himself, his life to spend

In vigil cold and wandering bold,
   Disdaining song and dalliance soft,
Seeking one purpose to behold,

And holding ever that aloft,
   Nor fearing God, nor heeding men.
So thus his hermit habit doffed
   Sir Palamede the Saracen.

VIII

KNOW ye where Druid dolmens rise
   In Wessex on the widow plain?
Thither Sir Palamedes plies

The spur, and shakes the rattling rein.
   He questions all men of the Beast.
None answer.   Is the quest in vain?

With oaken crown there comes a priest
   In samite robes, with hazel wand,
And worships at the gilded East.

Ay! thither ride!   The dawn beyond
   Must run the quarry of his quest.
He rode as he were wood or fond,

Until at night behoves him rest.
   —He saw the gilding far behind
Out on the hills toward the West!

With aimless fury hot and blind
   He flung himon a Viking ship.
He slew the rover, and inclined

SIR PALAMEDES, THE SARACEN KNIGHT

The seamen to his stinging whip.
  Accurs'd of God, despising men,
Thy reckless oars in ocean dip,
  Sir Palamede the Saracen!

IX

Sir Palamede the Saracen
  Sailed ever with a favouring wind
Unto the smooth and swarthy men

That haunt the evil shore of Hind:
  He queried eager of the quest.
" Ay ! Ay ! " their cunning sages grinned :

" It shines ! It shines ! Guess thou the rest !
  For naught but this our Rishis know."
Sir Palamede his way addressed

Unto the woods : they blaze and glow ;
  His lance stabs many a shining blade,
His sword lays many a flower low

That glittering gladdened in the glade.
  He wrote himself a wanton ass,
And to the sea his traces laid,

Where many a wavelet on the glass
  His prowess knows. But deep and deep
His futile feet in fury pass,

SIR PALAMEDES, THE SARACEN KNIGHT

Until one billow curls to leap,
  And flings him breathless on the shore
Half drowned.   O fool! his God's asleep,

His armour in illusion's war
  Itself illusion, all his might
And courage vain.   Yet ardours pour

Through every artery.   The knight
  Scales the Himalaya's frozen sides,
Crowned with illimitable light,

And there in constant war abides,
  Smiting the spangles of the snow ;
Smiting until the vernal tides

Of earth leap high ; the steady flow
  Of sunlight splits the icy walls :
They slide, they hurl the knight below.

Sir Palamede the mighty falls
  Into an hollow where there dwelt
A bearded crew of monachals

Asleep in various visions spelt
  By mystic symbols unto men.
But when a foreigner they smelt

They drive him from their holy den,
  And with their glittering eyeballs pelt
Sir Palamede the Saracen.

X

Now findeth he, as all alone
  He moves about the burning East,
The mighty trail of some unknown,
  But surely some majestic beast.

So followeth he the forest ways,
  Remembering his knightly oath,
And through the hot and dripping days
  Ploughs through the tangled undergrowth.

Sir Palamede the Saracen
  Came on a forest pool at length,
Remote from any mart of men,
  Where there disported in his strength

The lone and lordly elephant.
  Sir Palamede his forehead beat.
"O amorous! O militant!
  O lord of this arboreal seat!"

Thus worshipped he, and stalking stole
  Into the Presence: he emerged.
The scent awakes the uneasy soul
  Of that Majestic One: upsurged

SIR PALAMEDES, THE SARACEN KNIGHT

The monster from the oozy bed,
   And bounded through the crashing glades.
—But now a staring savage head
   Lurks at him through the forest shades.

This was a naked Indian,
   Who led within the city gate
The fooled and disappointed man,
   Already broken by his fate.

Here were the brazen towers, and here
   The sculptured rocks, the marble shrine
Where to a tall black stone they rear
   The altars due to the divine.

The God they deem in sensual joy
   Absorbed, and silken dalliance:
To please his leisure hours a boy
   Compels an elephant to dance.

So majesty to ridicule
   Is turned.   To other climes and men
Makes off that strong, persistent fool
   Sir Palamede the Saracen.

XI

Sir Palamede the Saracen
  Hath hied him to an holy man,
Sith he alone of mortal men

Can help him, if a mortal can.
  (So tell him all the Scythian folk.)
Wherefore he makes a caravan,

And finds him. When his prayers invoke
  The holy knowledge, saith the sage:
"This Beast is he of whom there spoke

The prophets of the Golden Age:
  'Mark! all that mind is, he is not.'"
Sir Palamede in bitter rage

Sterte up: "Is this the fool, 'Od wot,
  To see the like of whom I came
From castellated Camelot?"

The sage with eyes of burning flame
  Cried: "Is it not a miracle?
Ay! for with folly travelleth shame,

SIR PALAMEDES, THE SARACEN KNIGHT

And thereto at the end is Hell.
   Believe! And why believe? Because
It is a thing impossible."

Sir Palamede his pulses pause.
   "It is not possible" (quod he)
"That Palamede is wroth, and draws

His sword, decapitating thee.
   By parity of argument
This deed of blood must surely be."

With that he suddenly besprent
   All Scythia with the sage's blood,
And laughing in his woe he went

Unto a further field and flood,
   Aye guided by that wizard's head,
That like a windy moon did scud

Before him, winking eyes of red
   And snapping jaws of white: but then
What cared for living or for dead
   Sir Palamede the Saracen?

XII

Sir Palamede the Saracen
  Follows the Head to gloomy halls
  Of sterile hate, with icy walls.
A woman clucking like a hen
  Answers his lordly bugle-calls.

She rees him an ungainly rede
  Of ghosts and virgins, doves and wombs,
  Of roods and prophecies and tombs—
Old pagan fables run to seed!
  Sir Palamede with fury fumes.

So doth the Head that jabbers fast
  Against that woman's tangled tale.
  (God's patience at the end must fail!)
Out sweeps the sword—the blade hath passed
  Through all her scraggy farthingale.

" This chatter lends to Thought a zest "
  (Quod he), " but I am all for Act.
  Sit here, until your Talk hath cracked
The addled egg in Nature's nest! "
  With that he fled the dismal tract.

SIR PALAMEDES, THE SARACEN KNIGHT

He was so sick and ill at ease
    And hot against his fellow men,
    He thought to end his purpose then—
Nay! let him seek new lands and seas,
    Sir Palamede the Saracen!

XIII

Sir Palamede is come anon
   Into a blue delicious bay.
A mountain towers thereupon,
Wherein some fiend of ages gone

Is whelmed by God, yet from his breast
   Spits up the flame, and ashes grey.
Hereby Sir Palamede his quest
Pursues withouten let or rest.

Seeing the evil mountain be,
   Remembering all his evil years,
He knows the Questing Beast runs free—
Author of Evil, then, is he!

Whereat immediate resounds
   The noise he hath sought so long: appears
There quest a thirty couple hounds
Within its belly as it bounds.

Lifting his eyes, he sees at last
   The beast he seeks: 'tis like an hart.
Ever it courseth far and fast.
Sir Palamede is sore aghast,

THE HIGH HISTORY OF GOOD

But plucking up his will, doth launch
   A mighty poison-dippèd dart:
It fareth ever sure and staunch,
And smiteth him upon the haunch.

Then as Sir Palamede overhauls
   The stricken quarry, slack it droops,
Staggers, and final down it falls.
Triumph! Gape wide, ye golden walls!

Lift up your everlasting doors,
   O gates of Camelot! See, he swoops
Down on the prey! The life-blood pours:
The poison works: the breath implores

Its livelong debt from heart and brain.
   Alas! poor stag, thy day is done!
The gallant lungs gasp loud in vain:
Thy life is spilt upon the plain.

Sir Palamede is stricken numb
   As one who, gazing on the sun,
Sees blackness gather. Blank and dumb,
The good knight sees a thin breath come

Out of his proper mouth, and dart
   Over the plain: he seeth it
Sure by some black magician art
Shape ever closer like an hart:

SIR PALAMEDES, THE SARACEN KNIGHT

While such a questing there resounds
   As God had loosed the very Pit,
Or as a thirty couple hounds
Are in its belly as it bounds !

Full sick at heart, I ween, was then
   The loyal knight, the weak of wit,
The butt of lewd and puny men,
Sir Palamede the Saracen.

XIV

Northward the good knight gallops fast,
　　Resolved to seek his foe at home,
When rose that Vision of the past,
　　The royal battlements of Rome,
　　A ruined city, and a dome.

There in the broken Forum sat
A red-robed robber in a Hat.
　　"Whither away, Sir Knight, so fey?"
" Priest, for the dove on Ararat
　　I could not, nor I will not, stay!"

" I know thy quest.　Seek on in vain
　　A golden hart with silver horns!
Life springeth out of divers pains.
　　What crown the King of Kings adorns?
　　A crown of gems?　A crown of thorns!

The Questing Beast is like a king
In face, and hath a pigeon's wing
　　And claw; its body is one fleece
Of bloody white, a lamb's in spring.
　　Enough.　Sir Knight, I give thee peace."

SIR PALAMEDES, THE SARACEN KNIGHT

The knight spurs on, and soon espies
  A monster coursing on the plain.
He hears the horrid questing rise
  And thunder in his weary brain.
  This time, to slay it or be slain !

Too easy task ! The charger gains
Stride after stride with little pains
  Upon the lumbering, flapping thing.
He stabs the lamb, and splits the brains
  Of that majestic-seeming king.

He clips the wing and pares the claw—
  What turns to laughter all his joy,
To wondering ribaldry his awe ?
  The beast's a mere mechanic toy,
  Fit to amuse an idle boy !

XV

Sir Palamede the Saracen
   Hath come to an umbrageous land
Where nymphs abide, and Pagan men.
   The Gods are nigh, say they, at hand.
How warm a throb from Venus stirs
The pulses of her worshippers !

Nor shall the Tuscan God be found
   Reluctant from the altar-stone :
His perfume shall delight the ground,
   His presence to his folk be known
In darkling grove and glimmering shrine—
O ply the kiss and pour the wine !

Sir Palamede is fairly come
   Into a place of glowing bowers,
Where all the Voice of Time is dumb :
   Before an altar crowned with flowers
He seeth a satyr fondly dote
And languish on a swan-soft goat.

Then he in mid-caress desires
   The ear of strong Sir Palamede.

SIR PALAMEDES, THE SARACEN KNIGHT

"We burn," quoth he, "no futile fires,
  Nor play upon an idle reed,
Nor penance vain, nor fatuous prayers—
The Gods are ours, and we are theirs."

Sir Palamedes plucks the pipe
  The satyr tends, and blows a trill
So soft and warm, so red and ripe,
  That echo answers from the hill
In eager and voluptuous strain,
While grows upon the sounding plain

A gallop, and a questing turned
  To one profound melodious bay.
Sir Palamede with pleasure burned,
  And bowed him to the idol grey
That on the altar sneered and leered
With loose red lips behind his beard.

Sir Palamedes and the Beast
  Are woven in a web of gold
Until the gilding of the East
  Burns on the wanton-smiling wold :
And still Sir Palamede believed
His holy quest to be achieved !

But now the dawn from glowing gates
  Floods all the land : with snarling lip
The Beast stands off and cachinnates.
  That stings the good knight like a whip,

SIR PALAMEDES, THE SARACEN KNIGHT

As suddenly Hell's own disgust
Eats up the joy he had of lust.

The brutal glee his folly took
    For holy joy breaks down his brain.
Off bolts the Beast : the earth is shook
    As out a questing roars again,
As if a thirty couple hounds
Are in its belly as it bounds !

The peasants gather to deride
    The knight : creation joins in mirth.
Ashamed and scorned on every side,
    There gallops, hateful to the earth,
The laughing-stock of beasts and men,
Sir Palamede the Saracen.

XVI

WHERE shafts of moonlight splash the vale,
   Beside a stream there sits and strains
Sir Palamede, with passion pale,

And haggard from his broken brains.
   Yet eagerly he watches still
A mossy mound where dainty grains

Of gilded corn their beauty spill
   To tempt the quarry to the range
Of Palamede his archer skill.

All night he sits, with ardour strange
   And hope new-fledged. A gambler born
Aye thinks the luck one day must change,

Though sense and skill he laughs to scorn.
   So now there rush a thousand rats
In sable silence on the corn.

They sport their square or shovel hats,
   A squeaking, tooth-bare brotherhood,
Innumerable as summer gnats

SIR PALAMEDES, THE SARACEN KNIGHT

Buzzing some streamlet through a wood.
  Sir Palamede grows mighty wroth,
And mutters maledictions rude,

Seeing his quarry far and loth
  And thieves despoiling all the bait.
Now, careless of the knightly oath,

The sun pours down his eastern gate.
  The chase is over : see ye then,
Coursing afar, afoam at fate,
  Sir Palamede the Saracen !

XVII

Sir Palamede hath told the tale
  Of this misfortune to a sage,
How all his ventures nought avail,

And all his hopes dissolve in rage.
  " Now by thine holy beard," quoth he,
" And by thy venerable age

I charge thee this my riddle ree."
  Then said that gentle eremite :
" This task is easy unto me !

Know then the Questing Beast aright !
  One is the Beast, the Questing one :
And one with one is two, Sir Knight !

Yet these are one in two, and none
  Disjoins their substance (mark me well !),
Confounds their persons.   Rightly run

Their attributes : immeasurable,
  Incomprehensibundable,
Unspeakable, inaudible,

THE HIGH HISTORY OF GOOD

Intangible, ingustable,
  Insensitive to human smell,
Invariable, implacable,

Invincible, insciable,
  Irrationapsychicable,
Inequilegijurable,

Immamemimomummable.
  Such is its nature: without parts,
Places, or persons, plumes, or pell,

Having nor lungs nor lights nor hearts,
  But two in one and one in two.
Be he accursèd that disparts

Them now, or seemeth so to do!
  Him will I pile the curses on;
Him will I hang, or saw him through,

Or burn with fire, who doubts upon
  This doctrine, hotototon spells
The holy word otototon."

The poor Sir Palamedes quells
  His rising spleen; he doubts his ears.
"How may I catch the Beast?" he yells.

The smiling sage rebukes his fears:
  "'Tis easier than all, Sir Knight!
By simple faith the Beast appears.

SIR PALAMEDES, THE SARACEN KNIGHT

By simple faith, not heathen might,
  Catch him, and thus achieve the quest!"
Then quoth that melancholy wight:

"I will believe!" The hermit blessed
  His convert: on the horizon
Appears the Beast. "To thee the rest!"

He cries, to urge the good knight on.
  But no! Sir Palamedes grips
The hermit by the woebegone

Beard of him; then away he rips,
  Wood as a maniac, to the West,
Where down the sun in splendour slips,

And where the quarry of the quest
  Canters. They run like hippogriffs!
Like men pursued, or swine possessed,

Over the dizzy Cretan cliffs
  They smash. And lo! it comes to pass
He sees in no dim hieroglyphs,

In knowledge easy to amass,
  This hermit (while he drew his breath)
Once dead is like a mangy ass.

Bruised, broken, but not bound to death,
  He calls some passing fishermen
To bear him. Presently he saith:

SIR PALAMEDES, THE SARACEN KNIGHT

" Bear me to some remotest den
    To heal me of my ills immense ;
    For now hath neither might nor sense
Sir Palamede the Saracen."

XVIII

Sir Palamedes for a space
   Deliberates on his rustic bed.
" I lack the quarry's awful pace "

(Quod he); " my limbs are slack as lead."
   So, as he gets his strength, he seeks
The castles where the pennons red

Of dawn illume their dreadful peaks.
   There dragons stretch their horrid coils
Adown the winding clefts and creeks :

From hideous mouths their venom boils.
   But Palamede their fury 'scapes,
Their malice by his valour foils,

Climbing aloft by bays and capes
   Of rock and ice, encounters oft
The loathly sprites, the misty shapes

Of monster brutes that lurk aloft.
   O! well he works : his youth returns,
His heart revives : despair is doffed

D

THE HIGH HISTORY OF GOOD

And eager hope in brilliance burns
   Within the circle of his brows
As fast he flies, the snow he spurns.

Ah! what a youth and strength he vows
   To the achievement of the quest!
And now the horrid height allows

His mastery: day by day from crest
   To crest he hastens: faster fly
His feet: his body knows not rest,

Until with magic speed they ply
   Like oars the snowy waves, surpass
In one day's march the galaxy

Of Europe's starry mountain mass.
   "Now," quoth he, "let me find the quest!"
The Beast sterte up.   Sir Knight, alas!

Day after day they race, nor rest
   Till seven days were fairly done.
Then doth the Questing Marvel crest

The ridge: the knight is well outrun.
   Now, adding laughter to its din,
Like some lewd comet at the sun,

Around the panting paladin
   It runs with all its splendid speed.
Yet, knowing that he may not win,

SIR PALAMEDES, THE SARACEN KNIGHT

He strains and strives in very deed,
 So that at last a boulder trips
The hero, that he bursts a-bleed,

And sanguine from his bearded lips
 The torrent of his being breaks.
The Beast is gone : the hero slips

Down to the valley : he forsakes
 The fond idea (every bone
In all his body burns and aches)

By speed to attain the dear Unknown,
 By force to achieve the great Beyond.
Yet from that brain may spring full-grown
 Another folly just as fond.

XIX

THE knight hath found a naked girl
  Among the dunes of Breton sand.
She spinneth in a mystic whirl,

And hath a bagpipe in her hand,
  Wherefrom she draweth dismal groans
The while her maddening saraband

She plies, and with discordant tones
  Desires a certain devil-grace.
She gathers wreckage-wood, and bones

Of seamen, jetsam of the place,
  And builds therewith a fire, wherein
She dances, bounding into space

Like an inflated ass's skin.
  She raves, and reels, and yells, and whirls
So that the tears of toil begin

To dew her breasts with ardent pearls.
  Nor doth she mitigate her dance,
The bagpipe ever louder skirls,

SIR PALAMEDES, THE SARACEN KNIGHT

Until the shapes of death advance
   And gather round her, shrieking loud
And wailing o'er the wide expanse

Of sand, the gibbering, mewing crowd.
   Like cats, and apes, they gather close,
Till, like the horror of a cloud

Wrapping the flaming sun with rose,
   They hide her from the hero's sight.
Then doth he muse thereat morose,

When in one wild cascade of light
   The pageant breaks, and thunder roars:
Down flaps the loathly wing of night.

He sees the lonely Breton shores
   Lapped in the levin: then his eyes
See how she shrieking soars and soars

Into the starless, stormy skies.
   Well! well! this lesson will he learn,
How music's mellowing artifice

May bid the breast of nature burn
   And call the gods from star and shrine.
So now his sounding courses turn

To find an instrument divine
   Whereon he may pursue his quest.
How glitter green his gleeful eyne

THE HIGH HISTORY OF GOOD

When, where the mice and lice infest
   A filthy hovel, lies a wench
Bearing a baby at her breast,

Drunk and debauched, one solid stench,
   But carrying a silver lute.
'Boardeth her, nor doth baulk nor blench,

And long abideth brute by brute
   Amid the unsavoury denizens,
Until his melodies uproot

The oaks, lure lions from their dens,
   Turn rivers back, and still the spleen
Of serpents and of Saracens.

Thus then equipped, he quits the quean,
   And in a city fair and wide
Calls up with music wild and keen

The Questing Marvel to his side.
   Then do the sportful city folk
About his lonely stance abide :

Making their holiday, they joke
   The melancholy ass : they throw
Their clattering coppers in his poke.

So day and night they come and go,
   But never comes the Questing Beast,
Nor doth that laughing people know

SIR PALAMEDES, THE SARACEN KNIGHT

How agony's unleavening yeast
   Stirs Palamede. Anon they tire,
And follow an Egyptian priest

Who boasts him master of the fire
   To draw down lightning, and invoke
The gods upon a sandal pyre,

And bring up devils in the smoke.
   Sir Palamede is all alone,
Wrapped in his misery like a cloak,

Despairing now to charm the Unknown.
   So arms and horse he takes again.
Sir Palamede hath overthrown

The jesters. Now the country men,
   Stupidly staring, see at noon
Sir Palamede the Saracen

A-riding like an harvest moon
   In silver arms, with glittering lance,
With plumèd helm, and wingèd shoon,
   Athwart the admiring land of France.

XX

Sir Palamede hath reasoned out
Beyond the shadow of a doubt
   That this his Questing Beast is one;
For were it Beasts, he must suppose
An earlier Beast to father those.
   So all the tracks of herds that run

Into the forest he discards,
And only turns his dark regards
   On single prints, on marks unique.
Sir Palamede doth now attain
Unto a wide and grassy plain,
   Whereon he spies the thing to seek.

Thereat he putteth spur to horse
And runneth him a random course,
   The Beast a-questing aye before.
But praise to good Sir Palamede!
'Hath gotten him a fairy steed
   Alike for venery and for war,

So that in little drawing near
The quarry, lifteth up his spear
   To run him of his malice through.

SIR PALAMEDES, THE SARACEN KNIGHT

With that the Beast hopes no escape,
Dissolveth all his lordly shape,
  Splitteth him sudden into two.

Sir Palamede in fury runs
Unto the nearer beast, that shuns
  The shock, and splits, and splits again,
Until the baffled warrior sees
A myriad myriad swarms of these
  A-questing over all the plain.

The good knight reins his charger in.
" Now, by the faith of Paladin !
  The subtle quest at last I ken."
Rides off to Camelot to plight
The faith of many a noble knight,
  Sir Palamede the Saracen.

XXI

Now doth Sir Palamede advance
The lord of many a sword and lance.
   In merrie England's summer sun
Their shields and arms a-glittering glance

And laugh upon the mossy mead.
Now winds the horn of Palamede,
   As far upon the horizon
He spies the Questing Beast a-feed.

With loyal craft and honest guile
They spread their ranks for many a mile.
   For when the Beast hath heard the horn
He practiseth his ancient wile,

And many a myriad beasts invade
The stillness of that armèd glade.
   Now every knight to rest hath borne
His lance, and given the accolade,

And run upon a beast : but they
Slip from the fatal point away
   And course about, confusing all
That gallant concourse all the day,

SIR PALAMEDES, THE SARACEN KNIGHT

Leading them ever to a vale
With hugeous cry and monster wail.
   Then suddenly their voices fall,
And in the park's resounding pale

Only the clamour of the chase
Is heard : oh ! to the centre race
   The unsuspicious knights : but he
The Questing Beast his former face

Of unity resumes : the course
Of warriors shocks with man and horse.
   In mutual madness swift to see
They shatter with unbridled force

One on another : down they go
Swift in stupendous overthrow.
   Out sword ! out lance ! Cuirass and helm
Splinter beneath the knightly blow.

They storm, they charge, they hack and hew,
They rush and wheel the press athrough.
   The weight, the murder, overwhelm
One, two, and all. Nor silence knew

His empire till Sir Palamede
(The last) upon his fairy steed
   Struck down his brother ; then at once
Fell silence on the bloody mead,

SIR PALAMEDES, THE SARACEN KNIGHT

Until the questing rose again.
For there, on that ensanguine plain
   Standeth a-laughing at the dunce
The single Beast they had not slain.

There, with his friends and followers dead,
His brother smitten through the head,
   Himself sore wounded in the thigh,
Weepeth upon the deed of dread,

Alone among his murdered men,
The champion fool, as fools were then,
   Utterly broken, like to die,
Sir Palamede the Saracen.

XXII

Sir Palamede his wits doth rally,
  Nursing his wound beside a lake
Within an admirable valley,

Whose walls their thirst on heaven slake,
  And in the moonlight mystical
Their countless spears of silver shake.

Thus reasons he : " In each and all
  Fyttes of this quest the quarry's track
Is wondrous geometrical.

In spire and whorl twists out and back
  The hart with fair symmetric line.
And lo ! the grain of wit I lack—

This Beast is Master of Design.
  So studying each twisted print
In this mirific mind of mine,

My heart may happen on a hint."
  Thus as the seeker after gold
Eagerly chases grain or glint,

SIR PALAMEDES, THE SARACEN KNIGHT

The knight at last wins to behold
   The full conception.   Breathless-blue
The fair lake's mirror crystal-cold

Wherein he gazes, keen to view
   The vast Design therein, to chase
The Beast to his last avenue.

Then—O thou gosling scant of grace!
   The dream breaks, and Sir Palamede
Wakes to the glass of his fool's face!

" Ah, 'sdeath!" (quod he), " by thought and deed
   This brute for ever mocketh me.
The lance is made a broken reed,

The brain is but a barren tree—
   For all the beautiful Design
Is but mine own geometry!"

With that his wrath brake out like wine.
   He plunged his body in, and shattered
The whole delusion asinine.

All the false water-nymphs that flattered
   He killed with his resounding curse—
O fool of God! as if it mattered!

So, nothing better, rather worse,
   Out of the blue bliss of the pool
      Came dripping that inveterate fool!

XXIII

Now still he holdeth argument:
  "So grand a Beast must house him well;
Hence, now beseemeth me frequent
  Cathedral, palace, citadel."

So, riding fast among the flowers
  Far off, a Gothic spire he spies,
That like a gladiator towers
  Its spear-sharp splendour to the skies.

The people cluster round, acclaim:
  "Sir Knight, good knight, thy quest is won.
Here dwells the Beast in orient flame,
  Spring-sweet, and swifter than the sun!"

Sir Palamede the Saracen
  Spurs to the shrine, afire to win
The end; and all the urgent men
  Throng with him eloquently in.

Sir Palamede his vizor drops;
  He lays his loyal lance in rest;
He drives the rowels home—he stops!
  Faugh! but a black-mouthed money-chest!

63

SIR PALAMEDES, THE SARACEN KNIGHT

He turns—the friendly folk are gone,
    Gone with his sumpter-mules and train
Beyond the infinite horizon
    Of all he hopes to see again!

His brain befooled, his pocket picked—
    How the Beast cachinnated then,
Far from that doleful derelict
    Sir Palamede the Saracen!

XXIV

" ONE thing at least " (quoth Palamede),
  " Beyond dispute my soul can see:
This Questing Beast that mocks my need
  Dwelleth in deep obscurity."

So delveth he a darksome hole
  Within the bowels of Etna dense,
Closing the harbour of his soul
  To all the pirate-ships of sense.

And now the questing of the Beast
  Rolls in his very self, and high
Leaps his whole heart in fiery feast
  On the expected ecstasy.

But echoing from the central roar
  Reverberates many a mournful moan,
And shapes more mystic than before
  Baffle its formless monotone!

Ah! mocks him many a myriad vision,
  Warring within him masterless,
Turning devotion to derision,
  Beatitude to beastliness.

SIR PALAMEDES, THE SARACEN KNIGHT

They swarm, they grow, they multiply;
   The strong knight's brain goes all a-swim,
Paced by that maddening minstrelsy,
   Those dog-like demons hunting him.

The last bar breaks; the steel will snaps;
   The black hordes riot in his brain;
A thousand threatening thunder-claps
   Smite him—insane—insane—insane!

His muscles roar with senseless rage;
   The pale knight staggers, deathly sick;
Reels to the light that sorry sage,
   Sir Palamede the Lunatick.

XXV

A SAVAGE sea without a sail,
  Grey gulphs and green a-glittering,
Rare snow that floats—a vestal veil
  Upon the forehead of the spring.

Here in a plunging galleon
  Sir Palamede, a listless drone,
Drifts desperately on—and on—
  And on—with heart and eyes of stone.

The deep-scarred brain of him is healed
  With wind and sea and star and sun,
The assoiling grace that God revealed
  For gree and bounteous benison.

Ah! still he trusts the recreant brain,
  Thrown in a thousand tourney-justs;
Still he raves on in reason-strain
  With senseless " oughts " and fatuous " musts."

" All the delusions " (argueth
  The ass), " all uproars, surely rise
From that curst Me whose name is Death,
  Whereas the Questing Beast belies

SIR PALAMEDES, THE SARACEN KNIGHT

The Me with Thou; then swift the quest
  To slay the Me should hook the Thou."
With that he crossed him, brow and breast,
  And flung his body from the prow.

An end? Alas! on silver sand
  Open his eyes; the surf-rings roar.
What snorts there, swimming from the land?
  The Beast that brought him to the shore!

"O Beast!" quoth purple Palamede,
  "A monster strange as Thou am I.
I could not live before, indeed;
  And now I cannot even die!

Who chose me, of the Table Round
  By miracle acclaimed the chief?
Here, waterlogged and muscle-bound,
  Marooned upon a coral reef!"

XXVI

Sir Palamede the Saracen
   Hath gotten him a swift canoe,
Paddled by stalwart South Sea men.

They cleave the oily breasts of blue,
   Straining toward the westering disk
Of the tall sun ; they battle through

Those weary days ; the wind is brisk ;
   The stars are clear ; the moon is high.
Now, even as a white basilisk

That slayeth all men with his eye,
   Stands up before them tapering
The cone of speechless sanctity.

Up, up its slopes the pilgrims swing,
   Chanting their pagan gramarye
Unto the dread volcano-king.

" Now, then, by Goddes reed ! " quod he,
   " Behold the secret of my quest
In this far-famed stability !

SIR PALAMEDES, THE SARACEN KNIGHT

For all these Paynim knights may rest
   In the black bliss they struggle to."
But from the earth's full-flowered breast

Brake the blind roar of earthquake through,
   Tearing the belly of its mother,
Engulphing all that heathen crew,

That cried and cursed on one another.
   Aghast he standeth, Palamede!
For twinned with Earthquake laughs her brother

The Questing Beast. As Goddes reed
   Sweats blood for sin, so now the heart
Of the good knight begins to bleed.

Of all the ruinous shafts that dart
   Within his liver, this hath plied
The most intolerable smart.

" By Goddes wounds!" the good knight cried,
   "What is this quest, grown daily dafter,
Where nothing—nothing—may abide?

Westward!" They fly, but rolling after
   Echoes the Beast's unsatisfied
And inextinguishable laughter!

XXVII

SIR PALAMEDE goes aching on
  (Pox of despair's dread interdict!)
Aye to the western horizon,

Still meditating, sharp and strict,
  Upon the changes of the earth,
Its towers and temples derelict,

The ready ruin of its mirth,
  The flowers, the fruits, the leaves that fall,
The joy of life, its growing girth—

And nothing as the end of all.
  Yea, even as the Yang-tze rolled
Its rapids past him, so the wall

Of things brake down; his eyes behold
  The mighty Beast serenely couched
Upon its breast of burnished gold.

" Ah! by Christ's blood!" (his soul avouched),
  " Nothing but change (but change!) abides.
Death lurks, a leopard curled and crouched,

SIR PALAMEDES, THE SARACEN KNIGHT

In all the seasons and the tides.
　　But ah! the more it changed and changed"—
(The good knight laughed to split his sides!)

"What?　Is the soul of things deranged?
　　The more it changed, and rippled through
Its changes, and still changed, and changed,

The liker to itself it grew.
　　Bear me," he cried, "to purge my bile
To the old land of Hormakhu,

That I may sit and curse awhile
　　At all these follies fond that pen
My quest about—on, on to Nile!

Tread tenderly, my merry men!
　　For nothing is so void and vile
As Palamede the Saracen."

XXVIII

Sir Palamede the Saracen
  Hath clad him in a sable robe;
Hath curses, writ by holy men
  From all the gardens of the globe.

He standeth at an altar-stone;
  The blood drips from the slain babe's throat;
His chant rolls in a magick moan;
  His head bows to the crownèd goat.

His wand makes curves and spires in air;
  The smoke of incense curls and quivers;
His eyes fix in a glass-cold stare:
  The land of Egypt rocks and shivers!

" Lo! by thy Gods, O God, I vow
  To burn the authentic bones and blood
Of curst Osiris even now
  To the dark Nile's upsurging flood!

I cast thee down, oh crowned and throned!
  To black Amennti's void profane.
Until mine anger be atoned
  Thou shalt not ever rise again."

THE HIGH HISTORY OF GOOD

With firm red lips and square black beard,
Osiris in his strength appeared.

He made the sign that saveth men
On Palamede the Saracen.

'Hath hushed his conjuration grim:
The curse comes back to sleep with him.

'Hath fallen himself to that profane
Whence none might ever rise again.

Dread torture racks him; all his bones
Get voice to utter forth his groans.

The very poison of his blood
Joins in that cry's soul-shaking flood.

For many a chiliad counted well
His soul stayed in its proper Hell.

Then, when Sir Palamedes came
    Back to himself, the shrine was dark.
Cold was the incense, dead the flame;
    The slain babe lay there black and stark.

What of the Beast? What of the quest?
    More blind the quest, the Beast more dim.
Even now its laughter is suppressed,
    While his own demons mock at him!

SIR PALAMEDES, THE SARACEN KNIGHT

O thou most desperate dupe that Hell's
    Malice can make of mortal men!
Meddle no more with magick spells,
    Sir Palamede the Saracen!

XXIX

Ha! but the good knight, striding forth
  From Set's abominable shrine,
Pursues the quest with bitter wrath,
  So that his words flow out like wine.

And lo! the soul that heareth them
  Is straightway healed of suffering.
His fame runs through the land of Khem:
  They flock, the peasant and the king.

There he works many a miracle:
  The blind see, and the cripples walk;
Lepers grow clean; sick folk grow well;
  The deaf men hear, the dumb men talk.

He casts out devils with a word;
  Circleth his wand, and dead men rise.
No such a wonder hath been heard
  Since Christ our God's sweet sacrifice.

" Now, by the glad blood of our Lord!"
  Quoth Palamede, "my heart is light.
I am the chosen harpsichord
  Whereon God playeth; the perfect knight,

SIR PALAMEDES, THE SARACEN KNIGHT

The saint of Mary "—there he stayed,
   For out of Memnon's singing stone
So fierce a questing barked and brayed,
   It turned his laughter to a groan.

His vow forgot, his task undone,
   His soul whipped in God's bitter school!
(He moaned a mighty malison!)
   The perfect knight?   The perfect fool!

" Now, by God's wounds!" quoth he, "my strength
   Is burnt out to a pest of pains.
Let me fling off my curse at length
   In old Chaldea's starry plains!

Thou blessèd Jesus, foully nailed
   Unto the cruel Calvary tree,
Look on my soul's poor fort assailed
   By all the hosts of devilry!

Is there no medicine but death
   That shall avail me in my place,
That I may know the Beauteous Breath
   And taste the Goodly Gift of Grace?

Keep Thou yet firm this trembling leaf
   My soul, dear God Who died for men ;
Yea! for that sinner-soul the chief,
   Sir Palamede the Saracen!"

XXX

STARRED is the blackness of the sky ;
    Wide is the sweep of the cold plain
Where good Sir Palamede doth lie,
    Keen on the Beast-slot once again.

All day he rode ; all night he lay
    With eyes wide open to the stars,
Seeking in many a secret way
    The key to unlock his prison bars.

Beneath him, hark ! the marvel sounds !
    The Beast that questeth horribly.
As if a thirty couple hounds
    Are in his belly questeth he.

Beneath him ?   Heareth he aright ?
    He leaps to's feet—a wonder shews :
Steep dips a stairway from the light
    To what obscurity God knows.

Still never a tremor shakes his soul
    (God praise thee, knight of adamant !) ;
He plunges to that gruesome goal
    Firm as an old bull-elephant !

SIR PALAMEDES, THE SARACEN KNIGHT

The broad stair winds; he follows it;
   Dark is the way; the air is blind;
Black, black the blackness of the pit,
   The light long blotted out behind!

His sword sweeps out; his keen glance peers
   For some shape glimmering through the gloom:
Naught, naught in all that void appears;
   More still, more silent than the tomb!

Yet now the good knight is aware
   Of some black force, of some dread throne,
Waiting beneath that awful stair,
   Beneath that pit of slippery stone.

Yea! though he sees not anything,
   Nor hears, his subtle sense is 'ware
That, lackeyed by the devil-king,
   The Beast—the Questing Beast—is there!

So though his heart beats close with fear,
   Though horror grips his throat, he goes,
Goes on to meet it, spear to spear,
   As good knight should, to face his foes.

Nay! but the end is come. Black earth
   Belches that peerless Paladin
Up from her gulphs—untimely birth!
   —Her horror could not hold him in!

SIR PALAMEDES, THE SARACEN KNIGHT

White as a corpse, the hero hails
    The dawn, that night of fear still shaking
His body.   All death's doubt assails
    Him.   Was it sleep or was it waking?

"By God, I care not, I!" (quod he).
    "Or wake or sleep, or live or dead,
I will pursue this mystery.
    So help me Grace of Godlihead!"

Ay! with thy wasted limbs pursue
    That subtle Beast home to his den!
Who knows but thou mayst win athrough,
    Sir Palamede the Saracen?

XXXI

From God's sweet air Sir Palamede
   Hath come unto a demon bog,
A city where but rats may breed

In sewer-stench and fetid fog.
   Within its heart pale phantoms crawl.
Breathless with foolish haste they jog

And jostle, all for naught! They scrawl
   Vain things all night that they disown
Ere day. They call and bawl and squall

Hoarse cries; they moan, they groan. A stone
   Hath better sense! And these among
A cabbage-headed god they own,

With wandering eye and jabbering tongue.
   He, rotting in that grimy sewer
And charnel-house of death and dung,

Shrieks: " How the air is sweet and pure!
   Give me the entrails of a frog
And I will teach thee! Lo! the lure

THE HIGH HISTORY OF GOOD

Of light! How lucent is the fog!
  How noble is my cabbage-head!
How sweetly fragrant is the bog!"

"God's wounds!" (Sir Palamedes said),
  "What have I done to earn this portion?
Must I, the clean knight born and bred,

Sup with this filthy toad-abortion?"
  Nathless he stayed with him awhile,
Lest by disdain his mental torsion

Slip back, or miss the serene smile
  Should crown his quest; for (as one saith)
The unknown may lurk within the vile.

So he who sought the Beauteous Breath,
  Desired the Goodly Gift of Grace,
Went equal into life and death.

But oh! the foulness of his face!
  Not here was anything of worth;
He turned his back upon the place,

Sought the blue sky and the green earth,
  Ay! and the lustral sea to cleanse
That filth that stank about his girth,

SIR PALAMEDES, THE SARACEN KNIGHT

The sores and scabs, the warts and wens,
   The nameless vermin he had gathered
In those insufferable dens,

The foul diseases he had fathered.
   So now the quest slips from his brain:
" First (Christ !) let me be clean again ! "

XXXII

"Ha!" cries the knight, "may patient toil
Of brain dissolve this cruel coil!
   In Afric they that chase the ostrich
Clothe them with feathers, subtly foil

Its vigilance, come close, then dart
Its death upon it.   Brave my heart!
   Do thus!"   And so the knight disguises
Himself, on hands and knees doth start

His hunt, goes questing up and down.
So in the fields the peasant clown
   Flies, shrieking, from that dreadful figure.
But when he came to any town

They caged him for a lunatic.
Quod he: "Would God I had the trick!
   The beast escaped from my devices;
I will the same.   The bars are thick,

But I am strong."   He wrenched in vain;
Then—what is this?   What wild, sharp strain
   Smites on the air?   The prison smashes.
Hark! 'tis the Questing Beast again!

SIR PALAMEDES, THE SARACEN KNIGHT

Then as he rushes forth the note
Roars from that Beast's malignant throat
  With laughter, laughter, laughter, laughter!
The wits of Palamedes float

In ecstasy of shame and rage.
"O Thou!" exclaims the baffled sage;
  "How should I match Thee? Yet, I will so,
Though Doomisday devour the Age.

Weeping, and beating on his breast,
Gnashing his teeth, he still confessed
  The might of the dread oath that bound him:
He would not yet give up the quest.

"Nay! while I am," quoth he, "though Hell
Engulph me, though God mock me well,
  I follow as I sware; I follow,
Though it be unattainable.

Nay, more! Because I may not win,
Is't worth man's work to enter in!
  The Infinite with mighty passion
Hath caught my spirit in a gin.

Come! since I may not imitate
The Beast, at least I work and wait.
  We shall discover soon or late
Which is the master—I or Fate!"

XXXIII

Sɪʀ Pᴀʟᴀᴍᴇᴅᴇ the Saracen
  Hath passed unto the tideless sea,
    That the keen whisper of the wind
May bring him that which never men
  Knew—on the quest, the quest, rides he!
    So long to seek, so far to find!

So weary was the knight, his limbs
  Were slack as new-slain dove's; his knees
    No longer gripped the charger rude.
Listless, he aches; his purpose swims
  Exhausted in the oily seas
    Of laxity and lassitude.

The soul subsides; its serious motion
  Still throbs; by habit, not by will.
    And all his lust to win the quest
Is but a passive-mild devotion.
  (Ay! soon the blood shall run right chill
    —And is not death the Lord of Rest?)

There as he basks upon the cliff
  He yearns toward the Beast; his eyes
    Are moist with love; his lips are fain

SIR PALAMEDES, THE SARACEN KNIGHT

To breathe fond prayers ; and (marry !) if
  Man's soul were measured by his sighs
    He need not linger to attain.

Nay ! while the Beast squats there, above
  Him, smiling on him ; as he vows
    Wonderful deeds and fruitless flowers,
He grows so maudlin in his love
  That even the knaves of his own house
    Mock at him in their merry hours.

"God's death !" raged Palamede, not wroth
  But irritated, " laugh ye so ?
    Am I a jape for scullions ? "
His curse came in a flaky froth.
  He seized a club, with blow on blow
    Breaking the knave's unreverent sconce !

" Thou mock the Questing Beast I chase,
  The Questing Beast I love ?   'Od's wounds ! "
    Then sudden from the slave there brake
A cachinnation scant of grace,
  As if a thirty couple hounds
    Were in his belly !   Knight, awake !

Ah ! well he woke !   His love and scorn
  Grapple in death-throe at his throat.
    " Lead me away " (quoth he), " my men !
Woe, woe is me was ever born
  So blind a bat, so gross a goat,
    As Palamede the Saracen ! "

XXXIV

Sir Palamede the Saracen
   Hath hid him in an hermit's cell
Upon an island in the fen

Of that lone land where Druids dwell.
   There came an eagle from the height
And bade him mount. From dale to dell

They sank and soared. Last to the light
   Of the great sun himself they flew,
Piercing the borders of the night,

Passing the irremeable blue.
   Far into space beyond the stars
At last they came. And there he knew

All the blind reasonable bars
   Broken, and all the emotions stilled,
And all the stains and all the scars

Left him; so like a child he thrilled
   With utmost knowledge; all his soul,
With perfect sense and sight fulfilled,

SIR PALAMEDES, THE SARACEN KNIGHT

Touched the extreme, the giant goal!
   Yea! all things in that hour transcended,
All power in his sublime control,

All felt, all thought, all comprehended—
   " How is it, then, the quest " (he saith)
" Is not—at last!—achieved and ended?

Why taste I not the Bounteous Breath,
   Receive the Goodly Gift of Grace?
Now, kind king-eagle (by God's death!),

Restore me to mine ancient place!
   I am advantaged nothing then!"
Then swooped he from the Byss of Space,

And set the knight amid the fen.
   "God!" quoth Sir Palamede, "that I
Who have won nine should fail at ten!

   I set my all upon the die:
   There is no further trick to try.
Call thrice accursèd above men
Sir Palamede the Saracen!"

XXXV

"YEA!" quoth the knight, " I rede the spell.
This Beast is the Unknowable.
I seek in Heaven, I seek in Hell ;

Ever he mocks me.   Yet, methinks,
I have the riddle of the Sphinx.
For were I keener than the lynx

I should not see within my mind
One thought that is not in its kind
In sooth That Beast that lurks behind :

And in my quest his questing seems
The authentic echo of my dreams,
The proper thesis of my themes !

I know him?   Still he answers : No !
I know him not?   Maybe—and lo !
He is the one sole thing I know !

Nay! who knows not is different
From him that knows.   Then be content ;
Thou canst not alter the event !

SIR PALAMEDES, THE SARACEN KNIGHT

Ah! what conclusion subtly draws
From out this chaos of mad laws?
Am I, the effect, as I, the cause?

Nay, the brain reels beneath its swell
Of pompous thoughts. Enough to tell
That He is known Unknowable!"

Thus did that knightly Saracen
In Cantabrig's miasmal fen
Lecture to many learned men.

So clamorous was their applause—
"His mind" (said they) "is free of flaws:
The Veil of God is thin as gauze!"—

That almost they had dulled or drowned
The laughter (in its belly bound)
Of that dread Beast he had not found.

Nathless—although he would away—
They forced the lack-luck knight to stay
And lecture many a weary day.

Verily, almost he had caught
The infection of their costive thought,
And brought his loyal quest to naught.

It was by night that Palamede
Ran from that mildewed, mouldy breed,
Moth-eaten dullards run to seed!

SIR PALAMEDES, THE SARACEN KNIGHT

How weak Sir Palamedes grows!
We hear no more of bouts and blows!
His weapons are his ten good toes!

He that was Arthur's peer, good knight
Proven in many a foughten fight,
Flees like a felon in the night!

Ay! this thy quest is past the ken
Of thee and of all mortal men,
Sir Palamede the Saracen!

XXXVI

OFT, as Sir Palamedes went
   Upon the quest, he was aware
Of some vast shadow subtly blent
   With his own shadow in the air.

It had no shape, no voice had it
   Wherewith to daunt the eye or ear;
Yet all the horror of the pit
   Clad it with all the arms of fear.

Moreover, though he sought to scan
   Some feature, though he listened long,
No shape of God or fiend or man,
   No whisper, groan, shriek, scream, or song

Gave him to know it.   Now it chanced
   One day Sir Palamedes rode
Through a great wood whose leafage danced
   In the thin sunlight as it flowed

From heaven.   He halted in a glade,
   Bade his horse crop the tender grass;
Put off his armour, softly laid
   Himself to sleep till noon should pass.

THE HIGH HISTORY OF GOOD

He woke.   Before him stands and grins
   A motley hunchback.   " Knave ! " quoth he,
" Hast seen the Beast ?   The quest that wins
   The loftiest prize of chivalry ? "

Sir Knight," he answers, " hast thou seen
   Aught of that Beast ?   How knowest thou, then,
That it is ever or hath been,
   Sir Palamede the Saracen ? "

Sir Palamede was well awake.
   " Nay ! I deliberate deep and long,
Yet find no answer fit to make
   To thee.   The weak beats down the strong ;

The fool's cap shames the helm.   But thou !
   I know thee for the shade that haunts
My way, sets shame upon my brow,
   My purpose dims, my courage daunts.

Then, since the thinker must be dumb,
   At least the knight may knightly act :
The wisest monk in Christendom
   May have his skull broke by a fact."

With that, as a snake strikes, his sword
   Leapt burning to the burning blue ;
And fell, one swift, assured award,
   Stabbing that hunchback through and through.

SIR PALAMEDES, THE SARACEN KNIGHT

Straight he dissolved, a voiceless shade.
  "Or scotched or slain," the knight said then,
"What odds? Keep bright and sharp thy blade,
  Sir Palamede the Saracen!"

XXXVII

Sir Palamede is sick to death!
  The staring eyen, the haggard face!
God grant to him the Beauteous Breath!
  God send the Goodly Gift of Grace!

There is a white cave by the sea
  Wherein the knight is hid away.
Just ere the night falls, spieth he
  The sun's last shaft flicker astray.

All day is dark.   There, there he mourns
  His wasted years, his purpose faint.
A million whips, a million scorns
  Make the knight flinch, and stain the saint.

For now! what hath he left?   He feeds
  On limpets and wild roots.   What odds?
There is no need a mortal needs
  Who hath loosed man's hope to grasp at God's!

How his head swims!   At night what stirs
  Above the faint wash of the tide,
And rare sea-birds whose winging whirrs
  About the cliffs?   Now good betide!

SIR PALAMEDES, THE SARACEN KNIGHT

God save thee, woeful Palamede!
   The questing of the Beast is loud
Within thy ear. By Goddes reed,
   Thou hast won the tilt from all the crowd!

Within thy proper bowels it sounds
   Mighty and musical at need,
As if a thirty couple hounds
   Quested within thee, Palamede!

Now, then, he grasps the desperate truth
   He hath toiled these many years to see,
Hath wasted strength, hath wasted youth—
   He was the Beast; the Beast was he!

He rises from the cave of death,
   Runs to the sea with shining face
To know at last the Bounteous Breath,
   To taste the Goodly Gift of Grace.

Ah! Palamede, thou hast mistook!
   Thou art the butt of all confusion!
Not to be written in my book
   Is this most drastic disillusion!

So weak and ill was he, I doubt
   If he might hear the royal feast
Of laughter that came rolling out
   Afar from that elusive Beast.

SIR PALAMEDES, THE SARACEN KNIGHT

Yet, those white lips were snapped, like steel
    Upon the ankles of a slave!
That body broken on the wheel
    Of Time suppressed the groan it gave!

" Not there, not here, my quest!" he cried.
    "Not thus! Not now! Do how and when
Matter? I am, and I abide,
    Sir Palamede the Saracen!"

XXXVIII

Sir Palamede of great renown
  Rode through the land upon the quest,
His sword loose and his vizor down,
  His buckler braced, his lance in rest.

Now, then, God save thee, Palamede!
  Who courseth yonder on the field?
Those silver arms, that sable steed,
  The sun and rose upon his shield?

The strange knight spurs to him.   Disdain
  Curls the proud lip as he uplifts
His vizor. "Come, an end! In vain,
  Sir Fox, thy thousand turns and shifts!"

Sir Palamede was white with fear.
  Lord Christ! those features were his own;
His own that voice so icy clear
  That cuts him, cuts him to the bone.

"False knight! false knight!" the stranger cried.
  "Thou bastard dog, Sir Palamede?
I am the good knight fain to ride
  Upon the Questing Beast at need.

99

THE HIGH HISTORY OF GOOD

Thief of my arms, my crest, my quest,
  My name, now meetest thou thy shame.
See, with this whip I lash thee back,
  Back to the kennel whence there came

So false a hound." "Good knight, in sooth,"
  Answered Sir Palamede, "not I
Presume to assert the idlest truth;
  And here, by this good ear and eye,

I grant thou art Sir Palamede.
  But—try the first and final test
If thou or I be he. Take heed!"
  He backed his horse, covered his breast,

Drove his spurs home, and rode upon
  That knight. His lance-head fairly struck
The barred strength of his morion,
  And rolled the stranger in the muck.

"Now, by God's death!" quoth Palamede,
  His sword at work, "I will not leave
So much of thee as God might feed
  His sparrows with. As I believe

The sweet Christ's mercy shall avail,
  So will I not have aught for thee;
Since every bone of thee may rail
  Against me, crying treachery.

SIR PALAMEDES, THE SARACEN KNIGHT

Thou hast lied. I am the chosen knight
    To slay the Questing Beast for men ;
I am the loyal son of light,
    Sir Palamede the Saracen !

Thou wast the subtlest fiend that yet
    Hath crossed my path. To say thee nay
I dare not, but my sword is wet
    With thy knave's blood, and with thy clay

Fouled ! Dost thou think to resurrect ?
    O sweet Lord Christ that savest men !
From all such fiends do thou protect
    Me, Palamede the Saracen ! "

XXXIX

GREEN and Grecian is the valley,
  Shepherd lads and shepherd lasses
    Dancing in a ring
Merrily and musically.
  How their happiness surpasses
    The mere thrill of spring !

" Come " (they cry), " Sir Knight, put by
  All that weight of shining armour !
Here's a posy, here's a garland, here's a chain of daisies !
  Here's a charmer !   There's a charmer !
Praise the God that crazes men, the God that raises
  All our lives to ecstasy ! "

Sir Palamedes was too wise
  To mock their gentle wooing ;
He smiles into their sparkling eyes
  While they his armour are undoing.
" For who " (quoth he) " may say that this
Is not the mystery I miss ? "

Soon he is gathered in the dance,
  And smothered in the flowers.

SIR PALAMEDES, THE SARACEN KNIGHT

A boy's laugh and a maiden's glance
 Are sweet as paramours!
Stay! is there naught some wanton wight
May do to excite the glamoured knight?

Yea! the song takes a sea-wild swell;
 The dance moves in a mystic web;
Strange lights abound and terrible;
 The life that flowed is out at ebb.

The lights are gone; the night is come;
 The lads and lasses sink, awaiting
Some climax—oh, how tense and dumb
 The expectant hush intoxicating!
Hush! the heart's beat!   Across the moor
Some dreadful god rides fast, be sure!

The listening Palamede bites through
 His thin white lips—what hoofs are those?
Are they the Quest?   How still and blue
 The sky is!   Hush—God knows—God knows!

Then on a sudden in the midst of them
 Is a swart god, from hoof to girdle a goat,
Upon his brow the twelve-star diadem
 And the King's Collar fastened on his throat.

Thrill upon thrill courseth through Palamede.
 Life, life, pure life is bubbling in his blood.
All youth comes back, all strength, all joy indeed
 Flaming within that throbbing spirit-flood!

SIR PALAMEDES, THE SARACEN KNIGHT

Yet was his heart immeasurably sad,
For that no questing in his ear he had.

Nay! he saw all.   He saw the Curse
   That wrapped in ruin the World primæval.
He saw the unborn Universe,
   And all its gods coeval.
He saw, and was, all things at once
   In Him that is ; he was the stars,
The moons, the meteors, the suns,
   All in one net of triune bars ;
Inextricably one, inevitably one,
   Immeasurable, immutable, immense
Beyond all the wonder that his soul had won
   By sense, in spite of sense, and beyond sense.
"Praise God!" quoth Palamede, " by this
I attain the uttermost of bliss. . . .

God's wounds! but that I never sought.
   The Questing Beast I sware to attain
And all this miracle is naught.
   Off on my travels once again !

I keep my youth regained to foil
Old Time that took me in his toil.
I keep my strength regained to chase
   The Beast that mocks me now as then
Dear Christ! I pray Thee of Thy grace
Take pity on the forlorn case
   Of Palamede the Saracen!"

XL

Sir Palamede the Saracen
  Hath seen the All; his mind is set
To pass beyond that great Amen.

Far hath he wandered; still to fret
  His soul against that Soul.   He breaches
The rhododendron forest-net,

His body bloody with its leeches.
  Sternly he travelleth the crest
Of a great mountain, far that reaches

Toward the King-snows; the rains molest
  The knight, white wastes updriven of wind
In sheets, in torrents, fiend-possessed,

Up from the steaming plains of Ind.
  They cut his flesh, they chill his bones:
Yet he feels naught; his mind is pinned

To that one point where all the thrones
  Join to one lion-head of rock,
Towering above all crests and cones

THE HIGH HISTORY OF GOOD

That crouch like jackals. Stress and shock
   Move Palamede no more. Like Fate
He moves with silent speed. They flock,

The Gods, to watch him. Now abate
   His pulses ; he threads through the vale,
And turns him to the mighty gate,

The glacier. Oh, the flowers that scale
   Those sun-kissed heights ! The snows that crown
The quartz ravines ! The clouds that veil

The awful slopes ! Dear God ! look down
   And see this petty man move on,
Relentless as Thine own renown,

Careless of praise or orison,
   Simply determined. Wilt Thou launch
(This knight's presumptuous head upon)

The devastating avalanche ?
   He knows too much, and cares too little !
His wound is more than Death can staunch.

He can avoid, though by one tittle,
   Thy surest shaft ! And now the knight,
Breasting the crags, may laugh and whittle

Away the demon-club whose might
   Threatened him. Now he leaves the spur ;
And eager, with a boy's delight,

SIR PALAMEDES, THE SARACEN KNIGHT

Treads the impending glacier.
　　Now, now he strikes the steep black ice
That leads to the last neck.　By Her

That bore the Lord, by what device
　　May he pass there?　Yet still he moves,
Ardent and steady, as if the price

Of death were less than life approves,
　　As if on eagles' wings he mounted,
Or as on angels' wings—or love's!

So, all the journey he discounted,
　　Holding the goal.　Supreme he stood
Upon the summit; dreams uncounted,

Worlds of sublime beatitude!
　　He passed beyond.　The All he hath touched,
And dropped to vile desuetude.

What lay beyond?　What star unsmutched
　　By being?　His poor fingers fumble,
And all the Naught their ardour clutched,

Like all the rest, begins to crumble.
　　Where is the Beast?　His bliss exceeded
All that bards sing of or priests mumble;

No man, no God, hath known what he did.
　　Only this baulked him—that he lacked
Exactly the one thing he needed.

SIR PALAMEDES, THE SARACEN KNIGHT

"Faugh!" cried the knight. "Thought, word, and act
   Confirm me. I have proved the quest
Impossible. I break the pact.

Back to the gilded halls, confessed
   A recreant! Achieved or not,
This task hath earned a foison—rest.

In Caerlon and Camelot
   Let me embrace my fellow-men!
To buss the wenches, pass the pot,
Is now the enviable lot
   Of Palamede the Saracen!"

XLI

SIR ARTHUR sits again at feast
  Within the high and holy hall
Of Camelot.   From West to East

The Table Round hath burst the thrall
  Of Paynimrie.   The goodliest gree
Sits on the gay knights, one and all;

Till Arthur: " Of your chivalry,
  Knights, let us drink the happiness
Of the one knight we lack " (quoth he);

" For surely in some sore distress
  May be Sir Palamede."   Then they
Rose as one man in glad liesse

To honour that great health.   " God's way
  Is not as man's " (quoth Lancelot).
" Yet, may God send him back this day,

His quest achieved, to Camelot!"
  " Amen!" they cried, and raised the bowl;
When—the wind rose, a blast as hot

THE HIGH HISTORY OF GOOD

As the simoom, and forth did roll
   A sudden thunder. Still they stood.
Then came a bugle-blast. The soul

Of each knight stirred. With vigour rude,
   The blast tore down the tapestry
That hid the door. All ashen-hued

The knights laid hand to sword. But he
   (Sir Palamedes) in the gap
Was found—God knoweth—bitterly

Weeping. Cried Arthur : " Strange the hap !
   My knight, my dearest knight, my friend !
What gift had Fortune in her lap

Like thee ? Embrace me ! " " Rather rend
   Your garments, if you love me, sire ! "
(Quod he). " I am come unto the end.

All mine intent and my desire,
   My quest, mine oath—all, all is done.
Burn them with me in fatal fire !

For I have failed. All ways, each one
   I strove in, mocked me. If I quailed
Or shirked, God knows. I have not won :

That and no more I know. I failed."
   King Arthur fell a-weeping. Then
Merlin uprose, his face unveiled ;

SIR PALAMEDES, THE SARACEN KNIGHT

Thrice cried he piteously then
   Upon our Lord.   Then shook his head
Sir Palamede the Saracen,

As knowing nothing might bestead,
   When lo! there rose a monster moan,
A hugeous cry, a questing dread,

As if (God's death!) there coursed alone
   The Beast, within whose belly sounds
That marvellous music monotone

As if a thirty couple hounds
   Quested within him.   Now, by Christ
And by His pitiful five wounds!—

Even as a lover to his tryst,
   That Beast came questing in the hall,
One flame of gold and amethyst,

Bodily seen then of them all.
   Then came he to Sir Palamede,
Nestling to him, as sweet and small

As a young babe clings at its need
   To the white bosom of its mother,
As Christ clung to the gibbet-reed!

Then every knight turned to his brother,
   Sobbing and sighing for great gladness;
And, as they looked on one another,

THE HIGH HISTORY OF GOOD

Surely there stole a subtle madness
   Into their veins, more strong than death :
For all the roots of sin and sadness

Were plucked.   As a flower perisheth,
   So all sin died.   And in that place
All they did know the Beauteous Breath

And taste the Goodly Gift of Grace.
   Then fell the night.   Above the baying
Of the great Beast, that was the bass

To all the harps of Heaven a-playing,
   There came a solemn voice (not one
But was upon his knees in praying

And glorifying God).   The Son
   Of God Himself—men thought—spoke then.
"Arise! brave soldier, thou hast won

The quest not given to mortal men.
   Arise! Sir Palamede Adept,
Christian, and no more Saracen!

On wake or sleeping, wise, inept,
   Still thou didst seek.   Those foolish ways
On which thy folly stumbled, leapt,

All led to the one goal.   Now praise
   Thy Lord that He hath brought thee through
To win the quest!"   The good knight lays

SIR PALAMEDES, THE SARACEN KNIGHT

His hand upon the Beast.   Then blew
   Each angel on his trumpet, then
All Heaven resounded that it knew

Sir Palamede the Saracen
   Was master!   Through the domes of death,
Through all the mighty realms of men

And spirits breathed the Beauteous Breath :
   They taste the Goodly Gift of Grace.
—Now 'tis the chronicler that saith :

Our Saviour grant in little space
   That also I, even I, be blest
Thus, though so evil is my case—

Let them that read my rime attest
   The same sweet unction in my pen—
That writes in pure blood of my breast ;

For that I figure unto men
   The story of my proper quest
   As thine, first Eastern in the West,
Sir Palamede the Saracen !

George Raffalovich's forthcoming works.

THE HISTORY OF A SOUL.

Price 3s. 6d. Edition strictly limited.

THE DEUCE AND ALL.

A COLLECTION OF SHORT STORIES.

1s. net.

READY SHORTLY.

Through **THE EQUINOX** and all booksellers.

MR. NEUBURG'S NEW VOLUME OF POEMS.

Imperial 16mo, pp. 200.

Ready immediately. Order through The Equinox, *or of any Bookseller.*

THE TRIUMPH OF PAN.

POEMS BY VICTOR B. NEUBURG.

This volume, containing many poems—nearly all of them hitherto unpublished—besides THE TRIUMPH OF PAN, includes THE ROMANCE OF OLIVIA VANE.

The First Edition will be limited to Two Hundred and Fifty copies: Two Hundred and Twenty on ordinary paper, whereof less than Two Hundred are for sale; and Thirty on Japanese vellum, of which Twenty-five are for sale. These latter copies will be numbered, and signed by the Author. The binding will be half-parchment with crimson sides; the ordinary copies will be bound in crimson cloth.

The price of ordinary copies will be Five Shillings net; of the special copies, One Guinea net.

IV   *

PHOTOGRAPHS.

To be had of THE EQUINOX. Price Ten Shillings each.
Neatly framed in gold. The original panel Photographs :

THE STUDENT. (A reproduction faces "Aha!" in No. III.)

THE INTERPRETER. (Reproduced on p. 279 of No. IV.)

THE GUARDIAN OF THE FLAME.

THE GODDESS.

No student of the mysteries should be without one at least
of these remarkable and beautiful studies. Their presence
serves to remind the possessor of the constant quest and to
stimulate to more persistent Effort.

Essays of Prentice Mulford

Crown 8vo. Crimson cloth extra, 3s. 6d. net per volume.

THE GIFT OF THE SPIRIT. A Selection from the Essays of PRENTICE MULFORD. Reprinted from the "White Cross Library." With an Introduction by ARTHUR EDWARD WAITE. Third Edition.

CONTENTS.—God in the Trees; or the Infinite Mind in Nature. The God in Yourself. The Doctor within. Mental Medicine. Faith; or, Being Led of the Spirit. The Material Mind *v.* The Spiritual Mind. What are Spiritual Gifts? Healthy and Unhealthy Spirit Communion. Spells; or, the Law of Change. Immortality in the Flesh. Regeneration; or, Being Born again. The Process of Re-Embodiment. Re-Embodiment Universal in Nature. The Mystery of Sleep. Where you Travel when you Sleep. Prayer in all ages. The Church of Silent Demand.

"The Essays of Prentice Mulford embody a peculiar philosophy, and represent a peculiar phase of insight into the mystery which surrounds man. The essays were the work, as the insight was the gift, of a man who owed nothing to books, perhaps not much to what is ordinarily meant by observation, and everything or nearly everything to reflection nourished by contact with nature."—*E. A. Waite, in the Introduction.*

Under the title "Your Forces and How to Use Them," the Essays of Prentice Mulford have obtained the greatest popularity in America.

THE GIFT OF UNDERSTANDING. A Further Selection from the Works of PRENTICE MULFORD. Reprinted from the "White Cross Library." With an Introduction by ARTHUR EDWARD WAITE.

CONTENTS.—Introduction. Force, and How to Get it. The Source of your Strength. About Economising our Forces. The Law of Marriage. Marriage and Resurrection. Your Two Memories. The Drawing Power of Mind. Consider the Lilies. Cultivate Repose. Look Forward. The Necessity of Riches. Love Thyself. What is Justice? How Thoughts are born. Positive and Negative Thought. The Art of Forgetting. The Attraction of Aspiration. God's Commands are Man's Demands.

"This further selection has been prepared in consequence of the great popularity attained by the first series of Prentice Mulford's Essays, published under the title of "The Gift of the Spirit."

ESSAYS OF PRENTICE MULFORD. THIRD SERIES.

CONTENTS.—The Law of Success. How to Keep Your Strength. The Art of Study. Profit and Loss in Associates. The Slavery of Fear. Some Laws of Health and Beauty. Mental Interference. Co-operation of Thought. The Religion of Dress. Use your Riches. The Healing and Renewing Force of Spring. The Practical Use of Reverie. Self-Teaching: or the Art of Learning How to Learn. How to Push your Business. The Religion of the Drama. The Uses of Sickness. Who are our Relations? The Use of a Room. Husband and Wife.

The third and fourth series of Prentice Mulford's Essays have been prepared in response to a large demand for the complete works of the "White Cross Library" at a more reasonable price than that of the American edition in six volumes.

ESSAYS OF PRENTICE MULFORD. FOURTH SERIES. Completing the entire set of the Essays published in America under the title of "Your Forces and How to Use Them."

CONTENTS.—The Use of Sunday. A Cure for Alcoholic Intemperance through the Law of Demand. Grace Before Meat; or the Science of Eating. What we need Strength for. One Way to Cultivate Courage. Some Practical Mental Recipes. The Use and Necessity of Recreation. Mental Tyranny: or, How We Mesmerise Each Other. Thought Currents. Uses of Diversion. "Lies breed Disease; Truths bring Health." Woman's Real Power. Good and Ill Effects of Thought. Buried Talents. The Power of Honesty. Confession. The Accession of New Thought.

These four volumes constitute the cheapest and best edition of the Essays of Prentice Mulford published in the English language. Special care has been taken to eliminate the errors and mistakes with which the American edition abounds.

Write for full Catalogue to

WILLIAM RIDER AND SONS, Ltd., 164, Aldersgate Street, London, E.C.

A. CROWLEY'S WORKS

The volumes here listed are all of definite occult and mystical interest and importance.

The Trade may obtain them from

"The Equinox," 124, Victoria Street, S.W. Tel.: 3210 Victoria; and Messrs. Simpkin, Marshall, Hamilton, Kent & Co., 23, Paternoster Row, E.C.

The Public may obtain them from

"The Equinox," 124, Victoria Street, S.W.
Mr. Elkin Mathews, Vigo Street, W.
The Walter Scott Publishing Co., Paternoster Square, E.C.
Mr. F. Hollings, Great Turnstile, Holborn.
And through all Booksellers.

ACELDAMA. Crown 8vo, 29 pp., £2 2s. net. Of this rare pamphlet less than 10 copies remain. It is Mr. Crowley's earliest and in some ways most striking mystical work.

JEPHTHAH AND OTHER MYSTERIES, LYRICAL AND DRAMATIC. Demy 8vo, boards, pp. xxii + 223, 7s. 6d. net.

SONGS OF THE SPIRIT. Pp. x + 109. A new edition. 3s. 6d. net. These two volumes breathe the pure semi-conscious aspiration of the soul, and express the first glimmerings of the light.

THE SOUL OF OSIRIS. Medium 8vo, pp. ix + 129, 5s. net. A collection of lyrics, illustrating the progress of the soul from corporeal to celestial beatitude.

TANNHAUSER. Demy 4to, pp. 142, 15s. net. The progress of the soul in dramatic form.

BERASHITH. 4to, China paper, pp. 24, 5s. net. Only a few copies remain. An illuminating essay on the Universe, reconciling the conflicting systems of religion.

THE GOD=EATER. Crown 4to, pp. 32, 2s. 6d. net. A striking dramatic study of the origin of religions.

THE SWORD OF SONG. Post 4to, pp. ix + 194, printed in red and black, decorative wrapper, 20s. net. This is the author's first most brilliant attempt to base the truths of mysticism on the truths of scepticism. It contains also an enlarged amended edition of "Berashith," and an Essay showing the striking parallels and identities between the doctrines of Modern Science, and those of Buddhism.

GARGOYLES. Pott 8vo, pp. vi + 113, 5s. net.

ORACLES. Demy 8vo, pp. viii + 176, 5s. net. Some of Mr. Crowley's finest mystical lyrics are in these collections.

KONX OM PAX. See advt.

Collected Works (Travellers' Edition). Extra crown 8vo, India paper, 3 vols. in one, pp. 808 + Appendices. Vellum, green ties, with portraits, £3 3s.; white buckram, without portraits, £2 2s. This edition contains "Qabalistic Dogma," "Time," "The Excluded Middle," "Eleusis," and other matters of the highest occult importance which are not printed elsewhere.

AMBERGRIS. Medium 8vo, pp. 200, 3s. 6d. (Elkin Mathews.) A selection of lyrics, containing some of great mystical beauty.

www.ingramcontent.com/pod-product-compliance
Lightning Source LLC
Chambersburg PA
CBHW080827010225
21259CB00006B/21